THE GREENWOOD ENCYCLOPEDIA OF LOVE, COURTSHIP, & *Sexuality* THROUGH HISTORY

THE GREENWOOD ENCYCLOPEDIA OF LOVE, COURTSHIP, AND SEXUALITY THROUGH HISTORY

The Ancient World, Volume 1
James W. Howell

The Medieval Era, Volume 2
William E. Burns

The Early Modern Period, Volume 3
Victoria L. Mondelli and Cherrie A. Gottsleben, with the assistance of Kristen Pederson Chew

The Colonial and Revolutionary Age, Volume 4
Merril D. Smith

The Nineteenth Century, Volume 5
Susan Mumm

The Modern World, Volume 6
James T. Sears

THE GREENWOOD ENCYCLOPEDIA OF LOVE, COURTSHIP, *& Sexuality* THROUGH HISTORY

THE COLONIAL AND REVOLUTIONARY AGE
Volume 4

Edited by
MERRIL D. SMITH

GREENWOOD PRESS
Westport, Connecticut • London

Library of Congress Cataloging-in-Publication Data

The Greenwood encyclopedia of love, courtship, and sexuality through history / volume editors, James W. Howell ... [et al.].
    p. cm.
  Includes bibliographical references and index.
  Contents: v. 1. The ancient world / James W. Howell, editor—v. 2. The medieval era / William E. Burns, editor—v. 3. The early modern period / Victoria L. Mondelli and Cherrie A. Gottsleben, editors—v. 4. The colonial and revolutionary age / Merril D. Smith, editor—v. 5. The nineteenth century / Susan Mumm, editor—v. 6. The modern world / James T. Sears, editor.
  ISBN-13: 978–0–313–33359–0 (set : alk. paper)—ISBN-13: 978–0–313–33583–9 (vol. 1 : alk. paper)—ISBN-13: 978–0–313–33519–8 (vol. 2 : alk. paper)—ISBN-13: 978–0–313–33653–9 (vol. 3 : alk. paper)—ISBN-13: 978–0–313–33360–6 (vol. 4 : alk. paper)—ISBN-13: 978–0–313–33405–4 (vol. 5 : alk. paper)—ISBN-13: 978–0–313–33646–1 (vol. 6 : alk. paper)
  1. Sex—History—Encyclopedias. 2. Love—History—Encyclopedias. 3. Courtship—History—Encyclopedias. I. Howell, James W. II. Title.
  HQ21.G67125   2008
  306.703–dc22   2007023728

British Library Cataloguing in Publication Data is available.

Copyright © 2008 by Merril D. Smith

All rights reserved. No portion of this book may be reproduced, by any process or technique, without the express written consent of the publisher.

Library of Congress Catalog Card Number: 2007023728
ISBN-13:   978–0–313–33359–0 (set code)
           978–0–313–33583–9 (Vol. 1)
           978–0–313–33519–8 (Vol. 2)
           978–0–313–33653–9 (Vol. 3)
           978–0–313–33360–6 (Vol. 4)
           978–0–313–33405–4 (Vol. 5)
           978–0–313–33646–1 (Vol. 6)

First published in 2008

Greenwood Press, 88 Post Road West, Westport, CT 06881
An imprint of Greenwood Publishing Group, Inc.
www.greenwood.com

Printed in the United States of America

The paper used in this book complies with the Permanent Paper Standard issued by the National Information Standards Organization (Z39.48–1984).

10 9 8 7 6 5 4 3 2 1

Contents

List of Entries   vii

Set Preface   ix

Preface   xi

Acknowledgments   xiii

Introduction   xv

Guide to Related Topics   xix

Chronology of Selected Events   xxi

The Encyclopedia   1

Appendix   267

Selected Bibiliography   269

Index   273

About the Editor and Contributors   277

List of Entries

Abduction
Abortion
Actors
Adultery
African Slave Trade. *See* Atlantic Slave Trade
Alcohol
American Art. *See* Art, American/European
Anal Intercourse
Anti-Sodomy Law. *See* Sodomy and Anti-Sodomy Law
Aristotle's Masterpiece (1684)
Art, American/European
Art, Non-Western
Atlantic Slave Trade

Bastardy
Baths
Behn, Aphra (c. 1640–1689)
Berdache
Bestiality
Bigamy
Birth Control. *See* Contraception
Bisexuality
The Body
Breastfeeding
Byrd, William (1674–1744)

Casanova, Giacomo Girolamo (1725–1798)
Castlehaven, Earl of. *See* Touchet, Mervyn, Earl of Castlehaven
Castration
Celibacy
Cervantes Saavedra, Miguel de (1547–1616)
Chastity

Chevalier d'Eon (1728–1810)
Child Rape
Childbirth
Childhood and Adolescence
Chinese Theater. *See* Theater, Chinese
Circumcision
Clothing and Fashion
Concubines
Consent
Consumerism. *See* Household Consumerism
Contraception
Convents. *See* Monasteries
Cosmetics and Perfume
Courtship
Cross-Dressing

Dance
Death
D'Eon de Beaumont, Charles-Geneviève-Louis-Auguste-André-Thimothée. *See* Chevalier d'Eon
Diderot, Denis (1713–1784)
Divorce
Domestic Violence
Don Juan. *See* Tenorio, Don Juan
Dueling

Economics and Gender. *See* Household Consumerism
Education
Ejaculation
Elliott, Grace Dalrymple (1754–1823)

English Revolution. *See* Revolution and Gender
Enlightenment Thought on Sexuality
Erauso, Catalina de (1585–1650)
Eunuchs
Euphemisms and Slang
European Art. *See* Art, American/European
Explorers and Missionaries
Express Consent. *See* Consent

Fairy Tales
Fanny Hill (Cleland, 1749)
Fashion. *See* Clothing and Fashion
Flagellation
Folklore. *See* Myths and Folklore
Food
Footbinding
Fornication
Franklin, Benjamin (1706–1790)
French Revolution. *See* Revolution and Gender

Geisha
Gender. *See* Revolution and Gender
Gender Roles
Gossip, Eighteenth-Century England
Gossip, Seventeenth-Century America
Guadalupe, Virgin of. *See* Virgin of Guadalupe
Gynecology Manuals

Harems
Hermaphrodites

LIST OF ENTRIES

Hinduism
Hogarth, William (1697–1764)
Homosexuality
Household Consumerism
Hysteria

Implied Consent. See Consent
Impotence
Incest
Indentured Servants
India
Inés de la Cruz, Sor Juana (1651–1695)
Infanticide
Insanity. See Madness
Interracial Sex
Islam

Japanese Theater. See Theater, Japanese
Judaism

Laws
Libertine
Literacy. See Education
Literature

Madness
Maritime Culture
Marquis de Sade. See Sade, Donatien Alphonse François de
Marriage
Marvell, Andrew (1621–1678)
Masculinity
Masturbation
Mather, Cotton (1663–1728)
Medicine and Science
Men. See Masculinity
Menstruation
Mexico, Indigenous Women of
Mexico, Sexuality and Gender in
Midwives and Physicians
Milton, John (1608–1674)
Missionaries. See Explorers and Missionaries
Mistresses. See Royal Mistresses
Mixed Marriages, New France

Molly Houses
Monasteries
Murder
Myths and Folklore

Native Americans
Newspapers
Non-Western Art. See Art, Non-Western
Nudity. See The Body

Onanism. See Masturbation
Opera
Oral Sex
Orgasm
Orphans
Ottoman Empire

Paternity
Patriarchy
Perfectionists
Perfume. See Cosmetics and Perfume
Philosophy
Physicians. See Midwives and Physicians
Pirates
Polyandry
Pornography
Pregnancy
Premarital Sex
Prostitutes and Prostitution
Pueblo Indians
Puritans

Rape/Coerced Sex
Rape Law
Religion
Restoration Poetry (1660–1700)
Revolution and Gender
Romantic Love
Rousseau, Jean-Jacques (1712–1788)
Royal Mistresses

Sade, Donatien Alphonse François de (1740–1814)

Salons
Science. See Medicine and Science
Seduction Literature
Sex Crimes
Shakespeare, William (1564–1616)
Slander/Defamation of Character. See Gossip, Eighteenth-Century England; Gossip, Seventeenth-Century America
Slang. See Euphemisms and Slang
Slavery
Sodomy and Anti-Sodomy Law
Southeastern Indians
Swift, Jonathan (1667–1745)

Taboos
Taj Mahal
Tenorio, Don Juan
Theater, Chinese
Theater, European
Theater, Japanese
Thistlewood, Thomas (1721–1786)
Tobacco
Tom Jones (Fielding, 1749)
Torture
Touchet, Mervyn, Earl of Castlehaven (1593–1631)

Venereal Diseases
Virgin Mary
Virgin of Guadalupe
Virgins/Virginity
Virtue
Voyeurism

Wartime Rape
Widows and Widowhood
Wilmot, John, Earl of Rochester (1647–1680)
Witches and Witch Trials
Wollstonecraft Godwin, Mary (1759–1797)
Women, Changing Images of

Yorùbá Oral Poetry, Sexuality in
Yoshiwara

Set Preface

Sex and love are part of the very fabric of daily life—universal concepts that permeate every human society and are central to how each society views and understands itself. However, the way sex and love are expressed or perceived varies from culture to culture, and, within a particular society, attitudes toward sex and love evolve over time alongside the culture from which they arose. To capture the multicultural and chronological dimensions of these vital concepts, the six-volume *The Greenwood Encyclopedia of Love, Courtship, and Sexuality through History* explores the array of ideas, attitudes, and practices that have constituted sex and love around the world and across the centuries.

Each volume of alphabetically arranged entries was edited by an expert in the field who has drawn upon the expertise of contributors from many related disciplines to carefully analyze views toward sex and love among many cultures within a specified time period. Students and interested general readers will find in this work a host of current, informative, and engaging entries to help them compare and contrast different perceptions and practices across time and space. Entries cover such topics as customs and practices; institutions; legislation; religious beliefs; art and literature; and important ideas, innovations, and individuals. Users of this encyclopedia will, for instance, be able to learn how marriage in ancient Rome differed from marriage in Victorian England or in colonial America; how prostitution was viewed in medieval Europe and in the contemporaneous Islamic societies of Africa and the Middle East; and how or even if celibacy was practiced in eighteenth-century India, ancient Greece, or early modern Europe.

Edited by James W. Howell, Volume 1, *The Ancient World*, explores love and sexuality in the great societies of Europe, Africa, and Asia in the period before around 300 CE. Entries include Marriage, Homosexuality, Temple Prostitution, and Sex in Art. Volume 2, *The Medieval Era*, by William E. Burns examines sex and love in Europe, East Asia, India, the Middle East, Africa, and pre-Columbian Mesoamerica in the period between around 300 and 1400. Entries in this volume include Arthurian Legend, Concubinage, Eunuchs, Krishna, Seclusion of Women, *Thousand and One Nights*, and Virginity.

Volume 3, *The Early Modern Period*, edited by Victoria L. Mondelli and Cherrie Ann Gottsleben, with the assistance of Kristen Pederson Chew, focuses on sex and love in Europe, India, China, the Middle East, Africa, and the Americas in the fifteenth and sixteenth centuries. Some important entries in this volume are Bastardy, Confucianism, Dowries, Sex Toys, Suttee, and William Shakespeare. Edited by Merril D. Smith, Volume 4, *The Colonial and Revolutionary Age*, looks at love and sexuality in western Europe, eastern Asia, India, the Middle East, Africa, and the Americas in the seventeenth and eighteenth centuries. The volume offers entries such as Bestiality, Castration, Berdache, Harems, Pueblo Indians, and Yoshiwara.

Volume 5, *The Nineteenth Century*, edited by Susan Mumm, explores sex and love in the Victorian period, primarily in Europe and the United States, but also in India, Asia, and the Middle East. Entries in this volume include Birth Control, Courtship, Fetishism, Native Americans, and Ottoman Women. Edited by James T. Sears, Volume 6, *The Modern World*, explores major topics in sex and sexuality from around the world in the twentieth and twenty-first centuries. Entries include AIDS/HIV, Domestic and Relationship Violence, Internet Pornography, Politics and Sex, Premarital Sex, Television, and the Women's Movement.

Each volume is illustrated and several cross-references to entries are provided. The entries conclude with a list of additional information resources, including the most useful books, journal articles, and Web sites currently available. Other important features of the encyclopedia include chronologies of important dates and events; guides to related topics that allow readers to trace broad themes across the entries; bibliographies of important general and standard works; and useful appendices, such as lists of Chinese dynasties and selections of important films and Web sites. Finally, detailed subject indexes help users gain easy access to the wealth of information on sex, love, and culture provided by this encyclopedia.

Preface

Sex, love, and culture are central concepts of human life. This volume, *The Colonial and Revolutionary Age*, the fourth book in the six-volume *The Greenwood Encyclopedia of Love, Courtship, and Sexuality through History* that covers its topic from antiquity to the present, explores sex, love, and culture in the seventeenth and eighteenth centuries. The broad terms—sex, love, and culture—are covered here in many ways. Some of the entries, such as Ejaculation and Orgasm, cover the physical aspects of sex and sexuality. But this book encompasses more than just the physical, as important as it is. In this time of great political, religious, and social change, many movements, reforms, events, and individuals had an impact on sexuality and culture.

This volume is intended as a reference work for the general public and for students at various levels from high school through college who want to learn about the topic of sex and culture in the seventeenth and eighteenth centuries. For those who wish to learn more about the topic, each entry concludes with a list of further readings. In addition, the volume also includes a Select Bibliography of important information resources as well as an appendix offering annotated listings of relevant films and useful Web sites.

This encyclopedia includes 161 entries written by 53 scholars from around the world. Although many entries focus mainly on Western Europe and the Americas, others cover entries events, cultural practices, and art from around the globe. Within the confines of one volume, I have aimed to be as comprehensive as possible on such a broad subject. The coverage includes descriptions and explications of key terms, legal concepts, influential works of art and literature, and important movements, and people. Entries are listed in alphabetical order, from Abduction to Yoshiwara. Each narrative entry defines the term, provides an overview, and explains its importance to sex, love, and culture in the seventeenth and/or eighteenth centuries. All entries include cross-references in **bold** type, a listing of other related entries, and a suggested reading list provided by the author of the entry. The volume also includes a detailed subject index; a Guide to Related Topics that helps users quickly and easily trace broad themes and concepts across the entries; a chronology of key events, movements, and people in seventeenth- and eighteenth-century sex, love, and culture; and an introduction that helps provide context for the entries, many of which are also illustrated.

Acknowledgments

Grateful thanks to all the people who helped with this volume. John Wagner, my editor at Greenwood, helped guide this manuscript to completion and answered my many questions in a timely fashion.

To my friends, who acted interested, even when I went on and on about finishing "the book"—well, it's done, and now you can pretend to be interested in the next one. My husband, Doug, suffered through the process of my writing and editing, yet again, with cheerfulness, as we prepared for our daughter's high school graduation and took care of other family matters. My daughters, Megan and Sheryl, have become nonchalant about having my books about sex lying about the dining room and kitchen, even when their friends are here. Thanks, girls, for your support!

Finally, I want to thank all the contributors who wrote entries for this book. Several took on multiple, last-minute entries—a million thanks!

Introduction

Human sexuality has always existed. Without it, of course, humans would not have been able to reproduce. But sex and sexuality in humans is far more complicated than that. Men and women hate and love, feel happiness and anger, have creative urges, and try to explain and explore the unknown. Some men are attracted to other men; some women are attracted to other women. Some have chosen, for a variety of reasons, to remain celibate. In addition to biological needs and sexual desires, men and women are influenced by their cultures and the world around them. These influences have helped advise and proscribe conduct and behavior for both men and women. Over time and space, fashions in clothing, hairstyles, and even the size of body parts, such as breasts and feet, have dictated who might be considered a potential mate.[1]

Throughout human history, men and women have formed cultural constructs, such as marriage, within which there have generally been rules and rituals on how, when, and with whom they can have sexual relations. What exactly is allowed depends on the particular time, place, and society. In addition, various societies have interpreted how men and women should behave and determined what their roles are. Different civilizations have also used sex to conquer or abuse, as in the case of wartime rapes and slavery.

This volume of *The Greenwood Encyclopedia of Love, Courtship, and Sexuality through History* covers the seventeenth and eighteenth centuries, a time of enormous political, cultural, religious, and economic change. These transformations had a profound effect on men and women, and in the way they experienced sex or love, as they journeyed along newly defined paths—or struggled to maintain traditional values. For example, both church and state authorities in most of Western Europe and the American colonies considered premarital sex immoral and illegal. Yet many betrothed couples believed that they were not committing a sin in having sexual relations, since they intended to marry. That parents condoned some level of physical intimacy for courting couples, although probably not sexual intercourse, can be seen in the widespread practice of permitting them to spend the night together.

As the sixteenth century closed, the Renaissance was ending and the Age of Reason was beginning. Scientific discoveries such as Anton van Leeuwenhoek's discovery of male spermatozoa contrasted with continued myths about reproduction. Philosophers were questioning the existence of God, but religious differences led to separation movements, and even to wars.

INTRODUCTION

In England, a Protestant Separatist group, now commonly known as the Pilgrims, founded a colony in Plymouth, Massachusetts, where they could have their own church away from what they believed to be the corruptions of the Church of England. Following them came boatloads of Puritans, who established the colonies that later formed New England. Puritan beliefs challenged some English laws; for one thing, marriage was deemed a civil contract, not a sacrament, and divorces were more easily obtained than they were in England. Puritan rule in England followed the defeat of the royalists during the English Civil War (1642–1649) and led to the closing of London theaters and the avoidance of customary revels during Christmas.

But people believed in magic, demons, and witches. Witches, mainly women, were tried and executed throughout Europe and its colonies, in both Catholic and Protestant areas. Witches were accused of *maleficium*, doing evil by using supernatural means. They were frequently suspected of perverse sexual encounters with the Devil, animals, and their neighbors. Neighborly disputes and gossip were often the start of an investigation and accusation of witchcraft, and the bodies of suspected witches were inspected for marks of the Devil. In Spain and its colonies, witches were executed as part of the Inquisition. In England, witchcraft was made a capital crime in 1542. During the early years of New England's settlement, only unofficial charges of witchcraft were made, but, in 1648, Massachusetts executed a woman for witchcraft. Following that, a number of witchcraft scares occurred in New England. In 1692, nearly 200 people were accused of witchcraft in Salem, Massachusetts. Most of the accused and most of those claiming to be possessed were female.

Fear of the unknown and the unfamiliar went beyond the supernatural, and extended to the wilderness and the native people Europeans encountered in the Americas, and the Europeans tried to "tame" both of them. Europeans crossed the Atlantic, exploring and settling, forever changing the world, as microbes, animals, plants, and technology were exchanged between Europe and the Americas. Just as explorers, missionaries, and settlers were stymied in their understanding of the people and civilizations they encountered, so, too, are present-day scholars, who seek to know what the original inhabitants of the Americas were like, but often have only the biased reports of Europeans. Although French and Spanish explorers and missionaries wrote about the *berdache*, for example, they did not truly comprehend who they were. There was simply no place for a "two-spirited" person in the early modern Western world, which did not even acknowledge that homosexuality existed, merely that some people chose what many considered immoral—even evil—behavior.

Also problematical is terminology. The use of the word *berdache* is considered offensive to some. However, it must at least be used as a point of reference, since it was the term that the French and Spanish used for men who dressed and behaved as women. Then there is the problem of what to call the people who lived in the Americas and encountered Europeans. Indians? Native Americans? Amerindians? For most of the entries in this book, the contributors use the terminology that they feel is appropriate. In most cases, I have used Native Americans when referring to whole groups of people. This seems to be the term that is most commonly used in the sources that have been consulted. Indigenous people and native people are also frequently used terms.[2]

Africans were also brought over to the Americas, adding more complexity to sexual, racial, and gender relations. Although the status of the first Africans in what would become the United States was not much different from that of servants, it was not long before slavery was entrenched and codified in the New World. In the British colonies, slavery was an inherited state—the children of slave mothers were slaves (even if fathered by white owners or overseers). Slave owners could do as they wished with their slaves, which left women especially vulnerable to rape and sexual abuse.

Anglo-Americans viewed both African women and Native American women as promiscuous and sexually insatiable. Explorers, travelers, and plantation owners swapped stories about their encounters or near encounters with exotic temptresses. In the sixteenth and early seventeenth centuries, white women were also considered sexually aggressive and filled with lust. However, by the middle of the eighteenth century, beliefs about white women—at least "respectable" white women—would start to change, and they would be considered the virtuous mothers of the republic.

As this happened, concerns grew about the increased rates of premarital pregnancies. If young men seduced and then abandoned young women when they got pregnant, then towns would have to support the illegitimate children. Combined with growing literacy rates and anxiety about vice and immorality in the cities, these anxieties led to the popularity of seduction literature in both England and America.

Respectability and morality have often coexisted with vice and immorality. Even Puritan New England had prostitutes and men who patronized them. Young men and women throughout time have used their bodies to help themselves advance socially, and that was true of the seventeenth and eighteenth centuries as well. In seventeenth-century Japan, the Yoshiwara district became the area for prostitutes of various classes. Originally, "geisha" referred to male entertainers, but women became geishas in the eighteenth century. In the Ottoman Empire, some women asserted power from the harem. In Western Europe, some women, such as Grace Dalrymple Elliott and Nell Gwynne, gained a comfortable living because they were the mistresses of powerful men.

In this time of revolutions and revolutionary changes, some women stepped outside gender expectations. Catalina de Erauso escaped from a Spanish convent and traveled the world as a man for over twenty years. Aphra Benn wrote works filled with sexually charged themes. Mary Wollstonecraft defended rights for women, including the right to be educated and spoke out against marriage in her *Vindication of the Rights of Women* (1792).

Men also fought against the constraints of accepted masculine behavior. London homosexuals met and gathered in molly houses, such as Mother Clap's house. The poet and libertine, John Wilmot, earl of Rochester, frequently stepped outside the bounds of acceptable behavior and was even banished from Charles II's court for a time. Wilmot was a noted womanizer who finally succumbed to syphilis. In contrast, the Virginia planter, William Byrd, who also had numerous sexual encounters, wanted to be accepted as a gentleman. He spent his life imitating and emulating the lifestyle and manners of the English aristocracy.

Both women and men created works of art, literature, and music that expressed themes of sexuality. John Wilmot wrote sexually explicit poetry and John Cleland wrote his book about the sexual awakening of Fanny Hill to get out of debt. Artemisia Gentileschi painted works dealing with rape and sexual tension, following her own rape by the Florentine painter Agostino Tassi.

Throughout these two centuries, men and women explored the globe, and some settled in new lands, far away from their birthplaces. Wars and revolutions created, destroyed, and redefined nations. During this period, men and women continued to fall in love, have sexual encounters, and define and redefine their gender goals and ideals. This "Colonial and Revolutionary Age" truly had a profound impact on sex, love, and culture.

NOTES

1. For a study of how breast size was viewed in Western culture over centuries, see Marilyn Yalom, *A History of the Breast* (New York: Ballentine, 1997).

2. For a discussion on terminology, see Appendix A in Charles Mann, *1491: New Revelations of the Americas before Columbus* (New York: Alfred A. Knopf, 2005), 339–43.

Guide to Related Topics

ART, DANCE, THEATER
Actors
Art, American/European
Art, Non-Western
Dance
Opera
Theater, Chinese
Theater, European
Theater, Japanese

BODY AND BODY-RELATED
The Body
Breastfeeding
Castration
Childbirth
Circumcision
Cosmetics and Perfume
Death
Ejaculation
Eunuchs
Footbinding
Hermaphrodites
Orgasm

CHILDREN AND FAMILY
Breastfeeding
Childhood and Adolescence
Child Rape
Concubines
Orphans
Widows and Widowhood

FOOD, DRINK, TOBACCO
Alcohol
Food
Household Consumerism
Tobacco

INDIVIDUALS
Behn, Aphra (c. 1640–1689)
Byrd, William (1674–1744)
Casanova, Giacomo Girolamo
    (1725–1798)
Cervantes Saavedra, Miguel de
    (1547–1616)
Chevalier d'Eon (1728–1810)
Diderot, Denis (1713–1784)
Elliott, Grace Dalrymple
    (1754–1823)
Erauso, Catalina de (1585–1650)
Franklin, Benjamin (1706–1790)
Hogarth, William (1697–1764)
Inés de la Cruz, Sor Juana
    (1651–1695)
Marvell, Andrew (1621–1678)
Mather, Cotton (1663–1728)
Milton, John (1608–1674)
Rousseau, Jean-Jacques
    (1712–1788)
Sade, Donatien Alphonse
    François de (1740–1814)
Shakespeare, William
    (1564–1616)
Swift, Jonathan (1667–1745)
Tenorio, Don Juan
Thistlewood, Thomas
    (1721–1786)
Touchet, Mervyn, Earl of
    Castlehaven (1593–1631)
Virgin Mary
Virgin of Guadalupe
Wilmot, John, Earl of Rochester
    (1647–1680)
Wollstonecraft Godwin, Mary
    (1759–1797)

LAW AND LEGAL ISSUES
Abduction
Abortion
Adultery
Bastardy
Bestiality
Bigamy
Child Rape
Consent
Divorce
Domestic Violence
Dueling
Fornication
Incest
Indentured Servants
Infanticide
Laws
Murder
Paternity
Rape/Coerced Sex
Rape Law
Sex Crimes
Sodomy and Anti-Sodomy Law

POETRY, LITERATURE, REFERENCE
Aristotle's Masterpiece (1684)
Fairy Tales
Fanny Hill (Cleland, 1749)
Gynecology Manuals
Literature
Myths and Folklore
Pornography
Restoration Poetry (1660–1700)
Seduction Literature
Tenorio, Don Juan
Tom Jones (Fielding, 1749)
Yorùbá Oral Poetry, Sexuality in

GUIDE TO RELATED TOPICS

RELIGION AND RELIGIOUS ISSUES
Celibacy
Chastity
Death
Hinduism
Islam
Judaism
Monasteries
Perfectionists
Puritans
Religion
Virgin Mary
Virgin of Guadalupe
Witches and Witch Trials

SCIENCE AND MEDICINE
Aristotle's Masterpiece (1684)
Baths
Breastfeeding
Childbirth
Contraception
Gynecology Manuals
Hysteria
Medicine and Science
Menstruation
Midwives and Physicians
Venereal Diseases

SEX AND SEXUALITY
Anal Intercourse
Aristotle's Masterpiece (1684)
Baths
Berdache
Bestiality
Bisexuality
The Body
Celibacy
Chastity
Childbirth
Concubines
Contraception
Cross-Dressing
Eunuchs
Flagellation
Geisha
Harems
Homosexuality
Impotence
Incest
Interracial Sex
Masturbation
Molly Houses
Oral Sex
Orgasm

Premarital Sex
Prostitutes and Prostitution
Salons
Yoshiwara

SLAVERY AND SERVITUDE
Atlantic Slave Trade
Concubines
Eunuchs
Harems
Indentured Servants
Interracial Sex
Slavery

SOCIAL AND CULTURAL ISSUES
Baths
Berdache
Childbirth
Clothing and Fashion
Cosmetics and Perfume
Courtship
Cross-Dressing
Dance
Death
Education
Enlightenment Thought on
   Sexuality
Eunuchs
Euphemisms and Slang
Explorers and Missionaries
Geisha
Gender Roles
Gossip, Eighteenth-Century
   England
Gossip, Seventeenth-Century
   America
Harems
Household Consumerism
India
Libertine
Madness
Maritime Culture
Marriage
Masculinity
Mexico, Indigenous Women of
Mexico, Sexuality and Gender in
Mixed Marriages, New France
Myths and Folklore
Native Americans
Orphans
Ottoman Empire
Patriarchy
Philosophy
Pirates

Polyandry
Premarital Sex
Pueblo Indians
Revolution and Gender
Romantic Love
Southeastern Indians
Taboos
Taj Mahal
Torture
Virgins/Virginity
Virtue
Wartime Rape
Women, Changing
   Images of
Yoshiwara

WOMEN
Abortion
Behn, Aphra (c. 1640–1689)
Breastfeeding
Childbirth
Concubines
Divorce
Domestic Violence
Elliott, Grace Dalrymple
   (1754–1823)
Erauso, Catalina de (1585–1650)
Geisha
Gender Roles
Gynecology Manuals
Harems
Inés de la Cruz, Sor Juana
   (1651–1695)
Marriage
Menstruation
Mexico, Indigenous
   Women of
Midwives and Physicians
Polyandry
Pregnancy
Prostitutes and Prostitution
Rape/Coerced Sex
Rape Law
Revolution and Gender
Royal Mistresses
Virgin Mary
Virgin of Guadalupe
Wartime Rape
Widows and Widowhood
Witches and Witch Trials
Wollstonecraft Godwin, Mary
   (1759–1797)
Women, Changing Images of

Chronology of Selected Events

1599   Catalina de Erauso escapes from a Spanish convent and assumes life as a man.

1601   German brothels closed to prevent the spread of venereal disease.

1602   Michelangelo Merisi Caravaggio completes painting *Amor Vincit Omnia* ("Love Conquers All"), which features a realistic, nude Cupid.

1603   Queen Elizabeth I of England dies; London theaters closed due to plague; Tokugowu Shogunate established in Japan—rules until 1868.

1604   William Shakespeare produces the play *Measure for Measure*, commenting on contemporary concerns about premarital sexuality; James I publishes "Counterblast to Tobacco."

1605   Miquel de Cervantes writes *Don Quixote de la Mancha*, considered by many to be the first modern novel; Santa Fe, New Mexico, founded.

1607   Jamestown, Virginia, established—first permanent English colony founded in North America.

1609   First tea from China imported by Dutch East India Company.

1612   Tobacco first planted in Virginia.

1612   Trial of Florentine artist Agostino Tassi for the rape of artist Artemisia Gentileschi.

1613   Artemisia Gentileschi completes painting *Judith Slaying Holofernes*.

1613   First proclamation against dueling by James I of England; Globe Theater destroyed by fire.

1614   Second Globe Theater opened.

1616   William Shakespeare dies in Stratford; Miguel Cervantes dies in Madrid.

1619   First African slaves brought to Jamestown.

1620   Pilgrims arrive at Plymouth, Massachusetts, on the *Mayflower*; first English-language newspaper established.

1624   First Japanese theater opened in Edo (Tokyo).

1624   Pope Urban VIII gives Catalina de Erauso permission to continue dressing and living as a man.

1624   Richard Cornish tried and executed for sodomy in Virginia.

1631–1653   Taj Mahal built in India.

1631   Trial and execution of Mervyn Touchet, Earl of Castlehaven, for rape and buggery.

1640   First public opera house opened in Venice, Italy; first coffeehouse in Europe also opened in Venice; torture made illegal in England.

1642–1649   English Civil War.

1642   London theaters closed by Puritan government.

1649   Charles I beheaded in England; in China, Ming dynasty ends, and Quing begins.

1652   Completion of statue of *Ecstasy of St. Theresa* by Gian Lorenzo Bernini for Cornaro Chapel of Santa Maria della Vittoria in Rome.

CHRONOLOGY OF SELECTED EVENTS

1656	Jews permitted to live in England on an "unofficial" basis by Puritan government of Oliver Cromwell.
1657	First chocolate house opened in London—considered a drink only for the wealthy.
1657	First London synagogue founded.
1660	Restoration of the monarchy in England; theaters reopened—production of *Othello* cited as first time a woman, Margaret Hughes, as Desdemona, acted on stage in England.
1664	Nell Gwynne's stage debut.
1665	Great Plague of London kills 75,000; John Wilmot, Earl of Rochester, and noted libertine, attempts to abduct Elizabeth Malet, whom he marries in 1667.
1666	Great Fire of London destroys much of the city.
1669	Hindus rebel after Mogul Emperor Aurangzeb destroys Hindu temples and bans practice of Hindu religion.
1680	Largest *auto da fé* of the Spanish Inquisition—72 people are executed by burning.
1684	*Aristotle's Masterpiece*, a popular sex manual, first published in England.
1692–1693	Salem, Massachusetts, Witchcraft Trials.
1718	Coffee brought from Arabia and planted in Brazil.
1720	First public performance of famed castrato Farinelli (born Carlo Broschi) in Italy.
1724	Molly (Mother) Clap opens "molly house" in London.
1726	Mother Clap's is raided by authorities.
1737	Farinelli retires from public performances and becomes the official singer for Philip V of Spain, singing the same four songs to him every night for over two decades; Our Lady of Guadalupe made patron saint of Mexico City.
1740	China outlaws sex between men.
1742	Dr. John Halloway prosecuted and convicted for performing an abortion—his patient died and Halloway escaped to Rhode Island.
1745	Madame de Pompadour (born Jeanne-Antoinette Poissin) becomes influential royal mistress of Louis XV of France.
1748	Dr. William Cadogen publishes *Essay upon Nursing*, an influential essay on breastfeeding.
1749	Henry Fielding publishes *Tom Jones*.
1759–1767	Dressing as a man and using the name William Chandler, Mary Lacy serves on various English ships as a crewmember.
1762	Jean-Jacques Rousseau publishes *Émile*, in which he discusses the importance of women being mothers.
1765–1769	Sir William Blackstone publishes his *Commentaries on the Laws of England*, a work of great importance in determining how rape and marital laws were prosecuted in England and the United States.
1769	Wet nurse bureau established in Paris—wet nurses were paid.
1776	American Declaration of Independence.
1782	Pierre Choderos de Laclos publishes *Le Liaisons Dangereuses*.
1789	French Revolution begins.
1792	*Vindication of the Rights of Women* published by Mary Wollstonecraft; divorce legalized in France as part of republican reforms (abolished in 1816); sodomy decriminalized in France.

The Encyclopedia

ABDUCTION. The abduction of women by men seeking wives, **concubines**, or slaves is a practice that goes back to ancient times. One such example, the Rape of the Sabine Women, concerns the legendary founding of Rome. Facing a severe shortage of women and unable to get nearby cities to agree to alliances through intermarriage, the early Romans abducted the Sabine women during a religious festival. Despite being abducted and raped, the Sabine women formed attachments with their abductors. Some months later, when the Sabine men sought revenge, they found their sisters and daughters did not want to be rescued. Instead, they pleaded with their fathers and brothers not to attack the men who had become their husbands and the fathers of their unborn children. This story, recounted by both Ovid and Livy, justifies abduction and **rape** as a means to obtain brides and establish a city. This view of the episode has been immortalized over the centuries in numerous works of **art**, **literature**, and **theater** (including the musical *Seven Brides for Seven Brothers*, which sets the story in the American West).

One of the most famous portrayals of the Sabine women's abduction is the seventeenth-century painting by Nicolas Poussin, *Rape of the Sabine Women* (1633–1634). In this painting, Poussin portrays the rape and abduction in heroic terms. In fact, themes of "heroic rape" were common in the seventeenth century, as they were throughout the early modern period, emphasizing both the power of husbands over their wives and nobles over their subjects. In legal terms, rape was considered mainly a crime of property theft: the Sabine women were stolen from their fathers. Far from being objects of contempt or pity, the Sabine women became revered as the mothers of Rome.

The abduction of heiresses was one way in which some men increased their wealth and property. Abducted, forced into **marriage**, and consummation of the marriage, some wealthy women and girls found themselves legally bound to men who wanted only their land and money. One purpose of seventeenth- and eighteenth-century **child rape** laws was to protect the daughters of wealthy men by making sexual intercourse with girls under a particular age illegal. Since the girls could not legally **consent** to sexual relations, they also could not marry. Eighteenth-century laws against clandestine marriages, while serving to regularize marriage regulations and procedures within England, also attempted to prevent **bigamy** and the abduction of brides.

However, bride capture was not just an ancient Western tradition. Some Native American tribes stole women from neighboring tribes when they faced shortages of women within their own group. Historical evidence suggests that the Navajo and Pueblo at times exchanged women peacefully and at other times forcefully abducted them.

"The Rape of the Sabine Women," by Nicolas Poussin, 1637–38. © Erich Lessing/Art Resource, NY.

Similarly, some Native American and indigenous Mexican women were given as gifts to the Spanish, but at other times, Spanish soldiers and explorers seized them as spoils of conquest.

European women were also taken as captives by Native American men, as were men and children. Some women became "wives"; others were adopted by their captors, and still others probably held some indeterminate position, depending on how long they were held captive and by whom. Mary Rowlandson, in the first captivity narrative published in North America, declared that she was never raped, although she spent much time enumerating all the abuses of the Indians she considered to be savages.

Far from being repulsed, some European men, encountering Native American women, African women, and the indigenous women of various Pacific islands, viewed them as temptresses who were sexually voracious. Although some of these women were given to European men as wives or concubines in order to form trade or political alliances, others were simply abducted and raped. As the trade in African slaves grew and developed after the discovery of the New World by Europeans, millions of women and men were abducted, taken from their homelands, and forced across the Atlantic Ocean. See also Mexico, Indigenous Women of; Native Americans; Slavery; Wartime Rape.

Further Reading: Brooks, James F. *Captives and Cousins: Slavery, Kinship, and Community in the Southwest Borderlands.* Chapel Hill: University of North Carolina Press, 2002; Brownmiller, Susan. *Against Our Will: Men, Women and Rape.* New York: Fawcett Columbine, 1975; Wolfthal, Diane. *Images of Rape: The "Heroic" Tradition and Its Alternative.* New York: Cambridge University Press, 1999.

Merril D. Smith

ABORTION. An abortion is an intentional termination of a **pregnancy**. Desperate women who do not want to be pregnant have always sought abortions. While no one is sure when the practice first appeared, records have traced abortions as far back as 5,000 years ago when ancient Chinese women used herbs, poisons, and mercury as abortifacients, properties that were believed to terminate pregnancies. In the seventeenth and eighteenth centuries, common law in the American colonies and in Europe generally held that abortion was morally wrong and possibly dangerous, but it was rarely considered a criminal act. Sir William Blackstone's (1723–1780) landmark *Commentaries on the Laws of England* (1765–1769) codified the common law belief that early abortions were legal.

Rather than having women resort to abortions, colonial Americans used social persuasion to force men to marry the women they had impregnated. This practice ended in the mid-eighteenth century in response to difficulties over establishing **paternity**. Women who had sex outside marriage continued to face fines, jail sentences, or public humiliation. It was also considered a crime to conceal a pregnancy.

The move toward state control of reproduction that began in the late seventeenth century was due in large part to increasing numbers of desperate women who committed **infanticide** because they did not have access to abortion or had used unsuccessful methods or were simply afraid of using abortifacients. When such acts were discovered, they led to public outcry. The penalty for infanticide was usually execution. Governments were also concerned about increasing numbers of women being poisoned by taking alleged abortifacients and took steps to control access to dangerous substances.

As the eighteenth century drew to a close, abortions remained legal in America and most of Europe. France, which criminalized abortions in 1791, was the exception. This tacit acceptance of abortion ended in 1803 when England passed Lord Ellenborough's Act criminalizing abortion. This act served as the model for legislation passed in the United States. Initially, laws banning abortions were directed at physicians, but they were later amended to include women having abortions.

In 1742, Dr. John Hallowell of Pomfret, Connecticut, became the first physician in North America who was prosecuted for performing an abortion because it led to the death of his patient, nineteen-year-old Sarah Grosvenor. Although he was found guilty, Hallowell escaped punishment by fleeing to Rhode Island. By the middle of the eighteenth century, many physicians had become convinced of the necessity for therapeutic abortions, which was broadly defined to include pregnancies that were not wanted as well as those that were detrimental to the health of the mother.

From the beginning of the abortion debate, controversy surfaced over the issue of when exactly a fetus became a "person" or developed a soul. The common practice was to assume that personhood was established with "quickening," which generally occurs around the third or fourth month when the expectant mother feels the fetus move. The process of determining viability of a quickened fetus was complicated by the fact that no reliable tests for pregnancy existed, and some women did not recognize quickening when it occurred.

Some religions endorsed the concept of "simultaneous animation," the belief that the soul was present from the moment of conception, first advocated in 1658 by Hieronymus Florentinius, a Franciscan priest who argued that all fetuses possessed a soul and should be baptized. Other religions, however, maintained that ensoulment did not occur until quickening took place. During the seventeenth century, churches launched concentrated efforts to ban abortions on moral grounds.

Much of the knowledge about abortifacients was distributed through word of mouth, and most women had some knowledge of herbs that were readily available in gardens and woods and which were believed to restore interrupted menstrual flow, leading to termination of pregnancy. Doctors and apothecaries often helped women obtain herbs and drugs that had been identified as abortifacients. Material that advised women on what *not to do* while pregnant also served as resources on what pregnant women could do to cause abortions. By the mid-1700s, the use of abortifacients was so widely accepted that newspapers often advertised them.

Using abortifacients was commonly known as "taking the trade." These properties were ingested, rubbed on the skin, or placed on the body. The most popular abortifacients were ergot, savin, pennyroyal, and tansy. Other herbs used as abortifacients included marjoram, thyme, parsley, lavender, wormwood, aloe, asafetida, myrrh, rue, ginger, sage, savory, myrtle, hellebore, gentian root, nutmeg, common juniper, laurel, pepper, foxglove, catnip, balm, horehound, hyssop, willow, mustard, mint, and dittany. While most alleged abortifacients were harmless, they were also ineffective. Some were poisonous, ending pregnancies by killing the mother.

Binding, falling, running, lifting, leaping, excessive exercise, bleeding, blistering, purging, and vomiting were all used in the hopes of causing abortions. When no other method worked, women resorted to vigorous massage of the uterus or used instruments that perforated the uterus, frequently resulting in fatal infections for the mother.

Even in the American South where contraceptive knowledge often lagged behind the more industrial North, abortions were not unknown. Southern women accused of having abortions were required to appear before a "jury of matrons" that generally included a mid-wife. This unofficial jury determined whether a pregnancy had existed and the likelihood of termination, and then handed down recommendations based on their findings to official male juries for further action.

While abortions before quickening were legal throughout the sixteenth and seventeenth centuries in the United States and most of Europe, they were not readily available. Most abortions were attempted through the use of herbs, drugs, or practices thought to terminate pregnancy. Such methods were generally either ineffective or dangerous. Nevertheless, desperate women continued to abort unwanted fetuses as they had done since recorded history. By 1800, political and religious forces had created an environment in which access to abortions was destined to become restricted, and women who sought abortions and physicians who performed them were to be viewed as criminals. *See also* Childbirth; Contraception; Menstruation; Midwives and Physicians.

Further Reading: Brodie, Janet Farrell. *Contraception and Abortion in Nineteenth-Century America.* Ithaca, NY: Cornell University Press, 1994; Dayton, Cornelia Hughes. "'Taking the Trade': Abortion and Gender Relations in an Eighteenth-Century New England Village." *William and Mary Quarterly* (January 1991): 19–49; Olasky, Marvin. *Abortion Rites: A Social History of Abortion in America.* Wheaton, IL: Crossway, 1992; Riddle, John M. *Contraception and Abortion from the Ancient World to the Renaissance.* Cambridge, MA: Harvard University Press, 1992; Riddle, John M. *Eve's Herbs: A History of Contraception and Abortion in the West.* Cambridge, MA: Harvard University Press, 1997; Tone, Andrea, ed. *Controlling Reproduction: An American History.* Wilmington, DE: Scholarly Resources, 1997.

Elizabeth R. Purdy

ACTORS.   Until as late as the seventeenth century, the notion of *an actor* was reserved for men only; women were not allowed to perform on stage in most European countries. During the Restoration the notion widened to comprise both sexes, and the term *actress* was invented. The reputation of the profession also suffered from the fact that all female roles were played by men or boys before the seventeenth century; men in dresses on stage seemed proof that acting was "entertainment coming from the Devil" and that it encouraged **homosexuality**. Consequently, on the eve of the English civil war in 1642, the English Parliament officially closed theaters, although secret performances continued. According to some, the closing only improved dramatic performances. This period was also the dawn of female acting and, conversely, the dusk of male acting in female roles, which again caused controversy and protests. In 1656, William Davenant presented *The Siege of Rhodes*, which was not only the first English **opera** but also the first noted case of a woman performing on a public stage in England. Other sources claim that it was a performance of *Othello* in 1660 that first gave a woman the opportunity to act. The introduction of women onto the stage enhanced the realism of the plays and gave women a larger social role. On the other hand, from their very first roles women were cast and perceived mainly as sex objects.

Some of the most famous actors of the Restoration era are Charles Hart, Nell Gwynne, Catherine Coleman, Margaret Hughes, and Anne Bracegirdle—each of them having a great impact on the development of the profession. Charles Hart (1625–1683), according to some sources an illegitimate grandson of **William Shakespeare**'s sister Joan, was a soldier, but it was acting that proved more dangerous for him, for performing illegally earned him imprisonment on several occasions. In 1660, he became the leading man of the King's Company. Famed for his roles in heroic plays, Hart—together with Nell Gwynne, the most famous female actor of the time—also influenced Restoration comedy. Gwynne (1650–1687) was well known not only for being a pioneer female actor, but also for being a lover first to Charles Hart and then to Charles II. Also a friend of writers **Aphra Behn** and John Dryden, Gwynne was famous for her witticisms and bold remarks. Once, for example, she stopped a fight between a man who called her "a whore" and a man defending her honor by saying "I *am* a whore. Find something else to fight about." Gwynne was the most beloved female actor of the time and was also one of the few mistresses of Charles II who was popular with the English public.

Nell Gwynne, ca. 1907. Courtesy of the Library of Congress.

Not as lauded as Gwynne but perhaps even more important from the historical point of view were Catherine Coleman and Margaret Hughes. In 1656, Coleman became the first female actor to perform on a public stage in England, while Hughes's more remarkable portrayal of Desdemona in 1660 is most often referred to as the first ever performed by a woman. Another actor famous for playing *Othello*'s Desdemona was Anne Bracegirdle, a renowned member of the United Company, who was also a talented comedienne and had many roles written especially for her.

Outside England, the situation was similar. In seventeenth-century France, female actors were becoming increasingly popular, with Mlle Champmesle the most famous of them. However, in Italy, women were permitted to perform on stage in the sixteenth century when a true star of *commedia dell' arte* was born under the name of Isabella Canali, who was not only a great actor, but also a poet and writer of many of her own dialogues and monologues. *See also* Royal Mistresses; Theater; Theater, Chinese; Theater, Japanese.

Further Reading: Dasent, Arthur Irwin. *Nell Gwynne 1650–1687: Her Life's Story from St. Giles's to St. James's, with Some Account of Whitehall and Windsor in the Reign of Charles the Second.* New York: Benjamin Bloom, 1969; Howe, Elizabeth. *The First English Actresses: Women and Drama, 1660–1700.* Cambridge: Cambridge University Press, 1992; McAfee, Helen. *Pepys on the Restoration Stage.* New York: Benjamin Bloom, 1964; Powell, Jocelyn. *Restoration Theatre Production.* Boston: Routledge & Kegan Paul, 1984.

Bartlomiej Paszylk

ADULTERY. Adultery means voluntary sexual intercourse between a married individual and someone who is not his or her spouse. Western secular and ecclesiastical courts treated adultery as a serious offence in the seventeenth and eighteenth centuries. Generally, Western adultery **laws** focused on adultery committed by a married woman. This was due to a concern for property rights and legitimate inheritance, as well as the sexual double standard.

English society condoned infidelity in aristocratic men; it expected aristocratic women to put up with it. Generally, **divorce** fell under the purview of the ecclesiastical courts, which allowed annulments and separation of bed and board but not true divorce. Men could receive a separation if their wives committed adultery. Women had to prove adultery and another aggravating marital offence such as desertion or cruelty. By the end of the seventeenth century, patient noblemen could receive a true divorce through an act of Parliament. Meanwhile, the majority of Englishmen (and a few women) resorted to desertion and long-term adulterous affairs when their marriages broke down.

Continental Europe approached adultery in much the same way. The French moderated adultery law during the Revolutionary years, but the Napoleonic Code reinforced traditional condemnation and punishment of female adulterers. In Islamic countries some versions of *Shariah* required women and men convicted of *zina* (adultery) to be executed by stoning or severe whipping. Although Islam theoretically condemned adultery in both husbands and wives, wives faced swifter and more severe punishment in practice.

Most American colonies followed European law and custom with regard to adultery. Puritan-dominated New England, however, offers a unique case study in the history of adultery. Information on adultery in New England comes from court records. Unlike their Anglican and Catholic counterparts, Puritan courts allowed divorce in cases of adultery. These divorce cases do not tell us how often adultery occurred—fear, lack of resources, shame, and occasional apathy kept some men and even more women away from the courts. Nevertheless, seventeenth- and eighteenth-century family law provides a lens through which one can gauge changing attitudes about adultery. This lens suggests that two elements of American culture significantly altered the way many (though certainly not all) defined adultery: Puritan views on proper family governance and a patriotic rejection of upper-class British culture.

Seventeenth-century **Puritans** viewed the family as the primary unit of social control. Well-ordered families provided the foundation of political and ecclesiastical authority. Disorderly ones threatened the body politic. Unruly children must be controlled, disobedient wives corrected, and disorderly husbands reprimanded. Thus the Puritans demanded fidelity in husbands as well as wives. Moreover, because the Puritans defined marriage as a civil contract rather than a sacrament, women as well as men could sue for divorce. Indeed, four times as many women as men petitioned for divorce in seventeenth-century New England—many of them listing adultery as a reason for dissolution.

Although their laws punished adulterous husbands and allowed wives to seek a divorce, the Puritans certainly did not abandon the sexual double standard. Inequality in punishments suggests that adulterous wives were considered more dangerous than adulterous husbands. Social attitudes and financial dependence kept more wives with adulterous husbands than vice versa. Moreover, divorce laws favored men. While husbands could seek a divorce on the sole ground of adultery, wives had to combine adultery with another offence—usually desertion, bigamy, or failure to provide. Divorced women were expected to remarry more fit family governors.

Adulterers faced severe punishment. While only enforced thrice, seventeenth-century Puritan law prescribed the death penalty for adulterous wives and their partners. Adulterous husbands faced imprisonment. Those prosecuted for adultery were often convicted of lesser offences such as shameful and unchaste behavior. The convicted might find themselves publicly whipped, symbolically hanged, banished, branded, or compelled to wear Hawthorne's legendary scarlet letter. Whippings proved particularly humiliating for women who had to strip to the waist before receiving the customary thirty lashes.

Adultery was not a capital offence outside New England. In Pennsylvania, an adulterous spouse could receive twenty-one lashes and a prison term. Habitual offenders might be branded on their foreheads. Southern colonial courts were less interested in personal behavior—so long as it did not produce a bastard. Although true divorce was rare, a southern gentleman could secure a separation and occasionally a divorce from an adulterous wife. Wives had no such recourse. It comes as little surprise that men were not charged with adultery in a society that condoned sexual license with female slaves.

New England's adultery laws became less brutal over time. In the eighteenth century, "companionate marriage" became the ideal. Affection and friendship were important in such marriages. Cultural commentators put less emphasis on wifely submission and more on the emotional bonds between husbands and wives. Husbands who broke those bonds faced censure. Meanwhile women's "moral character" experienced a fundamental reevaluation. Fewer commentators portrayed women as morally suspect "Eves." Instead, they emphasized women's **virtue** and religiosity. Husbands had a more difficult time convincing people that they were the victims in an adulterous relationship.

Despite these developments, the sexual double standard lingered, making it difficult for wives to secure a divorce from adulterous husbands. Not that they did not try—more New England women than men sought divorce in the eighteenth century. But, men continued to enjoy legal, political, economic, and sociocultural advantages where divorce was concerned. That began to change during the American Revolution. The change had less to do with women's rising status than with a determination to distinguish the virtuous American Republic from the corrupt British empire. Corrupt English aristocrats engaged in vice; virtuous American republicans did not. The future of the Republic, argued many Founders, depended on female *and male* fidelity. *See also* Bastardy; Fornication; Gender Roles.

Further Reading: Cott, Nancy F. "Divorce and the Changing Status of Women in Eighteenth-Century Massachusetts." *William and Mary Quarterly* (1976): 586–614; Philips, Roderick. *Putting Asunder: A History of Divorce in Western Society.* Cambridge: Cambridge University Press, 1988; Turner, David M. *Fashioning Adultery: Gender, Sex, and Civility in England, 1660–1740.* New York: Cambridge University Press, 2002.

Tanis Lovercheck-Saunders

AFRICAN SLAVE TRADE. *See* Atlantic Slave Trade

ALCOHOL. Although alcohol has been known to affect people's sexuality throughout recorded history, it took on a special character in the colonial period, as its consumption at the time increased dramatically due to the sociocultural developments set in motion by the Industrial Revolution. The seventeenth century saw the invention and commercialization of a number of alcoholic beverages, including champagne in France and gin in Holland. But whereas champagne was slow to gain popularity, the discovery of gin provided cheap alcohol to masses who would not have been able to afford otherwise expensive wine or beer. Predictably, the ready availability of inexpensive spirits contributed to a mass-scale drinking problem in industrialized countries, which the moralists of the time considered to be a direct cause of moral depravation and sexual impropriety.

Excessive use of gin was a fairly common occurrence throughout the seventeenth- and eighteenth-century Western world—with the drink first becoming popular in Holland, France, and England, and eventually making its way to Australia and America—but the problem was arguably the most severe in the birthplace of the Industrial Revolution, England. Because gin sales taxes represented a substantial part of government revenues and gin production utilized large grain surpluses, the drink was seen as an important stimulus for the economy and its sale was initially encouraged by the authorities. This allowed gin production to develop into a major economic activity, making alcohol present on the streets, and giving rise to innumerable gin bars, a novel type of social venue frequented mostly by the lower classes. Thus there broke out the "gin epidemic," with gin bars being deplored as places of lewd misconduct documented in the **literature** and **art** of the time.

Also, apart from being a favorite recreational drug among the impoverished masses, gin did not go unnoticed by the emerging middle class. Driven by consumerism of capitalist society, curious of new commodities, wealthier citizens gradually succumbed to the allure of gin. But whereas gin was an affordable novelty for the rich, the poor indulged in drinking and sex as a form of desperate escapism, numbing themselves to their economic plight.

Large-scale binge drinking caused serious concern both among the government and the moralists of the time. The former tried to revert the trend by imposing high excise taxes on gin sellers; the latter offered exhortations to moral improvement through didactic art. An example of the latter approach, *Gin Lane* by **William Hogarth** is a print depicting all social ills believed to result from the alcohol abuse and sexual excess. According to Hogarth, gin was responsible not only for promiscuity, but also for poverty, crime, infant mortality, and **venereal diseases**, all demonstrated in graphic detail in the image of a street in ruin. In a similarly hortatory tone, a sizable proportion of Dutch painting of the time depicts alcohol-fueled debauchery. Many paintings by Jan Steen, Jacob Jordaen, or even Jan Vermeer show tavern interiors with drunken male and female revelers engaging in acts of explicit sexual contact.

Although alcohol was invariably present in scenes of wanton abandon, the link between alcohol abuse and loose sexual morals should be taken with some caution. Paintings and surviving reports on the question of alcohol and sex were produced by moralists, rarely characterized by objective observation, and they are currently approached with skepticism by scholars. It should be pointed out that moral liberation and sexual audacity were part and parcel of a larger cultural movement, libertinism, in

Europe which was motivated primarily by active opposition against Christian moral values. Libertinism was an intellectual attitude, in which alcohol played a merely incidental, not causal, role. It seems plausible that libertinism would have contested religious morality and resorted to sexual openness with or without indulgence in alcohol.

In America too, apart from being a ubiquitous commodity, alcohol was also a daily **food** staple. Because milk, water, tea, and coffee were either expensive or likely to be contaminated, wine and beer were consumed in large quantities. Later, in the course of geographic expansion, settlers unable to transport bulky cases of wine in their wagons increasingly switched to wieldier strong spirits. Thus in the early years of American history, the risk of alcohol abuse was a serious public concern. Temperance was considered a matter of Puritan responsibility for social stability and harmony. It was believed that an entire community faced damnation for failing to reform sinners, and thus alcohol misuse was censured by religious leaders. Puritan educator and minister Increase Mather argued that "Drink is in itself a good creature of God, and to be received with thankfulness, but the abuse of drink is from Satan." It was through appeal to religious values and ideals of rational self-control that community leaders encouraged moderate consumption of alcohol; temperance was not normally enforced under pain of punishment. *See also* Libertine; Tobacco.

Further Reading: Warner, Jessica. *Craze: Gin and Debauchery in an Age of Reason.* New York: Four Walls Eight Windows, 2002.

Konrad Szczesniak

AMERICAN ART. *See* Art, American/European

ANAL INTERCOURSE. Anal intercourse, condemned in the Bible, was considered a sin in Christian Europe. It was a crime against nature, that is, a sexual act from which reproduction could not occur, and was thus strongly condemned. Another reason that has been suggested for the condemnation of anal intercourse is that when two men engaged in anal intercourse the bounds of the male body were violated. Female bodies were meant to be penetrated not male bodies. Anal intercourse, therefore, blurred the boundaries between men and women in an era when these bounds were being ever more rigidly ascribed. It was during the early modern period that men who engaged in sexual relations with other men began to be viewed as feminine in dress and behavior.

It was also during the early modern era that many states began to enact legislation against anal intercourse between two men. In Castile, Aragon, and England, such laws were put into effect in the sixteenth century, whereas in the Dutch provinces of Holland and Groningen, such laws did not exist before the 1730s. Castilian Seville exempted boys under the age of fourteen and those who had been forced to commit **sodomy** from the death sentence, but in many places such distinctions did not exist. In England, anal intercourse between a man and a woman was made a crime in 1718. In Orthodox Russia, anal intercourse between men was considered a sin but not a crime until 1832 (though it had been condemned under Russian military law nearly a century earlier).

The penalty for committing anal intercourse with another man was generally severe. The death sentence was carried out across western Europe with burning being the method of choice in Seville while strangulation was preferred in the Netherlands. Sodomy was a crime that was considered highly contagious, and thus in the Netherlands, the authorities chose to perform executions in secret. In Seville, on the other hand, the authorities chose to make the burning of a sodomite a highly public display in an effort to warn others against committing such acts. By the end of the early modern era, the death penalty for sodomy was being abolished in many states, for example, Austria (1787), France (1791), and Prussia (1794).

Most of the men condemned for committing anal intercourse with other men in the eighteenth-century Netherlands were married with children. Exclusively homosexual men do not appear often in European records prior to the eighteenth century. In China, homosexual relations between men were considered acceptable throughout much of the empire's history so long as these men also married and had a family, as was their duty. Then, in 1740, the first laws against anal intercourse between men were enacted in China.

In many American native cultures, anal intercourse between men was perceived quite differently than in Christian Europe. In these cultures there existed an individual known as a **berdache**, who was a man living as a woman performing female duties (sometimes even including marriage to another man) and engaging in sexual relations with other men. In some societies, berdaches acted like male prostitutes and were supposed to satisfy the sexual desires of the young men and keep them away from the women until they were of a marriageable age. In others, berdaches performed anal intercourse on the ruler in public ceremonies designed to show the ruler's power. *See also* Bisexuality; Homosexuality; Oral Sex.

Further Reading: Gerard, Kent, and Gert Hekma, eds. *The Pursuit of Sodomy: Male Homosexuality in Renaissance and Enlightenment Europe.* New York: Harrington Park Press, 1989; Trexler, Richard. *Sex and Conquest: Gendered Violence, Political Order, and the European Conquest of the Americas.* Ithaca, NY: Cornell University Press, 1995.

Tonya Marie Lambert

ANTI-SODOMY LAW. See Sodomy and Anti-Sodomy Law

ARISTOTLE'S MASTERPIECE (1684). First published in England in 1684, *Aristotle's Masterpiece* was a widely reprinted and popular sex manual from its first appearance until the 1930s. Authorship of the work is unknown, but three men, Nicholas Culpepper, "Dr. Borman," and William Salmon, were associated with its printing and later editing, if not its composition. Claiming to represent that collected wisdom of English folk medicine, astrology and numerology, plus the scientific knowledge of Medieval, Renaissance, Greek, Roman, and Islamic physicians, the work was a compendium of sources translated and arranged in English with Aristotle's name to lend distinction and authority.

The book was originally intended for a well-educated, predominantly male audience, who had means to indulge in luxury goods and afford expensive ingredients for medicines. It also assumed mechanical knowledge of the sex act, offering advice on fine-tuning sex to aid in conception and mutual satisfaction. Unusually for the seventeenth century, the book ascribed parity in the desire of men and women, saw sex as a natural urge to procreate, and, using the humeral framework of medicine, insisted that for the birth of healthy children, both sexual partners should experience pleasure. To aid in this pursuit, the work suggested aphrodisiacs, soft lighting, sexy clothing, and thinking about seductive music. Partners should be chosen for attraction and love, and treated with respect, as in the book's suggestion that husbands give their wives benefit of the doubt when wondering about evidence of virginity or the parentage of premature children. Once conception was achieved, the book offered extensive suggestions on **pregnancy** management, diet, arranging a lying-in chamber, employing female midwives, and testing the sex of the unborn child.

In only a few places does *Aristotle's Masterpiece* veer into misogyny. Ignoring the sexual development of adolescent males, which readers would have experienced themselves, it offers an overheated view of teenaged girls, who were advised to marry extremely young and begin having children as soon as possible. It ascribes all infertility to women and follows the traditional idea that menstrual sex or viewing unpleasant things while pregnant would produce monstrous children. In a bizarre parallel to a mother's thoughts affecting a child, the book notes that an adulterous woman who thinks of her husband during sex with a lover will have a child resembling her spouse. On the contentious subject of the "ensouling" of children, the work authoritatively places the event not at conception, but at twenty-four days for a male child, fifty for a female. Because the point of the book is to encourage fertility, no contraceptive advice is given for either sex.

From its first printing, *Aristotle's Masterpiece* was a runaway success. It appealed to those wanting "tried and true" methods and avoided advocating modern innovations like the Chamberlein forceps. The book did change over time, with a second version appearing in the 1690s with a more pointedly witty tone and risqué remarks, although still studded with cautionary French woodcuts of "monster" children and cautionary quotations from the Scriptures. Although widely circulated in the American colonies as one of the few popular medical guides for pregnancy, a 1766 version was printed in America and enjoyed even greater readership. A third version, printed in England in the 1840s, bowdlerized the text and offered itself as an example of pleasures to be avoided outside **marriage** and to be moderated within, an almost total reversal of the original text. In this heated and "forbidden" form, the book became a popular masturbatory text for young men. As one of the longest-lived sex and pregnancy manuals, versions of *Aristotle's Masterpiece* only ceased to be printed for a popular audience in the 1930s. *See also* Childbirth; Food; Gynecology Manuals; Menstruation; Midwives and Physicians.

Further Reading: Beall, Otho T. "*Aristotle's Master Piece* in America: A Landmark in the Folklore of Medicine." *William and Mary Quarterly*, 3rd Series, 20 (April 1963): 207–22; D'Emilio, John, and Estelle B. Friedman. *Intimate Matters: A History of Sexuality in America.* New York: Harper and Row, 1988; Porter, Roy, and Lesley Hall. *The Facts of Life: The Creation of Sexual Knowledge in Britain, 1650–1950.* New Haven, CT: Yale University Press, 1995.

Margaret Sankey

ART, AMERICAN/EUROPEAN. The early period of European colonialism, the seventeenth and eighteenth centuries, was characterized by rich extravagance and high style during a time in America identified by Captain John Smith as "The Starving Time," and later, the struggle for independence. Early American paintings were generally portraits painted of lavishly dressed subjects in a flat style with firm lines. Eighteenth-century American art still focused on portraiture, but these portraits developed into realistic and dynamic images. Portrait miniatures served as intimate keepsakes given to family members, spouses, or secret lovers. Due to their private nature, portrait miniatures were often sexually charged. The Baroque Period was the hallmark of European seventeenth-century art, theatrically violent and erotic with rich colors and dynamic lines. In the eighteenth century, Baroque gave way to Rococo. Another extravagant style, Rococo is more playful, with ornate curly cues and soft pastels. With the revolution heralding in the late eighteenth century, Neoclassicism became the preferred style, discarding the erotic nature and opulence of before and focusing on serious political matters.

"Judith Slaying Holofernes," by Artemisia Gentileschi, ca. 1620. © Alinari/Art Resource, NY.

Seventeenth-century art in America was a chaste affair. Most colonists did not have the leisure time to practice art or the wealth to pay for it. Paintings were scarce, reminiscent of English styles, and nonsexual. By contrast, artists of seventeenth-century Europe painted religious or classical themes in an erotically charged manner. For example, Italian sculptor Gianlorenzo Bernini created *The Ecstasy of Teresa* (1647–1652). *The Ecstasy of Teresa* is a sculpture of the Christian saint in a moment of heightened passion as an angel prepares to thrust his golden spear into her. Teresa leans back, closes her eyes, and opens her mouth slightly in her blissful union of pain and pleasure. Bernini depicted the religious subject of Saint Teresa's mystical experience in a highly erotic, dramatic manner.

Other artists portrayed erotic Baroque images. Painter Michelangelo Merisi Caravaggio painted homoerotic images such as *Amor Vincit Omnia* ("Love Conquers All"). Commissioned from a private, homosexual patron, this painting depicts a nude Cupid slipping from a rumbled bed with clear anal erotic implications. Peter Paul Rubens, a Flemish artist, painted mythological themes with signature voluptuous women, emphasizing generous breasts and sensuous flesh. **Rape** was a common theme in Baroque art. Although male artists successfully depicted the violence of rape, the Italian painter Artemisia Gentileschi endured rape firsthand, and her paintings of sexual aggression, rape, anger, and retribution are some of the most poignant ones.

As America grew wealthier, the demand for portraiture rose in the eighteenth century; in addition, a cultural emphasis on **romantic love**, **marriage**, and familial affection developed. Baroque and Rococo influences are evident in portraits of this time. The portrait miniature exemplifies romantic love by its personal and intimate nature. Portrait miniatures, most of which could fit in the palm of a hand, were placed in delicate brooches or lockets and worn on the body. Artists painted the portraits on ivory, which lent painted skin a warm glow as light passed through. On the reverse, the sitter's braided hair was set under glass. The intimacy of miniatures made them ideal love tokens between secret lovers, serving as mementos of loved ones or as symbols of passion. The sitter's dress and pose could be seductive, culminating in the early nineteenth century when artist Sarah Goodridge painted *Beauty Revealed*, a portrait of her own breasts for her secret lover.

In eighteenth-century Europe, Rococo dominated until about 1775. Divided over whether Rococo is an independent style or a final form of Baroque art, scholars agree that Rococo began in the French palace Versailles. Rococo painter, Flemish-born Antione Watteau, painted shimmering images of *fêtes galantes*, or festive gatherings, that held thinly veiled sexual undertones. In his 1718 painting *The Dance*, Watteau depicts one of these festive gatherings with classical references. A stone ram head, a traditional symbol of lust, and a sculpture of a voluptuous woman, more voluptuously Rubens than Greek, watch the dancers. Jean-Honoré Fragonard's 1766 painting *The Swing* illustrates flirtation and **seduction**. In this image, a girl swings in an enclosed garden of lush, frilly leaves while her lover hides in the bushes, peeking up her dress. The girl is aware of his presence and kicks up her foot, opening her dress and kicking off a shoe in secret love play. *See also* Literature; Opera; Theater.

Further Reading: Batterberry, Ariane Ruskin. *Seventeenth & Eighteenth Century Art*. New York: McGraw-Hill, 1969; Bjelajac, David. *American Art: A Cultural History*. Upper Saddle River, NJ: Prentice Hall, 2005; Getlein, Mark. *Gilbert's Living with Art*. New York: McGraw-Hill, 2002.

Melissa K. Benne

ART, NON-WESTERN. Art frequently had a religious or social role in non-Western societies. In Indian temples, for example, the great gods appeared in many shapes, and by the time the Western colonizers and traders arrived, the temples of Khujarao, begun around the year 1000 CE, were being put up for the ordinary Indian, who thought of the old Vedic gods in homely ways. These massive pieces of architecture are covered with scenes of couples in the act of copulation. The gods are carved in stone along with great crowds of different sorts of people: dancers, singers, misfits, clowns, priests, and courtiers. The cults for which these temples were built were popular versions of the old cult of Siva and his wife, Parvati. The temples were designed as propaganda for the illiterate masses, showing that the government approved of their devotions to gods who were sexual like the worshippers. At the heart of the temple was a carving of Siva in the form of a great phallus. For the Indian mystic and for the public, Siva was being worshipped as a phallus; the phallus was the way to God.

In contrast to these huge religious statues are the small, everyday items created by pre-Columbian Andean people, although they, too, may have served a religious purpose. Small drinking vessels were placed in the graves of the dead. They depicted sexuality, with figures of heterosexual **anal intercourse** predominantly, as well as a substantial amount showing **oral sex**. Only third in quantity are those sculptures of heterosexual penis-vagina intercourse. The pots appear to have been made by women, and some of the pots have the spout as the penis, or the perforation for drinking as a vulva.

Still another form of art can be found in countries where **Islam** was practiced. Architecturally, the Islamic peoples put their efforts still into building mosques and palaces for the great Moguls and their multitudinous wives and members of their **harems**. Many of these were great pleasure palaces of beauty, specifically designed with love in mind. However, Islam forbids its followers from representing forms in sculptural or pictorial form: their brilliance in the fine arts turned to expressions of love, in nonpictorial forms.

Chinese art mixed the human mind with the truth of nature, which is part of the greater cosmic opposition between *yin* and *yang*. The mind had to be freed for this. Painting, sculpture, calligraphy, and other arts worked to permit the mind to blend into

Shiva appearing in the lingam, fiery pillar connecting heaven and earth, 12th–13th century. © The Art Archive/Musée Guimet Paris/Dagli Orti.

this cosmic Way (Tao), and this cosmic way would be attained by, but not exclusively by, sexual practices and union. The Chinese Taoist manuals on this subject, the first of their kind in written form, are florid and poetic accounts of precise and aim-based sexual practice, drawing on the similarity between the human essence and the essence of the facts of natural process. The reason why these sorts of art, these books, and this basis of Chinese culture were missed by Europeans who arrived in China in the seventeenth century is that a new dynasty had taken over the land and had reinstituted a superficial set of codes, a recrudescence of Confucianism, which takes no notice of the private life of the individual. Taoism went underground during this new Ch'ing dynasty. But despite the Enlightenment opinion that the Chinese were a restrained and eminently rational and asexual people, erotic art abounds. The delicate watercolor paintings of nature can be seen to describe the female reproductive organs in the hills and the delicacy of flesh in landscape. More obvious Chinese pottery and paintings resemble, in a distant way, ancient Greek pottery, decorated with images of couples in sexual union, as well as figurines of the same subject.

Japanese erotic art, or *shunga*, was popular throughout the Edo period (1603–1867). *Shunga* means spring or springtime pictures, and this type of art was generally done as woodblock prints or sometimes as painted scrolls. The prints were sexually explicit, featuring men and women, men and men, and women and women in a variety of sexual positions, performing anal intercourse, oral sex, as well as penis-vagina intercourse, and using sexual devices such as dildoes. Many artists, including those who were well known, painted *shunga*, but most of the works were done anonymously. *Shunga* were sometimes used as sex education manuals for the sons and daughters of the nobility, and brides often brought these erotic prints to their new homes, along with their wedding furniture. *See also* Art, American/European; Hinduism; India; Taj Mahal.

Further Reading: Bataille, Georges. *The Accursed Share*. 2 vols. Translated by R. Hurley. New York: Zone Books, 1991; Tannahill, Reay. *Sex in History*. London: Hamish Hamilton, 1980.

Jason Powell and Merril D. Smith

ATLANTIC SLAVE TRADE. The Atlantic slave trade refers to the forced removal and transportation of millions of Africans from their birthplaces in Africa to the Americas. Between 1450 and 1850, at least 12 million Africans crossed the Atlantic, enduring the infamous "Middle Passage." Generally, these slaves came from western and West central Africa and were traded for goods. Most often the slaves were sent to the Caribbean, Brazil, and Spanish-speaking areas of South and Central America. Less often, they arrived in English-speaking areas of North America or Europe. Once transported, they were forever separated from their families and homes.

Slavery existed in Africa before the start of the Atlantic slave trade. The system was not typically a hereditary system, although it could still be a violent one, as often slaves were captured during wars. Some people also became slaves as punishment or because they could not provide for themselves or their families.

Before the sixteenth century, most African slaves came from East Africa. Arab slave traders transported them to the Arabian Peninsula. Unlike the slaves transported in the later Atlantic slave trade, most of these slaves were women, as they were intended to be household or sex slaves. Nevertheless, the mechanisms for slave trading were already in place when the Atlantic slave trade began.

The Atlantic slave trade began and increased due to the need for an inexpensive and abundant labor force on plantations in the Americas. Most of these early plantations grew sugarcane, which was very labor-intensive, but plantations in the Western

Hemisphere also grew **tobacco**, cocoa, indigo, coffee, rice, and cotton. Plantation owners attempted to enslave **Native Americans**, but many of them died from European diseases to which they had no immunity. In addition, it was easier for them to run away, since they were not far from their homes and were familiar with the territory, unlike Africans.

The Atlantic slave trade began slowly in the 1440s. By the beginning of the eighteenth century, it began to increase. The Atlantic slave trade peaked in the 1780s, when approximately 80,000 Africans reached the Americas. Many tried to resist the voyage. There were sometimes mutinies aboard the ships, and sometimes slaves committed suicide by throwing themselves overboard. Fear of enslavement was not the sole motivation for resistance; many Africans believed that the Europeans were planning to kill and eat them.

The voyage across the Atlantic was filled with danger, and many died from diseases, such as dysentery. Shipboard hygiene and conditions were very primitive and insufficient. The voyage typically lasted from twenty-five to sixty days, depending on destination and weather conditions. Slaves were kept below deck at night and crammed tightly together. Male slaves were kept in shackles, but women and children were given more freedom during the day.

Often slaves were first brought to the West Indies, where they were "broken-in," before being sold elsewhere. Because plantation owners were generally looking for plantation laborers, most, but not all, of the slaves brought across the Atlantic were men. In mid-eighteenth-century Jamaica, England's most prosperous colony, most slaves were recent migrants from Africa. Their lives were filled with instability, as the slave population was constantly replenished with slaves from different parts of Africa, and many died from disease, insufficient food, overwork, and brutal treatment. White men on Jamaica routinely took black women as their sexual partners. The white population was mainly male, approximately 80 percent. White women's sexuality was heavily regulated, but white men could have numerous sexual encounters with black women without suffering any social stigma. Some scholars note that the few white women on the island were idealized as wives and mothers of future planters, but white men preferred black women as their sexual partners. Many believed that black women were sexually insatiable—and they were always available. Indeed, many white men moved to Jamaica because they could have sex whenever they wanted to with black slave women. Sometimes owners and overseers gave their sexual partners gifts or favorable treatment, but because they were slaves, the women could also be threatened, beaten, or abused.

It took time to abolish the Atlantic slave trade. Antislavery movements began appearing in Europe in the eighteenth century. Christian groups, such as the Society of Friends (Quakers) spoke out against the evils of slavery, and ideas of egalitarianism and brotherhood arose out of the American and French Revolutions. England outlawed the slave trade in 1807, the United States in 1808 (although not slavery itself), France in 1815, and Spain in 1820. Cuba was the last nation in the Western Hemisphere to abolish the slave trade in 1888. *See also* Indentured Servants; Interracial Sex; Revolution and Gender.

Further Reading: Burnard, Trevor. "The Sexual Life of an Eighteenth-Century Jamaican Slave Overseer." In *Sex and Sexuality in Early America*, edited by Merril D. Smith, 163–89. New York: New York University Press, 1998; Eltis, David and Philip Morgan. "New Perspectives on the TransAtlantic Slave Trade." Special Issue of *William and Mary Quarterly* 58 (January 2001).

Merril D. Smith

BASTARDY. Bastardy, the act of bearing or fathering an illegitimate child, was the cause for criminal prosecution in both England and its colonies during the seventeenth and eighteenth centuries. In the lexicon of criminal prosecutions for sexual offences, **fornication**, the act of engaging in extramarital sexual activity, whether it led to the birth of an illegitimate child or not, was the charge of choice in extreme Protestant jurisdictions. In these locations, the act of sexual intercourse itself was considered the criminal offence, not the production of an illegitimate child. Bastardy was an economic offence. With few exceptions, bastardy became a criminal offence only when the community into which the illegitimate child was born was required to provide for that child through the public purse. If child support was forthcoming from the putative father, or if the woman or her family were prepared to bring up the child independent of financial support from the community, bastardy charges were seldom levied, especially for a first offence. The most likely target of a bastardy prosecution was a single woman, usually a servant, who, having been impregnated by a fellow servant or a member of her employer's household, was unable to provide a home and financial support for her child. In most jurisdictions bastardy prosecutions came under the purview of church courts, both Protestant and Catholic. In England, presumably lax application of bastardy laws by the ecclesiastical courts established by the Church of England was a source of dissatisfaction to **Puritans**, who, in the seventeenth century, switched prosecutions for sexual offences from ecclesiastical to civil courts and extended the application of bastardy charges beyond the stereotypical prosecution of poor women to the general population. With the resumption of the monarchy in 1660, bastardy prosecutions reverted once more to the Church of England courts. These prosecutions comprised a small portion of prosecutions brought before the ecclesiastical or civil court systems in early modern England.

English colonies in North America provided a broad range of responses to bastardy dependent upon religious and economic concerns. In Puritan New England, women who bore bastards were more likely to be charged with fornication than with bastardy. The graver crime was considered to be the act of having sexual intercourse outside **marriage**, rather than the production of a bastard who would require public support. Punishment for fornication in New England ranged from a public whipping and a fine (the equivalent of a year's wages for a female servant in the seventeenth century), to a sixpence prior to the American Revolution. Prior to 1668 in New England, men were prosecuted along with their partners for fornication, when **paternity** could be proved. In 1668, the Massachusetts legislature passed a law that established a lower standard for a determination of paternity to be made, excused men from fornication prosecutions, and ensured that child-support payments were made.

In the remaining British North American colonies and in the Caribbean, the impetus for bastardy prosecutions was economic and diverged the least from contemporary English practice. Enforcement was irregular, gender specific, and status dependent. The majority of immigrants to these regions had been male **indentured servants** between the ages of seventeen and twenty-eight; single women were at a premium. Fortunes could be made using indentured servants in the production of tobacco and sugar, labor-intensive but very profitable crops. Planters were concerned about losing the labor of pregnant indentured servants and the expense of raising their children to a productive age. Women were prosecuted for bastardy when there were economic consequences to their withdrawal from field or household labor. Charges were not inevitable. Some cases appear in the court record as civil suits directed against the father of her child for compensation for lost labor. However, the economic implications of time lost through **pregnancy** and childcare meant that penalties for bastardy could be severe. As well as fines and whippings, indentures could be extended for an additional twelve to twenty-four months. The traditional double standard meant that their male partners would not be punished. *See also* Childbirth; Concubines; Infanticide; Midwives and Physicians; Laws.

Further Reading: Hambleton, Else L. *Daughters of Eve: Pregnant Brides and Unwed Mothers in Seventeenth-Century Essex County, Massachusetts.* New York: Routledge, 2004; Ingram, Martin. *Church Courts, Sex and Marriage in England, 1570–1640.* New York: Cambridge University Press, 1987.

Else L. Hambleton

BATHS. Baths and the ritual of bathing have existed since Greco-Roman times when huge elaborate facilities were built near places of exercise. As they evolved to become elaborate public meeting places and cultural centers, prostitutes found them to be a ready opportunity for soliciting customers. Lovers could meet in the ambiance of an environment where clothing was removed and cleanliness promoted. Meals and wine served tub side facilitated socialization, making the public bath an ideal activity. Public baths were associated with brothels and taverns. Medieval Europe hosted many erotic encounters in tubs of water, known as stews, until church fathers blamed sexual sin for the spread of plague and syphilis. Baths and bathing fell out of vogue, and attention to the **body**, particularly the naked body, was eschewed. Hot water was allegedly a venue for adventurous sperm to impregnate women and was blamed for inducing abortions as well. Few people bathed at all, and only when absolutely necessary because the body was considered vulnerable if wet. Europeans soon used powder, scents, and wipes to rid their bodies of smells and residues.

By the time English and French colonists established communities in America, bathing was not a normal part of everyday life. Uncommon in the Colonial world, baths gained more acceptance in the Revolutionary period particularly among the educated and upper classes. Cold water bathing was recommended as a therapeutic measure. But newly discovered natural mineral springs whose virtues were touted by **Native Americans** were embraced by those who sought new ways to improve their well-being. These springs, many high in sulfur and odiferous, were advertised originally for curing gout, sterility, **hysteria**, and a variety of unrelated problems. *Taking the waters* meant that one went to spas built on or near springs and drank from, rather than bathed in this liquid. News spread and resorts for the ailing or those who needed an additional boost to their health were opened; obviously these were for the affluent sick who could brag about their therapeutic choices. Boston boasted of Lynn Red Spring or the Cold Bath on Cambridge Street, and in Warm Springs, Standing Stone Valley, Pennsylvania, a resort, referred to as an Asylum, was built with one spring dedicated to women who were impatient at their ability to become pregnant. In Connecticut, in 1765, a man took a cold bath in the waters of Stafford Springs and was cured of the skin infection that he had had for many years. Almost overnight Stafford became a center of healing, and because of its success, Ebeneezer Guy searched for a spring and found one that he opened as a spa in nearby Mansfield, Massachusetts. However, some sexual activity may have been observed to prompt comments that appeared in local newspapers such as: "the waters are very improper for young people of a full habit of body … and are not to be used wantonly or in sport."

Europe, free from Puritan beliefs about morality and the body, had a very different worldview regarding bathing the body. Bathhouses and bathing never really totally disappeared after religious prohibitions; sensuality developed a new look, the private bathroom with a hot bath in preparation for a sexual encounter. Cold baths were therapeutic; hot baths sexy. In 1761, a public bathhouse using cold water was built on the banks of the River Seine in Paris for the affluent. The *Chateau de Madame Gourdan on Rue des Deux Portes*, was known to have a bath house in addition to a spanking room. Acolyte prostitutes were taken to the *Cabinet de Toilette*, where they were taught the arts of their profession.

Sexual associations of the bath are sacred as well as profane. For example, among religious Jewry of the world, an edifice known as a mikvah was built in order that women could purify themselves after each menstrual period. A mikvah was an essential part of a building and contained rainwater that was gathered and siphoned into a pool in accordance with certain rules. A woman was to immerse her entire body in the water. Only after total immersion was she considered pure enough to have relations with her husband.

It was not until the nineteenth century that taking a bath in a bathtub was an established ritual in most American homes, not just upper-class mansions. The first porcelain bathtub was built in 1850. *See also* Cosmetics and Perfume; Judaism; Medicine and Science; Menstruation; Prostitutes and Prostitution.

Further Reading: Bushman, Richard L., and Claudia L. Bushman. "The Early History of Cleanliness in America." *Journal of American History* 74, no. 4 (1988); Grieco, Sara. "The Body, Appearance and Sexuality." In *A History of Women*, edited by Georges Duby and Michelle Perrot. Cambridge: Belknap, 1994; Park, Edwards. "To Bathe or Not to Bathe: Coming Clean in Colonial America." See http://www.history.org/foundation/journal/Autumn00/bathe.cfm; Slonin, Rivkah. "The Mikvah." See www.chabad.org/women/the_jewish_woman.asp?AID=1541.

Lana Thompson

BEHN, APHRA (c. 1640–1689). Aphra Behn is best known as the first English woman to earn her living from her writing as a poet and playwright. Active during the Restoration era (1660–1688), when the newly restored Stuart monarchs reopened the theaters and thus initiated a period of sexually charged verse and revelry, Behn was also a novelist, literary critic, spy, and world traveler. Her exact birth year, family name (possibly Johnston), parents, rearing, and even the existence of the Mr. Behn who granted her the relatively "free" status of widowhood all remain open to conjecture and continued research.

Madame Aphra Behn, 1897. Courtesy of the Library of Congress.

Her Catholicism, command of French, and views on sexuality made Behn a popular figure during the Restoration and a favorite of Charles II's court (Nell Gwynne, one of Charles's mistresses, appeared in Behn's productions). Behn herself was a spy for Charles in Antwerp after becoming involved with an antimonarchist during a stay in a South American sugar colony. This trip to the "New World" also became fodder for her novella *Oronooko or, The Royal Slave, A True History*—published in 1688 and touted as the first English novel by critic Jane Spencer in *The Rise of the Woman Novelist*—and her play *The Widow Ranter*.

In all her works, Behn constructs an active female sexuality that though not as predatory as that of the stereotypical male "rake" of the period, like those that populated the plays of George Etherege and William Wycherley, and the poetry of **John Wilmot, Earl of Rochester**, still runs contrary to the idealized social norm of woman acting as a passive mirror for men. Behn's women defy sexual convention in order to actively search for, educate, and test potential mates instead of passively awaiting men's notice or the negotiations of their families. In *The Feigned Courtesans*, the female protagonist goes even further to present herself as a courtesan or highly paid prostitute to occasion her discourse with men.

Behn's verse also questions and blurs the lines of female sexuality with its echoes of Sappho (as in "To the fair Clarinda, who made Love to me, imagin'd more than Woman") and exposes the shortcomings of male sexuality in "The Imperfect Enjoyment," Behn's contribution to the Restoration subgenre known as the Premature-Ejaculation poem.

Late in the seventeenth century, Behn turned to prose fiction (the budding novel form) and criticism as the Glorious Revolution of 1688 and its cultural tastes swept with it the Restoration stage and comedies, which had been her forte.

For the greater part of the eighteenth and nineteenth centuries, Behn's life and work were deemed indecent and decried by even progressive female authors such as **Mary Wollstonecraft**. However, beginning with Virginia Woolf's recognition of Behn in *A Room of One's Own* as an important literary foremother ("All women ... ought to let flowers fall upon the grave of Aphra Behn ... for it was she who earned them the right to speak their minds"), studies of Behn have bloomed anew. *See also* Gender Roles; Libertine; Literature; Restoration Poetry; Royal Mistresses; Theater.

Further Reading: Duffy, Maureen. *Phoenix: The Passionate Shepherdess: The Life of Aphra Behn 1649–1680*. New York: Sterling Publishing, 2000; Hughes, Derek, and Janet Todd. *The Cambridge Companion to Aphra Behn*. Cambridge: Cambridge University Press, 2004; Todd, Janet M. *The Secret Life of Aphra Behn*. Piscataway, NJ: Rutgers University Press, 1997.

Samantha A. Morgan-Curtis

BERDACHE. Berdache is the name seventeenth-century French explorers gave to Native American men who dressed as and adopted the mannerisms of women. Today some Native American people feel the term is offensive or inaccurate, and they use other terms, such as "two-spirited" or "woman-man." Historians have also struggled with the term and the concept. Some historians believe the berdache was spiritually inspired to take on a different gender identity and that this is separate from sexual behavior.

Others define berdaches as homosexuals. It is very difficult though to comprehend the cultural identity of the berdache based on the limited sources available. Several early explorers did write about berdaches, but it was usually with disdain. To Europeans, men who took on women's roles were demeaning themselves, and men who had sex with other men were engaging in immoral, perverse behavior.

For Europeans of the seventeenth and eighteenth centuries, the concept of **homosexuality** did not exist. Nonprocreative sexual behaviors were lumped together as **sodomy**, and people who chose to engage in such behavior were punished if caught, sometimes even tortured or executed. Thus the concept of a person who was "two-spirited" was incomprehensible to the European explorers and missionaries who encountered berdaches.

However, not all berdaches had sexual relationships with other men, but all were interested in taking on the **gender roles** of women, as they were defined within their tribes. Thus, sometimes the berdache is considered a third gender, someone with the anatomical parts of a man, but acts as a woman. Berdache customs and rituals differed though. In some tribes, for example, a berdache might wear only female clothing and in other tribes a berdache wore items of both male and female clothing, but in all, they assumed the cultural tasks and behaviors of a woman.

Female berdaches did exist, but explorers seldom wrote about them. Like their male counterparts, female berdaches dressed and took on the gender roles of the other sex. Some female berdaches took wives. Among the Mohave, women who wanted to be treated as men were called hwames. Usually when they are girls, they refused to learn or participate in female activities. After undergoing a ritual, hwames were permitted to dress as, behave like, and learn the skills of boys. Hwames often took other women as their wives, and engaged in sexual relations, including **masturbation** with them. If the wife was pregnant at the time of marriage with the hwame, the hwame was considered the father of the child.

Male berdaches formed sexual attachments with other men, who were not berdaches. In sexual activities, male berdaches played a passive role. Sometimes male berdaches were casual sexual partners for men whose wives could not have sexual relations due to **menstruation**, **childbirth**, or illness. Berdaches rarely engaged in sexual relations with other berdaches. *See also* Bisexuality; Cross-Dressing; Mexico, Indigenous Women of; Native Americans; Pueblo Indians; Southeastern Indians.

Further Reading: Lang, Sabine. *Men as Women, Women as Men: Changing Gender in Native American Cultures*. Austin: University of Texas Press, 1998; Sayre, Gordon. "Native American Sexuality in the Eyes of the Beholders 1535–1710." In *Sex and Sexuality in Early America*, edited by Merril D. Smith. New York: New York University Press, 1998.

Merril D. Smith

BESTIALITY. Bestiality, or human-animal sexual interaction, was a source of social concern and regulation during the colonial and revolutionary periods. A strong correlation between "natural" laws and religious ideology influenced the creation and implementation of laws regulating sexual behaviors including bestiality, **homosexuality**, lewdness, and **adultery**. Bestiality and homosexual interaction were considered particularly heinous and were often referred to as "things fearful to name."

Fears about bestiality during this time period were fueled not only by religious beliefs, but also by misguided beliefs about the possibility of human-animal reproduction. The births of deformed animals served to enforce the beliefs in human-animal reproduction and at times also fueled accusations of bestiality based on physical similarities between a person and a deformed animal. The belief of interspecies reproduction was additionally enforced by folklore (such as the case of werewolves and other half-human, half-animal creatures).

Two prevailing acts considered "things fearful to be named" were buggery and **sodomy**. Primarily, buggery was used to refer to acts of bestiality, and sodomy was used to refer to homosexual acts, but several examples exist to point out the variable manners in which these terms were employed. The fluidity with which these terms were employed suggests the changing norms and efforts to control sexual expression at differing times and locations.

During the Colonial period the population of the New England colonies could be highly disproportionate with men outnumbering women as much as five or six to one (though this was not the case in all areas). This created a situation in which men, who may have also been constrained by issues of servitude and social class, were limited in their ability to marry or to be sexually involved with women. The limited ability to establish socially approved relationships, that is, **marriage**, may have resulted in increased occurrences of buggery (as well as sodomy). In fact, nearly all court records involving accusations of buggery, as well as sodomy, had male perpetrators. While both acts were illegal and viewed with social disapproval, there was more variability in the social tolerance and acceptance of sodomy. Initially there were more cases of buggery than sodomy, but over time this transitioned to few cases of buggery and more cases of sodomy.

Laws regulating buggery were problematic to enforce for a variety of reasons. Firstly, due to the largely agricultural lifestyle of much of New England, animals, especially farm animals, were fairly accessible and the ability to supervise every human-animal interaction was limited. Secondly, despite the close-living quarters of many New Englanders, the opportunity for some privacy was available. While the Puritan ideology of the day may have encouraged observing and regulating the behaviors of others on moral grounds, it was possible that individuals would have the opportunity to participate in variant sexual behaviors without observation. Thirdly, accusations of buggery were problematized by the variable requirements of different courts to have witness not only of potential buggery, but also of actual penetration.

Examination of the sentences involved in cases of buggery and sodomy in the New England colonies suggests that there was variable acceptance of these variant sexual acts. Courts may have taken various factors, such as age, marital status, mental capacity, and even race, into consideration when determining the likelihood of guilt and perhaps degree of punishment. In general, the punishment for those found guilty of buggery was death—though the official and practiced punishments varied. This sentence of death also extended to the animal(s) involved. The understanding was that buggery would leave a part of the human within the animal; thus, to eat the animal would have been tantamount to cannibalism, and so the animal needed to be destroyed. Buggery was seen as so loathsome socially that even to joke about this behavior was punishable by law.

Executions for bestiality within the New England colonies occurred throughout the first half of the seventeenth century. By the mid-seventeenth century, accusations and guilty findings in cases of buggery were declining. The last execution for buggery during this period occurred in 1673. During the second half of the seventeenth century, increased acceptance of variant sexual behaviors resulted in a decline in the acceptance of strict enforcement of moral codes by many citizens. While buggery was still regarded with disdain, it became increasingly difficult to definitively find a person guilty, so lesser charges, such as attempted buggery and lewd acts, may have been brought. The punishment for these lesser acts, while not death, was often harsh. These continuing harsh punishments suggest the strong social disapproval of this variant sexual act. *See also* Anal Intercourse; Laws; Oral Sex; Pornography.

Further Reading: Murrin, John M. "'Things Fearful to Name': Bestiality in Colonial America." *Pennsylvania History (Supplement)* 65 (1998): 8–43; Oaks, Robert F. "'Things Fearful to Name': Sodomy and Buggery in Seventeenth-Century New England." *Journal of Social History* 12, no. 2 (1978): 268–81.

Daniel Farr

BIGAMY. Bigamy is an individual's **marriage** to two or more people in a society where monogamous marriage is the only legal form. It differs from polygamy, which is a recognized custom in many societies, in that it is a criminal act. Acts of bigamy prominently disregarded the laws of both church and state in societies that strongly emphasized monogamous marriage, such as those of Christian Europe and its colonies.

Male bigamy was particularly characteristic of a young and mobile population and was associated with areas such as ports or border towns, where the population was often made up of transients whose past histories were not generally known. A common pattern was for men to have two wives in widely separated locations, often transoceanic. Other cases of bigamy involved men who deserted one wife in one area, then started a "new life" with a new wife elsewhere. The difficulty or impossibility of **divorce** in many areas of Europe and its colonies encouraged clandestine bigamy as "remarriage without divorce." This option was particularly available to the poor and landless, whose histories would not be known in the new area. Bigamists sometimes justified their actions by pointing out how their original marriage had failed to live up to the ideal of a loving, sexual Christian marriage. However, if a bigamous marriage was revealed, the second marriage was legally considered no marriage at all, and bigamy was grounds for annulment.

In Catholic societies, bigamy was treated as a religious offence against the sacrament of marriage, and bishop's and inquisitorial courts disputed jurisdiction over it with each other and with civil courts. Bigamy was not a capital crime (although some bigamists died in prison), and penalties ranged from service in the galleys to imprisonment to whippings carried out in public as a means of public shaming, as well as inflicting pain. The technical meaning of "bigamy" in Catholic canon law stretched to situations other than a person with two spouses. For example, a person under religious vows broke those vows by marrying, and the church considered him or her to have committed bigamy. Similarly, if a person married someone who was already married, or if a person remarried after being widowed, then religious vows could not be taken because the church considered it bigamous. (In the latter two cases, bigamy was not considered a crime or a negation of the validity of the marriage, but only an impediment if the person subsequently wished to take religious orders.)

Protestant societies did not treat marriage as a sacrament, but varied in whether bigamy fell under the jurisdiction of church or civil courts. Bigamy was made a civil felony in England by Parliamentary statute in 1604, which exempted from criminal penalties those who remarried after their spouse had been absent overseas for seven years or absent without the remarrier receiving word from the spouse for seven years. Bigamy was grounds for divorce in some Protestant societies that allowed divorce, such as New England.

Female bigamy, in which a woman was married to two or more husbands, was far less common than male bigamy but often attracted attention when it did occur. The English novelist Daniel Defoe made the title character of *The Fortunes and Misfortunes of the Famous Moll Flanders* (1722) a female bigamist. One celebrated English scandal was that of Elizabeth Chudleigh. Chudleigh had secretly married Augustus John Hervey in 1744 before marrying the Duke of Kingston in 1770. The Duke died in 1773, and his heir brought an action for bigamy against Chudleigh. In 1776, she was tried by the House of Lords, who had jurisdiction in the case of a peeress. They unanimously found her guilty, and she spent the rest of her life in travels on the European continent.

The definition of bigamy as a criminal act played a particularly important role in the imposition of European sexual mores and **laws** on **Native Americans** and other colonized societies, as multiple marriages were common in many non-Christian societies. A campaign by missionary friars to enforce monogamy on the Pueblo Indians was one of the causes of the Pueblo revolt of 1680.

Jewish law in the Ashkenazic world, which had abandoned polygamy in the eleventh century, distinguished between female bigamy, in cases of which the second marriage was invalid and the woman was required to divorce her original husband, and male bigamy, which violated rabbinic law but did not make the second marriage invalid. Jews in Islamic lands continued to allow for polygamous relationships. *See also* Adultery; Fornication; Harems; Islam; Polyandry; Puritans.

Further Reading: Boyer, Richard. *Lives of the Bigamists: Marriage, Family and Community in Colonial Mexico*. Albuquerque: University of New Mexico Press, 1995; Wiesner-Hanks, Merry E. *Christianity and Sexuality in the Early Modern World: Regulating Desire, Reforming Practice*. London: Routledge, 2000.

William E. Burns

BIRTH CONTROL. *See* Contraception

BISEXUALITY. Currently, the terms "bisexuality" and "bisexual" are used to encompass a variety of meanings. They may be used with reference to an individual who is sexually attracted to individuals of either gender or an individual who is sexually active with individuals of either gender. The terms may also used to denote a certain cultural or personal identity. However, these terms were only recently developed. The first recorded use of the term "bisexuality" was not until 1809, and that was in the field of botany. Before then, bisexuality as an attraction or as sexual behavior existed, but individuals were not labeled with the term "bisexual." Even within current research, there is a trend for historians to label those individuals who were sexually active with members of their own gender as homosexuals, without accounting for any sexual activity by that individual with members of the opposite gender. Thus, the history of bisexuality can be considered mostly incomplete.

The little history that does exist is based on an examination of the **laws** and social norms regarding **homosexuality**. For example, sexual behavior between women was illegal in many areas (such as the American colonies), but was rarely prosecuted against in this time period. Such behavior was seen to be an immature type of sexuality, with full maturity being indicated by later heterosexual relationships. Women who engaged in such behavior but later married and had children were seen as acting in a culturally acceptable manner. This was the case even with women who were married and simultaneously had romantic friendships with other women. However, it was not culturally acceptable for women to be seen as trying to assume masculine social or leadership roles. A woman who attempted to assume a male's social power, for example, through **cross-dressing**, would often be severely punished or even killed if found out.

A notable exception to this was Deborah Sampson, an American woman who was discharged on October 25, 1783, from West Point. While disguised as a male serving in the Massachusetts Regiment for seventeen months, she formed several relationships with women, but married and bore three children after her honorable discharge.

For men in the seventeenth and eighteenth centuries, sexual behavior with other men was also illegal in many areas, particularly those under the influence of European laws. Punishment for such behavior typically consisted of the death penalty. In China, laws against homosexual behavior were instated in 1740, but were more penalizing for men than women. A number of historians report that, prior to this time, male homosexual behavior was not publicly viewed as being central to masculine identity. However, an increase in the public's view that male homosexual acts were associated with femininity occurred in the eighteenth century. Notable men who had intense emotional or sexual relationships with both men and women include the Father of Modern Science Sir Francis Bacon (1561–1626), the author (and namesake for the sexual act of sadism) **Marquis de Sade** (1740–1814), English royalty such as King James I of England (1566–1625), and French royalty including Philippe I, Duke of Orléans (1640–1701), and King Louis XIII of France (1601–1643). *See also* Erauso, Catalina de; Hermaphrodites; Pirates; Sodomy and Anti-Sodomy Law.

Further Reading: Baird, Vanessa. *The No-Nonsense Guide to Sexual Diversity.* Oxford: New Internationalist Publications, 2001; Klein, Fritz. *The Bisexual Option.* Binghamton, NY: Harrington Park Press, 1993; Phillips, Kim M., and Barry Reay. *Sexualities in History.* New York: Routledge, 2002.

Dave D. Hochstein

THE BODY. Throughout the world in the seventeenth and eighteenth centuries, people decorated, changed, treated, and mistreated their bodies—and the bodies of others—in various ways. For example, **castration**, the removal of a male's testicles and sometimes his penis, was commonly performed on boys or young men in China and Islamic areas to provide **eunuchs** who guarded the **harems** of emperors and sultans. In eighteenth-century Italy, although it was illegal, boys were castrated to become the angelic-voiced singers known as castrati. In China, **footbinding** became increasingly popular during the Qing dynasty (1644–1911). Even peasant women had their daughters' feet bound, subjecting them to life-long pain so that they could marry well. People covered their bodies with furs, silk, linen, and other materials, and adorned them with jewels, shells, feathers, and tattoos, depending on the time and place, and the status and gender of the person involved. Prohibitions and rules surrounded how and when the body should be displayed, used, and cleansed.

Western **philosophy** conceived the body to be an illusion, so that the philosopher René Descartes (1596–1650) explained that it could indeed be an illusion that his body was real, but not that his mind was so. Part of a greater material universe, the objective character of the human body became the symbol for the age of the colonization of the globe. Characteristic images of the world incorporated the image of the human form and even appeared as literary metaphors. When the poet John Donne wrote of his love for his mistress, he did so in terms of his "new found land," his "America," comparing her female body and his desire to explore it, to the east coast of North America and the desires of explorers there.

Between 1500 and 1700 in Europe, new attitudes developed about the body and nudity, as a new emphasis was placed on **chastity** and modesty. Public **baths** were closed not only because they were seen as dissolute places where men and women cavorted in the nude, but also because they were deemed unhealthy. A naked, wet body was seen as particularly "open" to diseases that might travel through the water and permeate the skin. Instead of sleeping nude, people began to wear nightgowns, not only for warmth, but also to protect their skin and preserve modesty.

Europeans kept their bodies covered with layers of clothing, even in warm weather. They believed that the African and Native American women they encountered were promiscuous, or at least sexually passionate, because they were naked, or almost naked. But clothing determined more than just being "civilized." How a person dressed denoted social class and gender. Thomas Hall, a servant in seventeenth-century Virginia, at times dressed as a man, and at other times as a woman, upsetting the gendered society of colonial Virginia. Hall admitted to dressing and living as both a man and a woman, although he had been christened Thomasine in England and raised as a girl. When questioned by authorities, Hall said that he was both man and woman. A group of married women examined his body, and declared him a man. But noting Hall's explanation that his penis was not functional, the justices of the colony initially ruled him to be a woman. Finally, the General Court ordered him to wear men's breeches and women's accessories. Hall was not asked what he wanted to do. The idea of individual bodies not being distinctly male or female upset the worldview of Anglo Americans during this time and disrupted a society that believed so strongly in **gender roles**.

To the English, and to most Europeans of the seventeenth century, the body was a source of both sin and virtue. Puritans, in particular, believed the body was a temple of God, a physical house for the soul, and that it should not be abused or defiled. Nonprocreative sex and nonmarital sex were considered sinful uses of the body. Indeed, Puritans believed such practices as **masturbation** and **sodomy** weakened body and soul, and led one to the Devil. Some non-Puritans also held these beliefs, which extended beyond the seventeenth century. For example, in the eighteenth century, one evangelical preacher in the South had himself castrated because he so feared his bodily urges and lustful thoughts toward a recently converted married woman. *See also* Breastfeeding; Circumcision; Clothing and Fashion; Cross-Dressing; Hermaphrodites.

Further Reading: Brown, Kathleen M. *Good Wives, Nasty Wenches & Anxious Patriarchs: Gender, Race, and Power in Colonial Virginia*. Chapel Hill: University of North Carolina Press, 1996; Foucault, Michel. *The History of Sexuality*. Vol. 1. Translated by R. Hurley. London: Penguin Books, 1979; Godbeer, Richard. *Sexual Revolution in Early America*. Baltimore: Johns Hopkins University Press, 2002; Judovitz, Dalia. *The Culture of the Body: Genealogies of Modernity*. Ann Arbor: University of Michigan Press, 2001.

Merril D. Smith and Jason Powell

BREASTFEEDING. Breastfeeding began to assume great cultural importance during the early modern period in both England and the American colonies. Breast milk itself was considered an ideal **food**, not only for infants, but also for sick, weak, and elderly adults. Because it is so easily digestible, physicians advised breast milk for cases of decreased appetite or consumption. In addition, many of the medicinal recipe books written by early modern women list breast milk as a pain reliever for various ailments, such as ear and eye infections, and it was sometimes given to women during **childbirth** to make the delivery go faster.

Medical texts of this period describe breast milk as whitened blood—the same blood that nourished the fetus while it was inside the mother. Therefore, according to popular belief, mothers were literally feeding their babies with their own blood.

The purity and white color of breast milk contrasted with the red of menstrual blood, which was seen as foul, and even dangerous. Menstruating women were repulsive; breastfeeding mothers were selfless, giving, and loving. If **menstruation** was evidence of God's curse on Eve, then childbirth and breastfeeding meant redemption. To give birth, women risked death, but in nursing their babies, they continued to strain their bodies and give of themselves. Because a typical seventeenth- or eighteenth-century white American woman might spend twenty to twenty-five years pregnant or breastfeeding, the decision to breastfeed was of enormous significance and did affect a woman's health. Midwives frequently treated women for sore breasts and cracked nipples. Breast infections were painful and could be serious, and nipples could be permanently damaged.

During the Elizabethan period, many elite English women did not nurse their babies, but cultural attitudes about the importance of breastfeeding began to change. Protestant women in particular felt that breastfeeding was an important duty of mothers and that wet nursing was sinful, unless the mother was sick or incapacitated. However, even as cultural views toward breastfeeding changed and elite women desired to nurse their own babies, they faced some problems. In the seventeenth and early eighteenth centuries, physicians advised women not to nurse their babies until their milk came in. Colostrum, the fluid produced before milk, is now known to be filled with antibodies and important for newborns to have, but then it was considered harmful for babies. For one thing, its sticky, yellow appearance contrasted unfavorably with the pure appearance of breast milk. In addition, physicians directed their patients not to begin nursing their babies until after they stopped bleeding, following childbirth. Since sucking stimulates milk flow, and it might be several weeks until women stopped bleeding, women who did wait to nurse often found they could not produce enough milk to feed their babies. Since physicians usually attended only wealthier women at births during this time, and because poorer women could not afford wet nurses, insufficient milk flow and problems with breastfeeding were often seen as problems only more elite women encountered. In the mid-eighteenth century, physicians reversed course and began advocating that women nurse their babies right away, as that was following nature.

By the mid-eighteenth century, physicians, philosophers, and scientists throughout western Europe and the colonies promoted breastfeeding. Dr. William Cadogen's influential *Essay upon Nursing* (1748) went through many editions in England, France, and America. Books such as these gave helpful advice to women whose own mothers may not have breastfed, although most women in the colonies did nurse their babies. **Jean-Jacques Rousseau** published *Émile* in 1762. This book promoted the idea that women were meant to be self-sacrificing and nurturing mothers. In his 1752 taxonomy, the botanist Carolus Linnaeus used the term "mammalia" meaning "at the breast," to distinguish between animals formerly called quadripeds and now called mammals, in English. Breastfeeding began to be seen as patriotic and virtuous, and motherhood was seen as the highest calling for women.

In the United States, motherhood was tied to republican ideals about the new nation. It was up to mothers to raise healthy citizens for the new republic. They could do this by breastfeeding them. In France, breastfeeding also became linked to republicanism. Wet nursing was seen as another aspect of royal corruption, whereas breastfeeding was virtuous and pure. The iconography of the French Revolution featured bare-breasted women, in statues, on medallions, and in paintings. At the 1793 Festival of Regeneration held at the site of the old Bastille, water flowed from multibreasted goddess fountains. Toasts at the celebration invoked Mother Nature, and mothers in the crowd were urged to breastfeed their children to make them virtuous and to sustain the French republic. *See also* The Body; Contraception; Gynecology Manuals; Medicine and Science; Midwives and Physicians; Pregnancy; Women, Changing Images of.

Further Reading: Salmon, Marylynn. "The Cultural Significance of Breastfeeding and Infant Care in Early Modern England and America." *Journal of Social History* 28 (Winter 1994): 247–69; Yalom, Marilyn. *A History of the Breast.* New York: Ballentine, 1997.

Merril D. Smith

BYRD, WILLIAM (1674–1744). The Virginia planter William Byrd left a diary that provides a revealing picture of the life of an upper-class man in London and on a southern plantation. The diary, apparently intended only for Byrd's eyes, is significant because the South during the first half of the eighteenth century is so poorly documented. Byrd's writings offer rare insight into colonial sexual and emotional history.

Byrd, the son of William Byrd, was born on his father's plantation near Richmond, Virginia. At the age of seven, he was sent to England to obtain an **education**. He subsequently studied law in the Middle Temple in London and was admitted to the bar in 1695. Returning to Virginia that same year, Byrd was elected to the House of Burgesses. He went back to England in 1697. A gentleman of leisure, Byrd moved in fashionable London society. He regularly attended the **theater** and dances, while searching for a suitable bride. He is reputed to have been one of the four collaborators who wrote the play *The Careless Husband* (1704), a comedy about characters who resent the monogamous bonds of **marriage** and engage in a series of sexual affairs.

Upon his father's death in 1704, Byrd, as the sole heir, returned to Virginia to manage the family estate. He married Lucy Parke in 1706. After his marriage, Byrd did not always disguise his interest in other women and occasionally provoked his wife to tears by kissing other men's wives in front of her. In 1710, he recorded an unsuccessful effort to lure to his room the maid at a Williamsburg inn. In 1711, he asked a slave girl to kiss him. There is evidence that he engaged in sexual relations with slaves, although Byrd personally disliked the institution of **slavery**.

Byrd moved quickly into the highest ranks of Virginia society. In 1709, he was appointed to the Council of State, the supreme court of Virginia, and served on it for the rest of his life. In 1715, he went to London as a lobbyist for the interests of Virginia colonists. Lucy died in England the following year. Byrd, rebuffed in his efforts to establish courtships with several of England's eligible heiresses, was apparently lonely. During the years 1717 to 1719, he picked up prostitutes on the streets of London every few days. He paid one mistress two guineas a visit until he dismissed her for infidelity. He was also periodically remorseful and begged God in his prayers to forgive him for the sin of lust. Byrd married Maria Taylor in 1724 and returned permanently to Virginia in 1726.

An amateur physician and a scientific writer, Byrd indulged in bear meat as a source of virility. He remained an amorous man into old age, confessing that he had "played the fool" with a slave in 1741. In his diary, Byrd consistently took the blame for his actions and gave evidence of staunch Anglican religious faith. The model of a Virginia gentleman, he is one of the most prominent authors in early America. *See also* Courtship; Food; Masculinity; Prostitutes and Prostitution; Thistlewood, Thomas.

Further Reading: Godbeer, Richard. *Sexual Revolution in Early America.* Baltimore: Johns Hopkins University Press, 2002; Lockridge, Kenneth A. *The Diary, and Life, of William Byrd II of Virginia, 1674–1744.* Chapel Hill: University of North Carolina Press, 1987; Marambaud, Pierre. *William Byrd of Westover, 1674–1744.* Charlottesville: University Press of Virginia, 1971; Wright, Louis B., and Marion Tinling, eds. *The Secret Diary of William Byrd of Westover, 1709–1712.* Richmond: Dietz Press, 1941.

Caryn E. Neumann

CASANOVA, GIACOMO GIROLAMO (1725–1798). Giacomo Casanova was an Italian spy, soldier, diplomat, and writer. He is mainly known for his adventurous autobiography *History of My Life*, which is filled with descriptions of his many love affairs, but also gives readers a very interesting account of manners in the eighteenth century.

Casanova was born in Venice, and the first foreshadowing of his future reputation appeared when he was expelled from the seminary at St. Cyprian for scandalous conduct soon after he started studying there. Further scandals forced him to leave the places where he worked and travel throughout Italy and many other countries. From Rome he went to Naples, Corfu, Constantinople, and Venice, and then to Paris, Dresden, Prague, Vienna, and back to Venice. In 1775, he was jailed for five years for performing magic but escaped from prison the next year. He went to Paris where he met Louis XV, Mme. Pompadour, and **Jean Jacques Rousseau**. His job as a spy forced him to travel yet more throughout Europe, until finally he settled in Bohemia, spending his last years focusing on writing his autobiography.

Casanova's manuscript was sold to a German firm in 1822, but the first editions of the memoirs were either heavily cut or badly translated, and the first full English-language version of the autobiography was not published until 1966–1971 (six volumes, translated by W. R. Trask). Casanova's autobiography reveals him to be a serial seducer and sometimes rapist, concerned only with satisfying his own sexual urges and constantly seeking new thrills. Whenever he saw an attractive woman, Casanova could not control his desire toward her, feeling the urgency to have intercourse with her; however, as soon as he succeeded, his interest in the woman immediately faded, and he moved on in the search of another victim, always remembering to first indemnify the lover he was leaving. He was usually attracted to young women—or even to girls—but there were also affairs with older women in his life, the most notable of which is that with the Marquess of Urfé, a woman over seventy years old. As a lover he was insatiable and sometimes had intercourse so many times that he ended

Undated engraving of Giacomo Girolamo Cassanova. © The Granger Collection, New York.

up ejaculating blood; this used to shock his lovers, but it was an ultimate satisfaction for him. Having as much charm as he did, Casanova rarely had problems with seducing women; when one rejected his favors, though, he did not hesitate to threaten her with a knife to make her change her mind.

According to some critics, most of the adventures Casanova described in *History of My Life* never happened. Some others argue that although Casanova's life was undoubtedly adventurous, his memoirs do not hold much value as a work of **literature**. However, most of them agree that Casanova was a fascinating character, and the manuscripts he left are to be regarded as a window into life in the eighteenth century—and particularly as a window into the soul of a multiple seducer-rapist. *See also* Libertine; Seduction Literature.

Further Reading: Casanova, Giacomo. *History of My Life*. Translated by Williard R. Trask. Baltimore: Johns Hopkins University Press, 1997; Zweig, Stefan. *Casanova. A Study in Self-Portraiture*. London: Pushkin Press, 2001.

Bartlomiej Paszylk

CASTLEHAVEN, EARL OF. *See* Touchet, Mervyn, Earl of Castlehaven

CASTRATION. Castration is the procedure where an individual is deprived of his gonads and rendered sterile, unable to reproduce. Castration can be surgical, chemical, or performed with X-radiation. Although the term is used for both males and females in the animal kingdom, in humans, castration usually refers to orchiectomy, the surgical amputation of a man's testicles. In colonial and revolutionary America, only surgical castration was performed.

Animal castration, called gelding, results in a male animal that is more tractable and tame. Horses and farmwork animals were frequently gelded in Europe, and the tradition was continued in America. It was also observed that castrated livestock produced meat that was sweeter and more tender.

Early medical writings advised physicians to castrate men as part of surgery for hernia reduction. This was probably as a preventive measure so that the hernia would not recur. In Italy between the sixteenth and early nineteenth centuries, castration was performed on young boys so that their voices would remain high. These castratos could sing as high as sopranos but with greater strength because their vocal cords were thicker. They were much in demand in church choirs and as **opera** singers, especially before women were permitted to perform in these venues.

When castration is performed on a man, it has profound medical and psychological significance. During the Revolutionary period, castration was referred to as one of the "most melancholy operations in the practice of surgery" because it was associated with recurring diseases such as schirrhus, a hard, translucent cancerous tumor, a hydrocele, abscess, sarcocele, and certain hernias. The castration was performed by cutting or burning. Certainly a life-threatening tumor combined with a loss of masculine identity must have been a devastating circumstance, especially at a time when there were no antibiotics or reliable and safe anesthetics.

In addition to the medical necessity, castration was used to punish **rape**, **sodomy**, and other crimes during the settlement of America. The colonies were not consistent in their adherence to the legal system of England. Some crimes in England were punished more severely than in the colonies; others less so. New England's Puritan values differed from Philadelphia's, for example, where a predominantly Quaker population looked to rehabilitation rather than punishment as a way to deal with crime. However, in 1700, male sodomy was punishable there depending on the perpetrator's marital status. If a man were single, he was sentenced to life imprisonment with a whipping every three months; if married, castration. However, the Privy Council in 1705 disallowed the punishment of castration in 1705 because it was not part of English law, but it remained on the books until 1718.

A first offence rape was punishable with a seven-year imprisonment, thirty-one lashes, and property confiscation; on the second, the perpetrator was branded with an "R" on the forehead and castrated. However, after the Privy Council rescinded castration, the General Assembly substituted life imprisonment.

There was inequality in sanctions regarding social class and status especially with regard to slaves, servants, and **Native Americans**. Punishments given to the marginal members of society were always more severe. There was so much anxiety about the so-called hypersexual "black beast" during the seventeenth and eighteenth centuries that colonial legal codes provided castration, among other punishments, meted to blacks for sexual offences.

Symbolically, castration represents the power of an individual or political entity over another by forcing the altered person into a subordinate status. By cutting away a man's testicles, the alteration causes profound hormonal changes such as breast development and soft skin, lack of sexual desire, or ability to get or maintain an erection. In short, this renders a formerly virile man docile, and perceived as womanlike. It is particularly effective in cultures where gender inequality is extreme and the cultural bias favors men. Where men have more privileges and power, they are perceived as more important than women. To be deprived of that corporally is to lose one's dominant status. *See also* Eunuchs; Harems; Rape Law.

Further Reading: Cohen, Daniel A. "Social Injustice, Sexual Violence, Spiritual Transcendence: Constructions of Interracial Rape in Early American Crime Literature, 1767–1817." *William and Mary Quarterly* LVI, no. 3 (July 1999): 481–526; Preyer, Katherine. "Penal Measures in the American Colonies." *American Journal of Legal History* 26, no. 4 (1982): 326–53; Sharpe, Samuel. "Of Castration." In *Treatise on the Operations of Surgery*. London, 1750. See http://www.americanrevolution.org/surgery10.html.

Lana Thompson

CELIBACY. Celibacy is the voluntary or enforced state of not being involved in sexual activity. It has many purposes, the chief of them, in the West, being its religious function. During the early modern period, total abstention from sexual relations became a requirement for all Christian nuns, monks, and priests, who took vows promising to remain celibate. At the same time, the idea of Christian **marriage** based on love and fidelity, and sanctified by the church, grew stronger. As pronouncements about the duty of the laity to marry within the church and procreate intensified, new prohibitions were placed on **homosexuality** and all nonmarital, nonprocreative sex. Because the church demanded clerical celibacy and frowned on nonclerical celibacy, abstention from sexual relations was one way in which the clergy became distinct from the lay population.

As the Protestant Reformation took hold, Protestants abolished clerical celibacy. **Puritans** in particular, scorned the Catholic reverence for sexual abstinence and the belief that marital sex was a necessary evil. Although Puritan ministers conceded that procreation was one purpose of marital sex, they believed that the enjoyment of sexual union between husband and wife was a God-given right. This did not mean, however, that couples should engage in unbridled passion; instead, husbands and wives should practice **chastity**—or moderation—within marriage, and unmarried persons should remain celibate.

However, in the eighteenth century, some Protestant sects embraced and demanded celibacy of its members. One such sect was the Shakers, who came to America in 1774, after being persecuted in England. Like many other perfectionist groups, the Shakers awaited the second coming of Christ, and renounced sex to become closer to God.

Among some Native American tribes, men and women practiced celibacy, but not usually as a lifelong practice. The Iroquois, for example, believed that they could gain spiritual or physical strength by abstaining from sex. Before such activities as hunting or going to war, men abstained from sexual relations, and female virgins were sometimes given ceremonial roles.

In the **Ottoman empire**, the Janissaries, an elite group, worked for the sultans and were noted for their military prowess. Originally composed of young men who were conscripted from Christian families or taken as war captives, then converted to Islam, the Janissaries lived in almost monastic conditions and were expected to be celibate. By the sixteenth century, however, this was beginning to change, and some Janissaries did marry.

Then there were the massive quantities of **eunuchs** used in the royal **harems** and for government; enforced to celibacy in this way, societies such as the Chinese and Islamic depended on the eunuchs and used them to maintain order because they were considered totally trustworthy. Enforced celibacy was also found in some indigenous tribes in Australia. The procedure was carried out on indolent adolescent youths who were deemed useless to the tribe. The process involved mutilating the penis and rendering it either useless for sexual activity or else only useless for ejaculation. *See also* Native Americans; Perfectionists; Southeastern Indians; Virgins/Virginity.

Further Reading: Bataille, Georges. *Inner Experience*. Translated by L. A. Boldt. Albany: State University of New York Press, 1988; Godbeer, Richard. *Sexual Revolution in Early America*. Baltimore: Johns Hopkins University Press, 2002; Shoemaker, Nancy, ed. *Negotiators of Change: Historical Perspectives on Native American Women*. New York: Routledge, 1995; Tannahill, Reay. *Sex in History*. London: Hamish Hamilton, 1980; van Kessel, Elisja Schulte. "Virgins and Mothers between Heaven and Earth." In *A History of Women in the West*, vol. 3, edited by Natalie Zemon Davis and Arlette Farge. Cambridge, MA: Belknap Press of Harvard University Press, 1993.

Merril D. Smith and Jason Powell

CERVANTES SAAVEDRA, MIGUEL DE (1547–1616). Miguel de Cervantes Saavedra was a leading Spanish writer during the late sixteenth to early seventeenth centuries who created the famous character Don Quixote to parody the absurdities of chivalry.

Miguel de Cervantes Saavedra wrote short stories, long prose romances, plays, and poetry. Cervantes was involved in a string of brash love affairs, seductions, and scandals. His characters often reflected his own tumultuous romantic life. In his love stories, marriageable young women are beautiful but morally unstable, and handsome, macho young men tend toward sexual misbehavior. Although his writings present heterosexual relationships as an ideal goal, they attack traditional sixteenth- and seventeenth-century notions of chivalry.

Upon being captured by **pirates** during his military career, Cervantes was taken to Algiers, where he spent five years as a prisoner. There he was friends with a prisoner who was a homosexual. Some have suggested Cervantes had homosexual encounters with his captors and possibly others. When he left Algiers he was accused of filthy acts which remain unspecified. But suggestions that Cervantes specifically had homosexual experiences were not made in print until 1982 and remain mere theory. Cervantes did refer several times in his writings to sexual intercourse between men and boys, behavior that was prevalent in the **Ottoman empire**. It is also possible that Cervantes had a passionate love affair and a son with a beautiful Italian woman in Naples. He alludes to this in a semiautobiographical poem, "Voyage to Parnassus."

In his late thirties, he did have an affair with a twenty-year-old married actress, Ana Franca de Rojas. It seems Franca's husband married her for her dowry instead of for love, and therefore an extramarital affair with the exciting, heroic Cervantes has been termed inevitable by some. Cervantes tried to conceal the illicit affair, which was made more difficult by the birth of an illegitimate daughter, Isabel. Concerned over keeping Isabel's **paternity** a secret, Cervantes cut off the affair.

Just one month after Isabel's birth in 1584, he married Doña Catalina de Palacios Salazar, a woman half his age. Cervantes kept the recent affair and his daughter Isabel a secret from his new wife. However, both Palacios and the husband of Franca eventually found out the truth. Cervantes and Palacios had an unhappy, childless **marriage** and lived apart for long periods of time.

Cervantes is most famous for his classic European novel *El ingenioso hidalgo Don Quixote de la Mancha* (The Ingenious Gentleman Don Quixote de la Mancha). The first part was published in 1605, and the second part in 1615. The main character, Don Quixote, asserts that there cannot be a knight-errant (an adventure-searching knight) without a lady. He has dedicated himself to rescuing damsels in distress. As a chivalrous knight, Don Quixote is afflicted by rejection from the goddess-like women whom he loves. He must endure the pain of rejection under the code of chivalry, exalting the women as superior, and patiently and humbly serving them. Comically, the poor Dulcinea de Tobosa, whom Don Quixote imagined to be an elegant lady, and his lady at that, does not even know he exists.

Cervantes often played with names. The word *quijote* means a piece of armor that covers the thigh. In his time period, the thigh was traditionally used as a literary euphemism for the sexual area of the body. By naming his main character Quixote, Cervantes associates him with the anatomy surrounding the genital area and with covered or hidden sexuality. The name suggests that Quixote will prove his manhood on the battlefield rather than in the bedroom. His leg armor protects him from nudity on several occasions in the book.

Critics continue to analyze the roles Cervantes gave women in his works, arguing that he showed empathy for women who endured subordinate status in seventeenth-century Spain. Many female characters forcefully defend women's rights, unlike the characters of Cervantes's contemporaries. Cervantes died in 1616, in Madrid, probably of dropsy. *See also* Adultery; Literature.

Further Reading: Garcés, María Antonia. *Cervantes in Algiers: A Captive's Tale*. Nashville, TN: Vanderbilt University Press, 2002; McCrory, Donald P. *No Ordinary Man: The Life and Times of Miguel de Cervantes*. London: Peter Owen Publishers, 2002; Russell, P. E. *Cervantes*. Oxford: Oxford University Press, 1985; Weiger, John G. *The Individuated Self: Cervantes and the Emergence of the Individual*. Athens: Ohio University Press, 1979.

Elizabeth Jenner

CHASTITY.   Although often used synonymously with **celibacy** and virginity, chastity more often meant not engaging in *unlawful* sexual intercourse, that is, sex outside **marriage**, or in unseemly behavior. The word "chaste" was usually applied to women. English writers of the seventeenth century advised women to be modest in appearance and submissive to their husbands and fathers. In this way, both single and married women demonstrated their chastity.

CHASTITY

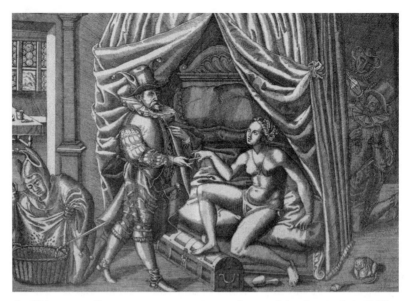

An 18th century German copper engraving on the use of the chastity belt. © The Granger Collection, New York.

Chastity in women helped to keep order in the family and, by extension, order in the community. Chaste women stayed at home taking care of their families and their domestic duties. They did not engage in wanton behavior, causing tension between neighbors, or have children out of wedlock, placing a burden on the community to support them. Witches, for example, might be seen as the most unchaste of women because they were believed to be sexually voracious, promiscuous, and able to upset the natural world around them. In addition to unseemly and lewd behavior, women accused of being witches were often blamed for such deeds as making men or women fall in or out of love, curdling milk, causing miscarriages and stillbirths, and even changing the weather, all of which would disrupt families and their community.

For a woman's chastity to be impugned was a serious matter. To be called a "whore" or "slut" was more than just trading insults. Sexual misbehavior was taken seriously in the British American colonies of the seventeenth century. On the strength of neighborhood **gossip**, women could be taken to court to testify or have their bodies examined by other women for signs of recent, illicit **childbirth** or witches' marks. If found guilty of a sexual crime, a woman might be whipped or fined. In the worst situation, after trial testimony based on rumors, a woman might be executed as a witch.

In defining chastity, Puritan writers emphasized that they were not extolling celibacy. Single men and women—whether never married or widowed—were expected to abstain from all sexual relations, but husbands and wives were supposed to have sex, and they were also meant to enjoy it. Seventeenth-century medical and religious authorities attributed **pregnancy** to the mixing of seeds from the man and woman. Women did not produce seeds unless they had an **orgasm**; therefore, husbands were supposed to ensure their wives enjoyed their intimate moments together.

To **Puritans**, chastity within marriage meant faithfulness to one's spouse, and it applied to both women and men. It also meant moderation. Although husband and wife were expected to love each other and enjoy intimacy, they were not supposed to love their spouses more than God, or to let their passion become too wild and unrestrained.

By the eighteenth century, the Puritan emphasis on premarital abstinence was losing its hold on young men and women. As these young adults began asserting their independence, they chose marriage partners based on love, regardless of their parents' wishes, and the bridal pregnancy rate rose. Although ministers condemned the licentiousness of young adults, by the mid-eighteenth century, many people accepted private intimate moments and even overnight visits for courting couples. At the same time, throughout the United States and England, many people were concerned about women being seduced and abandoned. This anxiety is reflected in the great popularity of **seduction literature** in the eighteenth century on both sides of the Atlantic.

Ideas of chastity did not apply to all groups of women. Because Native American women wore less clothing than Europeans and engaged in sexual encounters outside marriage, Anglo Americans viewed them as shameless and lewd. This view permeated European encounters with African and native women of other lands, as well. As slavery became codified, African and African American slave women were increasingly seen as promiscuous and "available," despite the fact that their status as slaves made them incapable of refusing the sexual advances of white men. White female servants who became pregnant were guilty of **fornication** and **bastardy**, and the courts ordered their terms of indenture extended in order to compensate their masters for any time lost. Black female slaves, however, found they were encouraged to bear children, as their children provided their masters with more slaves. *See also* Courtship; Indentured Servants; Interracial Sex; Native Americans; Slavery; Witches and Witch Trials; Women, Changing Images of.

Further Reading: Brown, Kathleen M. *Good Wives, Nasty Wenches, & Anxious Patriarchs: Gender, Race, and Power in Colonial Virginia.* Chapel Hill: University of North Carolina Press, 1996; Godbeer, Richard. *Sexual Revolution in Early America.* Baltimore: Johns Hopkins University Press, 2002.

Merril D. Smith

CHEVALIER D'EON (1728–1810). Charles-Geneviève-Louis-Auguste-André-Thimothée d'Eon de Beaumont, who is usually known as Chevalier d'Eon, was born in Tonnerre on October 5, 1728, the son of a wealthy nobleman. He had an eventful career as a diplomat and spy, but was to be remembered as one of the most famous cross-dressers of the eighteenth century.

D'Eon's career began under the service of King Louis XIV of France; then on behalf of his successor, Louis XV, he became an agent of the *Secret du Roi*, the royal secret service, which was to earn him the Order of Saint-Louis. During this time, he took up a commission as lieutenant of the Dragoons as a reward for his diplomatic work in Russia, followed up by the command of a company on the Rhine.

In 1762, d'Eon went to London appointed as secretary to the ambassador Comte de Guerchy, but jealous of d'Eon's successes on the Rhine at which the Comte himself had shirked his duties, Guerchy started a campaign of hostility against d'Eon. He first charged him with underhand plotting against the king, then accused d'Eon of being a hermaphrodite. Louis XV now distrusted d'Eon to the extent that he

Caricature of Charles Eon de Beaumont dressed as a woman, 1791. Courtesy of the Library of Congress.

became convinced that d'Eon was mad, and was worried he might reveal incriminating evidence about the king's secret service.

D'Eon published his *Lettres, mémoires, et négociations* in March 1764, further incurring the wrath of the king. Concerned about additional exposure, the French government came to an agreement whereby d'Eon would surrender all the French documents in his possession, in return for payments of all his debts and the provision of a royal pension. One further stipulation was added—that d'Eon must dress as a woman for the rest of his life, since the French court always believed that d'Eon was a woman who had fought in the army disguised as a man.

In England, during the 1770s, **gossip** about d'Eon's true sexual identity flourished with bets being taken on his gender. Public curiosity was fueled by British newspaper reports and French pamphlets about d'Eon. The *Public Advertiser* for March 12, 1771, noted, "The discovery of her sex was occasioned by her lately discharging a favorite footman, to whom she had entrusted the secret"; the *London Evening Post* for May 11–14, 1771, went as far as to declare "that a celebrated Chevalier [d'Eon] has with a few weeks past, been discovered to be of a different sex."

D'Eon returned to France in 1777 dressed as a woman, but in 1778 he was arrested for wearing his army uniform in a bid to win back his military position when France joined the American colonists against Britain in the War of Independence. D'Eon was ordered to return to his family home of Tonnerre to live with his mother.

In 1785, as a result of continued petition from d'Eon, the French government awarded him 6,000 livres in order to liquidate his debts in England, and he left France for good. Once back in London, his financial situation had so deteriorated that he was obliged to sell off his belongings at an auction at Christie's, including his favorite jewelry and his substantial collection of books. Still in the guise of a woman, he moved to 38 Brewer Street where he lived modestly. To finance himself, he teamed up with a former servant of his, Jacob de Launay, and a Mrs. Bateman and gave fencing lessons, teaching as a woman, touring the South of England, putting on shows, giving demonstrations, and inviting challenges from the audiences. A fencing accident left him unable to work, and he had to move back to London, setting up home with a Frenchwoman, Mrs. Marie Cole, at 33 Westminster Bridge in a purely domestic arrangement.

Unable to keep himself afloat on a pension of fifty pounds per year, in 1804 at seventy-five, d'Eon ended up in debtor's prison. Mrs. Cole managed to raise enough money to secure his release, and they both moved to 26 Milman Street where they continued living as platonic companions. Only on his death did she discover the person she had been sharing her life with for the last fifteen years was, in fact, a man. Throughout his life d'Eon displayed little sign of sexual passions and considered himself asexual. Even the doctor-priest who had looked after d'Eon throughout his last years was unaware of his real sexual identity, as was Italian libertine **Casanova**, alleged expert in women, who had mistakenly said of d'Eon, "I had not been a quarter of an hour in her company before I knew her for a woman. Her shape was too rounded for that of a man, and her voice was too clear." D'Eon died in Bloomsbury on May 21, 1810, aged eighty-two and was buried in the graveyard at St. Pancras church. *See also* Cross-Dressing; Hermaphrodites; Inés de la Cruz, Sor Juana; Newspapers.

Further Reading: Kates, Gary. *Monsieur D'Eon Is a Woman: A Tale of Political Intrigue and Sexual Masquerade*. London: HarperCollins, 1995; Nixon, Edna. *Royal Spy*. New York: Reynal, 1965; Peakman, Julie. *Lascivious Bodies. A Sexual History of the Eighteenth Century*. London: Atlantic, 2004.

Julie Peakman

CHILD RAPE. Most human societies have viewed childhood as a distinct stage of life and have granted children protections that they do not afford adults. From ancient times to the present, most cultures have tried to safeguard children from sexual violence and depredation, though they might understand what we currently refer to as child sexual abuse differently from era to era and from place to place. One way that seventeenth- and eighteenth-century societies tried to protect young girls was through laws that established an age of consent. The age of consent for a female specified the age under which a male could not engage in sexual relations with her. The age typically ranged from ten to thirteen years and coincided with the ages stipulated in both Canon Law and the Talmud. The age of consent also tended to coincide with female puberty, which was commonly the age at which a female could marry without parental consent. Age of consent laws functioned under the legal theory that females younger than the designated age could not comprehend the nature and consequences of the sexual act and thus needed special protection. Lawmakers, acting in the interests of society as well as of children, moved to prevent males from taking advantage of female naiveté and to punish them for child rape when they did such a thing.

Laws prohibiting sexual intercourse with females who were younger than the designated age commonly punished men on par with the crime of **rape**, even though the rape of a child was a unique and separate crime. While rape prosecutions required proof of force on the part of the man and proof of nonconsent on the part of the female, child rape merely required proof of sexual intercourse. A man did not have to employ any force to commit the crime, and it mattered not whether the child assented to the deed. In the eyes of the law, she was unable to give a legal consent, and the mere act of coition constituted the crime. Some scholars have asserted that the function of child rape laws was to protect the **virtue** and **chastity** of all young girls, and there is some evidence to support that contention. There is other evidence, however, that suggests that in the seventeenth and eighteenth centuries, another function of child rape laws was not to punish rapists, or what in modern times we call molesters, so much as to prevent the **abduction** of heiresses. Most societies of the seventeenth and eighteenth centuries were organized along a relatively rigid hierarchical social system and were strongly desirous of ensuring the legitimate transmission of property to legitimate heirs. One intent of child rape laws, then, was to prevent the "ravishment of wards," an act that entailed abducting a wealthy man's daughter and having sexual relations with her. The sexual intercourse could constitute a bona fide **marriage** and make the abductor the heir to his wife's father's wealth, even against parental wishes.

Underage girls who did not stand to inherit any wealth were not protected under the ravishment of ward statutes. There were, however, other laws designed to shield them from sexual depredation. Interestingly, conventional wisdom of the seventeenth and eighteenth centuries held that a man could not commit an actual rape upon an infant female. The legal and medical theory for this assertion stemmed from the belief that a mature, fully grown man could not *in fact* penetrate an infant female and penetration was integral to a charge of child rape. This made prosecutions difficult, though not impossible. And child rape prosecutions were necessary in the seventeenth and eighteenth centuries. Among the most common targets for these prosecutions were men who had contracted a **venereal disease**. There persisted a pervasive and widely held folkloric tradition, exported throughout the globe, that sexual intercourse with a virgin could cure a man of gonorrhea or syphilis. There was no cure for these diseases before the twentieth century, and so men who were infected sought whatever relief they believed was available to them. All too frequently, such men would solicit, purchase, or compel young girls to submit to them in hopes of curing their disease. Unfortunately, the historical record suggests that judges were more likely to show sympathy to the man rather than to the child and allowed him to use his illness as a mitigating circumstance to prosecution and conviction.

In the seventeenth and eighteenth centuries, rape and child rape both referred to the act committed by a man upon a female. This means that child rape statutes did not accord protections to young males. This does not mean that male children were entirely unprotected, for the historical record does contain a few instances where older men were prosecuted for **sodomy**, but the young male involved was not. As sodomy was a crime that required that both parties to the act be charged, this failure to indict suggests that officials felt the younger male had been coerced or was too young to understand the nature of the act, and thus was not culpable. It is also important to keep in mind that most societies in the seventeenth and eighteenth centuries did not adhere to the legal ideal of equal protection under the law. The law tended to privilege the upper classes over the lower with regard to child rape, thus making poor and working-class children more vulnerable to sexual depredation. Further, in an era of global exploration and exploitation, the female children of indigenous and enslaved populations were also disproportionately unprotected with respect to sexual depredations committed by their colonizers. *See also* Incest; Rape Law; Sex Crimes.

Further Reading: Laiou, Angeliki E., ed. *Consent and Coercion to Sex and Marriage in the Ancient and Medieval Societies.* Washington, DC: Dumbarton Oaks Research Library and Collection, 1993; Simpson, Antony E. "Vulnerability and the Age of Female Consent: Legal Innovation and Its Effect on Prosecutions for Rape in Eighteen-Century London." In *Sexual Underworlds of the Enlightenment,* edited by G. S. Rouseau and Roy Porter, 182–205. Chapel Hill: University of North Carolina Press, 1988.

Mary Block

CHILDBIRTH. Childbirth was a social occasion during the seventeenth and early to mid-eighteenth centuries in both the United States and Europe. Women came together to support one another through the birthing process and the lying-in period, which lasted from three days to two weeks. The lying-in period culminated with a religious ceremony in some areas or with a "groaning party" for those who had assisted the birth in others. While husbands occasionally made up part of the birthing support group, male participation in the process was not encouraged. Since knowledge of birth control was sketchy, ineffective, and often considered against the laws of God and nature, most women expected to give birth throughout their childbearing years. Nevertheless, women often faced childbirth with much trepidation. It was commonly believed that women who experienced severe pain or difficult births were reaping the consequences of sinful lives. Despite the fact that modern examinations of maternal death rates during this period indicate that deaths during childbirth were rare, particularly in America where overall good health and less interference by midwives produced less complications for both mothers and babies, women often approached childbirth in the belief that it would end their lives.

Prebirth preparations included purchasing valuable "childbirth linen" to be used during the birthing process, which later might be given to other women as wedding presents or in a will. As the time for birth drew near, a "birthing room" was prepared. In large homes, this was generally the master bedroom. In other situations, the room might simply be a section near a chimney that had been enclosed with quilts or other material. The enclosure represented a womb-like atmosphere in which the mother was warm and cosseted by a group of female friends and family, including a local midwife, who had gathered for that purpose. During the birth, the mother was fed broth, mutton, eggs, or toast and was given wine or tea to drink. In the so-called "normal births," little was done to relieve pain.

A variety of positions were used to facilitate birth, including sitting, standing, crouching, kneeling, or sitting in the lap of another woman. The birthing stool was frequently used because it protected the mother's modesty while supporting her back and allowing gravity to ease the infant's passage into the world. In New England, women often used the prone position, which sometimes resulted in shock-like symptoms as oxygen flow to the uterus was interrupted.

By the late 1700s, a professional midwives' kit was commonly available, containing syringes for enemas and various injections, skeins of thread to tie the umbilical cord, ergot to hasten birth, and different kinds of herbs and oils to make women more comfortable and to facilitate births. Laudanum and opium began to be used to relieve pain, and belladonna was used to stop hemorrhaging.

Traditional midwives usually lacked formal education but generally possessed a great knowledge of medicinal folklore. Many midwives were tried as witches because of their use of certain stones and herbs that had been considered since medieval times to have magical qualities to protect pregnant women and babies and to make childbirth easier. Midwives tended to be working-class women who had given birth themselves and who had assisted other women through the process.

Immigrant midwives brought knowledge, superstitions, and childbirth practices from their own cultures with them. In the American colonies, much of this knowledge and lore was European in nature. In the South, midwives were often slave women who delivered babies in surrounding areas as well as on their own plantations. These women brought both knowledge and practices from African cultures.

During the seventeenth and early eighteenth centuries, knowledge about childbirth spread slowly. In 1668, François Mauriceau (1637–1709) of Paris published *The Accomplisht Midwife*, which educated physicians on birth complications such as dealing with hemorrhage and puerperal fever. Three years later, British midwife Jane Sharp published *The Midwives Book*, the first childbirth manual written by a midwife.

Efforts to educate and license midwives began in France in the sixteenth century, fueled by midwife Louyse Bourgeois (1563–1626). Early in the eighteenth century, the first **laws** were passed elsewhere in Europe, requiring midwives to be able to read and write. Control of English midwives was placed in the hands of the Anglican Church. German midwives were organized under a senior midwife and were autonomous. In some areas, local governments often placed midwives on their payrolls. In New Amsterdam, for example, Anne Hutchinson (1591–1643) was paid 100 guilders annually by local authorities to assist poor women in childbirth. **Education** for midwives did not become common in the American colonies until 1760.

At this same time, physicians who had previously been called upon only when birthing complications occurred and a new group known as man-midwives began to wrest control of the birthing process from females. In response to new understanding of female anatomy and fetal development, increased attention to educating physicians in obstetrics and gynecology, and the appearance of lying-in hospitals for poor women led to a greater demand for professionalization of childbirth. Women were generally banned from educational and training institutions.

Expanded knowledge about the use of forceps, which had been closely guarded by the Chamberlain family who had invented them a century earlier, increased the likelihood that both the infant and the mother would survive in the latter half of the eighteenth century. The knowledge of the use of forceps was distributed in large part by Dr. William Smellie (1698–1763) through *Practice of Midwifery* (1752) and a series of lectures on childbirth. Students came from around the world to study under Smellie. In the past, infants had often been dismembered and killed to save the life of the mother. Smellie also developed a machine to teach physicians about the function of the uterus during childbirth.

While much progress was made in expanding knowledge of childbirth in the latter half of the eighteenth century, there was little progress in rural areas, where vestiges of seventeenth-century childbirth practices continued into the early twentieth century. In rural areas, childbirth continued to belong exclusively to women and was controlled by traditional midwives. In urban areas, this period produced a move toward physician-assisted births at home or in lying-in hospitals where the process became professionalized, excluding the traditional midwife. *See also* Gynecology Manuals; Medicine and Science; Menstruation; Midwives and Physicians; Pregnancy.

Further Reading: Gélis, Jacques. *History of Childbirth: Fertility, Pregnancy, and Birth in Early Modern Europe.* Boston: Northeastern University Press, 1991; Hay, Carla H. "Childbirth in America: A Historical Perspective." In *Who's Having This Baby? Perspectives on Birthing*, edited by Helen M. Serk, et al., 9–41. East Lansing: Michigan University Press, 2002; Rooks, Judith Pence. *Midwifery and Childbirth in America.* Philadelphia: Temple University Press, 1997; Shorter, Edward. *A History of Women's Bodies.* New York: Basic Books, 1982; Wertz, Richard C., and Dorothy C. Wertz. *Lying-In: A History of Childbirth in America.* New Haven, CT: Yale University Press, 1989; Wilson, Adrian. *The Making of Man-Midwifery: Childbirth in England, 1660–1770.* Cambridge, MA: Harvard University Press, 1995.

Elizabeth R. Purdy

CHILDHOOD AND ADOLESCENCE. Childhood and adolescence were life-stages epitomized by dependency. One attained independence through **marriage** or economic self-sufficiency. Society in the colonial and revolutionary era was profoundly young. In most towns and villages, people under thirty years of age comprised one-half to two-thirds of the overall population.

Many historians identify the late seventeenth and eighteenth centuries as the period in which Europeans recognized childhood as a distinct stage in life that was innately good and innocent. Puritan school books admonished children to avoid sin and idleness, characteristics that many contemporaries considered intrinsic to children. Breaking the will of a child, often through corporal punishment, was considered acceptable parental behavior through much of the colonial and revolutionary era. By the late seventeenth century, the English philosopher John Locke persuaded many Europeans that children's minds were blank slates formed primarily by their experiences. Educational philosophy thus slowly shifted toward fostering children's potential development instead of solely focusing on their capacity for evil.

Educational emphasis on early childhood development increased in the colonial and revolutionary era. In the introduction to *A Little Pretty Pocket Book* (1744), John Newbery taught parents that "the grand design on the nurture of children, is to make them strong, hardy, … virtuous, wise, and happy; and these good purposes are not to be obtained without some care and management in their infancy." The French Enlightenment philosopher **Jean-Jacques Rousseau** argued against the traditional practice of swaddling, stating that it limited children's natural freedom of movement. The practice of wet nursing—sending out a child to be nursed by another woman—steadily declined over the course of the eighteenth century as more middling and elite women decided to nurse their own children. Commercial development followed suit. By the end of the eighteenth century, there were established industries in children's toys and books on both sides of the Atlantic.

The term "adolescence" is a modern one, dating only to the end of the nineteenth century. But Europeans certainly had an understanding of the period of life between dependence and autonomy, that of the teens and twenties, as one fraught with particular challenges. They called the period of life from the teens to the mid to late twenties "youth." For many social classes, late marriage became the norm in the seventeenth and eighteenth centuries. This extended the length of time in which one lived as a youth and increased concerns about **premarital sex** and illegitimacy. Children and adolescents in a variety of cultures engaged in a series of symbolic life-stages that emphasized separation from childhood while they embarked on their variety of paths toward independence. European boys and girls both dressed in skirts until about the age of seven or eight. After this time, boys wore breeches and began to enter the man's world under the direction of their fathers, while girls continued to wear skirts and learned domestic chores. Further changes developed around puberty in a number of cultures. Native American girls were sent into isolated cabins upon their first **menstruation**, while boys endured episodes of fasting and isolation before they were welcomed among the men. African American slave children usually did light work until they turned ten or twelve years old. They were then introduced to adult slave work and were sometimes sold and separated from their families at this time. In their early teenage years, many European and colonial American teenagers were "put out" to become servants and apprentices in other homes. This period outside the home allowed young men and women to develop the skills they needed for independent living. Young men and women learned specific trades and domestic skills while living in a master's house. Youth were among the most mobile of the population. Young servants moved frequently from master to master, and journeymen often moved from city to city on the European continent. They also saved resources for future marriages and households, and learned how to make their own economic and social decisions. During this time, youth formed important peer relationships that taught them social skills necessary for later years. In continental Europe, male peer groups often helped to recreate support networks through professional or student organizations. These groups also occasionally maintained social and sexual norms in towns and villages by ritually shaming those who crossed cultural boundaries.

The length of childhood and adolescence also depended to a significant degree on gender and social class. Extensive schooling for elite boys extended the period of dependency on parents. For the poor or for slaves, many of whom were forced to work in some capacity from an early age, childhood was a short-lived affair. The end of adolescence was often accompanied by the acquisition of a trade or a set of land or goods. To be considered an adult, most young people would marry or form independent households. Most men and women in the American colonies married in their early to mid-twenties. In eighteenth-century France, many men and women married in their later twenties. *See also* Bastardy; Courtship; Education; Indentured Servants.

Further Reading: Ben-Amos, Ilana Krausman. *Adolescence and Youth in Early Modern England*. New Haven, CT: Yale University Press, 1994; Graff, Harvey J. *Conflicting Paths: Growing Up in America*. Cambridge, MA: Harvard University Press, 1995; Heywood, Colin. *A History of Childhood*. Malden, MA: Blackwell Publishers, 2001; Illick, Joseph E. *American Childhoods*.

Philadelphia: University of Pennsylvania Press, 2002; Plumb, J. W. "The New World of Children in Eighteenth-Century England." *Past and Present* 67 (1975): 64–93.

Christopher R. Corley

CHINESE THEATER. See Theater, Chinese

CIRCUMCISION. Circumcision is the surgical procedure used to remove the foreskin from a male's penis. The term has been used incorrectly to refer to other kinds of genital surgery, such as subincision on males in certain parts of Africa, and clitoridectomy, infundibulation, and removal of the labiae in females. In Western countries, circumcision is performed routinely, usually within the first week of life. One noncontroversial indication for circumcision is phimosis, a condition where the foreskin does not retract normally during erection, and surgical intervention is required in order to alleviate the pain caused by the tightness.

The rationale for male circumcision was religious at first, a symbolic covenant between the God of the Jewish people and Abraham. Over the next 2,000 years, the motivation to perform circumcision moved beyond religious edicts to include concerns about health, cleanliness, and sexuality. Thus, the surgery was performed to prevent the accumulation of smegma and to keep the penis clean. In the late eighteenth and early nineteenth centuries, circumcision was said to be a preventive and (sometimes) punitive strategy to prevent **masturbation**. But in the seventeenth and eighteenth centuries, this operation was viewed as both anathema to pleasure and a mutilation. The foreskin, described by Aristotle as moving up and down during sexual intercourse, was integral to pleasure in both men and women, and sex manuals promoted that information.

William Harvey (1578–1657), the famed anatomist who described the circulation of the blood and who was personal physician to Charles I, was the first to insist on the existence of the human ovum. He wrote that circumcised men had less sexual pleasure because the scar from the circumcision thickened the remaining membrane and blunted sensation.

The British thought circumcision was a disfigurement exclusive to alien people such as Jews and Turks. During the 1750s, the Jewish Naturalization Act in Britain was repealed because of the fear that Jews, once British citizens, would force Christians to undergo circumcisions instead of baptisms.

Tristram Shandy, the protagonist in a hilarious novel (1760) of the same name, sustains an injury to his penis when a window sash falls on it. There is a great deal of text devoted to Tristram's father as he informs the family about the history of circumcision. The immense horror and aversion to the procedure reflects British sentiments and fears of circumcision.

A Turkish text, the *Surname* was written by Vehbi to commemorate a fifteen-day celebration that was given to honor Ahmed III's sons. It is both a pictorial and verbal narrative with colorful illustrations by Levni. The most elaborate festivals in the **Ottoman empire** were for royalty, and this 1720 event is one of the most accurately recorded in Ottoman history. Invitations were sent, and a chief was appointed to supervise the construction of candy gardens and housing for thousands of guests. There were musicians and dancers, acrobats, performers, and special lighting arranged for the stages during performances and for the grounds and streets for the parade afterward. The celebration was held for four princes: a ten-year-old, a two-year-old, and three-year-old twins. In addition the sons of another high status family, as well as 5,000 boys from the lower classes were invited. All these children, regardless of age, were circumcised in a Circumcision Pavilion built especially for the surgery and then taken to the Baghdad Pavilion where they recuperated.

An unusual ink-and-wash work of art by Romeyn de Hooghe (1645–1708) titled "The Circumcision" was created in 1668. It is believed to reflect not only the procedure, but also an unusual depiction of the Sephardic Jews who lived in Amsterdam and whose mores allowed the production of images. Compared to the Ashkenazis, from eastern Europe, the Sephardim were more liberal and tolerant regarding art. And, although the United Provinces (former name for the Netherlands) allowed expelled and escaped Jews from Spain and Portugal to live there, there was still some prejudice. Because of de Hooghe's familiarity with Jewish culture, de Hooghe's wife was accused of having sexual relations with Portuguese Jews. Another artist, Bernard Picart (1672–1733), fifty years later, made a series of etchings of Jewish ritual, among them "The Circumcision." Compared to de Hooghe's solemn mood, Picart captures a more joyous celebration. Whether this is due to a change in the tenor of the ceremony or simply the artist's worldview, the two reflect different attitudes. *See also* Art; Ejaculation; Eunuchs; Judaism; Literature; Medicine and Science; Religion.

Further Reading: Atil, Esin. "The Story of an Eighteenth Century Ottoman Festival." *Muqarnas. Essays in Honor of Oleg Grabar* 10 (1993): 181–200; Bryk, Felix. *Circumcision in Man and Woman: Its History, Psychology and Ethnology*. New York: American Ethnological Press, 1934; Darby, Robert. "An Oblique and Slovenly Initiation: The Circumcision Episode in Tristram Shandy." *Eighteenth-Century Life* 27 (2003): 72–84; Golaher, David. *Circumcision: A History of the World's Most Controversial Surgery*. New York: Basic Books, 2000; Wilson, William. "The Circumcision, A Drawing by Romeyn de Hooghe." *Master Drawings* 13, no. 3 (1975): 250–57.

Lana Thompson

CLOTHING AND FASHION.   Within the area of European clothing and fashion in the seventeenth and eighteenth centuries, two tendencies seem to be combined—whereas clothing marked a visual representation of the wearers' social status, fashion was evolving toward enhancing their sexual attractiveness.

The seventeenth century witnessed French fashion taking over the leading position in Europe. As rulers sought to imitate the absolutistic ideal of the reign of Louis XIV, the Sun King, national differences and diversities in fashion were considerably diminished. Therefore, French fashion became the Western world fashion, and its dominance continued through the following century.

Male fashion was far more excessive and diverse than female fashion, marking women's inferior position in the society. In the seventeenth century, the fashion for men changed considerably from the military uniform style to showy ornamentation—the coats shrank and became more and more fitting to the figure at the upper body and tight at the waist. The breeches, or so-called *rhinegraves*, were so baggy and full that they actually resembled wide skirts: the trouser legs, using a large amount of fabric, were gathered below the knees with lace frills. This tendency indeed resulted in men wearing skirts over breeches, which led to their name *petticoat breeches*.

As for the female fashion of that period, the garments accentuated the curves of the female silhouette. *Stays* was the eighteenth-century name for corsets, a piece of clothing that gave the body a rigid cone shape. Corsets were not thought of as just underwear; they were visible at the front of the bodice, heavily decorated, and they ended in a pronounced V at the waist. The corset was not only a status symbol, but also seen as a moral and medical necessity; women, after all, were considered the weaker sex, so the corset was supposed to be both a protection of their feeble figures and a shield preventing easy seduction. Tight lacing was regarded virtuous; a loose corset was a sign of a loose woman. To keep her innocence and **virtue**, a lady had to be chaperoned everywhere she went. She needed to protect herself from lustful men (and her own morality) by wearing heavily reinforced layers of clothing and tight corsets that made getting undressed a long and difficult task. The décolleté was rather wide and low—usually a handkerchief would be worn to cover it, although for more dressy events in the evening it was customary to remove the handkerchief and show the cleavage. Like the cap, the handkerchief covering the neckline was regarded as guarding female virtue. Fashion required women to uncover their breasts, while decency and morality required the opposite, so the compromise was to wear low-necked dresses and kerchiefs.

The ladies' skirts at Louis XIV's court seemed to mark the rank of the wearer. The upper skirt, which was called robe or manteau ended in a train, and its length was determined by the status of the lady—the longer the train, the more aristocratic the person was. Although those court dresses were designed for representation, they still accentuated the female figure. The upper skirt was slit in the front, draped back on the hips, and supported by artificial round shapes at the back of the wearer, while the waist was extremely small. Thus the female figure seemed, despite the masses of fabric being used, to be more bared than actually covered.

The end of the seventeenth century saw the extreme popularity of wigs. They became compulsory in the fourth quarter of the century and immediately became status symbols of one's importance at the French court. Male wigs, especially those worn by the officers, tended toward a simple form, whereas the female wigs evolved toward rather orgiastic shapes, sophisticated constructions decorated with ostrich feathers or topped with a small hat.

The most fashionable accessories of the seventeenth and eighteenth centuries were patches. They formed an interesting contrast to ivory skin and were meant to enhance the facial attractiveness in the process of courting. As for other accessory examples, collapsible fans should be mentioned, as they were a truly efficient communicative device, used to convey many different meanings by the means of significant gestures, stances, or movements. *See also* Breastfeeding; Cosmetics and Perfume; Footbinding; Gender Roles; Women, Changing Images of.

Further Reading: Cumming, Valerie. *A Visual History of Costume: The Seventeenth Century*. London: Batsford, 1984; Hart, Avril, and Susan North. *Historical Fashion in Detail: The 17th and 18th Centuries*. London: V&A Publications, 1998; Picard, Liza. *Restoration London*. London: Weidenfeld & Nicolson, 1997.

Barbara Loranc

CONCUBINES. A concubine is a woman who cohabits with a man without legal marriage. Depending on the country and time period, concubinage had varying degrees of legal status and privileges.

The two defining phenomena of the Colonial Age—increasingly frequent travel and **slavery**—created conditions particularly conducive to the practice of concubinage. Travelers absent from home for long months or years found it hard to resist the temptations of carnal pleasures in remote lands. An obvious reason why seamen and traders entered into unions of sexual convenience was usually because the distance from home practically guaranteed that their actions would remain unseen and unknown. It was also not uncommon for discoverers and conquerors of new lands to live with the local women in free relationships. Such unions were in many cases consensual or were even formalized by **marriage**, but a lack of the women's express consent rarely stopped any colonizers from forcing them into concubinage. Although it is now hard to give precise numbers, it is estimated that thousands of Native American women were taken as concubines by Spanish conquistadors and other European settlers.

Thanks to seamen who were incisive observers of the sexual mores in lands newly discovered by Europeans during the Colonial Period, we know that concubinage was also practiced by the people they encountered. Captain James Cook's lieutenant, James Burney, gives a firsthand account of Maori social life, painstakingly describing details such as the number of wives and concubines of influential men.

Among the most famous events concerning concubinage and travel was the mutiny on the Bounty in 1789 in which the crew rebelled against their commander Lieutenant William Bligh and captured the ship. Although historians still debate the reasons behind the incident, it is now widely accepted that after a five-month stay at Tahiti, the seamen were angered by the commander's decision to set sail, forcing them to leave behind their Tahitian women. Several months after the mutiny, the seamen landed on Pitcairn Island, where they settled and formed a community based on concubinage with the women from Tahiti. Although within the first few years on the island, most of the mutineers, including their leader, were murdered in internecine conflict, their concubines and children survived, and their descendants live on Pitcairn to this day.

Slavery was another context in which concubinage took place. Always mindful of the inevitability of punishment at the slightest displeasure of plantation owners, female slaves usually had little real choice in responding to their masters' advances. Their predicament was doubly complicated by the fact that by yielding to their owners, they often incurred the wrath of the men's wives, who found it easier to vent their fury not at their unfaithful husbands but at the defenseless slaves. Whether a slave owner was caught in the very act or not, his wife would later see that the slaves' children were lighter-skinned than their slave mothers and strikingly similar to the master's legitimate children.

Although generally decried, interracial concubinage was sometimes loosely institutionalized. In New Orleans, a unique form of concubinage called *plaçage* was practiced to work around legal restrictions that forbade women of color to marry white males. During the so-called quadroon balls, lighter-skinned women of color were introduced to well-to-do gentlemen with the express intent to be joined in a relationship of plaçage, in which the man would ensure the financial security of his mistress. Because the mulatto women in question were usually very beautiful and highly educated, it was tacitly understood that their value had to be matched by a suitable price, which the future protector often had to negotiate with the woman's parents. Such unions were usually secret, and when the man officially married another woman, he and his plaçage partner would normally separate.

In China, concubines enjoyed an even more official status and a higher social standing. Although lower in rank than legitimate wives, and with fewer rights and privileges, they were nevertheless elevated socially by the fact of cohabitation with powerful men. Apart from several official wives, well-educated girls from the most elite families acted as regular sexual partners for Chinese emperors. Unlike in many parts of the world where children by concubines were often considered illegitimate and unworthy of respect, in China such children fathered by the emperor not infrequently became princes with significant political powers.

Concubines enjoyed a similarly high social standing in the **Ottoman empire**, where they played important political roles. *See also* Elliott, Grace Dalrymple; Geisha; Harems; Interracial Sex; Royal Mistresses; Thistlewood, Thomas.

Further Reading: Fossett, Judith Jackson, and Jeffrey A Tucker. *Race Consciousness: African American Studies for the New Century.* New York: New York University Press, 1997; Socolow, Susan Migden. *The Women of Colonial Latin America. New Approaches to the Americas.* New York: Cambridge University Press, 2000.

Konrad Szczesniak

CONSENT. Rape prosecutions have specific criteria that must be met before an indictment is even possible. One of those criteria centers upon the issue of the woman's consent. If a woman consented to sexual relations with a man, then she cannot accuse him of having raped her. In general terms, consent means to give one's permission. The law recognizes two kinds of consent. An *express consent* is direct and clear in demonstrating an agreement to an act or an omission to act and may be either verbal or written. An *implied consent* is an indirect or tacit indication of agreement that is typically demonstrated by a sign, silence, or an action or inaction. An implied consent must create a reasonable presumption that an accession of the will has been given to be legitimate.

The general legal principle regarding consent is that it is valid only when it is informed and given by a person who is mentally and physically competent to grant it. It is vital that the person understands and is knowledgeable as to what he or she is consenting to and that consent is given wholly of a person's own free will. If those criteria are not met, if the consent is uninformed, given in ignorance, or obtained through force, fraud, or coercion, it is not valid or binding. There are some exceptions to this general legal doctrine, and the exceptions occur mainly in rape law.

In the seventeenth and eighteenth centuries, rape was a crime that only a man could commit and only upon a woman. Rape trials hinged upon a man's word against a woman's. Defendants, whether they were prosecuted under the common law or civil law, could plead consent as a defense to the charge, and if they could show that the woman had given either an express or implied consent, then the charge could be dismissed or the jury could acquit the defendant. Defendants could prove the woman's consent in a number of ways, but the most common was to assert that she did not resist to her utmost ability. A woman's resistance to her assailant, or lack thereof, served as evidence of her willingness to accede to his desires. Though seventeenth- and eighteenth-century social norms depicted women as the weaker sex, the law presumed that women would somehow always be able to muster the necessary strength to defend their **chastity**. If a woman was raped, then courts concluded that she did not resist and that meant she had consented.

Courts considered other factors in determining consent. If the alleged assault occurred in or near a place where she could have been heard had she cried out, courts viewed her silence as an implied consent. When a woman did not immediately complain to friends, family, or the authorities, courts deemed the "stale complaint" as ruse to cover up her latent shame. Courts presumed that a woman who had consented to prior sexual relations outside marriage would submit to any man who solicited her afterward. Interestingly, courts presumed that any woman who became pregnant as the result of a rape had consented because conventional medical wisdom decreed that a woman could only conceive if she had an **orgasm** during coition, something no forced woman would have. If she became pregnant, she must have consented.

Not all females could give a legal consent to sexual intercourse. The law presumed that those under a designated age could not understand the nature and consequences of the act. Insane, unconscious, or intoxicated women could not give a lawful consent, but courts allowed defendants to claim that they did not know of the woman's incapacity to excuse or mitigate the offence. Some women simply could not be raped in the eyes of the law. There was no concept of marital rape, for a wife owed her husband total obedience and that included her perpetual consent to coition with him. Slave women were chattel property and hence could neither grant nor withhold consent, though a man who forced himself upon a slave woman without her master's permission had transgressed against him and might be punished under the law of trespass. *See also* Child Rape; Laws; Medicine and Science; Pregnancy; Slavery; Wartime Rape.

Further Reading: Simpson, Antony E. "The 'Blackmail Myth' and the Prosecution of Rape and Its Attempt in 18th-Century London: The Creation of a Legal Tradition." *Journal of Criminal Law and Criminology* 77 (Spring 1986): 101–50; Smith, Merril D., ed. *Sex and Sexuality in Early America*. New York: New York University Press, 1998.

Mary Block

CONSUMERISM. *See* Household Consumerism

CONTRACEPTION. Throughout history, women and their sexual partners who have been unwilling to become parents have practiced contraception of one sort or another, even when it was not considered socially or morally acceptable. During the Renaissance, European couples developed tolerance about sex outside **marriage**. Subsequently, the increased sexual freedom of the seventeenth and eighteenth centuries resulted in increased interest in contraception so that illicit couplings did not produce unwanted offspring. Many contraceptive methods used throughout the period were ineffective, and some were actually dangerous, as when toxic substances were ingested and with certain methods of **abortion**.

In seventeenth-century France, the salon atmosphere with its open discussion of women's rights led to public acknowledgement that many women were unwilling to have large families. During the following century, birth control knowledge and techniques began to be disseminated, and birth rates began to decline. The rest of Europe and the United State followed more slowly.

In colonial America, sex outside marriage occurred even though it was discouraged. The **Puritan** ethic stipulated that the use of contraceptives was against the laws of nature and was opposed to God's will. Practically, large families were desirable in the colonies because many hands were required to provide sustenance for families and communities. While it is impossible to know how many couples used contraceptives, it is clear from available records that colonial Americans practiced birth control.

Birth control methods varied. For instance, mothers of young infants sometimes prolonged **breastfeeding** for its contraceptive benefits. Women tried to abort unwanted fetuses, generally unsuccessfully. Other desperate women committed **infanticide**, knowing they faced execution. Some couples abstained from sex either on moral grounds or as the only fail-proof method of contraception.

Birth control information was spread chiefly through word of mouth and was handed down from generation to generation. Midwives and herbalists were also valuable sources for information on contraception. Apothecaries openly carried many herbs

"Cassanova and the condom," illustration from an edition of Casanova's memoirs published in 1872. Courtesy of the Library of Congress.

believed to prevent or end **pregnancy**. The most common contraceptive herbs, generally used in teas, ointments, and pastes, were ergot, savin, tansy, pennyroyal, and mints.

One of the earliest folklore methods of birth control involved tying knots in threads or sheets during a wedding ceremony to designate the number of children desired in a marriage. Some practitioners of magic taught that drinking teas made from the seeds of fruit trees prevented pregnancy. Other methods of contraception made popular by folklore included tossing seeds or stones equal to the number of desired pregnancies. Placing animal dung, deer's hearts, or children's teeth on a woman's body were also thought to prevent pregnancy in some cultures.

Both married and unmarried couples engaged in the practice of *coitus interuptus* in which the male withdrew during the sex act so that no semen was released. This form of birth control was referred to in Genesis 38:9 when Onan refused to impregnate his brother's widow to provide his brother an heir according to Hebrew law: "And Onan knew that the seed should not be his; and it came to pass, when he went in unto his brother's wife, that he spilled it on the ground, lest that he should give seed to his brother" (KJV). Couples also practiced what later became known as the rhythm method, refraining from sex at times that a woman was considered fertile.

Condoms were first used in the seventeenth century as protection against venereal diseases. The first condoms were simple linen sheaths. By the late seventeenth century, condoms made from sheep-gut or fish skins had also become popular. In his *Memoires*, Italian writer Giacomo **Casanova** spoke of using gold balls and cervical caps made from lemon halves to prevent pregnancies during his numerous sexual liaisons. Women were quick to see the contraceptive value of condoms, sponges, and tampons. They also tried suppositories, astringents, douches, cold baths, and bloodletting to prevent pregnancies.

Contraceptives were commonly used during the seventeenth and eighteenth centuries in the United States and Europe. Methods of contraception included those based on folklore and superstitions as well as newer methods such as condoms and cervical caps. Although many methods of birth control were ineffective, birth rates began to decline due to a general awareness of knowledge about contraception and a desire to limit family size. *See also* Childbirth; Gynecology Manuals; Midwives and Physicians; Myths and Folklore.

Further Reading: Brodie, Janet Farrell. *Contraception and Abortion in Nineteenth-Century America*. Ithaca, NY: Cornell University Press, 1994; Gordon, Linda. *Woman's Body, Woman's Right: A Social History of Birth Control in America*. New York: Grossman, 1976; Himes, Norman E. *Medical History of Contraception*. New York: Schocken Books, 1970; McLauren, Angus. *A History of Contraceptives: From Antiquity to the Present Day*. Cambridge: Basil Blackwell, 1991; Riddle, John M. *Contraception and Abortion: From the Ancient World to the Renaissance*. Cambridge, MA: Harvard University Press, 1992; Riddle, John M. *Eve's Herbs: A History of Contraception and Abortion in the West*. Cambridge, MA: Harvard University Press, 1997.

Elizabeth R. Purdy

CONVENTS. *See* Monasteries

COSMETICS AND PERFUME. Through much of the colonial and Revolutionary periods cosmetics, perfume, and efforts toward beauty by both sexes were strongly mitigated by social class. While the majority of the colonists did not have the time or financial ability to invest in expensive perfumes, cosmetics, and fashions, there was a greater availability for those of the upper classes. Cosmetics, perfumes, and beauty fashions not only served to convey ideals of beauty and attractiveness, but also served as a means to separate the well-to-do from the everyday person.

Colonial conceptions of beauty and fashion were strongly influenced by European culture. Many European societies reflected a strong class division with most cosmetic, perfume, and fashion products being consumed by the upper class. The upper class used perfumes and scents, often imported, to cover the foul scents that accompanied an expanding population with little infrastructure for bathing or waste removal. These scents were often quite strong, serving the dual purpose of covering one's own foul scent as well as helping to cover the foul environmental scents. In general the scents used were not highly gendered to reflect masculine or feminine scents—though there was some division occurring. Both men and women of the upper class wore cosmetics. One particular cosmetic used during this time period was the cake and powdered whitening face makeup (which was frequently lead based, thus ultimately harmful to one's health). This makeup served a dual purpose—to help smooth out complexions, as pox marks were common from the various plagues of the age, and to create a consistent and appealing color. Upon this base rouges were employed to redden lips and cheeks. Wigs were the final components to the fashion regime. These wigs served to create a pleasing and appealing mirage upon the natural hair that was seldom washed and likely infested with lice and other vermin. These fashion regimes served to create a clear demarcation between the classes and to enforce ideals of beauty. On the other side of the equation, the lower classes did not employ these extreme measures though they emulated them to varying degrees.

The Colonial period in America is often noted as a time of hardship. The majority of the early immigrants did not have the financial ability to purchase the expensive cosmetics available from Europe. Similar to Europe, the colonies had a strong division in the ideals of beauty and sexual appeal. The wealthy sought to emulate some fashions from Europe, while the nonwealthy had more fluidity in their physical adornments. Only the wealthy of this era were able to import cosmetics and perfumes from Europe. The nonwealthy, often limited in ability and time did incorporate modified versions of these beauty ideals into their own lives.

Ideals of beauty, hygiene, and scent are today strongly correlated, but in early America these were not highly associated. Bathing was not a common practice in early America. Few households had facilities specifically for bathing, or even owned bathing tubs. In fact, frequent bathing was considered a risk to one's health. Part of sexual and romantic life was the acceptance of body odor and dirt. Face and hand washing, while variable in their practice, was the extent of most bathing. Thus, perfumes and scents were employed to help foster greater allure by both sexes.

As America's infrastructure improved and the first glassblowing factory was established, perfumes and beauty tonics became more readily available in America. For the majority of the residents the cost of these products made them prohibitive. However, despite the inability to purchase commercially prepared perfumes, cosmetics, and fashion products many of the women and men would emulate upper-class fashion ideals as best they could. Lower-class women would use kitchen grease (bacon perhaps) to soften complexion and set hair, use flour to whiten complexion, and reddeners, such as beet juice, to color their lips and cheeks. Men also used greases to set and manage their hair (including facial).

During the Revolutionary period there was increasing departure from the European styles of the period, but these fashions remained highly influential. Over time the wigging practice fell out of favor. Cosmetic and perfume use continued in varying degrees within different communities as religious ideologies became more integrated into society and regulatory of sociosexual interactions. *See also* Baths; Clothing and Fashion.

Further Reading: Angeloglou, Maggie. *A History of Make-up*. London: Macmillan, 1970; Bushman, Richard L., and Claudia M. Bushman. "The Early History of Cleanliness in America." *Journal of American History* 74, no. 4 (1988): 1213–38; Horan, Julie L. *Porcelain God: A Social History of the Toilet*. Toronto: Carol Publishing Group. 1996.

Daniel Farr

COURTSHIP.   Courtship is the period of time during which a young man and a young woman get to know one another and are made mutually agreeable within the perspective of getting married. During courtship, the prospective mates strive to convince the other that he or she will make an admirable husband or wife. In the early American period, the first important factors were thus beauty and the appearance of good health. A father might recommend that his daughter avoid soldiers, old men, or sick men. The young man had to display a willingness to respect his future wife and to work hard to provide her with a comfortable life. As for the young woman, she must also show a will to please her future husband, while displaying the virtues of modesty and discretion. She must also demonstrate that she would be able to fulfill her duty as a wife, run a household, and raise children.

Historians generally hold that, in the upper class, mates were chosen by families. Indeed, restrictions existed on the inheritance a couple received if they married without the permission of their parents. In the wealthy aristocracy of the southern colonies, a young man would first talk to his father before turning his attention to a young woman. If the father approved, he or his son would write to the girl's father to explain who the young man was and why he would make a good husband, as well as the financial particulars of the match. When the girl's father had approved the match and revealed his own financial contribution, the courtship of the young people could start. Even then, love and companionship were taken into consideration, more and more so throughout the period.

In most cases, the young man initiated the courtship. For a young woman to do so would damage her reputation. However, older widows and older single women, if they were financially independent, had more freedom to join in a courtship without permission. Furthermore, young people with little or no property could choose whom they married. In general, parental influence declined throughout the eighteenth century with the emergence of a new ideal of **romantic love** as a basis for **marriage**.

The proper places for courtship were dances, church, and the girl's home. Careful of their reputations, the young couple would conduct their courtship in public in highly formal manners. They would call each other "Miss" and "Mister" followed by the last name. Public displays of affection were eschewed and liable to lead to punishment. The young people could take public walks together and exchange formal letters. The man would often write more than the woman, who had to remain discreet. He would come to visit his future wife's family and sometimes stay there for several days. As the couple became acquainted, their conversation would become more serious, and they would consider the more serious questions of marriage, property, and child rearing. The man would see that his future wife possessed the skills required to run the household, and he would help his future father-in-law with his trade to show that he was hardworking.

For couples who had pledged to marry, one accepted courtship practice was bundling. Although premarital sexual relations were proscribed, the custom of bundling, brought from England and northern Europe, allowed for some intimacy and physical contact. The young couple would sleep in the same bed, but with their clothes on and a bundling board between them, with the girl's legs wrapped in a bundling bag or duffel-like chastity bag. In some areas, the practice was so popular that a girl's social status was deeply affected if she didn't have a night visitor, or if she was above the age of eighteen and still at home.

The practice of bundling had not only emotional, but also practical reasons for existing. When the young man visited the girl he was courting, the distances and difficulty of travel would require him to stay at the house of his future in-laws. At night, it was often difficult to heat a house, so the young couple would bundle in bed to keep warm. But the best protection against sexual relations was when the parents slept in the same room.

Boards and bags may not have been completely efficient, however, as premarital relations occurred despite the public penalties. Toward the end of the Colonial period bridal pregnancy was on the increase, and a declining proportion of young men married the women whom they seduced and impregnated. The custom of bundling was abandoned by 1800.

When the couple decided to marry, and it may have been quickly given the ban on premarital sex, "Banns" were printed to make the intention of the parties public. It was posted at the church or meeting house, so that anyone who opposed the union could come forward. If no one did, the two could marry without delay.

Courtship was a crucial period of time in the social life of early Americans. If successful, it concluded in a wedding, the decisive event in the life of young men and women. Courtship was thus a major threshold in a young woman's life, whose *raison d'être* was marriage and childbearing and who, once married, would be completely subjected to her husband. *See also* Bastardy; Fornication; Seduction Literature.

Further Reading: Ingoldsby, Bron B., ed. *Families in Multicultural Perspective.* New York: Guilford Press, 1995; Middleton, Richard Robert. *Colonial America: A History, 1565–1776.* Oxford: Blackwell, 2002; Smith, Merril D., ed. *Sex and Sexuality in Early America.* New York: New York University Press, 1998.

Eve-Alice Roustang-Stoller

CROSS-DRESSING. People wore clothes normally appertaining to the other biological sex for many reasons. In some societies cross-dressing was related to institutionalized "third gender" roles such as those of the Indian Hijra **eunuchs**, the Native American **berdache**, or the Polynesian *mahu*. Cross-gender identity was sometimes associated with a strong connection to the spiritual realm, as in some Native American and shamanic societies. Shamanic initiation for both men and women was sometimes associated with the adoption of a new gender.

People also cross-dressed in societies that lacked institutional roles for them, including Enlightenment Europe. Women cross-dressed as men and adopted male identities for greater personal freedom and economic opportunity, or to pursue romantic and sexual relationships with women. Among the best-known biological females who adopted a male gender identity in the early modern period was the Basque **Catalina de Erauso** (1585–1650), who fled from a convent and adopted both male clothing and male identity. He served as a soldier in the Spanish army (soldiering was a common career choice for cross-dressed women) and eventually followed the male profession of mule-driver in Mexico. De Erauso, who became a minor celebrity in Europe, received permission from the Pope to continue living as a man. The documents surrounding De Erauso, including an autobiography, give little information concerning his erotic life, although there are indications that he was attracted to women.

Hannah Snell dressed as a soldier, ca. 1820. Courtesy of the Library of Congress.

There were also cases of "female husbands," women who cross-dressed and lived as men specifically to live with female lovers. One of the best-known examples in the eighteenth century was Maria of Antwerp, who was twice convicted of dressing and living as a man to marry a woman. Maria, who had also served as a soldier, seems to have been more interested in living in a male gender role than in having sex with women. Her case attracted much public attention, and she was the subject of a ghostwritten autobiography, *Heroine of Breda*. Men who lived as women seem to have been much rarer, as male-to-female cross-dressing offered none of the economic advantages of female-to-male.

Socially accepted transgendered people, such as De Erauso and the male-to-female Charles **d'Eon de Beaumont**, were exceptions in European society. Condemnation of cross-dressing and other forms of transgendered behavior goes back to the Jewish and Christian traditions as far as the book of Deuteronomy. Europe and its colonial offshoots had a marked hostility to the transgendered, whether within European society or outside it, as were the berdaches and others occupying "two-spirit" roles in Native American societies who ran afoul of missionaries and colonial authorities. The *mahu* were integrated into the overall European picture of Polynesian societies as dominated by sexual licentiousness.

Some theatrical traditions, such as the Japanese Noh and Kabuki theater or the pre-Restoration English **theater**, excluded women from the stage and filled female roles with cross-dressed men or boys. The first great *onnagata*, or man playing female roles in Kabuki, Yoshizawa Ayame (1673–1729), claimed in his influential manual for *onnagata* that to be successful in portraying women onstage, an actor should live as a woman offstage as well, advice followed by later *onnagata*. Kabuki had begun decades earlier as an all-woman's theater, but the danger presented by women playing male roles was a reason that the Japanese government gave for suppressing it in 1629. Although for women cross-dressing for theatrical purposes was not usually as institutionalized as male cross-dressing, some actresses, notably the Englishwoman Charlotte Charke, were known for their performances as men in "breeches roles." (Charke spent some time living as a man in her offstage life as well, but this was very unusual behavior for an actress.)

Temporary assumption of clothing of the opposite gender was also common for specifically sexual reasons. Female prostitutes also sometimes cross-dressed, not to conceal their gender identity but to appeal to potential customers. The rise of urban gay male culture in eighteenth-century Europe was accompanied by that of men who temporarily cross-dressed in the confines of **"molly houses,"** adopting feminine personae and referring to each other by female names and pronouns while maintaining male identities on the outside. *See also* Native Americans; Prostitutes and Prostitution; Theater, Japanese.

Further Reading: Bullough, Vern L., and Bonnie Bullough. *Cross-Dressing, Sex and Gender*. Philadelphia: University of Pennsylvania Press, 1993; De Erauso, Catalina. *Lieutenant Nun: Memoirs of a Basque Transvestite in the New World*. Translated from the Spanish by Michele Stepto and Gabriel Stepto. Boston: Beacon Press, 1996; Dekker, Rudolf M., and Lotte Van Der Pol. *The Tradition of Female Transvestism in Early Modern Europe*. New York: St. Martin's Press, 1989.

William E. Burns

DANCE. Dance as recreation and entertainment was a significant part of most people's lives in eighteenth-century Europe and America; social dance in particular was a favorite pastime of all classes. For the upper class, a mark of a refined man and woman was the ability to dance well. Dancing was an important aspect of the education of middle- and upper-class young women. At this time teachers and choreographers were known as dancing masters, and the English and French monarchs employed the best dance masters to choreograph dances for special occasions. Throughout Europe, dance halls were built, and many dance manuals and dance instruction books were published. As ballet became admired, theaters began to showcase professional dancers. Many of the period's most renowned composers, such as Beethoven and Mozart, wrote music for dancing.

At the beginning of the eighteenth century, "formal" dances with complex and prescribed steps such as the minuet were the most popular, but gradually "contredanse" or "English country dances" and "cotillion" (that involve two or four couples in formation) emerged as favorites in Europe and in America. Many of these country dances were "line dances" or "longways formations." In other words, men and women stood in lines facing each other. The first couple started the dance by performing a series of steps called figures; they then moved to the back of the line as the next couple completed the figures. The dance ended when all the dancers had had a turn and the first couple returned to the head of the line. Depending upon the number of dancers, a dance might take from five minutes to over sixty. As a result, country dances afforded the dancers the chance for conversation, and because a dance might take a long time, choosing the right partner was important. Contemporary jokes compare being coupled with a dull, quarrelsome, or unpleasant partner to being married to a bad spouse. Usually accompanied by chaperons, unmarried people loved these dances, it seems, as opportunities for private talk. A lengthy country dance gave them precious time for conversation away from mothers, older sisters, or aunts, moments highlighted in the novels of the time such as those by Jane Austen (1775–1817). These line dances remained popular until the nineteenth century, when "couple dances" such as the polka and especially the waltz became the rage.

The popularity of social dancing spread throughout Europe and America. In the country, the gentry (property owners without titles) and their workers danced at birthday parties and wedding receptions, one of the few instances where different classes mingled at leisure. In England, upper-class political candidates held balls for the voters as key campaigning events. These dances were to show the candidates' lack of pride as they danced with the voters' wives and daughters, and as the politicians' wives danced with voters. In towns and cities, dance halls (known in England and in America as assembly rooms) were built as public places for entertainment open to men and women, although unmarried women were expected to be chaperoned. **Opera** houses used masked balls to supplement their revenue.

Because dancing was so important, dance masters were held in high regard. Most of them were primarily instructors, teaching young women in their studios or in their students' homes. To many masters and their students' parents, dancing was more than a fun-leisure activity; it was a method for "refinement." The dance master taught his student etiquette, the right posture, the appropriate manner of dress for social situations, and a graceful walk. Many books by dance masters were published throughout the century, and one from 1785 exemplifies the common view that dance was an integral part of a young person's **education**; it begins, "It has been universally allowed, that Dancing is one of the most useful accomplishments a well-bred person can be possessed of. No gentleman or lady can be said to be qualified for a court, an assembly, or even any public line of life, without some knowledge of this art: a man or woman, cannot even walk with any degree of the graces ... without having been taught at least the rudiments of Dancing." Along with moral instruction some dance masters also included in their books steps for popular dances, "choreography" then possible to record after they developed a new system of notation. These books are extremely valuable now as the only records of eighteenth-century social dances. Throughout Europe and America, dance was important—as entertainment, as recreation and exercise, as social ceremony, and as instruction. *See also* Courtship; Marriage; Theater.

Further Reading: Franks, A. H. *Social Dance: A Short History*. London: Routledge & Kegan Paul, 1963; Sadie, Stanley, ed. *The New Grove Dictionary of Music and Musicians*. 2nd ed. Oxford: Oxford University Press, 2001.

Timothy J. Viator

DEATH. Western Europeans in the seventeenth and eighteenth centuries were intimately acquainted with death. Women frequently died in **childbirth**; babies often died before their first birthday. In an era when medical knowledge was scanty and incomplete, people could expect to die from even minor illnesses, while unhealthy conditions in European cities and periodic epidemics took their toll, as well. In the summer of 1665, for example, the Great Plague struck London, and 15 percent of the population there perished.

For those Europeans who crossed the Atlantic to live in the New World, there were additional fears of death through disease, starvation, and attacks by **Native Americans** or soldiers of foreign powers when European wars carried over to the colonies. Some geographical areas or populations were more susceptible to disease, or encountered particularly unhealthy conditions. For instance, settlers in the Chesapeake colonies of Virginia and Maryland in the seventeenth century faced high mortality rates. Those new to the area almost always became ill, probably with malaria. Women who survived the "seasoning" period were often weakened by recurring bouts of malaria, making them more vulnerable to other diseases and less able to withstand childbirth. Many more men than women came to the Chesapeake, but both the men and the women who came were mainly young—in their late teens or early twenties—and single, and most arrived as **indentured servants**. Most did not live past their early forties. Since they came as servants, they could not marry until their terms of indenture had been completed.

The high mortality rates, early age of death, late **marriage** age, and sexual imbalance led to unique demographic conditions that affected family formation in these colonies. Because the young people arriving as servants had no families on this side of the Atlantic, they did not have parents to approve or disapprove of their marital choices— or to place restrictions on their behavior. Although servant women who bore illegitimate children faced fines, whippings, and increased time added to their indentures, free women, whether single or widowed, could be fairly certain that they would not face such risks, since the lack of women in the colony meant they would not be single for long. However, the high mortality rates also meant that few mothers or fathers survived to see their babies grow to adulthood. Widows and widowers quickly remarried, so that many families were composed of stepparents, stepchildren, and half brothers and sisters.

Conditions in the New England colonies were not as dire. Mortality rates were lower than in the Chesapeake and European cities: people lived longer, and fewer women died in childbirth. In addition, **Puritans** generally arrived in family groups, and single men or women who did not have families usually lived in a household with a family and were subject to the patriarch's discipline. However, Puritans connected illness and dying much more directly with sin and temptation. Ministers urged sick people to fast and to confess their sins, but their prayers and confessions had to be sincere.

Because death could come suddenly and without warning, Puritan ministers and writers warned men and women to live pious lives and not wait until it was too late to change their behavior. Those with serious illnesses and women in childbirth frequently used the experience to meditate, repent, and vow to improve. Dying men, women, and children were attended by family and neighbors, who gathered to see if the afflicted person behaved appropriately. They looked, too, for wonders and amazing sights. Puritans believed that the Devil sent temptations to the dying, and that God might send miracles.

For Africans brought over to "the New World" as slaves, death came during the "Middle Passage" across the Atlantic, where it is estimated that 10–20 percent of the Africans packed into each ship died. Death also came through suicide for those trying to escape bondage, and from the deplorable working conditions they endured as slaves, as well as from disease. Native Americans died in epidemics for which they had no immunity. It is believed that 90 percent of the Aztec population died from direct or indirect exposure to diseases brought by the Spanish explorers and soldiers.

The five nations of the Iroquois were struck by successive waves of epidemics in the seventeenth century, as Europeans from England, France, and the Netherlands settled in their territory and had families. Epidemics of smallpox, influenza, and other diseases killed at least half of the population by the 1640s, with higher death rates occurring within some tribes. Iroquois burial customs changed during this period, most likely due to the large number of deaths occurring from epidemics. Whereas prior to the sixteenth century, it was unusual to find artifacts in Iroquois graves, the practice became widespread by the seventeenth century. During the mid-seventeenth century when the epidemics were most lethal, the graves of young children were lavishly stocked with presents, indicating the Iroquois belief in the need to aid the most vulnerable victims in their journey to the afterworld.

Although death, especially epidemics, changed and affected all societies, death itself was frequently associated with sex in the Western world. In London in 1739 according to one hospital's records, one woman died in childbed for every sixty births; but then this rate was much higher for any given woman, since she might face these odds six or seven times in her life, having several children, so that sex would, if resulting in **pregnancy**, result in a one-in-ten chance of death.

Syphilis is thought to have come from the Americas with Christopher Columbus in 1493, and Italy was rampant with it two years later; only a decade later there were reports of it in **India** and China. From the first it was known to be a disease transmitted by sexual union and was seen by Christians and Western minds in general, as part of the death in the **body**, the nothingness lying beneath a life without **chastity** or God.

In French, an **orgasm** was known as "la petite mort," or the small death, because it wiped out most of the ingredients of a normal consciousness and threw the person back into a vacant, empty condition. The "greater death" is foreshadowed in this "lesser death." On the other hand the Chinese manuals of this time see intercourse as strengthening a man's vital essence and prolonging his life and do not associate sex with death.

Many cultures and religions were concerned with how the body would fare in the afterworld. Hindu Indians ideally placed the dead body in the river Ganges, which, as the great provider, would also resurrect the body in its next life. In contrast, Muslims placed the body speedily into the ground, where it would be reborn into another world, to face a life of continual sexual happiness. Many religions, such as this one, considered that the physical completeness of the body was important to this process of rebirth, so that, if a part were missing at death and burial, it would not be part of the body on its rebirth. Muslim **eunuchs** therefore, were buried with their extracted penis so as to be reborn in Paradise with it refitted. *See also* Atlantic Slave Trade; Orphans; Religion; Slavery; Taj Mahal; Venereal Diseases.

Further Reading: Carr, Lois Green, and Lorena S. Walsh. "The Planter's Wife: The Experience of White Women in Seventeenth-Century Maryland." In *A Heritage of Her Own*, edited by Nancy F. Cott and Elizabeth H. Pleck, 25–57. New York: Simon & Schuster, 1979; Hall, David D. *Worlds of Wonder, Days of Judgment: Popular Religious Belief in Early New England*. Cambridge, MA: Harvard University Press, 1990; Richter, Daniel K. *The Ordeal of the Longhouse: The Peoples of the Iroquois League in the Era of European Colonization*. Chapel Hill: University of North Carolina Press, 1992; Tannahill, Reay. *Sex in History*. London: Hamish Hamilton, 1980.

Merril D. Smith and Jason Powell

D'EON DE BEAUMONT, CHARLES-GENEVIÈVE-LOUIS-AUGUSTE-ANDRÉ-THIMOTHÉE. *See* Chevalier d'Eon

DIDEROT, DENIS (1713–1784). Denis Diderot, a leading thinker and writer of Enlightenment France and the editor of the *Encyclopdie*, vigorously attacked what he viewed as the sexual hypocrisy and repression of European Christian society. However, Diderot was not a consistent or systematic thinker, and his thought on sexuality is no exception.

Diderot's ethics drew from materialist philosophy, science, and psychology. Human desire was the ultimate arbiter of good and evil, or ugliness and beauty, and these designations had no reality transcending humanity. Humans were material beings, with no "cosmic destiny" or "free will," and as material beings they needed to follow their natural biological and social instincts. **Religion**, which restrained humans' sexual nature, was at best suspect, at worst destructive to natural human happiness. **Chastity** and **celibacy**, rather than being the virtues that Catholicism claimed they were, were positively evil, depriving society of citizens and corrupting morals by contributing to **adultery**.

Diderot married Anne Toinette Champion in 1743. The **marriage**, the result of a youthful passion, was clandestine, and Diderot concealed it from his family for years. It was not a success and colored Diderot's generally negative view of the institution. Marriages, he claimed, were inspired by a momentary physical passion, yet often yoked two incompatible people together for life. He praised marriage as a source for children and as preferable to celibacy, but was highly skeptical about the possibility of marriages based on companionship and mutual affection. He favored **divorce**, forbidden in Catholic France, and easy remarriage. Diderot endorsed the "double standard," by which female adultery was punished more harshly than male adultery. He believed that marriage, and society generally, was unfair to women, but that women's subordination to men was a natural phenomenon based on women's comparative physical weakness and necessary roles as mothers. His longest and most fulfilling sexual relationship was that with his mistress, Sophie Volland, which began in the mid-1750s and lasted until her death only a few months before his.

Much of Diderot's fiction is erotic. His first published novel, *The Indiscreet Jewels* (1748), is a fantasy about an African king (modeled on Louis XV with a mistress modeled on Louis's mistress Madame Du Pompadour) who acquires a jewel that can make women's vaginas, or "jewels," speak. It was suppressed as **pornography**. *The Nun*, which was too controversial to be published until after the French Revolution, contains one of the most explicit treatments of lesbianism scenes in eighteenth-century **literature**, in the desire for the nun of the title exhibited by the prioress of one of her convents. It too was suppressed as pornographic. Diderot's *Supplement to the Voyage of Bougainville* (written in 1772, but not published until after Diderot's death, in 1796) paints a familiar eighteenth-century picture of Tahiti as a utopia of sexual freedom, contrasting the Tahitians's frank acceptance of sex with the repression and hypocrisy of European visitors who bring both sexual shame and **venereal disease**. He even went so far as to endorse intergenerational incest, particularly if a father begets children on a daughter too ugly to attract men. In *Rameau's Nephew*, Diderot suggests that a savage given the passions of a man of thirty and lacking social mores would kill his father and have sex with his mother. Sigmund Freud later credited him with anticipating the idea of the "Oedipus complex." So radical was Diderot's *Supplement* that during his life it circulated only in manuscript to his closest friends.

Diderot's sexual utopianism is bound up with the natalism, which he shared with many other Enlightenment thinkers. (He claimed to find pregnant women particularly attractive.) For Diderot and his fictional Tahitians, sex is largely valuable because it leads to the conception and birth of children. The Tahitans frown on sex with women who cannot conceive, and sterile or menstruating women wear particular clothing to indicate their sexual unavailability. Sterile women who have sex are punished. However, in other contexts, Diderot was more favorable to nonprocreative sexuality. The lesbian prioress of *The Nun* received some authorial sympathy, but lesbianism is presented as a consequence of the highly "unnatural," and undesirably monogendered environment of the convent. He was also less opposed to **masturbation** than were many Enlightenment thinkers. In *D'Alembert's Dream*, Diderot suggested that even **bestiality** might be harmless. *See also* Enlightenment Thought on Sexuality; Literature; Philosophy.

Further Reading: Diderot, Denis. *Diderot's Letters to Sophie Volland: A Selection*. Translated from the French by Peter France. London: Oxford University Press, 1972; Goodde, Angelica. *Diderot and the Body*. Oxford: Legenda, 2001.

William E. Burns

DIVORCE. Divorces were almost nonexistent in western Europe prior to the seventeenth and eighteenth centuries. Following the Reformation, some Protestant reformers promoted divorce as a means of cleansing the church of abuses and of helping to promote order. **John Milton**, for example, wrote in defense of divorce, calling it a "law of moral equity." However, divorces remained rare even in most Protestant states.

France, which remained a Roman Catholic country, did not permit divorce until 1792. Then, as part of revolutionary reforms and anti-Catholicism, it passed a liberal divorce law that made divorce available and affordable to nearly everyone. Napoleon placed restrictions on the law, and it was abolished in 1816, with the return of the monarchy and Roman Catholicism.

In England, divorces were expensive, complicated affairs that could be granted only through the ecclesiastical courts or by act of Parliament. Only if a **marriage** was declared invalid to begin with due to sexual incapacity, **bigamy**, or consanguinity, could a petitioner receive a total divorce from the bonds of matrimony (*divotium a vincula matrimonii*). For **adultery**, desertion, or excessive cruelty, a partial divorce from bed and board (*divortium a mensa et thoro*) might be granted. In addition, although civil courts deemed the testimony of one witness sufficient, ecclesiastical courts demanded testimony from two witnesses. Late in the seventeenth century, Parliament began to grant divorces permitting remarriage—but only to men whose wives had committed adultery. Women could not receive a complete divorce from their adulterous husbands. Parliament did not grant divorces to women until 1801, and even then it was uncommon. However, throughout the seventeenth and eighteenth centuries men and women self-divorced, or simply deserted their spouses.

In several of the English colonies, however, divorce **laws** were more flexible, and divorces, while still rare, were more common than they were in England. In New England, under Puritan law, marriage was a civil contract, not a religious sacrament, and so the courts granted divorces for adultery, bigamy, and desertion. New Haven also granted divorces for sexual incapacity in the husband. To **Puritans**, marriage and the family were of prime importance. By permitting divorce, the New England colonies kept households stable, and by extension, the community and commonwealth were also stabilized. If a husband or wife deserted his or her spouse, could not have sexual relations, or was engaging in adulterous affairs, then the household suffered. However, if a deserted wife, for example, was having illicit sexual encounters, it was important that the state permit her to remarry (usually after a period of seven years), so that she would no longer be involved in sinful behavior.

In Pennsylvania, divorce was also encoded among the earliest laws in the colony. Here, too, marriage was considered a civil contract, although marriage before a clergyman was permitted. Divorces could be obtained by petitioning the governor and assembly, but few people actually attempted to do so, and only a handful of divorces were granted. In 1785, as part of the new state's republican reforms, a divorce act was passed that permitted the state's Supreme Court to grant divorces. Divorces could be sought for adultery, bigamy, desertion, and sexual impotence of the husband. Wives could also receive a divorce from bed and board with alimony if they could prove they had experienced "cruel and barbarous" treatment by their husbands. Following the passage of this act, more women than men applied for—and received—divorces in Pennsylvania.

In contrast to New England and Pennsylvania, some states did not allow divorce until much later. Virginia did not grant divorces from bed and board until 1827 or complete divorces until 1848. South Carolina did grant any divorces at all until after the Civil War.

Among **Native Americans**, marriage and divorce customs varied. In some tribes, marriage was a loose agreement, less permanent than European/American arrangements, causing European and colonial observers to consider Native Americans promiscuous. Among the Iroquois, couples could divorce as they wished. Marriages were often of brief duration. Because households were matrilineal, they did not focus around the couple, and the mother's brothers often took over the roles of fathers. *See also* Courtship; Widows and Widowhood.

Further Reading: Norton, Mary Beth. *Founding Mothers & Fathers: Gendered Power and the Forming of American Society.* New York: Vintage Books, 1997; Richter, Daniel K. *The Ordeal of the Longhouse: The Peoples of the Iroquois League in the Era of European Colonization.* Chapel Hill: University of North Carolina Press, 1992; Smith, Merril D. *Breaking the Bonds: Marital Discord in Pennsylvania, 1730–1830.* New York: New York University Press, 1991.

Merril D. Smith

DOMESTIC VIOLENCE. In the seventeenth and eighteenth centuries, family violence was often considered an accepted element of the patriarchal system. As a group, women lacked the power to call for public scrutiny of the issue. Slaves, both male and female, had even less power. While violence against male slaves was generally restricted to physical beatings, slave women were subject to rapes as well as beatings.

Because it was a male's responsibility to maintain order, it was frequently assumed that men had an inherent right to "moderately" punish their wives, children, slaves, and servants for whom they were legally responsible. Abusive behavior, therefore, was often seen within the context of correcting recalcitrant behavior rather than as physical attacks. By the end of the nineteenth century, social agencies had been established to deal with the growing problem of family violence, and **slavery** had been abolished as an institution in the Western world. Before this time, abused women received some assistance from the courts, but more often they turned to family, neighbors, servants, and the church for less formal assistance. Children and slaves had almost no protection against violence.

According to the English legal concept of *coverture*, which applied in the American colonies as well as in the mother country, husbands "owned" their wives' bodies, as well as their property and possessions. Sex without a wife's **consent** was not considered **rape**, since she belonged to her husband, and similarly, most people considered it acceptable for a husband to give his wife a moderate beating. Even though single women had more legal rights than married women, fathers could force their daughters to marry against their will or prevent them from marrying men who were considered unsuitable. **Incest** was not easily proved and was rarely punished.

Unwritten law required that men punish their wives only from the desire to correct rather than from a love of violence. Nevertheless, domestic violence was often tolerated because under the patriarchal system of *coverture*, married women had no separate existence from their husbands. If a woman ran away from an abusive husband, she was not allowed to take her children and often had no means of financial support. Divorces were rare and difficult to obtain. In the American colonies, the courts sometimes granted the so-called "bed and board" divorces so that abused wives could live apart from their husbands. As **Enlightenment thought** with its emphasis on individuality progressed, women began to be perceived in a more positive light. By the mid-nineteenth century, wives had begun obtaining divorces for mental as well as for physical cruelty.

Before the Enlightenment, the practice of considering women as property led to passage of laws in which rape and **abduction** of young girls were considered theft of a man's property rather than violation of a woman's body and rights. Women were sometimes seen as equally culpable in **sex crimes**. In Holland, for instance, young girls past puberty were considered participants rather than victims of sex crimes, and girls could be charged as accessories to their own rapes. It was not until the latter half of the seventeenth century that the focus in sex cases shifted toward the individual rights of women and away from property rights of their husbands and fathers.

Popular opinion often dictated that abused women were responsible for causing their husbands to resort to violence. As a result, abused women often remained silent about domestic violence because of the perceived shame involved and/or because they feared further violence. Nevertheless, neighbors were sometimes an abused wife's strongest allies because they reported domestic discord to local magistrates since it interfered with their own desires to live in peaceful communities.

If someone other than her husband attacked a woman, she and her husband could join in bringing charges against the other individual(s). The husband could ask for damages if the injuries were severe enough to interfere with a wife carrying out her wifely duties. A wife could not, however, recover damages if her husband were unable to perform his husbandly duties.

During the early seventeenth century, **Puritans** and Calvinists began to grapple with the morality of accepting domestic violence as a male prerogative. In England, William Gouge (1575–1653), known as the "father of the London Divines," was instrumental in banning wife beating as a form of justifiable punishment rather than as a crime.

In 1609, in response to an antifemale talk by Latin dramatist William Gager at Oxford University, William Heale (c. 1581–1627), a chaplain at Exeter College, published a well-researched tract, "An Apologie for Women," in which he contended that no legal basis for wife beating existed. He did not go so far as to denounce **patriarchy**. In 1682, Heale's tract was reprinted, and the Puritans condemned wife beating in even stronger language. By the latter half of the seventeenth century, church courts had begun prosecuting abusive husbands. In more traditional cultures, however, the church often provided little more than emotional support for battered women, continuing to uphold a man's right to beat his children and his servants.

The Puritan influence in the American colonies resulted in some condemnation of wife beating in New England, but most southern colonies remained locked in the patriarchal mode that upheld a man's right to punish members of his household. Lyle Koehler notes that between 1630 and 1699, 128 men and fifty-seven women were tried for spousal abuse in Massachusetts, Connecticut, New Hampshire, Plymouth, Maine, and New Haven.

In 1641, Massachusetts Bay followed the English example and adopted the Body of Liberties that prohibited husbands from violent forms of correction but retained the right for husbands to hit their wives in self-defense. In 1650, a stronger law banned physical violence within marriage, establishing fines of up to ten pounds or whippings as punishment. In 1671, Plymouth passed a similar law, but other colonies failed to follow suit. Domestic violence continued to be dealt with on a case-by-case basis throughout most colonies.

Even when **laws** that were designed to end domestic violence existed, punishment was light, consisting of fines, admonishments, or court orders that prevented abusers from being in close physical contact with their victims. In many cases, the abusers returned to their households and continued the abusive behavior. Men were rarely sentenced to prison, partially because courts recognized that imprisoned men were unable to support their families.

In the seventeenth and eighteenth centuries, the court of public opinion was often more effective than law courts in dealing with domestic violence. It was believed that violence demonstrated a man's inability to control his family in acceptable ways. When domestic discord became intrusive, neighbors often interfered in order to maintain the public peace rather than through efforts to protect women. Even when battered women received some protection from the courts and society, violence against children continued to be accepted until the nineteenth century. *See also* Child Rape; Divorce; Indentured Servants; Marriage.

Further Reading: Baer, Judith. *Our Lives before the Law: Constructing a Feminist Jurisprudence*. Princeton, NJ: Princeton University Press, 1999; Clark, Anna. *Women's Silence, Men's Voices, 1770–1945*. London: Pandora Press, 1987; Fletcher, Anthony. *Gender, Sex, and Subordination in England, 1500–1800*. New Haven, CT: Yale University Press, 1995; Koehler, Lyle. *A Search for Power: The "Weaker Sex" in Seventeenth-Century New England*. Urbana: University of Illinois Press, 1980; Norton, Mary Beth. *Founding Mothers and Fathers: Gendered Power and the Framing of the American Society*. New York: Vintage Books, 1997; Yalom, Marilyn. *A History of the Wife*. New York: HarperCollins, 2001.

Elizabeth R. Purdy

DON JUAN. See Tenorio, Don Juan

DUELING. Ritual dueling between men was a well-known practice in colonial America. The dispute in question could be based on class, nationality, or ethnicity, but most often what drove men to bloodshed was a challenge of sexual honor.

Dueling and its strict and revered rules of engagement arrived in North America with the first colonial settlers. The first recorded duel in North America was fought between two servants, and the object of the quarrel was a young woman whom both the men fancied. On June 18, 1621, Edward Leister and Edward Doty dueled with rapiers; both survived their wounds and were immediately arrested and prosecuted, though ultimately pardoned, lending credence to the tradition that the colonists had brought from England.

Like the Lester/Doty duel, most clashes were fought over a perceived impingement of honor or civility, fueled by matters of jealousy, love, sex, or ridicule. Something as innocent as a casual remark regarding a nearby lady's hat could lead to an exchange about the woman's looks, then her reputation, and contested by the men first with words, then with swords or pistols.

Dueling quickly became an institution in America. Castle Island, in Boston Harbor, was once a fashionable dueling ground for "hot-headed sons of Old England." Although landed gentry assumed the ritual was theirs alone, armed contests in America were not limited to aristocrats—male servants and even slaves fought as well. A woman's honor was defended staunchly by fighting men, even though women themselves would not take part.

Noncompliance with the strict regulations of dueling was considered a worse crime than participating in the contest itself. A 1711 duel between two men was fought over the attentions of two women who apparently played the men against one another, until one challenged the other—a challenge to which the other responded by fleeing the village. The scorn cast against the action of cowardice was greater than against those who murdered their opponent, but numerous instances of rejected or rebuffed challenges existed.

Dueling remained a common, if not completely accepted occurrence throughout much of the eighteenth century. Duels were frequently mentioned in the newspapers of the time. One such duel was fought in 1765 between rivals Alexander Simpson and Thomas Whitehurst, who after service in the British Navy, became enamored with the daughter of a prominent North Carolina landowner. Animated discussion of the lady's merits soon turned to violence, and the two met at the edge of the town of Brunswick. Simpson's first shot only injured Whitehurst, and in his fury, Simpson summarily clubbed his adversary to death. Brought before a jury in October 1765, Simpson was convicted of manslaughter, not murder, as Simpson's counsel argued convincingly that the passion of the situation had driven him to an unreasoning fit of anger—in sharp contrast to the duel itself, held under rigorous, almost passionless rules of conduct.

Public opinion began to turn against dueling at the close of the eighteenth century. George Washington forbade his officers from dueling; **Benjamin Franklin** vehemently denounced the practice, and the death of Alexander Hamilton at the hands of Aaron Burr in an 1804 duel caused an outcry. Dueling was not abolished, but it was clear that the old barbarous custom would not be welcome in the more enlightened republic. A Congressional Act passed in 1806 forbade dueling in the military, and many states, New York and New Jersey among the first, passed legislation outlawing duels altogether. In the southern United States the tradition held firmer. One of the most popular publications of the mid-nineteenth century was a pamphlet outlining the "Code Duello," published in 1838 in South Carolina. *See also* Adultery; Gender Roles; Laws; Murder.

Further Reading: Cochran, Hamilton. *Noted American Duels and Hostile Encounters.* Philadelphia: Chilton, 1963; Peltonen, Markku. *The Duel in Early Modern England: Civility, Politeness and Honour.* Cambridge: Cambridge University Press, 2003.

Doug Krehbiel

ECONOMICS AND GENDER. *See* Household Consumerism

EDUCATION. Before the seventeenth century, the education of lower-class males was rudimentary, and education for females of all classes was restricted. By the seventeenth century, middle- and upper-class European families had begun to send their daughters as well as their sons to boarding schools. Other children were educated at home or in small public or private schools. The quality of education varied greatly among these forms of education. Public education, therefore, came to be seen as a means of leveling out some of the class and gender differences evident in the hit-or-miss system.

The delayed recognition that education was essential to society as well as to individuals led to a movement in England in which **orphans** and children of poor and indigent parents were placed under the care of the so-called "masters" who taught them to read and write and the rudiments of a trade. In addition to language skills, basic education consisted of building character, instilling morals, and encouraging self-discipline.

As the Industrial Revolution gained momentum in England, a group of literate women began to propose that all young girls be educated. Educators who fueled this debate over education for women included Englishwomen Hannah Wooley and Bathsua Makin and Dutch educator Anna Maria Van Schurman.

Anna Maria Van Schurman developed a curriculum for educating women in the Netherlands that included grammar, logic, rhetoric, physics, metaphysics, history, languages, mathematics, poetry, and **art**. Van Schurman influenced Bathsua Makin, who as a tutor of Princess Elizabeth, was in a unique position to wield influence upon the developing field of women's education. In 1673, Makin's *An Essay to Revive the Ancient Education of Gentlewomen* presented comprehensive arguments for educating women. The book also served as an advertisement for Makin's recently established school for girls.

Like Bathsua Makin, Hannah Wooley, who had established her own school at the age of fifteen after being orphaned, believed that men conspired together to keep females ignorant. Well known in the field of home economics, Wooley interspersed her domestic instructions with progressive ideas on women's education.

Feminists of the period were also at the forefront of the debate on women's education. Writers such as Mary Astell and ex-patriot **Mary Wollstonecraft**, who had migrated to France, broadened the debate to examine education from a theoretical, as well as from a practical perspective. As women began to speak for themselves in the works of women writers, it became clear that intelligence and rationality were not restricted to males.

Mary Astell, who had been greatly influenced by the French *salonnieres*, published *A Serious Proposal to the Ladies* (1694) in which she proposed the establishment of a college for women to be supported by a wealthy group of her friends. Astell also offered practical suggestions for educating women that were designed to narrow the existing gap between educated males and barely literate women. For Astell, the focus of educating women was always on preparing them for future employment. The Chelsea Charity School, a pet project of Astell's, concentrated on educating the daughters of English veterans. Many of her students were orphans who found it necessary to support themselves.

Mary Wollstonecraft, the author of *A Vindication of the Rights of Woman*, was the most influential feminist of her day. Like Astell, Wollstonecraft believed that it was as important for girls to learn to support themselves as it was for boys. She proposed that coeducational public day schools be made available to all children. Coeducation was essential, in her view, because each sex learned things from the other that better prepared both sexes for their lives as adults.

All proponents of education for females were not women. Philosopher John Locke and writers **Jonathan Swift**, Daniel Defoe, and William Law also called for increased attention to the education of women. Defoe was particularly interested in the need for educating women and developed a plan for an academy for women. Defoe, like Wollstonecraft, believed that both sexes were socialized into believing that women were inferior.

The prevalent idea that education for girls benefited males by producing better wives and mothers was more palatable to the general public than the idea that men and women were equally entitled to basic rights and that women were not biologically and mentally inferior.

In colonial America, literacy rates were low, but they increased in the years immediately before the American Revolution. The increase in literacy was due in part not only to an interest in the volatile political situation but also to the conviction that democracy required an educated public.

Before the American Revolution, girls in the American colonies were educated either at home or in what came to be known as "dame schools." Or, in the case of the upper class, daughters were sometimes sent abroad to be educated or were enrolled in English-style boarding schools. In the South, it was not uncommon for a group of plantation owners to band together to support a school in which children of both sexes were taught the basics. Classes generally consisted of ten to twenty-five students of all ages learning together in a single room.

Basic education for girls generally went no further than reading, writing, and perhaps French. In addition to these subjects, girls were taught needlework, singing, dancing, and deportment. The goal of women's education, of course, was to teach girls how to become wives and mothers and how to behave in proper society.

At the same time that girls' education was restricted to basics and domestic arts, young boys were trained to enter the work world. In addition to the basic subjects, they were taught mathematics and Latin, and later on science and other languages were added to their curriculum.

As the need for literacy spread, girls were allowed to attend summer sessions of public schools, along with younger children, while older boys were put to work in the fields. Decision makers slowly realized that it would be impossible for young girls who received no education to grow into women who could educate their sons to become good citizens in the new democracy. This realization led to greater educational opportunities for girls of all classes. The opportunity for higher education, however, continued to be generally restricted to middle- and upper-class males. Even though the numbers of female educators grew, salaries of females lagged behind those of their male counterparts.

As the eighteenth century drew to a close, the establishment of female seminaries opened new avenues of learning to young girls who, for the first time, were taught **literature** and classical languages. The realization that women possessed intelligence and imagination and that women were deserving of political rights paved the way for the organized women's movement of the nineteenth century, which considered education for women a high priority.

In the early modern period, education beyond the basic level was generally considered a prerogative of middle- and upper class-males in both Europe and America. During the last decades of the early modern period, as the Industrial Revolution began to expand throughout Europe, the demand for literate workers increased. The emphasis on individuality, rationality, and Lockean rights also articulated the need for basic education for females as well as for males. *See also* Childhood and Adolescence; Gender Roles; Marriage; Philosophy; Women, Changing Images of.

Further Reading: Boulding, Elise. *The Underside of History: A View of Women through Time.* Vol. 2. New York: Sage, 1992; Defoe, Daniel. "An Essay upon Projects." http://etext.library.adelaide.edu.au/d/defoe/daniel/d31es/part16.html, 1697; Evans, Sara M. *Born for Liberty: A History of Women in America.* New York: Free Press, 1989; Spruill, Julia. *Women's Life and Work: In the Southern Colonies.* New York: Norton, 1938; Wollstonecraft, Mary. *A Vindication of the Rights of Woman.* New York: Norton, 1988.

Elizabeth R. Purdy

EJACULATION. Ejaculation, the expulsion of seminal fluid during the male orgasm, was, in **William Shakespeare**'s phrase, "the expense of spirit in a waste of shame." Dr. Edward Ville, a seventeenth-century surgeon and researcher at the Elizabethan Academy of Science in London, courtier, and literati was plagued by Shakespeare's artistic expression in sonnet (129) about ejaculation. Ville saw Shakespeare's expression as playing much into the hand of the church by confirming the common views that frequent ejaculation leads to madness. To discredit such common views, Ville embarked on his first study of the ejaculation of various male species and was the first renaissance scholar to establish a link between the frequency and speed of ejaculation and the size of the species' penis.

His research took him to places outside Europe. He traveled into Africa, the Middle East, and **India**. In his travels he observed the sexual behavior and sexual anatomy of various species of animals in their natural habitats. He discovered that the erection of a seventy-kilogram man is larger than that of a 200-kilogram gorilla, and that the volume and amount of the sperm produced by men are much more than that of the gorilla. Ville linked penis size and volume of ejaculate to frequency of copulation. The reason why gorillas carry such a small penis, Ville observed, "is that they rarely have sex." Humans, he affirmed, have sex often and, equally important, have descended from humans who had sex even more often. He hailed men who ejaculate fast and related them to their prehistoric ancestors. He speculated that in primitive times when a woman probably mated with many men, often in rapid sequence, the fastest ejaculator with the largest penis would win the competition to fertilize the woman and ensure the survival of his seeds.

Opposing the prevailing medical view, endorsed by traditional Christianity, that frequent ejaculation weakens the body and leads to loss of sight, among other physical problems, Ville coupled ejaculation with life, virility, **masculinity**, and power. While his views on ejaculation and sexuality were held immoral by the orthodoxy and cost him his place at the Academy, they were subtly echoed in the works of several seventeenth- and eighteenth-century poets. John Dryden in "The Flee" and **Andrew Marvell** in "To His Coy Mistress" present men in pursuit of their sexual pleasures trying to persuade their unwilling women to yield to their sexual desires. Samuel Johnson, the renowned eighteenth-century critic, attributed the apparent promiscuity of conservative poets such as John Donne and John Dryden to the views of Dr. Edward Ville that were in vogue in the court and among the laity in England. Jean Baudrillard wittingly remarks in *Seduction* that Ville's views on ejaculation changed the "eighteenth century man's view of his tool of production the way postmodern erection industry enabled the postmodern man to hold his manhood in his hand," taking charge of his erections whenever he desires and for the length he desires (65). Dr. Ville's views liberated men from their sense of shame and disgust embodied in the obtuse Shakespearian sonnet and motivated them to grow more promiscuous by promising them a larger tool in proportion to the frequency of their ejaculations. *See also* Medicine and Science; Midwives and Physicians; Rape; Religion.

Further Reading: Baudrillard, Jean. *Seduction*. New York: St. Martin's Press, 1990; Dandalero, Roberto. *The Phallus: The Male's Creative Power*. Milan: Zibuwawa Publishing, 1971; Goodwill, Hansen. *Sexuality of Men and Mice*. Manchester: Carole Publishing, 1982; Johnson, Samuel. *Selected Writings*. Edited by Patrick Cruttwell. London: Penguin, 1987; Maclean, Riley. *Eighteenth-Century Sexuality*. Edinburgh: Edinburgh University Press, 1963.

Wisam Mansour

ELLIOTT, GRACE DALRYMPLE (1754–1823). Born in Edinburgh, Scotland, in 1754, Grace Elliott was one of the most celebrated courtesans of the late eighteenth century, among a number of such women who made a very good living as the paid companions of wealthy and/or titled men. Successful English courtesans—like their European counterparts, especially the French—were not always great beauties, but they had charm, wit, and social savvy. The more intelligent among them were also business women, for courtesans were professionals, who had the foresight to plan for their future.

They were businesswomen who secured annuities (a kind of life-long alimony payable quarterly) that enabled them to live comfortable lives when their halcyon days were over. Grace, who was painted at least twice by the great portrait painter Thomas Gainsborough, was a beauty by the standards of the Georgian era in all but her height. She was dubbed "Dally the Tall," and may have been six feet in stature. But she fit the age's other criteria for beauty: clear, white skin, large eyes, long neck, small hands and feet, and full bosom. She had an erect and graceful carriage that showed to perfection in the late panniered gowns of the late eighteenth century and, later, in the Empire fashion of the early nineteenth century.

Grace Elliott's notoriety lies in the **divorce** action taken against her by her husband Dr. John (later Sir John) Elliott, owing to her public **adultery** with Arthur Annesley, Viscount Valentia. Her claim to fame lies in having had a child, Georgiana, by the Prince of Wales (later King George IV), although another claimant was her longtime lover, the Marquess of Cholmondeley. She also survived the French Reign of Terror. She wrote about the latter experience in her posthumous memoir, *Journal of My Life during the French*

Revolution (1859). She died in Ville d'Avray, France, in 1823. *See also* Clothing and Fashion; Concubines; Geisha; Prostitutes and Prostitution; Royal Mistresses; Taj Mahal.
Further Reading: Manning, Jo. *My Lady Scandalous*. New York: Simon & Schuster, 2005.

Jo Manning

ENGLISH REVOLUTION. *See* Revolution and Gender

ENLIGHTENMENT THOUGHT ON SEXUALITY. The term "Enlightenment" is common in discussing the progressive and (mostly) secularly minded intellectuals, or "philosophes," of eighteenth-century Europe and North America including **Benjamin Franklin**, Voltaire, **Denis Diderot**, and **Jean-Jacques Rousseau**. However, enlightened individuals and movements varied in their opinions of many things, including sex, and the Enlightenment should not be treated as a set of dogmas. Certain common themes are clear. Enlightenment thought challenged the prevailing sexual order in its secularity and emphasis on the positive aspects of sex. It was conservative in its support for male domination and its emphasis on procreation, but even in these areas it found new ways to express and uphold old ideas.

Enlightenment thinkers held many religious positions, ranging from Christianity to atheism, but all mistrusted clerical authority. This mistrust extended to clerical control over sexuality, very much a live issue in an eighteenth-century Europe where church courts exerted authority over many sexual matters, such as **marriage** and illicit sex. The philosophers of the Enlightenment rejected the traditional Christian suspicion of sex, particularly the Catholic idea that **celibacy** was a higher, more spiritual state than being sexually active. However, most did not argue that the proper sexual order was one of unfettered license. Sexual life should be regulated, not by the precepts of the Bible or the decrees of the church, but by the laws of nature. Sexual desire was a natural phenomenon, and sex, particularly procreative sex, was an innately praiseworthy activity. Refraining from sex was "unnatural," not spiritual. **Medicine and science** were often invoked in place of **religion** as the proper guides in sexual matters. To challenge bad ideas about sex, sexual matters had to be openly discussed. The writings of many Enlightenment philosophers were sometimes censored for that reason. Pornographic books circulated along the same distribution networks as the works of the Enlightenment and were also referred to as "philosophic books."

Although some Enlightenment thinkers adopted a broadly tolerant attitude toward different sexual behaviors, belief in natural law often entailed rejecting not only celibacy but also sexual behaviors considered "unnatural," because they were unprocreative. The violent hostility to **masturbation**, which emerged in eighteenth-century Europe, was endorsed by many Enlightenment thinkers, who also employed homophobic attacks on their enemies, particularly the Jesuit order. Celibacy was often blamed for promoting same-sex relations, and neither celibates nor homosexuals produced offspring.

In fact, many Enlightenment thinkers, particularly in France, believed that one of society's main problems was underpopulation. Sexual repression, particularly in the institutionalized form of celibacy, contributed to this situation. Celibates were parasites on society in their refusal to participate in the creation of the next generation. This was one difference between the Enlightenment in Catholic countries, with their legions of celibate priests, nuns, and monks, and the same movement in Protestant countries, where celibacy had much less presence and was less of an issue. Abolition of celibacy and the acceptance of sex as a natural phenomenon would lead to an increase in population, thus strengthening the state. For the same reason, some advocated the abolition of the stigma against unmarried women having children.

Although many championed **education** for elite women, with a few scattered exceptions, the Enlightenment thinkers did not challenge male dominance in society, marriage, and the civil law. They did not root male dominance in divine law, however, but in the "naturally" different functions of the sexes. Woman's natural function was domestic, as a wife and mother, while man's was public. Sexual desire was as natural and praiseworthy for women as it was for men, particularly since sex led to motherhood, but though many male Enlightenment thinkers had affairs with married women and showed some sympathy for women trapped in unhappy marriages, few questioned the double standard—the idea that oaths of marital fidelity are more binding on women. Enlightenment thinkers also emphasized the positive role of sex and the relations of men and women in creating and sustaining human society. Sociability was an important Enlightenment value. This was particularly the case in France, where **salons**, open to males and females, were an important venue for enlightened sociability. (Enlightenment belief in sociability was also another reason for rejecting masturbation—it was not merely unnatural, but antisocial.) *See also* Divorce; Homosexuality; Philosophy.

Further Reading: Darnton, Robert. *The Literary Underground of the Old Regime.* Cambridge, MA: Harvard University Press, 1982; Gay, Peter. *The Party of Humanity: Essays in the French Enlightenment.* New York: Knopf, 1964; Trouille, Mary Seidman. *Sexual Politics in the Enlightenment: Women Writers Read Rousseau.* Albany: State University of New York Press, 1997.

William E. Burns

ERAUSO, CATALINA DE (1585–1650). Catalina de Erauso was a Basque noblewoman who escaped from the convent and spent most of her life dressed as and living as a male lieutenant. The autobiography of Catalina de Erauso is one of the earliest known autobiographies by a woman. In it, Erauso describes her life as a transvestite. She lived a wild existence as a roving soldier, murderer, gambler, thief, and woman chaser. In the end, she emerged as a hero of the Spanish-speaking world.

Erauso began her transvestite life in 1599 when she escaped from the Spanish convent at San Sebastián just before she was to take her final vows to become a nun. For more than twenty years, she continued to disguise herself successfully and was thus able to roam the country and travel to the New World with all the freedoms held exclusively by men of the time.

Erauso was a violent, crafty bandit with a bad temper. Not only did she gamble, cheat, lie, brawl, frequently steal money and property, and spend time in jail, but she also maimed and murdered opponents in duels. In fact, she murdered around a dozen men off the battlefield.

Erauso was also a military hero; a fearless lieutenant who led subordinates into bloody battles. She was reported to be one of the first to leap onto an enemy ship, evidence of her extraordinary bravery. Fifteen years of service fighting for the Spanish empire in Peru and Chile earned her a military pension.

In her autobiography, Erauso consistently referred to herself with masculine pronouns. Only in rare instances did she choose to use feminine pronouns. While she never explicitly declared her sexual preference, she did describe erotic same-sex encounters that included physical caressing and petting.

Hardened and impassioned, she followed her desires, even if they cost her. After remeeting her brother in her male disguise, the two became close friends. He was never aware of her true identity. A few years into the friendship they became enemies due to a conflict over her brother's mistress. She simply would not stop visiting the mistress even when threatened.

Erauso expressed recurrent romantic involvement with a variety of women in the Spanish New World colonies. And not only did she flirt with women, but she was also pursued by women who wanted to marry her. On several different occasions, parents tried to arrange marriages between Erauso and their daughters.

When she finally revealed that she was a woman, and a virgin at that, she was not condemned by Baroque society, but rather was viewed as a celebrity. In 1624, she visited Pope Urban the Eighth in Rome, who gave her permission to continue her life dressed as a man, admonishing her only to live an honest existence and not to harm others. Her fame had spread everywhere; she was a spectacle followed about by crowds that included princes, bishops, and cardinals. Erauso was an anomaly, both male and female, who emerged as an adored hero despite her extreme cultural and gender deviance. The only record of the last few decades of Erauso's life highlights her erotic obsession with another woman. *See also* Cross-Dressing; Gender Roles; Homosexuality.

Further Reading: De Erauso, Catalina. *Lieutenant Nun: Memoir of a Basque Transvestite in the New World*. Translated by Michele Stepto and Gabriel Stepto. Boston: Beacon Press, 1996; Velasco, Sherry. *The Lieutenant Nun: Transgenderism, Lesbian Desire, & Catalina de Erauso*. Austin: University of Texas Press, 2000.

Elizabeth Jenner

EUNUCHS. Castrated males, or eunuchs, played many roles in early modern societies. Eunuchs exercised great political influence through their connections to courts in many polities, particularly in China and Islamic countries. They lost considerable ground in China in the transition from the Ming to the Qing dynasty beginning in 1647. The Ming had made extraordinarily heavy use of eunuch royal servants, as generals, admirals, arms manufacturers, trade supervisors, mining superintendents, engineers, and judges. Self-castration even became a common strategy for desperate men seeking Imperial employment, despite Imperial prohibitions. It was estimated that there were over 80,000 eunuchs in China when the Ming were overthrown. Chinese Confucian scholars and officials, always suspicious of eunuch power, condemned the Ming's heavy reliance on eunuchs, and the new Manchu Qing dynasty relegated eunuchs to the political sidelines as part of its attempt to present itself as a reforming Chinese dynasty. Europe and Japan lacked the institution of the court eunuch entirely. In both Islamic societies and China, eunuchs were often members of peripheral or foreign ethnic groups, and a considerable portion of the early modern Indian Ocean slave trade was devoted to supplying courts with eunuchs. Europe, and particularly Japan, did not have a large foreign immigration in the early modern period, which may explain the minor (in the case of Japan, nonexistent) role of eunuchs in their culture.

In Islamic societies where eunuchs were prominent, the keeping of **harems** was traditionally entrusted to them. The chief harem keeper of the **Ottoman empire** was the Lord of the Black Eunuchs, a powerful official in the Ottoman government. In the Mogul empire of India, harem eunuchs played a smaller role, as more of the administrative

Eunuch of the Ottoman court, from a 17th century Ottoman Turkish manuscript on Turkish Costumes. © The Art Archive/Biblioteca Nazionale Marciana Venice/Dagli Orti.

burden of the harem was borne by women. The idea of the eunuch-guarded harem played a powerful role in the European Orientalist fantasies of the lascivious Orient. However, eunuch officials were not restricted to the harem, but served as military leaders and administrators throughout the Islamic regions, in some periods in Ottoman history even functioning as *de facto* rulers of the Empire.

Although Europe lacked court or household eunuchs, it had another culturally prominent population of castrated males, the *castrati*. *Castrati* were boys, almost always from poor families in southern Italy, brought up to sing, then castrated before their voices could break. **Castration** was illegal, but widely practiced. Catholic churches in Italy had castrato choirs, as women were forbidden to sing in church. The castrato repertoire broadened to include **opera**. The most famous operatic castrato of the eighteenth century was Carlo Broschi (1705–1782), known as Farinelli, an international celebrity honored by royalty. Successful operatic *castrati* toured Europe and attracted romantic interest from women; at least one, Giusto Tenducci (c. 1735–1790) actually married a woman. Although Italian *castrati* were strongly associated with the Catholic Church, they could not become priests. The church maintained its prohibition against ordaining eunuchs, which dated back to late antiquity. Changes in musical style in the late eighteenth century led to the rise of the tenor lead and the waning of the *castrati* as international stars, but they persisted in Italy into the early twentieth century.

Some societies accorded eunuchs a sacred status. In the *hijra* community of **India**, males (not all of whom were castrated) who adopted female garments and were numerous enough to form their own communities were associated with a particular Hindu goddess, Bahucarah Mata, although some were Muslim. The sacrifice of the male organs was seen as an ascetic act, and in line with the traditional Indian view of asceticism, as one that brought power. The *hijra* functioned as a caste in India's corporatist society and supported themselves partly as entertainers during celebrations like those families had at the birth of a son. The Russian Christian perfectionist sect of the Skoptsi, or "eunuchs," which emerged in the late eighteenth century, also practiced male self-castration as a means of spiritual ascent, but without the adoption of female garments or a feminine role. In **Islam**, the traditional guardians of Mohammed's tomb in Medina were the Eunuchs of the Prophet, a group whose origin dates back to the twelfth century. The Eunuchs of the Prophet were the only ones allowed to enter the tomb. A similar though less prestigious group of sacred eunuchs emerged in Mecca in the eighteenth century. *See also* The Body; Circumcision; Ejaculation.

Further Reading: Scammel, Elsa. "All You Would Like to Know about the Castrati." See http://www.velluti.org/index.htm; Tsai, Shih-Shan Henry. *The Eunuchs in the Ming Dynasty*. New York: State University of New York Press, 1996.

William E. Burns

EUPHEMISMS AND SLANG. Asked for the most common euphemism or colloquialism for the act of sexual intercourse, most would undoubtedly say, "fuck." That word, whose brevity and earthiness probably were reasons it has remained so popular and naughty throughout the centuries, was certainly in use in the eighteenth century, but it is one of many such words that existed at the time.

Thought to be of Old Germanic origin, according to the *Oxford English Dictionary* (OED), it was banned from the OED for years and was not even included in the premier source of vulgar words in the eighteenth century, *The 1811 Dictionary of the Vulgar Tongue*, subtitled *Buckish Slang, University Wit and Pickpocket Eloquence*. The original edition of this rich dictionary was published in 1785 by Captain Francis Grose

(c. 1730–1791), and bore the title *Classical Dictionary of the Vulgar Tongue*. Grose was a bit of a bowdlerizer—he defined "cunt," for instance, as "a nasty name for a nasty thing" and used dashes, so "c - - t."

Grose, with his assistant, Tom Cocking, was one of the first lexicographers to gather and collect words from the underbelly of society. He also included cant words, the often impolite and secret language of thieves and beggars; one of his sources was undoubtedly Richard Head's *The Canting Academy*, a source dating back to 1673. Head (1637–1685) said he collected his words from rogues, vagabonds, pickpockets, prisoners, and other urban scoundrels, but much of it probably came from earlier dictionaries of cant. Head was a bookseller, hack writer, and gambler. Grose, sometimes misnamed Gross, was a classically educated man and a member of the Society of Antiquaries. The military title came from his Surrey Militia stint.

Another term in Grose's volume is "shag," often mistakenly thought to be a 1960s term from its use in the recent Austin Powers films. Grose's compendium defines it as "to copulate," enlarging further on the definition with "He is but bad shag; he is no able woman's man." Some have speculated that that irrepressible punster, **William Shakespeare**, signed his name as "William Shagspeare" in the church register in 1582 on purpose, as a joke, although spelling was so erratic then that Shakespeare could be spelled in a number of ways.

Of course, there were prevalent euphemisms—nicer expressions like "sleep with," "to bed," "amorous rites," "amorous congress," "amorous sport," "dalliance," "conversation" (as in "conjugal conversation"). "Making love" did not have the sexual connotation until the mid-twentieth century; from the sixteenth century on it meant simply "to woo." "**Fornication**" had a harsher, ruder, more judgmental tone and was also used as a legal term for men and women accused of engaging in premarital sexual relations. It has been in use since at least the fourteenth century.

Other terms for the sex act from Grose's dictionary that were perhaps not so nice include "to flourish," with the meaning of taking/enjoying a woman "in a hasty manner, to take a flyer," perhaps with her clothes on and without benefit of a bed. But the eighteenth-century Virginia planter **William Byrd** also used the word "flourish" as a term denoting a stylish gesture and as a sign of his gentility. In diary entries, he described giving his wife "a flourish." Other terms from Grose's book include "to tup," "the two-handed put," "tiffing," "to swive," "to strum," "strupping," " to stroke," "to stitch," "to snooze, snoodge," "to screw," "rutting," "to roger" (from the word "roger" meaning a bull's penis), "riding St. George," "to ride rantipole" (refers to a specific position with a woman uppermost), "to be proud" (with the meaning of desirous of copulation), "occupy" (as in to occupy/have carnal knowledge of a woman), "nub" (coition), "mutton" (as "in her mutton," i.e., to have carnal knowledge of a woman), "melting moments" (a fat man and a fat woman in the amorous congress), "to knock," and "making the beast with two backs." In seventeenth-century Massachusetts, "frogging" was a term frequently used by young men to describe sexual intercourse.

There were also many colloquial terms used for the genitals. Another term for the vagina, perhaps nicer than the rude "cunt," was "Miss Laycock"; terms for the penis included "yard" and "arbor vitae" (tree of life). A bizarre expression for **masturbation** was "to box the Jesuit, and get Cock Roached." "Flying fuck"—sex on horseback—was depicted as one in a series of bawdy etchings by Thomas Rowlandson, the famed caricaturist, and published in 1845 as *Pretty Little Games for Young Ladies and Gentlemen: With Pictures of Good Old English Sports and Pastimes*. Cunnilingus and fellatio are also depicted.

Words for homosexual men included "Molly" and "Sodomite." There were hundreds of words for prostitutes and courtesans; among them are "the frail sisterhood," "trollop," "on the town," "dollymop," "wife in water colors," "strumpet," "demi-rep," "demi-mondaine," and "squirrel." "Nunneries" referred to brothels; the women who worked within these confines were "nuns," and madams were called "mother" or "abbess." *See also* Molly Houses; Prostitutes and Prostitution.

Further Reading: Godbeer, Richard. *Sexual Revolution in Early America*. Baltimore: John Hopkins Press, 2002; *The 1811 Dictionary of the Vulgar Tongue; Buckish Slang, University Wit and Pickpocket Eloquence*. Foreword by Max Harris. London: Senate Books, 1994.

Jo Manning

EUROPEAN ART. *See* Art, American/European

EXPLORERS AND MISSIONARIES. As male explorers and missionaries traversed the globe during the early modern period, they encountered the indigenous populations of the lands they intended to explore and conquer. Starting with Christopher Columbus's voyages to the Caribbean, European men coaxed, coerced, threatened, and forced native women to have sexual relations with them. They wrote about their encounters for the voyeuristic delight of male readers back home. In these accounts, they usually described the women as sensual and filled with desire for European men.

That the women may not have been willing was not emphasized, and rape scenes were often written about as scenes of seduction. Raping indigenous women was an effective military strategy for Spanish military commanders who were attempting to conquer a region. In addition, soldiers expected women as part of their reward. Some of the Catholic missionaries, however, spoke out against men raping indigenous women, often in front of their husbands and families.

In contrast to the erotic reports that many explorers wrote, some of the French Catholic missionaries in Canada emphasized the **chastity** of the Indians they observed. Several commented favorably on the custom of newlyweds in waiting six months to one year before consummating their **marriage**. For some missionaries, however, it was the chastity of the Indians who had become Christians that was noticeable, in contrast to the promiscuous behavior of the unconverted.

Most Europeans considered Indians savages, albeit sometimes delightful ones, because of their lack of clothing and apparent sexual freedom. However, in his 1705 promotional piece, *History and Present State of Virginia*, written to attract settlers, Robert Beverly conveys a different view of Indians. Beverly portrays the **Native Americans** he has encountered as innocent creatures. The young women described as prostitutes in other accounts, Beverly describes as merely playful and free with their bodies.

Other explorers encountered new lands and people in different parts of the world. Captain James Cook made three voyages to the Pacific Ocean, "discovering" Australia and the Hawaiian Islands, which he named the Sandwich Islands for the Earl of Sandwich. During his third voyage, he was killed in a skirmish with Hawaiians.

One of the men who sailed with Cook was William Bligh, who served as navigator on Cook's third voyage. In 1787, Captain Bligh sailed for Tahiti. His mission was to obtain breadfruit plants and bring them to the West Indies, where they could be transplanted and provide inexpensive food for the slaves there. After months at sea, many of the sailors considered Tahiti a paradise, and the women beautiful and engaging. While in

Tahiti, the shore party, including Fletcher Christian, formed romantic attachments with some of the Tahitian women. When the Bounty left Tahiti with the breadfruit plants, many crewmembers were unhappy. Led by Christian, they mutinied and placed Bligh and some of the crew on a launch. Bligh ultimately made it back to England. Christian and the other mutineers settled on Pitcairn Island with several Tahitian women. Their descendents still live there, despite periods of strife. *See also* Atlantic Slave Trade; Maritime Culture; Mexico, Indigenous Women of; Pirates; Wartime Rape.

Further Reading: Sayre, Gordon. "Native American Sexuality in the Eyes of the Beholders, 1535–1710." In *Sex and Sexuality in Early America*, edited by Merril D. Smith, 35–54. New York: New York University Press, 1998; Wood, Stephanie. "Sexual Violence in the Conquest of the Americas." In *Sex and Sexuality in Early America*, edited by Merril D. Smith, pp. 9–34. New York: New York University Press, 1998.

Merril D. Smith

EXPRESS CONSENT. *See* Consent

FAIRY TALES. Fairy tales refer to stories with supernatural characters and with no specific time or place as a setting. Folklorists and historians have debated its definition; some maintain that only stories that feature a fairy as a character should be classified as a fairy tale, yet for the most part most folklorists accept the more general definition. Many of the most popular tales were derived from "oral narratives." Before the eighteenth century they were intended for adult audiences; only after they were revised and censored for young readers did they become children's literature. Many dismiss them as escapism fantasy that children outgrow, but some argue that they teach morals and behavior. Well-known examples include "Cinderella," "Snow White," and "Little Red Riding Hood."

In the seventeenth century aristocratic intellectuals in France, particularly women, grew interested in the magic tales they heard from their servants and nurses, stories they came to call *les contes de fees* (Tales of the Fairies). The world of seventeenth-century French aristocrats was highly structured, and women were limited by that **patriarchy**, especially by arranged marriages. With "public" space closed to them—**education** and government—women met at their homes to discuss **literature** and politics; usually these meetings took place in the living rooms or **salons**, and consequently these women became known as *salonnières*. Meeting in their salons afforded the *salonnières* a venue to educate themselves and voice their opinions.

These factors perhaps explain the women's interest in fairy tales. They first learned the narratives from their nurses and servants, women who often played more important roles in their childhoods than their aristocratic mothers. At that time in France, fierce debates about learning and knowledge pitted those who favored "modern" or contemporary learning against those who argued for the "ancient" or the supremacy of Greek and Roman thinkers. Some welcomed the folktales as unique French literature and therefore "modern." As many recent scholars have suggested, the *salonnières* might have been attracted to the tales because many female characters display wit, cunning, and strength. Furthermore, these characters by their situations call into question the arbitrary and stifling social institutions, the very limits that the *salonnières* encountered and criticized. Finally, the folktales allowed the women to channel their creativity as they selected, updated, and adapted to narrate these "new" stories to their companions.

The most notable of these *salonnières* is Marie-Catherine Baronne d'Aulnoy (c. 1650–1705). Her life resembles a story out of romance, with a forced **marriage** to an alcoholic **libertine**, an escape to Spain, a long exile, then a return to Paris nearly twenty years later. Her salon was one of the most popular and important of her time.

She was a leader creating the vogue for fairy tales, and her several books include *Les Contes des Fees* (1697) and *Contes Nouveaux ou Les Fees a la Mode* (1698), volumes of fairy tales popular in France and translated into English and published in London in 1699. Admired and influential, her tales with their ironic and satiric stance exemplify the fairy tales written by the *salonnières*, and they clearly show that they were intended for adults and not for children.

A frequent guest of D'Aulnoy's salon was Charles Perrault (1628–1703). He reworked, then published some fairy tales in *Histoires ou contes du temps passé, avec des moralités: Contes de ma mère l'Oye* (1697). Perrault's book is by most measures the most influential early collection of fairy tales. It offers Perrault's versions of "Puss in Boots," "Sleeping Beauty," "Cinderella," and "Little Red Riding Hood." It was translated into English and published in London by 1730. Its subtitle translates to "tales told by Mother Goose," and the success of Perrault's book mostly likely introduced the character of Mother Goose to England and the United States.

By the middle of the eighteenth century fairy tales evolved from literature for adults to literature for children. A clear example of this transition is the tale of "Beauty and the Beast." In 1740 Madame Gabrielle de Villeneuve wrote a long version of the tale for her collection, *La jeune ameriquaine, et les contes marins*. Typical of fairy tales of the previous generation, Villeneuve's version is complex, addressing the issue of arranged marriages. In 1756 Madame Le Prince de Beaumont published her much different, much shorter, simpler version. Her purpose was without a doubt to teach young readers lessons. The genre is then children's literature by the turn of the century when the familiar and famous versions of the tales emerge, especially after the publication of the Grimm Brothers' books in 1812 and 1815 in Germany and *Fairy Tales Told for Children* by Hans Christian Andersen in 1835. *See also* Seduction Literature.

Further Reading: Warner, Marina. *From the Beast to the Blonde: On Fairy Tales and Their Tellers*. New York: The Noonday Press, 1996; Windling, Terri. "Les Contes de Fées: The Literary Fairy Tales of France." *Realms of Fantasy*, 2000. See http://www.endicott-studio.com.rdrm/forconte.html.

Martha Graham Viator

FANNY HILL (Cleland, 1749). *Fanny Hill*, first published in 1749 under the title *Memoirs of a Woman of Pleasure*, was written by British author John Cleland, who, at the time, was in jail for having created a debt he could not pay back. The book's many erotic scenes were, as the writer later admitted, aimed at winning as large a readership as possible and in effect bringing him enough money to be set free. Nowadays, *Memoirs of a Woman of Pleasure* is widely recognized as a sharp political satire and critique of the mores in eighteenth-century England.

The book is usually labeled as a "vivid description of sexual awakening," and its main part starts with a **rape** attempt that, rather surprisingly and to much controversy, triggers the heroine's search for erotic pleasures. It must be explained, however, how this attempt is shown in the book. At the beginning, Fanny Hill is a fifteen-year-old girl, who has lost both her parents and has to travel to London to find accommodation and a job. She ends up in a house without realizing that it is actually a brothel, and therefore her first contact with the opposite sex happens soon after her arrival in London. One Mr. Crofts cannot control his desire, and after dinner, when all other women have left the room, he attacks Fanny, forcing his kisses and attempting to undress her. The young girl is shocked but tries to defend her virginity. In the ensuing fight, Mr. Crofts suffers premature **ejaculation**, which changes him back into a shy and silent person. After the event, Fanny falls ill, spends several days in bed, and only gets better after hearing the news of Mr. Crofts being arrested (for a crime unrelated to the attempted rape). As soon as she leaves the bed, her pursuit of erotic pleasures begins; it starts with **voyeurism** and **masturbation**, and ends in sadomasochism. Further in the book, the reader encounters another rape scene, even more controversial than the first one, as it eventually appears that were it not for the social status gap between the rapist and one of Fanny's friends, the incident would result in a perfect relationship.

Owing to its many disputable and explicit sex scenes, such as the two mentioned above, the book could not be published in the United States until 1966, when Charles Rembar, a lawyer who also defended *Lady Chatterley's Lover*, proved in court that it cannot be banned for obscenity, as it does not lack literary merit. The year 1966 was then called "the end of obscenity," and the court's decision opened the doors for the publication of more sexually explicit fiction and nonfiction (*The Way to Become the Sensuous Woman* by J. and *The Joy of Sex* by Alex Comfort). In Britain, the book first appeared in a heavily censored version (as *Memoirs of Fanny Hill*), and only after 1966 an edition more true to the original was released. However, it was not until 1985 that the last missing scene (between two homosexual men) was finally restored to the novel. *See also* Flagellation; Pornography; Sade; Virgins/Virginity.

Further Reading: Cleland, John. *Fanny Hill or Memoirs of a Woman of Pleasure*. London: Penguin Books, 1986; Rembar, Charles. *The End of Obscenity: The Trials of Lady Chatterley, Tropic of Cancer and Fanny Hill*. New York: Granite Impex, 1987.

Bartlomiej Paszylk

FASHION.   See Clothing and Fashion

FLAGELLATION.   Although often claimed to have originated in France, flagellation became known as "the English vice" during the eighteenth century and was to be advocated as a cure for **impotence**, used as a school discipline, and as a public punishment. It would be dispensed to wives and servants as a household correction, taken up as a sexual activity in the home and in the brothel, and developed as a theme in erotic **literature**.

German doctor Johann Heinrich Meibom (1590–1655) promoted flagellation as a curative measure for impotence believing it to aid erection through the improved circulation of blood. His essay, *De Usu Flagrorum in Re Medica & Veneria & Lumborum Renumque Officio* (1629), or "On the Use of Rods in Venereal Matters and in the Office of the Loins and Reins," was reprinted in English by pornographer Edmund Curll as *A Treatise of the Use of Flogging in Venereal Affairs* (1718), but it was originally intended as a serious medical work. The idea that medicinal properties of flagellation could be combined with discipline was a topic expounded upon in both the *Gentleman's Magazine* of the 1730s and the *Bon Ton* in the 1790s. The *Bon Ton* December issue of 1795 reported, "Physicians strongly recommend punishing children with birch for faults which appear to proceed from a heavy or indolent disposition, as nothing tends more to promote the circulation of the blood than a good rod, made of new birch, and well applied to the posteriors."

In his *Confessions* (1782), French philosopher **Jean-Jacques Rousseau** recollected the effect of the beatings from his nanny when he was a child, which led to a predilection for flagellation in later life. "Who would believe that this childish punishment, inflicted upon me when only eight years old by a woman of thirty, disposed of my tastes, my desires, my passions, and my own self for the remainder of my life?"

Middle-class homes were becoming locations for more private flagellation. Although not a crime itself, the flagellation activities of a group of young professionals in Norwich came to light in a trial in 1709; Samuel Self was reported to have put Jane Morris over his knee in the kitchen or on the upstairs bed and spanked her naked buttocks. Specialized brothels emerged; Journalist Ned Ward reported his visit to a flagellation brothel in *The London Spy* in 1709 where he came across "flogging-cullies." *The London Journal* for May 14, 1726, referred to whores who provided a flagellation service. The trial of Mary Wood in September 1719 involved John Tenants, who had supplied his own rods when he paid her to whip him "in front and behind." Likewise, Susan Brockway related how John Richmond offered her ten shillings if she would get a pennyworth of rods to whip him "and make him a good boy."

In the memoirs of Theresa Berkeley, *Venus School-Mistress, or Birchen Sports* (c. 1808–1810), the addresses of flagellation brothels were published as an advertisement to readers. Machines were invented for the purposes of flagellation; one called the "Berkeley horse" allowed the prostitute to strap in her client and thereby turn him to any position for being whipped; the original machine was presented to the Society of Arts at the Adelphi. Another flagellation machine designed by Chase Price was claimed to be able to take care of forty victims at once. Actor Samuel Foote had a long debate with the inventor of this contraption in the brothel of bawd Charlotte Hayes, over a machine Price wanted to patent.

The *Bon Ton Magazine* for December 1792 reported that a club of "Female Flagellants" met on a Thursday evening in London's Jermyn Street. Allegedly the women were married and, having grown tired of the routine of their marriages, took up the activity. About twelve women were supposedly involved in the group, six flogging the other half dozen. It is however, impossible to tell whether the *Bon Ton* was relating fact or fiction since it was notorious for relating **gossip**.

Early French **pornography** had influenced eighteenth-century English material; its flagellation scenarios derived from Catholic penitential practices. Erotica such as *Venus dans la Cloître* (1683), *Histoire de Dom B* (c. 1742), and *Thérèse Philosophe* (1748) would set their scenes within nunneries or **monasteries** to enable the arena of religious flagellation to develop into a sexual one. John Cleland was one of the first authors in England to write pornographic flagellation scenes in *Memoirs of a Woman of Pleasure* (1749) where **Fanny Hill** related her experience with her client, Mr. Barville; "At last, he twigg'd me so smartly as to fetch blood in more than one lash."

A new wave of pornographic fiction emerged in England between 1770 and 1830 in which flagellation themes ran throughout the entire text. Pornographic novellas such as *The Birchen Bouquet* (1770), *Exhibition of Female Flagellants* (1777), *The Spirit of Flagellation; or The Memoirs of Mrs. Hinton, Who Kept a School Many Years at Kensington* (c. 1790), and *Manon La Fouëtteuse, or the Quintessence of Birch Discipline* (c. 1805) became increasingly popular and would remain so throughout the nineteenth century. Boarding schools, parlors, governesses, and stepmothers became integral to the setting, as did nosegays and purple gloves, which

Eighteenth and nineteenth century erotic books owned by author and art collector Roger Peyrefitte. The original gouaches of *Thérèse Philosophe* were later engraved. *Thérèse* was one of the favorite erotic books of the Marquis de Sade. © Erich Lessing/Art Resource.

indicated a predilection for flagellation in the wearer. This pornography involved themes of defloration, blood, and positioning of the body, and explored erogenous zones beyond the genitalia, with white thighs, snowy bellies, red buttocks, and plump forearms all coming into focus. *See also* Molly Houses; Prostitutes and Prostitution; Sade.

Further Reading: Cooper, Rev. Wm. M. *History of the Rod.* London: William Reeves Bookseller, 1870; Peakman, Julie. "Initiation, Defloration and Flagellation: Sexual Propensities in *Memoirs of a Woman of Pleasure.*" In *This Launch into the Wide World: Essays on Fanny Hill*, edited by Patsy Fowler and Alan Jackson, 153–72. New York: AMS Press, 2003; Peakman, Julie. *Lascivious Bodies, A Sexual History of the Eighteenth Century.* London: Atlantic, 2004; Peakman, Julie. *Mighty Lewd Books, The Development of Pornography in C18th England.* Basingstoke: Palgrave Press, 2003; Scott, G. Riley. *Flagellation: The History of Corporal Punishment.* London: Tallis Press, 1968; Stone, Lawrence. "Libertine Sexuality in Post-Restoration England: Group Sex and Flagellation among the Middling Sort in Norwich in 1706–07." *Journal of the History of Sexuality* 2, no. 4 (1992): 551–25.

Julie Peakman

FOLKLORE. *See* Myths and Folklore

FOOD. When the European **explorers**, conquistadors, then colonists, set foot in the New World they brought their traditional foods with them, while seeking the unknown and exotic. In addition to nutritional and gustatory value, food had symbolic, often sexual connotations. Like roots, leaves, flowers, and other plant material, certain foods were eaten for their healing, stimulant, or sedative properties. Without chemical equipment to analyze their foods, their empirical experiences worked well enough to keep traditions going. Folk knowledge was useful and "wives tales" often contained truths. Advice to drink milk as a sleep aid was found to be scientifically valid: it contains tryptophan, an amino acid useful in sleep disorders. Substances believed to have stimulant properties, such as coffee and tea, increase energy and alertness because they contain caffeine. However, other foods were assigned attributes because of the "doctrine of signatures" or "simples" since they created intense sensory perceptions in the mouth or other parts of the body.

The "doctrine of signatures" was a belief that a plant that looked like a body part or organ would have a corresponding use because God had left a mark on everything in the universe as a clue. Toothwort was believed to be good for toothache. Maidenhair fern allegedly could restore a bald man's hair growth. Foods that are dramatic tasting—hot, sour, bitter, or extremely sweet—cause bodily changes such as sweating or salivating. The hot pepper's fiery reputation is associated with the sex act because it first causes the eater to salivate, sweat, and feel hot in the face, all visceral changes that occur during a vigorous sexual act.

Europeans adapted many new foods from **Native Americans** because of necessity: geographic and environmental conditions were different from those in Europe. Although the Indians were referred to as savages because of their public nakedness and non-Christian belief system, their ability to survive cold barren winters without food taught the early settlers a lesson. English settlers who arrived in the northern woodlands of New England were accustomed to year-round food such as beef, venison, beer, wheat bread, peas, root vegetables, apples, and other fruits grown on trees. On the other hand, the Native Americans were accustomed to lean periods where food was minimal. Corn (*zea maize*) had long been a staple of Native Americans and was soon adopted with skepticism by the new settlers because, although grown in England, it was fed to pigs. However, as they learned more about their new world, European colonists readily adapted. Since summers were shorter, hotter, and more humid than in the British Isles, mildew grew on wheat and rye crops. Corn soon replaced wheat and rye, and cornbread, a new bread, was eaten.

The three sisters, corn, beans, and squash, cultivated by Native American women had spiritual significance. Among the Pueblo, corn was the cosmic principles of femininity. The Corn Mother was worshipped throughout the indigenous cultures of America as the basis of life. Corn was not only a realistic staple but also the symbolic basis of fertility.

Virginia settlers were impressed and thrilled that there was an abundance of fish. Chesapeake Bay, the site of the first English settlement in Maryland, was named *Chesepiook* by the Algonquin for the abundance of crabs, oysters, clams, and eels. Seafood had long been considered to have aphrodisiac qualities because a fishy smell is often associated with vaginal odors and because both clams and oysters unmistakably resemble female genitalia. Eels are associated with phallic themes. However in all of human history, no food or substance other than cantharides, that is, Spanish fly, or a medical hormone replacement when a deficiency exists, has ever been found to possess true aphrodisiac properties. And the real reason that the Spanish fly appears to act on the genitals is that it irritates the bladder, which the body interprets as sexual.

The potato (*Solanum tuberosum*), according to the "doctrine of signatures," resembled testicles and its hidden virtue was supposed to enhance male potency. **Cotton Mather** allegedly maligned potatoes because they had aphrodisiac qualities. Tomatoes (*Lycopersicon esculentum*), originally from South America, were believed to be the forbidden fruit of the Bible. And for many years because they belonged to the same family as deadly nightshade they were believed to be poisonous. After that myth was discounted, they were called *poma d'Moro* or Moor's apples. But the French mistakenly thought the name of the plant was *pomme d'amour* or apples of love having aphrodisiac qualities. American farmers called it the "wolf peach" and used it for decorative purposes until its poisonous reputation was dismissed. Tomatoes do contain tomatin, a poison which could be harmful if tomatoes are eaten in excess.

Coffee originated in Ethiopia sometime between 500 and 900 BCE. It did not come to Europe until the seventeenth century and from there, John Smith who founded Jamestown is said to have introduced coffee to North America. Coffee, although bitter, gained popularity and, in 1773, became the official national beverage after Americans revolted against the tax on tea from Britain. Because of its stimulant properties, some eighteenth-century authorities believed coffee in excess allegedly caused priapism (prolonged and painful erection), lascivious dreams, and involuntary seminal emissions.

Chocolate, from the cocoa bean, originated in Mexico. It was adopted by the Spanish and in the sixteenth century used as a drink for medicinal and aphrodisiac purposes. From there it spread throughout Europe until it was reintroduced to Dorchester, Massachusetts, by John Hanan. By that time, it was mixed with sugar and vanilla, another substance with sexual connotations. *See also* Alcohol; Tobacco.

Further Reading: Coffee History: www.discountcoffee.com/coffeehistory.htm; Farb, Peter, and George Armelagos. *Consuming Passions: The Anthropology of Eating*. Boston: Houghton Mifflin, 1980; Lowe, Benno. "Body Images and the Politics of Beauty." In *Ideals of Feminine Beauty: Philosophical, Social and Cultural Dimensions*, edited by Karen Callaghan. Westport, CT: Greenwood Press, 1994; McWilliams, James E. *A Revolution in Eating: How the Quest for Food Shaped America*. New York: Columbia University Press, 2005; Oliver, Sandra. "New England." In *Encyclopedia of Food and Culture*, vol. 3, edited by Solomon H. Katz. New York: Thomson-Gale, 2003; Tannahill, Ray. *Food in History*. New York: Stein and Day, 1973.

Lana Thompson

FOOTBINDING. Footbinding has ingrained itself, particularly in the minds of the Western population, as a powerful symbol of the subjection of Chinese women, who, by means of severe mutilation, were taught their inferior social and intellectual position, passivity, and ignorance of the outside world.

There is no doubt that to a certain extent footbinding was meant as a restrictive device—after all, women who could barely walk were more likely to be dependant on their husbands. At the same time, however, it cannot be denied that footbinding should also be viewed in terms of its particular sexual appeal to Chinese men. Their well-documented admiration of small feet not only resulted in parents subjecting their daughters to unimaginable pain in hope of attracting a potential husband, but also produced generations of women willing to maim themselves to achieve male-defined standards of beauty.

In practice, footbinding amounted to a skilful application of bandages around each foot in such a way as to force the small toes in and toward the sole. The largest toe was left unbound but the bandages were wrapped so tightly that the heel and toes were drawn closer together, making the foot arch and more than often resulting in the breaking of the bones. Since the healing process was quickened if the flesh became putrescent and fell off, frequently the girl was forced to walk on broken glass or had sharp objects inserted into the binding to cause open wounds and speed the decaying of skin. The pain continued for about two to three years after which time the foot was practically dead. All this was done to girls aged five to eight.

Originally traced back to the twelfth century BCE and the last empress of the Shang dynasty, footbinding was mainly an elite upper-class practice. Briefly banned in the mid-seventeenth century by the Manchus, it reached its peak during the Qing dynasty (1644–1911), when peasant women began to imitate it in growing numbers. In the eighteenth century, small feet, popularly referred to as "golden lotuses," were praised in several essays by a man known as Fang Hsûn (Xun), who enumerated fifty-eight "lotus" varieties with regard to three qualities: plumpness, softness, and fineness.

According to Fang Hsûn, who called himself Lotus Knower or the Doctor of the Fragrant Lotus, perfectly bound feet must meet seven qualifications—be small, slim, pointed, arched, fragrant, soft, and straight. Apart from being aesthetically pleasing to the eye, Hsûn regarded tiny feet as an important element of sexual intercourse and described eighteen sexual positions involving their active use. As the names of the erotic techniques such as "Encircling Twin Lotuses," "Two Dragons Playing with a Pearl," and "A Head Inserted in Lotus Petals" suggest, bound feet were not only touched and squeezed during the penetration of a woman. In fact, the little crevice between the crushed toes and the heel was frequently treated as another vagina, whose penetration was doubly stimulating for men since they could gaze into the exposed female genitals. Although, it should be noted that in some provinces the sight of female genitals was considered unlucky.

Apart from praising the feet as such, Fang Hsûn mentioned the pleasures connected with lotus slippers, in particular drinking games involving their use. That practice was later to become an integral part of sex with prostitutes and result in fetishizing tiny shoes even more. In fact, lotus slippers (especially red silk ones) were in such demand that frequently women had to sew them to their socks to avoid having them stolen in the dark.

Last but not the least, bound feet were the source of other types of pleasure. Their obvious connotation with pain inspired cruelty. They appealed also to men with odor fetishes since they continued to exude a sickly sweet fragrance of decay. As women with bound feet were forced to walk with a gait, such posture resulted in the tightening of the muscles in their upper legs, hips, and vagina. That only increased their attractiveness to Chinese men, fitting their general preference for voluptuous female shapes and making each act of intercourse seem like one with a virgin. The sensuous sound of tiny bells attached to the heels of the shoes made male satisfaction complete. *See also* Clothing and Fashion; Prostitutes and Prostitution; Virgins/Virginity.

Further Reading: Jackson, Beverly. *Splendid Slippers*. Berkeley, CA: Ten Speed Press, 1977; Ko, Dorothy. *Every Step a Lotus*. Berkeley: University of California Press, c. 2001; Levy, Howard S. *The Lotus Lovers*. Buffalo, NY: Prometheus Books, 1992; Wang, Ping. *Aching for Beauty: Footbinding in China*. Minneapolis: University of Minnesota Press, 2000.

Katarzyna Ancuta

FORNICATION. The pejorative term "fornication" was used to describe heterosexual intercourse between two unmarried persons or two persons who were not married to each other. It was also used in the legal sense as a criminal charge levied in ecclesiastical or secular courts against such persons following the discovery of an out-of-wedlock **pregnancy**. Fornication was prosecuted in extreme Protestant jurisdictions such as Switzerland, Germany, Scotland, Puritan England (1640–1660), and New England from the mid-sixteenth century to the mid-eighteenth century. These prosecutions peaked in all jurisdictions during the seventeenth century. Married couples whose first child arrived before thirty-two weeks of **marriage** were also prosecuted in some locales. Penalties for fornication varied by jurisdiction and time period, ranging from a public whipping and/or a fine equivalent to a year's wages for a female servant, to a token fine, to judicial and ecclesiastical censure.

With the advent of the Protestant Reformation, the centuries-old system of **bastardy** prosecutions that prevailed in the ecclesiastical courts of Europe was criticized for being too lenient. In seventeenth-century England, for example, **Puritans** pressed for a broader range of sexual offences, the uniform application of existing fornication laws, and harsher penalties for offenders. During the Interregnum, Puritans instituted criminal prosecutions in secular courts for bastardy and fornication. English ecclesiastical courts had not presented married couples whose first child was born early, nor did they customarily present single men or women for lewd behavior.

While in English ecclesiastical courts the charge was bastardy, the female defendants were poor, and the primary motivating factor behind prosecution was economic, a harsher regimen developed in Puritan England and New England. Similar punishment patterns prevailed in Scotland, Geneva, and Germany. In these jurisdictions, female bastard-bearers from all status groups were charged with fornication, not bastardy. Their crime was not that they had produced an illegitimate child that needed support from the public purse, but that they had engaged in sexual intercourse while single. In Massachusetts, the laws governing sexual offences were written and administered by men who had been rebuffed in their efforts to reform the English system of prosecution for sexual offences. The initial impetus, then, behind the criminalization of consensual sexual intercourse outside marriage was moral, not economic, although clearly Puritans made no finite distinction between the two issues.

Massachusetts was not the only British North American colony that tried to prevent unmarried persons from engaging in sexual activity by making sexual intercourse outside marriage a criminal offence. The types of sexual behaviors, though, that were criminalized, the motivating factors for the legislation, and the penalties assigned varied by colony. Not surprisingly, New England sexual legislation diverged the most from that of customary English practice; Virginia and the Caribbean, the least. In the southern colonies the motivation for fornication prosecutions appears to have been primarily economic. Whatever legislation existed on the books in other British North American colonies, enforcement was irregular, gender specific, and status dependent.

Virginia provided a very different ideological and physical environment than Massachusetts. Unlike New England, where most settlers emigrated in family groups, the majority of immigrants to Virginia were male **indentured servants** between the ages of seventeen and twenty-eight, and single women were at a premium. Fortunes could be made growing a labor-intensive crop, **tobacco**, through the exploitation of indentured servants, both male and female. Planters were more concerned about losing the services of pregnant female servants and the expenses of raising their children than they were with the moral issues involved. For this reason, judicial activity was directed against indentured servants who bore illegitimate children. These women were charged with bastardy, as in England, because their crime lay not so much in having engaged in coitus, as in producing an illegitimate child, which reduced their ability to work and, temporarily, created another drain on their master's resources in the form of an infant who had to be raised to a productive age. Sexual misconduct that did not have economic consequences, such as premarital fornication, which formed the largest category of offence in New England, was seldom prosecuted elsewhere in British North America and the Caribbean.

The typical fornication defendant was an unmarried female servant between the ages of seventeen and twenty-five. She faced certain prosecution and punishment. In the seventeenth century, she would most likely be stripped to the waist and whipped in public, or, if from a prominent family, fined the equivalent of a year's wages. Only one-fifth of single women prosecuted for fornication in Massachusetts between 1640 and 1685 married subsequently, and while most were required to pay child-support equivalent to that paid by the father in the instances where **paternity** was assigned few were able to maintain custody of their illegitimate child. Their sexual partners were seldom prosecuted for fornication because of difficulties in proving paternity although, technically, a **childbirth** declaration made by the laboring mother to her midwife was sufficient legal proof. Ironically, men who married pregnant women were prosecuted for fornication, and both partners faced corporal punishment or significant fines.

By the mid to late eighteenth century, the religious climate had changed radically in Europe and America. The early modern rhetoric that had posited women as inherently sexually voracious had been replaced by an idealized view of women who became pregnant out of wedlock as the victims of male sexual predators. Occasional bastardy charges were levied, but the fine had become a token sixpence. Nevertheless, while the consequences of an act of extramarital sexual intercourse differed, and the types of sexual behaviors that were criminalized varied by region, gender, and the decade or century in which the offence occurred, a generalized philosophical assumption existed throughout Europe and the British Atlantic world that coitus prior to marriage presented a moral and an economic threat. *See also* Courtship; Infanticide; Laws; Midwives and Physicians.

Further Reading: Hambleton, Else L. *Daughters of Eve: Pregnant Brides and Unwed Mothers in Seventeenth-Century Essex County, Massachusetts.* New York: Routledge, 2004; Hambleton, Else L. "The Regulation of Sex in Seventeenth-Century Massachusetts: The Quarterly Court of Essex County vs. Priscilla Willson and Mr. Samuel Appleton." In *Sex and Sexuality in Early America*, edited by Merril D. Smith, 89–115. New York: New York University Press, 1998; Ingram, Martin.

Church Courts, Sex and Marriage in England, 1570–1640. New York: Cambridge University Press, 1987.

Else L. Hambleton

FRANKLIN, BENJAMIN (1706–1790). Benjamin Franklin is best known for the scientific experiments that made him famous throughout the English world of his day. His posthumously published *Autobiography* and his political role as one of the Founding Fathers of the United States had made him one of the most renowned Americans in history.

Born on January 16, 1706, in Boston, Franklin later resided in Philadelphia from 1723 until his death. Retiring from a successful printing business at the age of forty-two, he achieved prominence as a scientist, politician, and man of affairs in the second half of his life. He gained entry to both English and French society for more than the quarter century that he spent overseas as a colonial agent and then minister plenipotentiary before returning home to Philadelphia for the last five years of his life.

Franklin had a common-law **marriage** to Deborah Read from 1726 until her death in 1774. Recent scholarship portrays Franklin as an eighteenth-century gentleman who served as patriarch of his family, but whose wife shared in his businesses, both in his early life when they were together and later when he was in England. Through extensive correspondence, we are able to see how the two related over the decades, especially since Franklin resided overseas fifteen out of the last seventeen years of their marriage, and was still away when she died suddenly in 1774.

Franklin had only three children (one who died at age four), a small number considering the families of the day. The limited number proved to be advantageous to Franklin in his role as father and later as a public figure who resided for many years away from his family. Franklin had a different relationship with each of his children. His eldest illegitimate son, William (mother unknown), received an English **education**, became royal governor of New Jersey, and was a loyalist during the Revolution, resulting in his estrangement from his father during his lifetime. Franklin assisted and was generous with his male grandchildren, William Temple Franklin and Benjamin Franklin Bache. Franklin did not expound rights for women. For his daughter, Sarah (nicknamed Sally), he provided only some music education, sent her various gifts from England, and disapproved at first her marriage to Richard Bache rather than his selection of his London friend's son William Strahan, Jr. Later, in Philadelphia, in the years before his death on April 17, 1790, Franklin favored his visitor Polly (Stevenson) Jewson rather than his own daughter. Franklin left a significant part of his estate to Sally, which she dissipated over a twenty-year period.

Franklin's life in England and then France led to speculation about his many affairs. In England, he resided at the home of Margaret Stevenson and her daughter Polly; later in France, he stayed with Leray de Chaumont. Current scholars ascertain that he probably did not have any sexual affairs with any one apart from his wife, and his relationships with women close to him were platonic. In France, he had a wide range of associates, participated in the **salons**, but there is no evidence of affairs, except when he sought a relationship with Madame Brillion, who rejected his advances. In France, many of the women he met called him "Papa." His relationships with several younger women—Polly Stevenson, Catharine Ray, and Georgiana Shipley—were of a mentor-student relationship.

From the age of seventeen, Franklin published various letters, parodies, and pamphlets under anonymous names and his own. In his writings, from the Silence

Dogood letters of his teenage years to his writings late in life, he transcended genders, appearing sometimes in a female role. His posthumously published "Old Mistress Apologue" (Reasons for Preferring an Old Mistress to a Young One) written in 1745, but not published until 1926, served as a partial reason for historians' view of Franklin's relationships with women. His made-up tale of the trial of Polly Baker (1747) was critical of the colonial legal system and its treatment of unwed mothers, but it was popular enough for the Frenchman Rabelais to include in his *Encyclopedia*. Historian Jan Lewis notes in an essay on Franklin that he "was caught between the imperatives of his republicanism, which negated the distinctions of gender, and his own evident appreciation of human sexuality, which, of course, delighted in those very distinctions" (Tise, p. 71). *See also* Enlightenment Thought on Sexuality; Gender Roles; Household Consumerism; Revolution and Gender.

Further Reading: Brands, W. H. *The First American: The Life and Times of Benjamin Franklin*. New York: Doubleday, 2000; Issacson, Walter. *Benjamin Franklin: An American Life*. New York: Simon & Schuster, 2003; Labaree, Leonard, et al., eds. *The Autobiography of Benjamin Franklin*. New Haven, CT: Yale University Press, 1964; Labaree, Leonard W., et al., eds. *The Papers of Benjamin Franklin*. 37 vols. New Haven, CT: Yale University Press, 1959–; Lemay, J. A. Leo. *Benjamin Franklin Writings*. New York: Library of America, 1987; Lemay, J. A. Leo, and P. M. Zall, eds. *Benjamin Franklin's Autobiography: An Authoritative Text, Backgrounds, and Criticism*. New York: Norton, 1986; Lopez, Claude-Anne, and Eugenie W. Herbert. *The Private Franklin: The Man and His Family*. New York: Norton, 1975; Tise, Larry, ed. *Benjamin Franklin and Women*. University Park: Pennsylvania State University Press, 2000; Wood, Gordon S. *The Americanization of Benjamin Franklin*. New York: Penguin Press 2004.

Joel Fishman

FRENCH REVOLUTION. *See* Revolution and Gender

GEISHA. The *geisha*, often treated as the erotic symbol of Japan, is a woman who can be seen as the embodiment of male fantasies of mysterious, alluring, intellectual companions, set in contrast to the almost managerial position of the wife in the culture where marriage is frequently described in terms of filial duty rather than a passionate affair.

The geisha can be traced back to the *shirabyoshi* (dancing women), who were, in fact, performing female courtesans popular at the height of the Heian period (794–1195). The word "geisha" itself is recorded to have first appeared in Edo during the Genroku Era (1688–1704), although some sources date its development at around 1760. Originally coined to describe male entertainers, better known as *taikomochi* (drum-bearers), the term "geisha" is usually translated as "artiste," "entertainer," or "arts person."

During the Horeki Era (1751–1764), male geisha enjoyed unrivalled popularity, frequently favored over female entertainers, since they were not seen as direct competition to the courtesans. Initially performing the function of "party masters" responsible for ensuring that the visitors received the entertainment they had paid for, the male geisha soon became an independent profession. From then on they were usually referred to as *hokan* (comedians), or the said *taikomochi*, and were much appreciated for their skills in music and their suggestive buffoonery, often with overtly sexual undertones.

Sources differ with regard to the appearance of the geisha as we know them today. Some claim that the first female geisha came into existence in Kyoto and Osaka with the beginning of the Horeki Era. Other sources record the appearance of the regular female *geiko* (the term often translated as "woman of art" and used particularly in Kyoto) at around 1754. As early as the 1680s many lords and more significant samurai began to hire the *odoriko* (dancing girls) to perform before the guests at parties. By the 1760s the dancing odoriko were so popular that even the **Yoshiwara** courtesans felt threatened by their presence.

Female geiko, originally hired for the task of competing with the odoriko often were, in fact, older odoriko themselves, although, reportedly, the term "geiko" was used for the first time to describe female drum-bearers (*taiko-joro*) who appeared within the walls of the Shimabara, in the famous pleasure district of Kyoto. Soon the new term caught on. In time the geisha were recognized as female entertainers whose performance frequently included playing a three-stringed musical instrument called *shamisen* and singing little lyrical songs known as *ko-uta*, many of which described male-female relations in the pleasure quarters.

Undated portrait of Uchitsutsumae playing a zither, by Shigenaga Nishimura. Courtesy of the Library of Congress.

The first female geisha is said to have been a woman called Kikuya from the town of Fukagawa, remembered as a prostitute with a reputation for her exquisite *shamisen*-playing and singing. Her popularity as an entertainer is said to have contributed greatly to the fact that Fukagawa was allegedly teeming with female geishas by the 1750s. In the Yoshiwara, however, all geishas were male until around 1760. The first recorded female Yoshiwara geisha was Kasen of the Ogiya house (1761). Just like in the case of Kikuya, little is in fact known about her, apart from perhaps that she was a prostitute who had earned her freedom and established herself as an independent entertainer. In the following years the number of female geisha in the Yoshiwara increased dramatically, and by the end of the eighteenth century the term itself began to primarily mean a woman not a man.

The increasing popularity of the geisha ties in with the disappearance of the great courtesans from the pleasure quarters. By the mid-1700s most modern men were attracted to the more understated geisha rather than to the overwhelming extravagance of the courtesan with her ornate kimono and elaborate headdress. Originally the geisha were ordered to wear a plain kimono and a simple hairstyle in order to eliminate competition. They were frequently expected to be less physically attractive than the courtesans, hired to work in twos and threes and not allowed to sit near the guests. Any geisha working in the pleasure quarters who was found propositioning a customer risked losing her license, sometimes even permanently. Such restrictions, of course, did not apply to independent geishas who could sleep with whoever they liked. At the same time the distinction was clear: prostitution was never anything the geisha were forced to participate in. *See also* Concubines; Molly Houses; Prostitutes and Prostitution; Theater, Japanese.

Further Reading: De Becker, Joseph Ernest. *The Nightless City of Geisha*. London: Kegan Paul, 2002; Downer, Leslie. *Geisha*. London: Headline, 2001; Seigle, Cecilia Segawa. *Yoshiwara*. Honolulu: University of Hawaii Press, c. 1933.

Katarzyna Ancuta

GENDER. *See* Revolution and Gender

GENDER ROLES. From 1600 to 1800, gender roles underwent a number of watershed changes that redefined women's roles in significant ways. For instance, in the 1600s in the American colonies, where men outnumbered women six-to-one, women possessed more freedom of action than their counterparts in England, where gender behavior differed greatly across class lines. By the end of the early modern period, as women were delegated to the private sphere, middle- and upper-class women were restricted by what was seen as "proper" roles for women.

In France, although women were thought of as more emotional and less logical than men, a number of women achieved fame in French **salons. Mary Wollstonecraft**, author of *A Vindication of the Rights of Woman* (1792), left her native England to take up residence in France where, she contended, women were more respected. Wollstonecraft maintained that women were socialized into appearing weak and dependent. She rejected Jean-Jacques Rousseau's notion that giving women rights would give them power over men, insisting that equality for women would only give them the desired power over themselves.

Patriarchy continued to flourish throughout the early modern period in Europe and North America. Married women lost their legal identities through the legal system of *coverture*, which gave their husbands control over their wives' lives, bodies, offspring, and property. In the home, men exercised almost total control over their wives, children, and servants. While *femme sole* status gave single women more legal freedom, their status still lagged behind that of men.

Puritans were so convinced of male superiority that they believed that male fetuses took longer to develop into their higher life forms. It was thought that males received their souls on the fourth day, while females were without souls until the eightieth day. Even such common Puritan names as Patience, Prudence, Verity, and Comfort established what was considered women's proper roles.

Women immigrated to the New World for many of the same reasons that men came: religious freedom, economic opportunity, and a better quality of life. Many women sold themselves as **indentured servants** to win entry into the new land associated with freedom and opportunity. Others worked on farms or as seamstresses, midwives, printers, merchants, milliners, or teachers. In general, as the colonies became more established, the ideal role for white women was a domestic one. Women were supposed to master the skills of being a housewife, which might also include tending the kitchen garden, taking care of a dairy, and nursing sick family members, servants, or slaves. In areas away from the frontier, and as **slavery** assumed a more important role in the southern colonies, white women seldom worked in the fields, although black women, poor white women, and women in frontier areas did.

By the late eighteenth century, more women chose not to marry, but generally young women were encouraged to do so because it was believed that women realized their true destinies only through **marriage**. Within the private sphere of the home, women were concerned with their roles as wives, mothers, and homemakers. Femininity came to be associated with emotionalism, dependence, piety, passivity, modesty, meekness, charity, tenderness, and inferiority.

In contrast, men's roles and duties were outside the home. Men worked in the fields—if they did not own slaves—hunted, or tended to business concerns. Men also fought in wars, served as judges, and held political posts. By the eighteenth century, men such as **William Byrd** of Virginia followed a code of gentlemanly behavior, and they and their wives sought to display their status by how they dressed and behaved.

In England, despite restrictions on gender roles, early feminists such as Mary Astell, **Aphra Behn**, Hannah Wooley, and Lady Mary Chudleigh focused attention on the rights of women. The bluestockings of the English salons also played a significant role in allowing women to define themselves rather than being defined by prevalent views on gender roles. The women's movement in the United States did not become formalized until the mid-nineteenth century, but individual women defined themselves as feminists and rebelled against rigid gender roles. Before, during, and after the American Revolution, for example, women went beyond their domestic roles and became involved in the conflict and politics around them. Abigail Adams, wife of John Adams, who later became the second president of the United States, famously reminded him to "remember the ladies" when articulating the rights of the new republic.

Mercy Otis Warren, known as the First Lady of the Revolution, went even further with her political writings, influencing both directly and indirectly the general public and such luminaries as John Adams, Samuel Adams, and John Hancock. Warren was an important Anti-Federalist and was instrumental in forcing the Federalists to add a Bill of Rights to the new constitution.

Throughout the early modern period, the patriarchal system defined women to restrictive gender roles. Feminists in Europe and the United States rebelled against these restrictions, demanding to be treated as equals. During the late eighteenth century, Enlightenment thinkers who espoused classical liberalism with its emphasis on individuality paved the way for the organized women's movement of the nineteenth century that would begin to break down legal barriers to the subordination of women shaped by the restrictive gender roles of the past. *See also* Education; Masculinity; Rousseau, Jean-Jacques; Women, Changing Images of.

Further Reading: Evans, Sara M. *Born for Liberty: A History of Women in America*. New York: Free Press, 1989; Norton, Mary Beth. *Liberty's Daughters: The Revolutionary Experience of American Women, 1750–1800*. Boston: Little-Brown, 1980; Stone, Lawrence. *The Family, Sex, And Marriage in England, 1500–1800*. New York: Harper and Row, 1977; Wollstonecraft, Mary. *A Vindication of the Rights of Woman*. New York: W. W. Norton, 1988.

Elizabeth R. Purdy

GOSSIP, EIGHTEENTH-CENTURY ENGLAND. England in the eighteenth century was a scandalous age; no one disputed that. People behaved in flamboyant ways, and others eagerly observed it, read, and gossiped about it. The juicy *on-dits* made the rounds of the fashionable world and trickled down to *hoi polloi* in no time. Even the illiterate and poor—those who could not afford **newspapers**—could view the graphic cartoons posted for sale in the print shop windows illustrating the outrageous antics of the *Bon Ton*. It was a public and dirty trough, filled to the brim daily by the gossip columnists and caricaturists, the Georgian *paparazzi*. Those who could read enjoyed the thinly veiled remarks in the newspapers—every newspaper reported at least a line or two of gossip—or more detailed articles in one of the period's many burgeoning general-interest magazines.

One of the most successful print shops in London had an intimate connection to arguably the most outrageous of these caricaturists, James Gilray. This was the shop of Hannah Humphrey, with whom Gilray had been living since 1793, first on Old Bond Street and later on New Bond Street the next year, and finally on St. James's Street beginning in 1797. Gilray's relationship with Humphrey was exclusive both personally and professionally. His *Hannah Humphrey's Print Shop* or *Very Slippery Weather*, drawn in 1808 and showing a gentleman falling in front of a bow window full of Gilray caricatures, insured immortality to both the little print shop and the daring artist.

Women are routinely and carelessly tarred with the gossip brush, but London gossip seems to have started in the men's coffee houses, then migrated to the tabloids for publication. Most newspaper-gossip columnists masked their identities with pen names to protect themselves from being attacked in the streets, as was Dr. James Hill, a newspaper personality almost on par with Henry Bate, the controversial editor of several gossip-filled London newspapers. Hill wrote under the *nom de plume* of "The Inspector," producing a gossip column for the *London Advertiser* and *Literary Gazette*. He was described as "a rakish figure in his early thirties [who] criss-crossed fashionable London in a magnificent chariot, picking up paragraphs and sowing mischief in his daily column.... He made many enemies along the way, and his column was ... littered with retractions and apologies."

Captain Philip Thicknesse, a writer of travel and gardening pieces, became another notable gossip columnist, but, unlike Bate and Hill, whom people could identify, he was well hidden behind the pseudonym "A Wanderer" in the *St. James's Chronicle* and "Polyxena" in the *Gentleman's Magazine*. Thicknesse not only wrote truly scurrilous material, but was also a blackmailer; he was paid handsomely to keep gossip from his columns. Even James Boswell, the noted biographer of his friend Dr. Samuel Johnson, stooped to write gossip between 1777 and 1783 for the *London Magazine*, under the pseudonym of "The Hypochondriack."

A great source for gossip of the anonymous sort was the *tete-a-tetes*, full name "Histories of the Tete-a-Tetes," in the *Town and Country Magazine*. They were, in fact, the most popular feature of the magazine. The features—there were to be 312 *tetes-a-tetes* in total, ceasing publication after the August 1795 issue—were compiled from information sent in by what today would be called stringers, and who were then termed "correspondents." The features were of doubtful accuracy at best, again, not so very unlike what surfaces in today's gossip sheets. Some were probably revenge pieces, such as the one that purported to detail a love affair between Horace Walpole and the actress Kitty Clive, but was instead full of innuendo about Walpole's possible **homosexuality**.

Servants were also a likely source of information about their employers and may have been bribed by these correspondents. A number of the correspondents may have been women, who were protected by the anonymity of the series. As with contemporary scandal and gossip, these juicy articles were read avidly and discussed widely, not only in London, but also in the smaller cities and into the far-flung provinces.

The scandalous doings of the *ton* supplied more than enough fodder for the series. The editors boasted that monthly sales exceeded 11,000 copies, and that through shared copies the readership was at least 30,000. Two vis-à-vis engravings of a gentleman and his mistress normally illustrated the article, and these engravings were actually collected by readers, who cut them out and pasted them into albums, much as we would collect and paste pictures into photo albums. (A vis-à-vis was also a kind of carriage in which the passengers faced each other.)

More aware readers noted the subtle body language between those depicted in the vis-à-vis engravings. Were they smiling at each other and gazing fondly, eye-to-eye, or was one of them looking away, distracted, or, worse, frowning? There were all kinds of attitudes displayed, which could be interpreted as clues to the relationship. In the engraving illustrating the piece on one such couple whose relationship came to a sorry end, the adulterous wife **Grace Dalrymple Elliott** and her paramour, the equally married Arthur Annesley, Lord Valentia, Grace is shown in profile looking at the Viscount, who is in full face, but blatantly ignoring her. In a later article showing the same Mrs. Elliott with her new lover, George James, Lord Cholmondeley, they are both in three-quarter view, but, while she is turned toward him, he is looking away from her. Again, clues to where the relationship is going are clearly given by the lack of communication implied.

Political and personal satires often went hand in hand, as the line between politics and personal lives in the eighteenth century was at all times thinly drawn. Contemporary **literature**, both plays and novels, did not ignore the pervasive and popular gossip features promulgated by *Town and Country Magazine*. In his play *School for Scandal*, the playwright Richard Brinsley Sheridan has his character Snake rightly say of Mrs. Clackit, "Nay, I have more than once traced her causing a Tete-a-Tete in the *Town and Country Magazine*, when the Parties, perhaps, had never seen each other's Faces before in the course of their Lives." Sheridan, who was part of the Prince Regent's inner circle, knew more than most of whereof he spoke.

All strata of society participated in the laying out of the age's dirty linen. Aided by the advent of print media like newspapers and magazines, no one had—nor could find—a place to hide. Gossip and scandal were the order of the day, and it was lapped up eagerly. *See also* Actors; Gossip, Seventeenth-Century America; Royal Mistresses; Theater.

Further Reading: Wilkes, Roger. *Scandal, A Scurrilous History of Gossip*. London: Atlantic Books, 2002.

Jo Manning

GOSSIP, SEVENTEENTH-CENTURY AMERICA. Gossip served an important function in the seventeenth-century British American colonies. The steady chatter of women and men about their neighbors kept people informed about one another, their activities, and their misbehavior. For women, whose access to magistrates and courts were limited, and especially for married women, who could not take independent legal action, gossip was one way of exerting some control or revenge. However, men also gossiped and were the targets of gossip.

Negative rumors could affect a man's business affairs by presenting him as someone who was untrustworthy or who engaged in unscrupulous practices. A bad reputation could cause a man to lose status, as well as profits. Deals were often made with oral agreements, making it necessary for the parties involved to trust each other. "Rogues" or "knaves" were common insults used for men, both terms meaning someone who was dishonest or deceitful.

The slanderous terms that most concerned women alluded to their sexual behavior. The most common insults hurled at women were "whore," "slut," or similar terms, and most often these insults were made by other women. A good reputation for a woman was just as essential as it was for a man in order for her to live in the community, and rumors suggesting sexual misbehavior or loose morals could follow a woman for years, sometimes even across the Atlantic.

Gossip served, too, as a sort of informal policing method. With these informal networks, women could gain some influence over other women—and men—and align themselves within a community of women. On occasion, disputes between women grew into larger community disagreements, fueled by the women's gossip network. The remarks made by women could upset the social order at times, as even powerful men were gossiped about.

Gossip also came to the attention of justices and church leaders, and when the rumors and allegations involved criminal behavior, which included among other things, **fornication**, **sodomy**, and **adultery**, these authorities felt it necessary to investigate. As a result, some people were prosecuted, tried, and punished as a result of their "ill fame," and witnesses before the bar might repeat the gossip they had heard, rather than report events that they had actually observed.

Although charges of immorality were taken very seriously in the seventeenth century, an accusation of witchcraft was even more serious. **Witches** also were usually accused of dissolute or depraved sexual practices, such as consorting with the Devil and animal familiars, as well as enticing formerly respectable citizens into erotic encounters. Because of this, it was believed that witches could destroy marriages and families, and by extension, destroy the very structure of society, as well as turn God against the community. Those accused of being witches were generally married women who were at odds with their neighbors and already a source of gossip, sometimes because they had overstepped their bounds as submissive, quiet wives.

However, women did hold some power within the courts, as they were called upon to examine the bodies of women who were accused of witchcraft or of having given birth illicitly. Because men were excluded from some events, such as **childbirth**, midwives and other women attending births were the only ones who could testify as to what was said there—for example, if a woman named the father of her child—or what the women had seen. In fact, near the end of the sixteenth century, women who gathered together at births became known as "gossips." The importance of women's testimony can be seen in several court cases of the era. One important case began when Mary Dyer, a supporter of the religious dissenter, Anne Hutchinson, gave birth in October 1637 to a stillborn child who was grossly deformed. Following the occurrence, the women's gossip network whispered to one another about the "monstrous birth." Male authorities, however, did not hear about the birth until several months later, and then only by chance. The issue of monstrous births later assumed enormous importance in the Massachusetts Bay Colony, as Puritan leaders believed them to be a physical sign of how people were straying from Puritan religious doctrine. *See also* Bastardy; Gossip, Eighteenth-Century England; Midwives and Physicians; Newspapers; Witches and Witch Trials.

Further Reading: Brown, Kathleen M. *Good Wives, Nasty Wenches & Anxious Patriarchs: Gender, Race, and Power in Colonial Virginia*. Chapel Hill: University of North Carolina Press, 1996; Norton, Mary Beth. *Founding Mothers & Fathers: Gendered Power and the Forming of American Society*. New York: Vintage Books, 1996.

Merril D. Smith

GUADALUPE, VIRGIN OF.   *See* Virgin of Guadalupe

GYNECOLOGY MANUALS.   The number of treatises discussing women's anatomy, sexuality, and fertility increased in Europe and North America during the early modern period. Drawing on ancient texts such as Soranus's *Gynecology*, and the medieval writings of Trotula, early modern writers described the structure of the genitals, offered advice about how to determine whether a woman was a virgin or not, and noted various illnesses associated with **menstruation**, **pregnancy**, and **childbirth**. The audience for this kind of information extended far beyond official medical circles to include female healers, laypeople of both sexes, and readers simply in search of a sex manual. Modern scholars continue to be fascinated by the publications, gleaning from them historical understandings of gender, health, sexuality, and the female **body**. It is difficult to determine, however, the extent to which gynecology manuals reflect everyday beliefs in the past. Most books were written by male physicians and surgeons, proffering a specifically medical and masculine comprehension of the female body. Though a few texts were penned by female midwives, the books typically lack a female point of view. Moreover, these publications proliferated precisely when male practitioners were becoming more active in gynecological and obstetrical activities, long the exclusive domain of female midwives. For the most part, scholars consider gynecology manuals part of male efforts to professionalize and legitimate their practices by claiming a specialized knowledge of the female body.

Many books, even some written by female authors, portray the female body as inferior to the male body. This approach is in keeping with the dominant humoral theory, which understood bodies to be constituted by four humors or fluids (yellow bile, blood, phlegm, and black bile). Men were considered replete with blood and yellow bile, embodying the healthy qualities of hotness and dryness. Women, on the other hand, tended to be naturally phlegmatic, and consequently colder and more prone to disease. Instead of "burning" up excess blood like men, women menstruated to rid themselves of malevolent humors. Though menstruation was a sign of female inferiority, it was also crucial to women's health. A woman who was hotter than her female counterparts was not necessarily healthier, for she would likely not menstruate and therefore be infertile. Her dry uterus could also compress her heart in its upward search for moister organs, though it might not wander throughout her body at will—theories about the actual movement of the womb varied. Gynecological texts described cures for such unruly wombs, including sexual activity. A penis anointed with scented almond oil could both moisten the womb and lure it downward.

According to some feminist scholars, gynecology manuals were part of a broader effort by male medical practitioners to render the female body visible, knowable, and manageable. Many books contain visual images as well as written descriptions of the female body, portraying the reproductive organs, and sometimes even the external genitalia. This revelation of the female body was linked with power, according to Lynne Tatlock, for example, who contends that once women's bodies were exposed to invasive observation, they became objects of masculine medical knowledge. Yet even as men were clearly attempting to expand their practices, they were normally prohibited from looking at the exposed female body throughout the early modern period. Female clients were covered with linens, requiring men to work with their hands rather than their eyes. The images in gynecology manuals thus simultaneously compensated for the limited nature of men's scrutiny of the female body and revealed the male desire for unimpeded visual access. At the same time, numerous case studies in gynecology manuals indicate that women who invited male practitioners to their homes were not merely objects on display. They looked back at the men, appraising their appearance, clothing, facial expressions, and manual activities for signs of competence.

Gynecology manuals offer complex representations of the female body. These important historical sources shaped understandings of feminine sexuality, portraying women as not only passive and prone to illness, but also potentially resistant to male authority. *See also* Ejaculation; Hysteria; Medicine and Science; Midwives and Physicians; Orgasm.

Further Reading: Green, Monica H., ed. and trans. *The Trotula: A Medieval Compendium of Women's Medicine*. Philadelphia: University of Pennsylvania Press, 2001; King, Helen. *Hippocrates' Woman: Reading the Female Body in Ancient Greece*. London: Routledge, 1998; McTavish, Lianne. *Childbirth and the Display of Authority in Early Modern France*. Aldershot: Ashgate, 2005; Soranus. *Gynecology*. Translated and introduced by Owsei Temkin. Baltimore: Johns Hopkins University Press, 1956; Tatlock, Lynne. "Speculum Feminarum: Gendered Perspectives on Obstetrics and Gynecology in Early Modern Germany." *Signs* 17, no. 4 (1992): 725–60.

Lianne McTavish

H

HAREMS. The term *harem* signifies a section of a palace inhabited by the usually many women of one powerful man. Although the term itself which comes from Arabic is normally associated with the traditions of the Arab world, harems have been a historically universal fact. Anthropologists agree that polygamy was practiced throughout history in over 80 percent of human cultures, and even during and after the seventeenth and eighteenth centuries, harems were found in parts of what is considered the Western world. Because they served as an ultimate power symbol and guaranteed exclusive rights to polygamous carnal pleasures, harems could not but figure prominently in the ambitions of men in the many countries where they continued to exist.

In the seventeenth and eighteenth centuries, the harem was an essential part of the culture and law system of the **Ottoman empire**. The Turkish sultans kept huge and expensive harems housing hundreds of **concubines**, or odalisques, some of whom they chose to marry, the others remaining for the sultan's sexual convenience. Most of the women were slaves from the conquered territories in Asia, Africa, and Europe, but many were also sold by their impoverished parents or were encouraged to join a harem willingly, and thus secure a life of luxury. The sultan's odalisques were generously remunerated, with their daily rank-based allowances ranging from a few to a few thousand *aspers*, amounts sufficient to buy costly furs and jewels.

A harem was also staffed by **eunuchs**—males castrated for the purpose of reliably guarding their master's women, and thus vouching for his **paternity** of the children born there. **Castration** would generally take two forms. Although a male could be deprived of both his penis and testicles, in most cases only the testicles were removed. It was commonly assumed that a castrated male was incapable of and uninterested in copulating with the women of a harem, a view almost certainly mistaken, given reports that odalisques often preferred intercourse with a eunuch, as his erection was not limited in time by **ejaculation**. The sultan's false sense of exclusivity was further belied by the fact that, through daily contact and mutual massaging, the odalisques often became secret lovers.

The harem and its inhabitants had no small influence on the political fate of the Ottoman empire. Historians agree that its allure contributed to the downfall of the state. After a period of greatness, the empire's sultans gradually abandoned their responsibilities and retired to the comforts of the harem, leaving some of their decision-making powers to viziers, their high state officials. Moreover, in the power struggle, many princes with ascension prospects were on purpose confined to and raised in harems, where they obtained little else than carnal knowledge, and were most often denied the knowledge of state affairs. Inexperienced, they were either easily sidelined or came under the influence of their harem concubines, whose expertise on state matters they valued over that of seasoned advisers. The women of the royal harem had extraordinary political power in an era known as "The Sultanate of Women," which spanned throughout the sixteenth and seventeenth centuries, a period marked by political instability and a gradual decline of the empire.

The Ottoman harems are the best-documented examples of harems of the seventeenth and eighteenth centuries, but harems existed in many other societies at the time and afterward. The Keeling Islands, located Northwest of Australia, settled by the English adventurer Alexander Hare became home to his magnificent Malay harem. Another famous example is the nineteenth-century Mormon traditional harem-like household characterized by polygamy, which was later outlawed by the American government. Especially common were the harems of the Arab world, whose rulers were also among the most fertile. The Sultan of Morocco called Moulay Ismail the Bloodthirsty (1672–1727) is said to have sired 888 children with his harem women. Apart from their obvious procreative aspects, the Arab harems had special status for one more reason. Because **dance** in public is prohibited in most Muslim societies, the harem was one place where traditional dances could be performed.

Toward the end of the nineteenth century, harems were being abolished in most places in the world, or they disappeared, along with their "host" societies. Such was the case of the South American *Cumanagoto* culture, whose chiefs were entitled to many wives living in harem-like formations. Due to the Spanish domination, the group gradually lost its language, identity, and customs, including that of polygamy. *See also* Islam; Marriage; Polyandry.

Further Reading: Croutier, Alev Lytle. *Harem: The World behind the Veil.* New York: Abbeville Press, 1989.

Konrad Szczesniak

HERMAPHRODITES.   The term "hermaphrodite" has been replaced in medical and lay contexts by the term "intersex" since the 1990s. "Hermaphrodite" had always been a problematic word conjuring a mythical creature, for the early modern definition of a hermaphrodite was a person born with a perfect set of both male and female genital organs. Because this designation required two "perfect" sets of genitalia, no one who fit this definition was ever found. This led some early medical authorities to believe that hermaphrodites did not exist in the human species. Earthworms, snails, and some reptiles could be hermaphrodites, these experts argued, but not humans. Nevertheless, some people were born with ambiguous genitalia that allowed them flexibility in living variously as male and female. Although their bodies did not fit the criteria exactly, these individuals were sometimes considered hermaphrodites.

Before "hermaphroditism" became a medical condition inevitably necessitating medical intervention, early medical, legal, and religious authorities had opinions on how people with atypical genitalia should be regarded. There were a range of responses to "hermaphrodites," including a conception of the bodily expression of a "monstrous" birth, signaling the parents' sinful nature, to a worry that hermaphrodites were really women with enlarged clitorises, potentially able to copulate with other women. Even if true hermaphrodites did not exist according to medical authorities, the idea of *one* body exhibiting *two* sexes, able to couple with either sex, raised a host of anxieties about gender and sex.

In early America, doctors neither had the social status nor the medical knowledge that they would come to acquire in the nineteenth century, and laypeople typically managed illness and disease without professional help. Because most people tended to their own health needs, extensive medical records are not available for this era. Consequently, historians are left with a comparative dearth of such sources from this period. Later, in the nineteenth century, as doctors professionalized, they wrote journal articles about various conditions their patients endured, including atypical genital anatomies, and so, since the early 1800s, historians have had rich medical material to interpret. Some American **midwives and physicians** read European medical manuals, and their understanding of various conditions was no doubt influenced by a European intellectual tradition going back for centuries. The handful of early American authors who wrote their own books cited these European writers, whether or not they agreed with their ideas or not. Early American readers, we know, also read European and British treatises; in fact, some of these books, like Jane Sharp's *The Midwives Book: or the Whole Art of Midwifery Discovered* and Nicholas Culpeper's *The Compleat Practice of Physick*, became quite popular in the colonies. Fortunately, medical treatises are not the only available sources to mine. At least in New England, sermonic literature reflecting the religious interpretation of illness and disability exists, and throughout the colonies there were legal records, which sometimes involved charges of impotency related to what we now see as intersex conditions. In addition, there are **newspapers** and literary sources, such as Alexander Hamilton's *Itinerarium*, that can offer clues as to how colonists understood "hermaphrodites" in an era before "hermaphroditism" was considered a medical condition requiring treatment.

The first case of ambiguous sex that has been found in early American sources concerned an adult, Thomas/Thomasine Hall, who came to the attention of the Virginia court in 1629 for dressing in women's apparel. During the course of the investigation into the matter, it became clear that Hall had lived some years as male and some years as female, and that his or her genitals were sufficiently ambiguous so that authorities could not determine a permanent gender category. Ultimately, the court ordered an unusual and paradoxical punishment, mandating a costume that incorporated both male and female clothing, thus marking Hall as an indeterminate being, neither male nor female. Hall's case was unique; the more typical response encouraged the choosing of one sex only.

Early European treatises had emphasized the legal regulations, including laws of **marriage**, which should be applied to hermaphrodites. Using both Jewish Talmudic law and ancient Latin canon and civil law as guides, eighteenth-century medical manuals typically addressed the legal issues that hermaphrodites or their parents might have faced, all of which required that a hermaphrodite or guardian choose one sex. For example, James Parsons's 1741 English treatise, *A Mechanical Inquiry into the Nature of Hermaphrodites*, outlined the standard regulations in great detail. Despite his contention that hermaphrodites did not exist in the human species, Parsons nevertheless listed each possible legal question, from whether a hermaphrodite should be given a male or female name at birth to whether a hermaphrodite should be allowed to marry or **divorce** or not. The answers to most questions required that hermaphrodites or their parents select and maintain one sex. Later in the nineteenth century, when doctors professionalized, they assumed the authority of deciding the sex of people with ambiguous genitals, sometimes even suggesting that their patients had been mistaken in their own assessments and urging them to switch genders. By contrast, in early America, though people were strongly urged to choose one sex and stick to it, this vital

HINDUISM

decision was left to the patient. *See also* Cross-Dressing; Gender Roles; Gynecology Manuals; Impotence; Laws; Medicine and Science.

Further Reading: Brown, Kathleen. "'Changed ... into the Fashion of Man': The Politics of Sexual Difference in a Seventeenth-Century Anglo-American Settlement." *Journal of the History of Sexuality* 6 (1995): 171–93; Dreger, Alice Domurat. *Hermaphrodites and the Medical Invention of Sex*. Cambridge, MA: Harvard University Press, 1998; Fausto-Sterling, Anne. *Sexing the Body: Gender Politics and the Construction of Sexuality*. New York: Basic Books, 2000; Kessler, Suzanne J. *Lessons from the Intersexed*. New Brunswick, NJ: Rutgers University Press, 1998; Laqueur, Thomas. *Making Sex: Body and Gender from the Greeks to Freud*. Cambridge, MA: Harvard University Press, 1990; Norton, Mary Beth. *Founding Mothers and Fathers: Gendered Power and the Forming of American Society*. New York: Alfred A. Knopf, 1996, 183–97; Reis, Elizabeth. "Impossible Hermaphrodites: Intersex in America, 1620–1960." *Journal of American History* 92 (2) (September 2005): 411–41.

Elizabeth Reis

HINDUISM. One of the oldest religions of humankind, Hinduism has accommodated various contradictions in its fold. Sex and sexuality is permissible, but not lust and deviant behavior. On the one hand, it glorifies women to the highest pedestal, but on the other hand, many of its proponents relegate the female gender to a marginalized space. In the seventeenth and eighteenth centuries, it was witnessing an already entrenched **Islam** and the coming of Christianity along with the European colonial powers.

Hinduism has revolved round the *varnashramadharma* (four stages of life) and *purushartha* (four goals of life) since time immemorial. Ideal stages of life pass through four phases: *bramacharya* (**celibacy**), *grihasthya* (household life), *vanaprastha* (hermit), and *sanyasa* (ascetic). The philosophical speculation of Hinduism sets the agenda for *moksha* (liberation or enlightenment) from this *samsara* (mundane world/phenomenal existence), which is superior to the other three: *dharma* (duty/moral harmony), *artha* (wealth/fame), and *kama* (sensual/emotional pleasure). It is the life of a householder and the goal of sensual or emotional pleasure that sets the norm of sex and sexuality in Hinduism. According to the Hindu *dharma sastras*, the three prescribed functions of marriages are: *prajaa* (progeny for family or generativity), *dharma* (meeting religious goals), and *rati* (sensual and emotional pleasure). The desire to be with the opposite sex is but natural. The sexual union between married people for the purpose of procreation is the ideal norm. Kama is an eternal force physically uniting two people. Love may be also on a romantic or platonic level.

In Hinduism, Kama is the god of love with wings, bow, and flower-decked arrow. His wife, Rati, is represented not as a passionate woman, but as a mental stage of love. An open display of passion, love, and sexuality is hallmark of Hinduism, along with its erotic icons on the temples and in texts like the *Kama Sutra*. It explores sex, and at the same time controls it. Sexuality is energy to be channeled not toward **adultery**, intense passion, and debauchery, but should be practiced within the norms of a society and under a sanctified **marriage** system. There would be societal harmony and a balanced life for an individual. Like any other **religion**, this ideal frame of reference is not adhered to always, and human nature overcomes limitations of religious sanctions, as there are differences

Erotic scene of lovemaking from an 18th century Indian manuscript of the *Kama Sutra*. © The Art Archive/JFB.

between the theory and practice of religion, both in the seventeenth and eighteenth centuries and today.

Although sexual union with a prostitute was regarded as *adharma* (antireligion), red-light areas were prevalent in the urban centers of North and South India. The *devadasis* (temple dancers) were wedded to God, but examples are not wanting, where there was immorality and debauchery. But for most Hindu women, sexuality was suppressed with veiling of the face and limits on public appearances. Its role was marginalized in the rigid doctrinaire approach of Hinduism in a patriarchal society. Strict adherence to religion resulted in remaining chaste, observing fasting for the good of the spouse after marriage and confining themselves to the *antapura* (secluded atmosphere of the house). Restrictions were severe for the high-status families. Women belonging to the have-not groups did the manual work outside the home. In many ways, a woman was to be an *asuryampasya* (confined in a dark corner, where there is not even a ray of sunshine). In addition, certain abominable practices entered into the fold of Hinduism like **infanticide**, child marriage, polygamy, and the burning of widows at the funeral pyre, but these were not of a universal nature.

In the domain of **literature**, the position of women was not within the parameter of Hinduism. The poetry espousing the passionate love between Krishna and Radha and erotic poetry in vernacular languages celebrated the *parakiya priti* (love outside marriage). A woman was portrayed as a person having her own emotional and sexual longing to be united with her beloved. There were also instances of the third sex or hijras indulging in homoeroticism. They were tolerated at the auspicious functions of marriage and the birth of a baby. The transgendered and castrated man, donning the apparel of a woman was a part of Hindu society in spite of religious sanctions. Same-sex love among women was less frequently portrayed.

Hinduism tries to build a harmonious society with its prescribed agenda, as per the religious texts. In spite of retrogressive ideas that crept into it, it tries to adapt to the phenomenon of sex and sexuality in a continuous process. *See also* Berdache; India; Polyandry; Romantic Love; Taj Mahal; Widows and Widowhood.

Further Reading: Ballhatchet, Kenneth. *Race, Sex and Class under the Raj: Imperial Attitudes and Policies and Their Critics, 1793–1905*. London: Weidenfeld & Nicholson, 1980; Basham, A. L. *The Wonder That Was India*. Reprint ed. Calcutta: Rupa, 1992; Kakar, Sudhir. *Intimate Relations, Exploring Indian Sexuality*. Chicago: University of Chicago Press, 1990; Meena, Khandelwal. *Women in Ochre Robes: Gendering Hindu Renunciation*. New York: State University of New York Press, 2003; Mitter, Sara. *Dharma's Daughters: Contemporary Indian Women and Hindu Culture*. Piscataway, NJ: Rutgers University Press, 1991; Nanda, Serena. *Neither Man nor Woman: The Hijras of India*. Belmont, CA: Wadsworth Publishing, 1990; Teltscher, Kate. *India Inscribed, European and British Writing on India 1600–1800*. New Delhi: Oxford University Press, 1997; Vanita, Ruth, and Saleem Kidwai, eds. *Same-Sex Love in India: Readings from Literature and History*. New York: St. Martin's Press, 2000.

Patit Paban Mishra

HOGARTH, WILLIAM (1697–1764). William Hogarth was a British painter, engraver, and social commentator. Born on November 10, 1697, in London, Hogarth was the eldest child of Richard and Anne Gibbons Hogarth. A schoolmaster and printer, Richard Hogarth was imprisoned for debt after the failure of his coffeehouse, spending 1708–1712 in the Fleet prison, a family experience his son remembered vividly in his later works. Hogarth became an apprentice silversmith, moving over to engraving after enrolling in drawing school. His first successful prints were a series of illustrations to Samuel Butler's *Hudibras* (1726), followed by the popular plates for John

"Marriage à la mode—the toilette," by William Hogarth, 1745. Courtesy of the Library of Congress.

Gay's subversive *Beggar's Opera* (1728), which played up the rowdy, sexualized plot of highwaymen, whores, and corruption.

After marrying Jane Thornhill in 1729, Hogarth was introduced to the circle of Whig politicians and wealthy patrons surrounding her father, James Thornhill, who was a member of Parliament (MP) and a painter. Although Hogarth accepted commissions for stately portraits of powerful Whigs like Mary Edwards and Benjamin Hoadley, the Bishop of Winchester, his most profitable works were engravings of London's underside. He illustrated George Oglethorpe's report to the House of Commons on the sorry state of the Fleet prison, a filthy holding pen overrun with prostitutes, debtors, and thieves. Hogarth's most famous engravings were detailed, sexually frank, and cynical attacks on city morality, beginning with *The Harlot's Progress* (1732), in which Molly Hackabout, a country girl, finds her ambitions as an actress subverted into prostitution and death by syphilis. *The Rake's Progress* (1734) tells the parallel story of Tom Rakewell, a middle-class man whose grandiose behavior leads him to marry a grotesque heiress for her money, become ensnared by gambling and whores, and eventually succumb to madness in Bedlam.

In 1735, Parliament passed an Act protecting the works of engravers from copyright violation by their publishers and imitators, a law generally believed to have been made to protect Hogarth's increasingly coveted and collected works. In 1743, he produced his masterpiece satirizing the behavior of the British ruling class, *Marriage a la Mode*, in which an earl's son and a merchant's daughter marry by family arrangement and self-destruct, the noble through sexual excess, drinking, and dueling, his parvenu wife through **adultery** and the poor advice of society flunkies. Hogarth also supported the unpopular 1751 Gin Act with a series of prints, *Beer Street and Gin Lane*, exposing the crude lives of London's underclass with vivid scenes of women neglecting or selling their children for gin; lives ruined through prostitution and thievery, and pathetic deaths through starvation and disease.

Hogarth, who had been most associated with Whigs in the patronage of former Prime Minister Robert Walpole, was increasingly sidelined by a new generation of politicians and their propagandists, most significantly William Pitt the Elder and John Wilkes. Wilkes skewered Hogarth for supporting George III's first Prime Minister, the Earl of Bute, in his paper, the *North Briton*, and effectively pushed him from the center of politics. On October 26, 1764, Hogarth died at his home in Leicester Fields, London. *See also* Alcohol; Art, American/European; Molly Houses; Prostitutes and Prostitution; Venereal Diseases.

Further Reading: Lindsay, Jack. *Hogarth: His Art and His World*. New York: Taplinger Publishing, 1979; Paulson, Ronald. *Hogarth: His Life, Art and Times*. New Haven, CT: Yale University Press, 1971; Uglow, Jennifer. *Hogarth: A Life and a World*. New York: Ferrar, Straus and Giroux, 1997.

Margaret Sankey

HOMOSEXUALITY.   A product of the transforming definition of sex, the social status of homosexuality was in a state of epistemic shift in the seventeenth and eighteenth centuries. From antiquity to the Enlightenment, sex was assumed to be a cultural rather than an *a priori* category. Namely, it was assumed that there was a single axis of sex upon which both genders were situated. Since the Enlightenment, however, metaphysical claims ushered in the two-sex model, which was strategically cohesive to the emerging values stemming from classical liberalism and modern science. The most significant notion of this new model was "the triumph of complimentarity" (Schiebinger 214). That is, males and females were conceived to be ontologically different, yet when their gendered roles were juxtaposed against one another they were understood as being complimentary. Within this paradigm the institutionalized patriarchal **marriage** was deemed the ideal union for intimate relationships. To ensure the primacy of these unions, there was a stringent conflation of biological sex and cultural gender; thus, males have a natural sexual predilection toward females, and similarly females have a natural sexual predilection for males. Sexual relations with members of the same sex were accordingly rendered as being aberrations, and duly ostracized. Thus, in this discursive purview, heterosexuality was normalized as to guarantee its dominance, while homosexuality was relegated to the periphery of social mores.

This period which reconceptualized sex and reified heteronormativity affected homosexuals and homosexual experiences in very tangible ways. The Buggery Act (1533)—which was the first decree against homosexuals enacted in any Germanic country—alongside other antisodomy laws ratified thereafter, collectively established a pejorative environment for homosexual activity. **Sodomy** in this orthodox context was considered one of those *deviant* sexual practices because it does not culminate in procreation. The legal ramifications against same-sex relations resulted in more state prosecution of homosexuals during the seventeenth and eighteenth centuries than had been ever seen before. Moreover, with the intensifying role of the Catholic Church over sexual governance, sodomy was constructed to be both a crime against **religion** and society. Consequently, men were increasingly required to publicly pronounce their heterosexuality, whilst adolescent boys were socialized into an ideology of reverent homophobia.

The codification of homophobic sentiments into public policy coupled with the rise of groups whose sole mission was the rectification of puritanical morality, compelled men to carry out homosexual activities in progressively more circumspect venues. A popular example of this, at least in England, were **molly houses**—places, usually taverns or private homes, where men seeking homosexual sex or transgression from conventional masculinity could meet others who sought the same. Partly because of the harrying cast against their body politic, molly houses became the first modern sites in which the gay subculture cultivated a sense of community, though they did not operate without violent harassment. Agents of antisodomite groups were recruited to surveil and identify locations at which homosexuals gathered. In 1726, for example, the information accumulated by the agents of the Societies for Reformation of Manners led to numerous raids, the most infamous of which being Margaret Clap's molly house. From here over forty people were arrested and tried, of which several were convicted under antisodomy laws and subsequently hanged. Similar methods of persecution were invoked by other Western countries in their efforts to purge homosexuality.

The contemptuous treatment for homosexuality that was ensconced in Judeo-Christian states was affixed, perhaps most problematically, to the ethos of Western imperialism, a phenomenon that had been congealed by the mid-1700s. A plethora of anthropological evidence suggests that many precolonial indigenous traditions sanctioned homosexual expression, and did not strenuously demarcate such activities from what was conservatively regarded, by the imperialists, to be strictly heterosexual. Thus, these indigenous cultures often assumed that both same- and opposite-sex relations contributed to an individual's holistic sexual experience. The missionary movement, which was a segment of the social dimension of imperialism, either assimilated or associated colonized subjects into Christianity. Incidentally, homosexual practices were demonized, and its etiology was depicted to be rooted in imprudent, primitive culture. In the process, indigenous peoples came to negate homosexuality and embody a sexual template that closely reflected that of their Western colonizers. Indeed, much of the homophobia that has been apparent in the developing world is the noxious legacy of imperialism.

During this era, the vernacular of social and legal debates effectively reframed how sexual practices were to be understood. Prior to the Enlightenment, homosexual activity was interpreted in terms of isolated acts. By the end of the eighteenth century, however, for a man to partake in same-sex relations imposed upon him an overarching homosexual identity—an identity which was the very invention of the hegemonic discourses of the day and had not been delineated prior. This was certainly part of a broader social project that endeavored to bolster the mandate for sex complimentarity. In short, the fluidity in sexual behavior that had existed hitherto was, in this period, superseded by the essentialist heterosexual/homosexual dichotomy. The nuances between these two binary sites were likewise silenced. What ought to be underscored is that the marginalization of homosexuality was functional to the epistemological transitions of the time, which dogmatically claimed opposite-sex coupling to be natural and thereby labeled all other sexual behavior as aberrations. From this premise, the seventeenth and eighteenth centuries can be interpreted as the epochs in which compulsory heterosexuality gained supremacy yet at the detriment of homosexual experiences. *See also* Anal Intercourse; Berdache; Cross-Dressing; Masculinity; Native Americans; Prostitutes and Prostitution.

Further Reading: Bray, Alan. *Homosexuality in Renaissance England.* New York: Columbia University Press, 1982; Hird, Myra J. *Sex, Gender and Science.* New York: Palgrave Macmillan,

2004; Norton, Rictor. *Mother Clap's Molly House: The Gay Subculture in England, 1700–1830*. London: Gay Men's Press, 1992; Schiebinger, Londa. *The Mind Has No Sex? Women in the Origins of Modern Science*. Cambridge, MA: Harvard University Press, 1989; Talley, Colin L. "Gender and Male Same-Sex Erotic Behavior in British North America in the Seventeenth Century." *Journal of the History of Sexuality* 6, no. 3 (1996): 385–408.

Ajnesh Prasad

HOUSEHOLD CONSUMERISM. In recent decades, historians have dispelled the myth of the self-sufficient colonial household whose members grew and produced all the goods they needed to survive. Instead, scholars now recognize that households in British North America engaged in increasing rates of consumer spending to obtain goods throughout the seventeenth and eighteenth centuries. Falling prices and the manufacture of cheaper quality goods made it possible for Americans across the economic spectrum to make purchases for personal and household use. Motivated by their desire to make life easier and more comfortable, as well as their desire to emulate their social betters, colonial and revolutionary–era Americans eagerly participated in the consumer marketplace. Especially after the middle of the eighteenth century, merchants offered for sale both an increased number and greater variety of commodities: cloth, ceramic tableware, cutlery, hats, ribbons, glassware, accouterments for serving tea, jewelry, books, wine, spices, chocolate, sugar, and other groceries were some of the items which colonial and revolutionary–era Americans could choose to purchase. This proliferation of goods opened a world of consumer choice to the residents of British North America, and their actions in the consumer marketplace had significant implications for American culture, the household economy, and household gender relations. In particular, women's increased access to consumer goods held the potential to threaten male household authority, authority that most colonial and revolutionary–era Americans believed was necessary to restrain women's "natural" disorderliness, sinfulness, and sexuality.

Anglo Americans both embraced and feared the new consumer possibilities. While consumer goods held the promise to enrich life, excessive consumption threatened to overturn established class and gender hierarchies. Throughout the colonial era, elites distinguished themselves and solidified their leading position in society by acquiring and displaying consumer goods. Expensive consumer goods were visible marks of social status and authority. However, as the prices of goods fell and as cheaper imitations of expensive commodities became more widely available, the middling and even lower classes were able to purchase goods that had defined elite status. Fearing this threat to their social position, elites throughout British North America passed sumptuary laws that regulated the clothing of the various social classes. By reserving the finest fabrics and most fashionable styles for themselves, colonial elites hoped to preserve their visible social superiority to their countrymen and uphold the established social order. The expanding consumer market doomed the sumptuary laws to failure, however, and colonial elites instead developed complex codes of behavior that were less easily imitated than were styles of dress to distinguish themselves and maintain their social position.

Increased participation in the consumer market also profoundly affected gender hierarchies. Consumption altered the gendered division of labor within British North American households, the vast majority of which engaged in agricultural production. Never a rigid system that completely precluded men and women from performing certain tasks, this gendered labor arrangement nevertheless assigned men and women work roles supposedly suited to their different abilities and natures. Men were responsible for the fieldwork: they planted, tended, harvested, and marketed crops; they cared for livestock; they cut firewood; they maintained and repaired tools, fences, and buildings. Women's duties included bearing and caring for children, food production and meal preparation, and depending on family resources and access to markets, the production of a vast array of items necessary for household survival including clothing, bedding, other household linens, soap, and candles. Legally, the male household head owned the products of his wives' and daughters' labors. He was also legally entitled to sexual access to his wife. This "ownership" of his female dependents' labor and of his wife's sexuality encumbered the male head of the household with the responsibility to provide economically for his female dependents and to control their sexuality within acceptable boundaries. Increased access to the consumer market, however, threatened male authority over both women's labor and women's sexuality.

Particularly after the middle of the eighteenth century, women increased the amount of market-oriented productive labor in which they engaged *and* increased their consumer spending, producing greater amounts of cheese and butter, for example, to finance purchases of cloth and tableware. Increased consumption changed households' relations with the market and had the potential to change relations between men and women. Accustomed to commanding the labor of their wives and daughters, male household heads did not necessarily welcome women's increased access to consumer commodities. Women's ability to purchase goods—and their ability to finance those purchases with the products of their own labors—could threaten men's economic authority over their female dependents. In addition, the associations that Anglo Americans drew between women's consumer activities and women's supposedly greater affinity for luxury, a concept freighted with sexual connotations, made male control of female sexuality problematic in a world of increasing consumer options.

Increased rates of consumer spending led to an outpouring of social commentary on household consumerism which revealed the often troubling connections colonial and revolutionary–era Americans made among consumption, the household economy, and women's position within the household. Women's ability to purchase goods appeared to threaten households' economic status as well as traditional patterns of male household authority. The excessive spending of wives and daughters could involve households in crippling amounts of debt, a circumstance that could threaten the economic independence of the male household head. Anglo Americans believed that women, by nature, were disorderly, weak, and more likely to give in to temptation. For these reasons, wives and daughters were subject to the authority of their husbands and fathers. According to these beliefs, women were more apt to succumb to the temptations presented by the increased availability of consumer goods. Husbands and fathers unable to control the spending habits of their female dependents exposed their households to possible economic ruin and the degradation associated with the pursuit of luxury and its attendant vices.

For Anglo Americans, luxury was associated with the sins of covetousness, envy, greed, sensuality, and lust, sins that threatened not only individuals but also the entire social fabric. In addition, colonial and revolutionary–era Americans believed that luxury was a peculiarly feminine vice, one with distinctly sexual overtones. In Western **literature** and **art**, luxury was portrayed as a sensual, lustful woman who commanded power through her sexuality and ability to arouse desire. Given these cultural associations, Anglo Americans posited the potentially corrupting influence of women's pursuit of luxury through excessive consumption against the orderly, prosperous household where male authority kept female luxury and sexuality under control. Essays critical of consumption also expressed fears that excessive consumer spending threatened to blur the lines that distinguished men and women from each other. When they defied their husbands and fathers by purchasing needless luxuries, women acted in a bold, assertive manner not in keeping with traditional gender prescriptions. Likewise, essayists feared that consumer finery and extravagance would create soft, effeminate men who would be unable to wield the authority necessary to maintain orderly, stable households. The pursuit of luxury through consumption, then, threatened to unleash forces that could disrupt economic prosperity, traditional gender distinctions, and gender hierarchies within the household.

In the last third of the eighteenth century, household consumerism became entangled in political tensions between the North American colonies and Great Britain. British taxes on consumer goods precipitated the crisis that eventually led to revolution and independence. Colonial Americans responded to British attempts to tax consumer goods with a variety of nonimportation and nonconsumption agreements. The dispute with Great Britain added new layers of meaning to Americans' consumer spending by tying consumer goods to an explicitly political agenda. Leaders of the protests against British taxes urged men and women to support the patriotic cause by refusing to buy British-manufactured goods. Patriots claimed that denying themselves consumer goods would enable colonists to reclaim their rights within the British empire, as well as to restore economic prosperity to individual households. As tensions with Great Britain grew, signing and adhering to nonconsumption agreements became important acts defining colonists' political allegiances.

By the end of the colonial period, household consumerism was freighted with a host of meanings regarding economic roles, gender relations, patriarchal authority, and political allegiance. As Americans declared and won their independence, they recognized that the consumer activities of ordinary men and women would play an important role in shaping the economic, political, and gender relations of the new nation. *See also* Gender Roles; Laws; Marriage; Masculinity; Women, Changing Images of.

Further Reading: Breen, T. H. *The Marketplace of Revolution: How Consumer Politics Shaped American Independence.* New York: Oxford University Press, 2004; Brewer, John, and Roy Porter, eds. *Consumption and the World of Goods.* New York: Routledge, 1993; Carson, Cary, Ronald Hoffman, and Peter J. Albert, eds. *Of Consuming Interests: The Style of Life in the Eighteenth Century.* Charlottesville: University Press of Virginia, 1994; Shammas, Carole. *The Pre-Industrial Consumer in England and America.* Oxford: Clarendon Press, 1990.

Mary Beth Sievens

HYSTERIA. Until relatively recently hysteria was perceived as an affliction regulating, to a certain extent, the emotional behavior of women, who were identified as the primary if not the only sufferers. The initial association of hysteria with women may be traced to the term itself, coined from the Greek word *hystera*, meaning "uterus." Ancient speculations of the uterus being the source and the primal site of the disease gave rise to a number of prominent theories reflected in the works of numerous seventeenth- and eighteenth-century physicians, clinicians, anatomists, and psychiatrists.

According to the classical definition, hysteria was blamed on the rising and falling of the uterus, traveling, so to speak, all over the female body. The disordered uterus was responsible for emanating vapors, which in turn, floating upward, resulted in producing various somatic manifestations of hysteria, mainly convulsive and paroxysmal in form. So convincing was the above explanation that in time "the vapors" in question began to serve as the term equivalent with the disease in its entirety. Not surprisingly also, to begin with, the treatment of hysteria was aimed at "convincing" the migrating uterus to return to its original place.

Though the uterus continued to be quoted as an occasional starting point of the disease by many seventeenth- and eighteenth-century physicians and physiologists, returning even in the most influential theories of such celebrated medical scientists as the English neurologist, William Cullen (1712–1790), or the Dutch physician, Gerhard van Swieten (1700–1772), soon it became obvious that the study of hysteria was to take a completely different route.

One of the pioneers of the new approach to the disease was a physiologist and neuroanatomist, Thomas Willis (1622–1675), who formulated the theory that hysteria, understood by him as a convulsive distemper, originated in and affected the brain. The identification of the cerebral origin of hysteria, in turn, allowed him to suggest that the affliction was not limited to women only, although, due to their weaker physical constitution, women were still believed to be predominant sufferers. The definite recognition of hysteria as the affliction of the mind, however, came with the work of the eminent English clinician, Thomas Sydenham (1624–1689), whose *Epistolary Dissertation* introduced a fresh approach to the debate.

Sydenham went beyond the earlier discussions of convulsive hysteria describing a number of other hysterical manifestations such as headaches, coughing, vomiting, stomachaches, stiffening of the muscles, pain in the back, or swelling of various body parts. He observed that the said physical disturbances were frequently accompanied by an upsetting of emotions, and that the lack of balance in the mind-body relationship was responsible for the disorders in that part of the body which was the weakest at the moment. Sydenham's belief that hysteria and hypochondriasis (the male-related form of hysteria) gave rise to "putrid humors" preventing blood purification led to the clinician's insistence of the treatment relying on fortifying and purifying the blood.

"Weak nerves" and "passions of the mind" were quoted as the cause of hysteria in the works of Giogrio Baglivi (1668–1706) and Robert Whytt (1714–1766), and the suggested treatment often included soothing and humoring the patient. According to Baglivi's *Practice of Physick*, since all "nervous diseases" were seen as deriving from emotional distress, disorder of emotions was considered not as much a symptom of hysteria, as its cause. Whytt's treatise *Nervous, Hypochondriac or Hysteric Disorders*, on the other hand, clarified the expression "nervous" as dependant on the "uncommon delicacy of nerves."

Even if women still remained to be seen as potential sufferers, it is interesting to notice that they were not the only ones. In 1733, a Scottish physician, George Cheyne (1671–1743) in his treatise *The English Malady or a Treatise of Nervous Disorders of All Kinds as Spleen, Vapours, Lowness of Spirits, Hypochondriachal and Hysterical Distempers* identified the said afflictions as characteristic of the English, attributing them to the complexity of modern civilization. Among the many factors which contributed to the weakening of the English nervous system Cheyne quoted the increasing import of foreign customs and substances (such as tea, coffee, chocolate, or snuff), lack of exercise, overeating, climate, lack of sunshine, and, last but not least, the development of London into a large urban center.

The end of the eighteenth century saw the recurrence of the classical uterine theories, strengthened occasionally by the expanding on the theme in the like of Cullen's revelations of ovaries being particularly affected by the disease. At the same time, however, Philippe Pinel (1745–1826), who was in charge of Salpêtrière from 1794, was already beginning to gather his detailed records and interviews with patients, for the first time treated as individuals, which were to form the research basis for many psychologists and psychiatrists to come. *See also* Food; Madness; Medicine and Science; Midwives and Physicians.

Further Reading: Gilman, Sander L., Helen King, Roy Porter, G. S. Rousseau, and Elaine Showalter. *Hysteria beyond Freud.* Berkeley: California University Press, 1993; Porter, Roy. *Mind-forg'd Manacles.* London: Penguin, 1990; Veith, Ilza. *Hysteria: The History of a Disease.* Northvale, NJ: Jason Aronson, 1993.

Katarzyna Ancuta

I

IMPLIED CONSENT. *See* Consent

IMPOTENCE. Although most attention centered on male impotence, **marriage** could also theoretically be annulled owing to female impotence in the early modern period. Impotence did not equal sterility, but rather a physical inaptitude on the part of the male to depose his seed in the female, and on the part of the female to receive the male member and seed. The topic of impotence raised anxieties concerning reproduction and the role of marriage. The ability not only to achieve an erection but also to ejaculate and to produce the right kind of seed was called into question, and the moral and legal ramifications of marriage for **hermaphrodites**, **eunuchs**, and castrati were hotly debated.

Various causes for male impotence were cited in seventeenth- and eighteenth-century Europe. Medical explanations blamed the lack of sufficient heat to produce an erection and **ejaculation**. Overwork, ill health, and fatigue, as well as excessive sexual activity, could deplete a man's vital heat and render him (temporarily) impotent. The Catholic and Protestant Churches cited lascivious behavior—prostitutes were not believed capable of conception for instance as their wombs were made too slippery through overuse. The abandonment of God was also seen as a cause of impotence as a form of divine punishment, and heretics were often symbolically castrated before execution. Witchcraft was a common explanation expressed as theft of the *membrum virile* by a witch or the presence of a witch tying a knot in a piece of cord (nouer l'aiguillette) during the marriage ceremony. In seventeenth- and eighteenth-century England the effects of coffee and tobacco on male reproductive health were discussed in periodicals such as the *Athenian Mercury*. In 1674 a *Women's Petition against Coffee* argued that coffee dried up the body's moisture and provided too much heat, inhibiting the production of semen and resulting in an epidemic of impotent men.

In many European cultures the aim of marriage was procreation, and the absence of children brought shame and dishonor on a couple. Men who failed to impregnate their wives and whose virility was doubtful were often mocked publicly in the form of charivari, rumors, neighborhood **gossip**, and in the case of royalty and the aristocracy, even pamphlets ridiculing their sexual dysfunction and subsequent lack of heirs. Such cases could also lead to judicial trials and petitions for annulling marriages. Up until 1677 impotence trials in France took place in ecclesiastical courts and involved a process known as trial by congress. Both parties were interrogated before proceeding to the intervention of medical experts. Women petitioners were obliged to bathe in order to ensure that they had not used astringents to procure the appearance of virginity.

Male and female genitalia were examined by surgeons, physicians, and midwives. The couple was then led to a chamber where they were required to perform the sexual act in front of the medical witnesses. Ecclesiastical judges would then rule on evidence of the woman's virginity or defloration and aptitude to receive the male member: the man's ability to produce and sustain an erection, and also on his capacity to ejaculate and the quality and appearance of the seed produced. Post-1677 this final test was reduced to proof of physical erection and ejaculation in the presence of four surgeons and physicians.

In sharp contrast, eunuchs played important social roles in many Eastern cultures. Although **castration** was forbidden in Islam, eunuchs from Byzantium and Africa were observed by Western travelers, such Johann Wild and Lady Mary Wortagu, guarding **harems**, acting as lady's servants in the Middle East, and guarding sacred sites in Mecca and Medina, including the prophet Mohammed's grave. In western Europe, it became popular in the seventeenth and eighteenth centuries to have vocal castrati at court and in church choirs. Usually Italian, these operatic singers and **theater actors** were found at the French court of Louis XIV, the Spanish courts of Philip V and Ferdinand VI, and also at the Vatican. In 1586 Pope Sixtus V had prohibited eunuchs from marrying and from any form of sexual relations. It was deemed that he who was incapable of intercourse could not enter the sacrament of marriage. However, a compilation of debates, *Eunuchi conjugium*, printed in 1685 in defense of the marriage of castrati Bartolomeo de Sorlisi to a noble Protestant of Saxony, raised various questions regarding the legal and ethical position of eunuchs according to the method of castration used (the severing of the spermatic cords, removal of the testicles or of all the sexual organs) and the extent of impotence. *See also* Divorce; Food; Opera; Puritans; Religion.

Further Reading: Darmon, Pierre. *Trial by Impotence: Virility and Marriage in Pre-Revolutionary France*. London: Hogarth, 1985; Scholz, Piotr O. *Eunuchs and Castrati. A Cultural History*. Princeton, NJ: Markus Weiner, 2000.

Cathy McClive

INCEST. Incest is a sexual relationship between closely related people, such as between a father and his daughter, but which relationships are deemed incestuous depend on the time, place, and society under discussion. In early modern Europe, incest was generally defined as an unlawful **marriage** made between individuals whose blood relationship was considered too close for marriage. Modern definitions of incest as **child rape** did not emerge until the mid-nineteenth century, and even then, authorities rarely pursued incest charges and often did not believe the stories of children who were the victims of **rape** by family members. However, the Puritan colonies in New England did consider incest to be grounds for **divorce**, and the New Haven colony made incest a capital offence, as well.

In contrast, among some native tribes, kin marriages were a general rule. The idea was to share wealth amongst a family, and yet to form alliances. By one marriage whole dynasties of peasant families were brought into relationship with each other. This careful sharing of wealth, and yet sharing it only in a semi-familial way, made tribes of South America draw up lists of cousins who were not only not incestuous partners, but were expected marriage partners. To avoid wealth merely being passed directly from father to son, or to stop the father keeping hold of his daughters, and thus maintaining his wealth, or finally, to stop humans from thinking only of their own offspring, incest rules were observed.

The same rule applied to distant and ancient tribes across the globe: marriageable partners for a male or female can be put into codes or tables which more or less specify who the partner will be. The basis for this is usually that the partner be part of the family, but not immediately so. Marriage completely outside the family may be forbidden. Prescribed partners could be detected. For example, in one tribe of the Himalayas, the double meaning of a name for a relative: "mother's brother's daughter" also meant, for this tribe, "sweetheart" or "preferred marriage partner." But, while this practice was common in some non-Christian societies, and took place as a rule, there was never any written or conscious evidence that it was a rule in England or the West in general.

Royal families were sometimes exempt from a society's laws against incest. For example, an Inca ruler maintained his purity by practicing incest. The Inca ruler could only marry another distant descendant of the Sun—that meant his sister. However, when incest was practiced amongst the common people, it was harshly punished. The **taboo** on incest is very cloudy. Some scholars think that it is a genetic inheritance, a behavior mechanism that increases genetic health in the product of sexual reproduction. The Western churches and the sensibility of people in general have interpreted the taboo on incest in various ways. The church justified the ban on incest on grounds that it was "unnatural," and that it was not God's intention. Along with **sodomy** and other "unnatural" acts, incest was believed to create ruinous progeny, or no progeny at all. However, the power and dominance that slaveholders in the southern colonies held over their black slaves, permitted some of them to ignore laws and nature, and to have sex with their daughters, the offspring of the slave women they had impregnated. *See also* Fornication; Pregnancy; Puritans; Religion; Slavery.

Further Reading: Brown, Kathleen M. *Good Wives, Nasty Wenches & Anxious Patriarchs: Gender, Race, and Power in Colonial Virginia*. Chapel Hill: University of North Carolina Press, 1996; Lévi-Strauss, Claude. *The Elementary Structures of Kinship*. Translated by J. H. Bell, J. R. von Sturmer, and R. Needham. London: Eyre and Spottiswoode, 1969.

Jason Powell and Merril D. Smith

INDENTURED SERVANTS.   An indentured servant was a person, male or female, who sold his or her labor for a fixed period of time, usually four to seven years, in British North America in the seventeenth and eighteenth centuries. The majority of indentured servants were English men who obtained passage to America by selling their time to a ship's captain, who, in return, sold them upon arrival to local planters as agricultural laborers. Some persons had their labor sold involuntarily: Scots prisoners of war, Irish men and women kidnapped for the purpose, convicts, paupers, **orphans**, and illegitimate children. Since their owners had a limited period of time in which to recoup their investments, working conditions were often exploitative. Female indentured servants faced additional risks in the form of **rape** by their masters or other servants and in having their terms of indentures increased for bearing illegitimate children. In the seventeenth century, most indentured servants shipped from London or Bristol to Virginia and the British West Indies. A smaller number of indentured servants went to New England, but the family labor system and the lack of a labor-intensive and profitable crop like **tobacco** in Virginia or sugar in the West Indies limited the demand for indentured servants. In the eighteenth century, Pennsylvania became a popular destination for indentured servants.

Indentured servants received food, clothing, and shelter in return for their labor. While they were unable to change masters, their masters could reassign them and collect any wages they made. Younger men who served as apprentices in Virginia fared even worse. Seven years of indentured servitude was followed by seven more years as a tenant, under which terms they received one-half of their wages for the second seven-year period. Since the length of time a master had to recoup his investment was limited by the number of years assigned in the indenture, indentured servants were often subjected to onerous working conditions. Upon completion of their indentures, servants received suits of clothing, perhaps a land grant, and the right to marry.

The majority of servants who signed indentures to secure passage to the New World were male. In New England, indentured servants tended to arrive as prisoners of war or to be free labor forced into indentured servitude by debt. In Massachusetts, a child could be indentured from the age of two, and this became the common fate of orphans and illegitimate children who, in the case of boys were indentured until twenty-one, girls till eighteen.

Since indentured servants were not allowed to marry, and since New England Puritans criminalized sexual intercourse between unmarried persons and persons who were not married to each other, illicit sexual intercourse, which manifested itself in the form of an illegitimate pregnancy, led to criminal conviction on a fornication charge. Punishment for fornication fell most heavily upon female indentured servants since, while pregnancy provided irrefutable evidence of a sexual misdemeanor, **paternity** was harder to prove. If their partner was free and could afford to purchase the time remaining on the female servant's indenture, pay dual fornication fines, perhaps endure a mutual public whipping, and face the community censure that followed a fornication conviction, there was the possibility of **marriage**. If a male indentured servant was found guilty of engaging in sexual intercourse, he was punished severely, since he was unable to marry or to provide financially for his child. Men who engaged in sexual intercourse while free to court were treated more leniently.

Female indentured servants in Massachusetts faced the sexual importunities of their employers and their employers' and neighbors' sons, and their fellow indentured servants. Not all these sex acts were consensual. Added to the power imbalance that prevailed between master and servant was the peculiar nature of seventeenth-century **rape law**. If a woman conceived during a rape, the act was assumed to be consensual, for it was believed that conception was not possible unless both parties had achieved **orgasm**.

What happened to the indentured servant who bore a child out of wedlock? Midwives were required to learn the name of the baby's father during childbirth. He would be most likely prosecuted if he was a married man or if he was an indentured servant, because in both those instances marriage was impossible. After a change in the law in 1668, men were no longer prosecuted for fornication if they agreed to pay one-half of the child-care expenses for two years, after which the child could be indentured until it reached the age of twenty-one. If the mother refused to have the child indentured, she became responsible for paying the entire child support herself. Female indentured servants lost custody of their babies because they could neither support nor take care of them. They were employees and owed their labor, until the end of their indenture, to their employer. It was common, too, to extend the period of a pregnant servant's indenture to compensate for labor lost during pregnancy. In one instance, a female indentured servant had her term of service extended for two years following the birth of a son. Her son was indentured to her master for twenty-one years. While she had the comfort of retaining her son in the household in which she worked, she had no authority over him. Ordinarily the child was taken into charge by the town and given to the resident who required the least amount of money to raise it.

A relatively equal male/female ratio prevailed in Puritan New England from the outset. This was not the case in Virginia and Jamaica, where the number of emigrating male indentured servants outnumber women by 4:1. Vastly different working conditions prevailed for indentured servants in Virginia and the British West Indies also. Tobacco and sugarcane were both labor-intensive crops, requiring year-round attention. The death rate was high; many indentured servants died within a few months of their arrival. The heat, humidity, and the physical intensity of field labor were debilitating to English men and women. Diseases like yellow fever, which was especially hard on pregnant women, took a toll on unseasoned labor as well, and ship captains learned to land immigrants during the winter months when acclimation was easier. Moreover, since labor was limited, masters had a vested interest in getting the greatest possible amount of work from these men and women before they became free, when, in theory, they were granted land and were able to set themselves up as competitors to their former masters. In 1662, to get a few more years of labor from indentured servants, the age at which young servants were to be freed from their indentures was raised from twenty-one to twenty-four.

Indentured servants were forbidden to marry in Virginia as well as in New England, but the limited number of free women, especially in the seventeenth century, and the amount of money to be made growing tobacco, increased the chance that female indentured servants might have their contract purchased and be able to enter into marriages. Women in Virginia worked in the fields alongside men in some facets of tobacco production, as well as provided housewifery skills. As slaves from Africa gradually replaced white indentured servants in the tobacco fields, women's labor was concentrated within the households of small planters and plantation owners. In the seventeenth century the scarcity of women provided upward mobility for female indentured servants who could be assured of marriage, often to their master, when their term was completed. In the eighteenth century, rich gentlemen planters like **William Byrd** considered servants their social inferiors whose responsibilities included sexual duties as well as cooking, cleaning, and laundry.

If an indentured servant became pregnant, the father was likely to be her master, a neighboring free man, or a fellow indentured servant. As in New England, the servant would be required, while in labor, to name the father of her child. Rather than a fornication charge, however, in which the act of engaging in sexual intercourse while unmarried was criminalized as in Massachusetts, the female servant and the man she named while she was in labor would be prosecuted for **bastardy** if the child became a public charge on the local parish. Pragmatic Virginians were more concerned with the economic than the moral implications of out-of-wedlock sexuality. There were still penalties, however. Bastardy was punishable by a public whipping and a fine. An indentured servant who bore a white child had her indenture extended to age twenty-four. If she bore a black child, her length of service was extended to age thirty. If her partner was an indentured servant, he was also whipped and fined, and his indenture could also be extended. If the father was a free man, he could buy her contract from her master and the couple could marry, or if the indentured servant's master was the father of her child, he was required to marry her or free her to marry another man who would provide a home for her and her child.

Children who had been placed with the parish, and native-born orphans, were indentured as infants. These indentures specified, in many cases, that girls were to be trained in domestic trades such as spinning, carding, and knitting, and were to be released from their indentures at age eighteen or marriage. Boys who were indentured in infancy served until the age of twenty-one. Parish officials, who may have come to America themselves as indentured servants, sometimes specified, while indenturing infants, that they were not to be put to agricultural labor. *See also* Courtship; Fornication; Laws.

Further Reading: Brown, Kathleen M. *Good Wives, Nasty Wenches, & Anxious Patriarchs: Gender, Race, and Power in Colonial Virginia*. Chapel Hill: University of North Carolina Press, 1996; Burnard, Trevor. "European Migration to Jamaica, 1655–1780." *William and Mary Quarterly*, 3rd Series, 53, no. 4 (October 1996): 769–96; Hambleton, Else L. *Daughters of Eve: Pregnant Brides and Unwed Mothers in Seventeenth-Century Essex County, Massachusetts*. New York: Routledge, 2004.

Else L. Hambleton

INDIA. Sex and sexuality in seventeenth- and eighteenth-century India present a contradictory picture of rigidity stemming from religious and moral sanctions on the one hand, and an outburst of human passion on the other. The period was a reflection of continuity, as well as changes in various areas.

The expression of sexuality was restricted by ethical, moral, and religious norms for both Hindus and Muslims. **Hinduism** had prescribed a strict agenda of family life along with century-old conventions. **Islam** with its Qur'an and Shariyat did not tolerate any deviant behavior of its adherents. Nevertheless, the period witnessed expression of human desire, lust, passion, and lovemaking outside the parameters of both religions.

Restrictions were imposed on womenfolk with their movements checked outside the domain of the house. Hindu and Muslim women had to cover their bodies and put on veils. This custom was stronger among the high-caste Hindu families of northern India. Linked to a patriarchal society, the system of restrictions put a bar on access to public life and command over resources in a male-dominated society. The Muslim women had to put on *burqa* (a garment covering the whole body with slits for eyes). The Hindu woman was *asuryampasya* (confined to a dark corner, where sunlight does not penetrate). Some practices, such as **infanticide**, child marriage, and the *satee* system (burning of widows at the funeral pyre) also existed in some quarters. Among certain Rajput royal ladies, the *jauhar* (mass suicide in burning fire) was practiced after the death of the King in a battlefield so as to protect their honor. The early **marriage** of girls, severe restrictions on widows, and absence of **divorce** severely suppressed female sexual expression among Hindu women. Liaisons outside marriage and going to prostitutes for fulfilling male sexual desire were looked down upon, but tolerated. The *devadasi* (temple dancers) system was misused, and it became an outlet for prostitution.

The life of upper-class Muslim women was confined to the **harem**, sharing a husband with many wives, **concubines**, and *bandis* (slave girls). Divorce was rare among the Muslim nobility. The King distributed property after the death of a noble among the sons. In the family dwellings, there was segregation of *mardana* (man's quarters) and *zenana* (woman's quarters). Compared to the stunted

The master of the house proudly shows his harem to a trusted visitor; the ladies are impressed, one even drops the knife with which she's peeling oranges. © Mary Evans Picture Library.

expression of female sexuality among Muslim women, the men belonging to the aristocratic families and royalty had a free reign in meeting their carnal desire. They visited courtesans and brothels, where *muzzara* (dancing sessions) was a source of attraction. Kings took defeated rulers' wives and daughters as war booty, placing the women in their harems. The nobles and officers had slave girls for enjoyment. Life for both Hindu and Muslim women belonging to the lower strata of society was one of hardship.

There were instances, where sex, sexuality, and love were expressed in different ways. The **literature** of the period saw a flourishing of love poetry, where lovers' *viraha vedana* (pain in separation), amorous descriptions of lovemaking, eroticism, and ornamental delineation of female beauty and body were described in vivid detail. Love poetry was written in the vernacular languages. The Oriya poet Upendra Bhanja (1670–1720) wrote in an ornate style celebrating love, lovemaking, and eroticism. The powerful feeling of love in a spontaneous manner was the hallmark of the rhetorical school in Hindi poetry, with lyrical couplets mentioning the beauty of woman from *nakha* to *sikha* (nails of the toes to hair of the head), *nayika veda* (different varieties of lady in love), and *milana* (lovers in union). The lyrical Padavali songs in Bengali dealt with *parakriya priti* (love outside marriage). In the *Farebi-i-Ishq* (The Deceit of Love), Shawq (1783–1871) described the pleasure of love and lovemaking between men and women.

Both Hindu and Muslim ladies took care to beautify their bodies with sixteen types of *shringars* (makeups) with ingredients like gram flour, sandalwood paste, butter, kohl, and turmeric. Mud baths and hot ashes were used to wax hair. Lotus stems and honey were applied to develop vital parts of the body. *Urad dal* (one type of cereal) was avoided to keep the body trim, and broken earthen pitchers were used for shaping the derriere. The makeup assortment and apparel of a rich woman consisted of anklets, bracelets, bangles, girdles, eye-darkeners, ivory combs, and different types of beautiful dresses. The consort of Jehangir, Nur Jehan was a trendsetter in fashions, and the Queen of Shahjahan, Mumtaz Mahal, bewitched the Emperor with her makeup. Jahandar Shah was captivated by the swishing of the dancing girl, Lal Kanwar's dress.

Certain locations served as meeting places for men and women. The Meena bazaars were fairs, where the Mughal ladies displayed their products for sale, and it also served as a meeting point for flirtations. Jehangir fell in love with Nur Jehan after looking at her in such a place. It was not uncommon for the ladies of the royal family, who displayed remarkable personalities, to play an active part in politics: Rani Durgavati of Gondwana, Nur Jehan, Ahilya Bai Holkar, Kittur Rani Chennamma, and Jahanara Begam. Begam Samru married General Walter Reinhar, and her tomb still attracts tourists.

Homoerotic behavior in certain quarters was not lacking, although female-to-female sexual activity was rare and confined to the secluded atmosphere of harems in seventeenth- and eighteenth-century India. The *rekhti* poems were written describing the love between lesbians. The third sex or the hijras were employed in the Mughal court and harem as porters and bodyguards. They along with the *amrads* (beardless boys) catered to the needs of homosexual men. Fellatio was not uncommon among these **eunuchs**, and they were passive partners. They were pejoratively called in a vulgar way, *gandus*, or the anus beaters. The transgendered man who put on women's clothes was part of Indian society. However, the British outlawed **sodomy** in 1860, and presently as per the Indian Penal Code, it is still illegal. The notion of sex and sexuality in Indian society is a continuous process with various changes and adaptations. *See also* Clothing and Fashion; Cosmetics and Perfume; Cross-Dressing; Homosexuality; Oral Sex; Patriarchy; Romantic Love; Taj Mahal.

Further Reading: Barr, Pat. *The Memsahibs: The Women of Victorian India.* London: Secker and Warburg, 1976; Ballhatchet, Kenneth. *Race, Sex and Class under the Raj: Imperial Attitudes and*

Policies and Their Critics, 1793–1905. London: Weidenfeld & Nicholson, 1980; Hambly, Gavin. *Women in the Medieval Islamic World: Power, Patronage, and Piety.* New York: St. Martin's Press, 1998; Kate, Teltscher. *India Inscribed, European and British Writing on India 1600–1800.* New Delhi: Oxford University Press, 1997; Kausar, Zinat. *Muslim Women in Medieval India.* Patna: Janaki Prakashan, 1992; Lall, John. *Begam Samru: Fading Portrait in a Gilded Frame.* New Delhi: Roli Books, 1997; Mishra, Patit Paban. "India-Medieval Period." In *Encyclopedia of Modern Asia*, vol. 3, 22, 25. Edited by Karen Christenson and David Levinson. New York: Charles Scribner's Sons, 2002; Misra, Rekha. *Women in Mughal India, 1526–1748 A.D.* Delhi: Munshiram Manoharlal, 1967; Mujeeb, M. *The Indian Muslims.* London: George Allen and Unwin, 1967; Mukherjee, Soma. *Royal Mughal Ladies and Their Contributions.* New Delhi: Gyan Pub. House, 2001; Nanda, Serena. *Neither Man nor Woman: The Hijras of India.* Belmont, CA: Wadsworth Publishing, 1990.
Web Sites:
 http://www.bharatvani.org/books/mssmi/ch12.htm.
 http://www.jadski.com/keralaf4femalesexuality.htm.
 http://www.india-emb.org.eg/section%203/sec%203%20eng%5CMuslim%20Women%20in%20India.htm.

Patit Paban Mishra

INÉS DE LA CRUZ, SOR JUANA (1651–1695). Sor (Sister) Juana Inés de la Cruz (J. I.) was a seventeenth-century Mexican nun and pioneer feminist writer whose themes often played with sexual identity. She argued for **education** and equality for women long before feminism had a name. Inés was famous for her feminist writings in a misogynist culture where women were not allowed an intellectual identity and when writing was considered a taboo occupation for women. She was the first person in North America to argue in writing for women's right to education. She claimed neither gender was superior and denied fixed sexual roles.

 Inés was born Juana Inés Ramírez de Asbaje in a period of history when women were often subjugated to men. As a child, Inés begged her mother to disguise her in boy's clothing so she could sneak into the University in Mexico City. Her mother refused, so the child prodigy educated herself. By age fifteen she was one of the most learned women in Mexico.

 Marrying a man would have required Inés to devote herself to her husband and a family, rather than pursue her love affair with knowledge. Feeling a total disinclination toward **marriage**, she entered the convent. Illegitimate women were not allowed to become nuns, so Inés told the convent her parents were married, although they were not.

 In the convent, Inés deconstructed the gender-filled language of her contemporaries and declared the *concept* of a woman to be a tyrannical, man-made category. A Peruvian man wrote suggesting Inés should live as a man if she were to be a poet. To turn herself into a man would be to metaphorically **rape** herself, to commit sexual violence against her own being, she replied.

 However, Inés did manipulate traditional sexual identity. She considered herself genderless and abstract. Using the legend of Hermaphroditus, she commented that she was a spiritual androgyne. And her soul could love anyone, regardless of gender.

 Inés idealized and promoted love between women. She addressed erotic love poems to women with whom she carried on emotionally intimate relationships. At times, she played with gendered words to keep the gender of a recipient of a poem secret.

 Inés wore a ring given to her by Maria Luisa de Manrique, the married *Countess de Paredes*, to whom she wrote erotic poetry. Although it was prohibited for nuns to have visitors, Inés often did, including the Countess.

In her erotic poems, Inés suggested that gender was not important when it came to love, that the beauty of her close women friends enslaved her, and that she loved them with passionate, unstoppable madness. She concluded there was little difference between feelings of pure and profane love.

In seventeenth-century New Spain (Mexico), knowledge was a commodity controlled by the religious hierarchy. Church leaders believed knowledge and theology belonged only to men by Divine Order. They viewed female intelligence with hostility and feared Inés as an enactor of change.

Despite the hostility of the church, Inés became famous. Her works were published on two continents and were best sellers in Spain. Threatened, jealous church leaders criticized Inés for writing the same kinds of secular material as themselves. She responded by openly defending her academic abilities, declaring them equal to men's. Nuns were expected to be silent observers, but she would not silence herself.

A superior, Don Miguel Fernández de Santa Cruz y Sahagún, Bishop of Puebla, wrote an attack against Inés. He felt she had strayed too far from her naturally subordinate female position and crossed into the male order. He saw Inés as an impersonator of male identity, so he chidingly impersonated the female. Pretending to be a sister nun, he attacked her under the pseudonym Sor Filotea de la Cruz.

Inés knew the identity of her accuser. She replied with La Respuesta de la poetisa a la muy ilustre Sor Philotea de la Cruz (*Response to the Most Illustrious Poetess Sor Philotea de la Cruz*), in which she cited more than forty women who had made significant contributions to history. She countered that it was not a sin for her, as a woman, to write, but it was a holy gift and mandate from God.

After years of resisting misogyny, Inés renounced writing and surrendered her collection of 4,000 books, the largest library in Mexico at the time. After her death, an unfinished poem was found carefully hidden in her room. *See also* Gender Roles; Homosexuality; Monasteries; Romantic Love; Women, Changing Images of.

Further Reading: Inés de la Cruz, Sor Juana. *Poems, Protest, and a Dream: Selected Writings.* Translated with notes by Margaret Sayers Peden. New York: Penguin Books, 1997.

Elizabeth Jenner

INFANTICIDE. Infanticide, or "child murder," as it was commonly known during this period, refers to the killing of a newborn infant by its birth mother. Before the advent of widespread and reliable birth control, unwanted pregnancies were common. Such pregnancies could be disastrous for women, and many resorted to infanticide in an attempt to avoid having a child outside **marriage**. Social historians can reconstruct a partial picture, but infanticide is generally a private, secret act, difficult to account for, and difficult to police. Demographic records are sketchy to nonexistent, and historians must turn to the legal record. For example, there were forty-two cases in sixteenth- and seventeenth-century Nuremberg; there were twenty-four in Amsterdam between 1680 and 1811. In Geneva between 1599 and 1712, thirty-one women were convicted of child murder, twenty-five of whom were executed. In northern England, there were approximately two to three cases a year throughout the eighteenth century. In Sweden between 1749 and 1778 there were 617 death sentences handed down; over 200 were for infanticide.

The practice of infanticide cannot be fully accounted for by any one of the common explanations: poverty, illegitimacy, **madness, seduction** and abandonment, or shame. Illegitimacy, particularly, was generally believed to have had a strong causal link with the practice, but only a very small proportion of women dealing with unwanted pregnancies resorted to this solution. But while it is difficult to assess who was committing infanticide and how frequently, it is certainly possible to determine who was accused of it and who stood trial. A high proportion of infanticides seem to have occurred when different classes came into conflict, particularly when laboring-class women were constrained to reconcile the conflicting demands of their own cultural practices around **courtship**, sexuality, and marriage with newer received notions of middle-class respectability. These conflicts occurred within a wider context of the poverty and dislocation of the industrial revolution and its aftermath. Middle- and upper-class women could be said, with the practices of clandestine birth and sending newborn infants to "baby-farmers," to have been committing "indirect infanticide." Overwhelmingly, however, the criminal justice system concerned itself with, and sought to regulate, the sexual and reproductive practices of single working women. Infanticide was almost uniformly considered to have been their provenance.

There was one group that seemed to have been particularly vulnerable to the pressures that induced women to commit infanticide: contemporary observers and current commentators alike note that a disproportionate number of domestic servants committed the crime. Or perhaps they were simply caught more often. Certainly as a group they lived under particularly close surveillance and so were more likely to be apprehended, but it was those very disciplinary conditions that would have pushed them toward such a desperate solution in the first place. The bulk of the poor and laboring classes by and large had no reputations to lose, as the middle classes understood the term, and the women who *had* reputations to maintain were most vulnerable to infanticide. Many women in the general population did indeed return to work after the birth of an illegitimate child, but servants, and upper servants in particular, would not have had that option, given both the occupational requirement for moral rectitude and the limited market in which they sold their services. "Honor," for these women, was materially interwoven with economics, sexual and cultural politics, and laboring-class self-respect.

Infanticide has long been seen, in the West, as a threat to the authority of the church, the state, and the family. The sixteenth and seventeenth centuries saw a series of laws enacted across Europe that criminalized the concealment of a **pregnancy** or birth when the resulting infant died or was missing, as such was considered adequate proof of criminal intent: for example, France in 1556, England in 1624, and Scotland in 1690 all enacted **laws**, rigorously enforced, which placed the burden of proof on the suspected woman, and in France, unmarried women who became pregnant were legally required to register their pregnancies. The English law also specifically targeted unmarried women, and it was not until 1828 that it was amended to include all women. Significant numbers of women were executed under these statutes, second only to the numbers of women executed for witchcraft in the same period, and frequently these executions involved **torture**. Prosecutions for infanticide, in most European states, increased in the sixteenth and seventeenth centuries. The eighteenth century, however, saw a widespread leniency in the treatment of accused and suspected women, due in large measure to the perception in many jurisdictions that the laws were excessive. In eighteenth-century England, for example, the laws against concealment were the subject of much contention. After the first decades of the eighteenth century the English law "seems to have been largely disregarded" (Malcolmson 197). Nevertheless, four attempts to repeal it between 1772 and 1773 failed until finally it was replaced by Lord Ellenborough's Offenses Against the Person Act of 1803 (43 Geo. III, c.58). Scotland followed suit and repealed the 1690 statute in 1809 (49 Geo. III c.14). Under these new laws, women were either to be tried under existing legislation against **murder** or for the lesser crime of concealment, the maximum penalty for which was reduced to two years, though few in practice received the full sentence. These new laws, however, rather than altering the experience of women in the courts, merely gave official sanction to the leniency that had by then become common practice.

Infanticide was written into law in a way that reflected laboring-class practice since illegitimacy, the frequent result of different mores and increased vulnerability, and concealment, a practical necessity given working women's lives, were specifically targeted. In practice it was unmarried women of poor and laboring-class backgrounds who were prosecuted, the class of women perceived to be most in need of regulation and most dangerous in their fertility if left unchecked. There was, as noted, a shift to greater leniency in the courts, but there were exceptions. There is indication, for example, that women who were considered recalcitrant or irreligious were treated more harshly. Women accused of infanticide were required to *demonstrate* to the court that they were fit subjects for mercy. Confessions and admissions of wrongdoing were taken as signs of "goodness," and displays of extreme emotion were demonstrations of proper femininity and maternal feelings. The women charged with infanticide throughout both the eighteenth and nineteenth centuries who did not receive acquittals or pardons generally fell afoul, not of the law necessarily, but of normative ideas of femininity on the one hand, and class-based deference on the other.

Public attitudes were, to a certain extent, sympathetic to the concerns of impoverished, pregnant women. Although there is a long history in many jurisdictions of alarm about infanticide, it is not uniform. In the English statute of 1624 women who committed infanticide were characterized as "lewd," and a century later vocal social critics like Defoe were unrelenting: "Not a sessions passes but we see one or more merciless mothers tried for the murder of their bastard children" (*Augusta Triumphans: Or, the Way to Make London the Most Flourishing City in the Universe*, 1728). However, Bernard de Mandeville was perhaps more representative when he commented in 1714 that modest rather than shameless women were tempted to commit infanticide because only they had reputations to lose (*The Fable of the Bees*, 74). William Hunter, whose forensic work, and in particular his *On the Uncertainty of Signs of Murder in the Case of Bastard Children* (1783), was instrumental in developing an enlightened, humanitarian response to women suspected of infanticide, wrote that he saw it as his duty to publish his critiques of common forensic practices in order to save "some unhappy and innocent women." Humane attitudes such as this were by no means universal, but they were more and more in evidence by the end of the eighteenth century. Infanticide was no longer automatically the unnatural crime of an immoral woman; the woman herself was now also seen as a victim. *See also* Abortion; Bastardy; Childbirth; Fornication; Indentured Servants; Puritans.

Further Reading: Backhouse, Constance. *Petticoats and Prejudice: Women and Law in Nineteenth-Century Canada*. Toronto: Osgoode/Women's Press, 1991; Hoffer, Peter Charles. *Murdering Mothers: On Infanticide in England and New England, 1558–1803*. New York: New York University Press, 1981; Jackson, Mark Andrew. *New-Born Child Murder: Women, Illegitimacy and the Courts in Eighteenth-Century England*. Manchester: Manchester University Press, 1996; Kertzer, David I. *Sacrificed for Honor: Italian Infant Abandonment and the Politics of Reproductive Control*. Boston: Beacon, 1993; Malcolmson, R. W. "Infanticide in the 18th Century." In *Crime in England, 1550–1800*, edited by J. S. Cockburn, 187–211. Princeton, NJ: Princeton University Press, 1977; Rose, Lionel. *The Massacre of the Innocents: Infanticide in Britain, 1800–1939*. London: Routledge, 1986.

Miriam Jones

INSANITY. *See* Madness

INTERRACIAL SEX. The history of sexual relations between different races has provoked different reactions from the seventeenth and eighteenth centuries to the present day. Miscegenation, from Latin *miscere*, "to mix," and *genus*, "kind," is used to refer to the mixing of different ethnicities, especially when that mixing refers to **marriage**, cohabitation, and/or sexual relations. The word "miscegenation" came into popular usage in the late 1800s by David Croly in a pamphlet written by him titled *Miscegenation: The Theory of the Blending of the Races, Applied to the White Man and the Negro*. The contemporary usage of the term is often expressed as interracial marriage and interracial dating. In the English colonies, miscegenation had a negative connotation, which led to a variety of racist attitudes, ordinances, and **laws** forbidding interracial sexual relations and intermarriage. However, in the Spanish and French colonies, words such as *mestizaje* and *metissage* tend to refer to the mixing of cultures in the form of a melting pot. Moreover, in the Portuguese colonies, sexual relations and intermarriage were not only common but also often times encouraged, and citizenship was granted to some of the children based on their skin color. Some Portuguese colonies in Brazil, Cape Verde, and Sao Jome e Principe had large open mixed-race populations. As these countries established colonies throughout the world, the spread of **slavery**, especially the triangular trade in North America and the Caribbean, led to a dramatic change in the racial and ethnic landscape of the western hemisphere.

Colonial court records in Pennsylvania document a white servant as being indicted for sexual interaction with a black servant in 1677. In 1698 the colonial court in Chester County, Pennsylvania, laid down the principle that the mixing of the races was not to be allowed. Several colonies passed strict penalties for persons offending race-mixing laws. In New Amsterdam, an order dated April 15, 1638, stated: "Each and everyone must refrain from fighting, from adulterers intercourse with Heathens, Blacks, and other persons."

Intermarriages also occurred between **Native Americans** and African Americans during the colonial period. One such union occurred between Sarah Muckamugg, a Nipmuc from Hassanamisco, Massachusetts, and Aaron, a slave of African ancestry. The union between slaves, former slaves, freedmen, and women of color resulted from a combination of circumstances including Native Americans working alongside slaves and indentured servants in colonial New England; some Native American societies accepting escaped slaves, or maroons, into their societies, and, in colonial Florida and Louisiana, explorers remaining in the colonies, marrying, and producing families. Several Native American-European and Native American-African unions occurred as well.

French and Spanish colonial Louisiana represented a special case of mixing in North America. Under the rule of Spain and France, the population in the city of New Orleans had about 20,000 people. Mulattoes, individuals who were the product of mixed-race sexual encounters, and Negroes were openly protected by the colonial government. Anyone doing harm to a Mulatto or Negro would be subject to penalties of law. Women of color were highly sought after by white men,

"The white boy I love." An early 19th century engraving from Martinique. © The Art Archive/Bibliothèque des Arts Décoratifs Paris/Dagli Orti.

and white women of high esteem sought after some prominent men of color. For the men, it was easy to engage in such sexual relationships. Rich white men had one or more **concubines** and supported them and the children they had with these women, in addition to their legitimate wives and offspring. So common was this practice in the colony of Louisiana that Quadroon and Octoroon societies held prominent places in society and frequently were the hosts of society balls and dances. To be considered quadroon, one must have one-quarter African or black ancestry; Quadroons were considered "colored." Octoroons were also considered "colored" if their genetic makeup was seven-eights white and one-eights black. This race classification system existed in French and Spanish colonies. Any child resulting from interracial relations of an octoroon and a white person was considered a quadroon. Quadroon balls were hosted by light-complexion Creole women and used as a means of social advancement (some received extraordinary gifts, living expenses, and their children sent to Europe for education) because marriage was forbidden between white, Creole, and colored populations.

A famous play, *The Octoroon*, dramatizes the moral economy of a social system in which some characters accept prohibiting interracial marriage, but allow the sexual relations that ultimately produced the octoroon society. These practices persisted well into the nineteenth century when described by Alexis de Tocqueville: "To debauch a Negro gal hardly inquires an American reputation; to marry her dishonors him" (590).

During the seventeenth and eighteenth centuries, several state statutes attempted to ensure racial purity. However, with more mixed-raced persons entering the American colonies, the control of sexual behavior became harder to regulate among free people. Many colonies viewed the issue as **fornication**. A 1662 Virginia act fined both white men and women who engaged in interracial fornication, but it was the behavior of the men that prompted new laws and further regulation of sexual activity. In fact, interracial sexual relationships extended beyond slave/servant and master or prostitute, but rather were common to some parts of colonial America between free people of different races. *See also* Bastardy; Mixed Marriages, New France.

Further Reading: Hodes, Martha, ed. "Miscegenation." In *Reader's Companion to US Women's History*. New York: Houghton Mifflin Company, 1998; Hollinger, David. "Amalgamation and Hypodescent: The Question of Ethnoracial Mixture in the History of the United States." *American History Review* 108 (2003): 1363–91; de Tocqueville, Alexis. *Democracy in America*. Translated and edited by Harvey C. Mansfield and Delba Winthrop. Chicago: University of Chicago Press, 2000; Rogers, J. A. *Sex and Race: A History of White, Negro and Indian Miscegenation in the Two Americas*. Vol. II. New York: Helga M. Rogers, 2000.

DeMond S. Miller

ISLAM. Islam is a **religion** founded in the seventh century based on the teachings of the Prophet Muhammad, encompassing a variety of interpretations and practices. The followers of Islam are called "Muslims" and worship is restricted to one divine being called "Allah," the Arabic word for "God." Islam affects every aspect of a worshipper's life in his or her pursuit to attain peace, deferring to the holy book, the Qur'an, to understand their laws and rights. The Qur'an dictated sex and sexuality in the seventeenth and eighteenth centuries, listing which sexual activities were lawful. Also spelled *Koran* or *Quran*, the Qur'an presented very clear guidelines concerning sex and sexuality for the followers of Islam. In itself, sexuality neither represented any inborn evil nor caused negative consequences.

In Islam, sexual intercourse between a husband and wife was encouraged. Although the Qur'an permitted men to have up to four wives and a multitude of **concubines**, it was difficult to meet the conditions required to have multiple wives, as each wife may require her own household. Even imperial rulers of the time were allowed only four wives; all the other women within their **harems** were legal concubines. While both men and women have the right under the Qur'an to have satisfying sex, the holy book forbid some sex acts including **anal intercourse**, sex during **menstruation** or during bleeding after **childbirth**, sex during the month of Ramadan during daylight hours, or sex that could be harmful or prolong recovery from an illness. **Oral sex**, fellatio, or cunnilingus between a husband and wife was lawful, but often considered unclean and of low morality. After sexual intercourse, a bath or ritual cleansing was required as an expression of respect for Allah.

Muslims of the seventeenth and eighteenth centuries accepted birth control, conditionally. Islam encouraged followers to welcome many children but family planning was permissible for certain reasons, such as preserving health, desirable child spacing, or waiting for a more financially responsible time to have children. The lawful use of birth control did not apply to permanent use or for the fear of losing wealth. The primarily endorsed contraceptive method was coitus interruptus, in which the couple interrupted sexual intercourse by withdrawal of the penis from the vagina prior to **ejaculation**. In Islamic tradition, the Prophet Muhammad practiced coitus interruptus. In addition, artificial contraceptive methods were equally permissible with the exception of sterilization and **abortion**. In certain circumstances, usually regarding health or honor, abortion was sometimes allowed and encouraged during the first trimester.

Homosexuality in Islamic cultures during the seventeenth century was common and expected, although Islamic cultures defined homosexuality differently from Christian cultures. Homosexuality, male or female, was forbidden, yet seventeenth-century visitors to Islamic societies claimed that Muslims were bisexual by nature and gave descriptions of lesbianism among women in harems and bathhouses. Not allowed in such places, visiting male authors most likely did not witness such instances, yet they caused homosexuality in general to be known in Europe as the "Persian" or "Turkish" vice. Sex involving penetration typically took place between dominant, free adult men and anyone else considered subordinate to them, such as wives, concubines, boys, male and female prostitutes, and male and female slaves. Sexual partners did not necessarily define homosexuality. Islamic tradition forbid male homosexuality only if the two men were considered equals in status and power. Muslims viewed women as naturally submissive; male prostitutes submitted for personal gain and were not forbidden. Pederasty, sexual relations and intercourse between a man and a boy, usually an adolescent, was common in the seventeenth century. Islamic cultures did not consider pederasty damaging to boys, those who were not yet men, since their **masculinity** was not at stake. Men sometimes voluntarily gave up their dominant role to live publicly as women; while these men lost their respectability as men, they could be valued as poets or singers. The treatment of homosexual activity changed in the late seventeenth and eighteenth centuries as European colonialism brought Christian views to Islamic cultures. Existing **gender roles** and relationships remained largely unaffected, but hostility to previously acceptable homosexual acts emerged in many areas. *See also* Baths; Contraception; Hinduism; Judaism; Prostitutes and Prostitution; Sodomy.

Further Reading: Bouhdiba, Abdelwahab. *Sexuality in Islam*. Translated by Alan Sheridan. London: Routledge, 1985; Esposito, John L. *The Oxford History of Islam*. New York: Oxford University Press, 1999; Musallam, B. F. *Sex and Society in Islam: Birth Control before the Nineteenth Century*. New York: Cambridge University Press, 1983; Robinson, Francis. *The Cambridge Illustrated History of the Islamic World*. New York: Cambridge University Press, 1996.

Melissa K. Benne

JAPANESE THEATER. *See* Theater, Japanese

JUDAISM. Judaism consecrates the love of God and the love of one's neighbor as fundamental ethical values according to Moses's commandments. Homosexuality is prohibited; sexuality is strictly heterosexual, confined to marriage, and regulated according to the wife's impure periods (menstruation and childbirth).

The seventeenth and eighteenth centuries were a turbulent period for Jewry. Bogdan Khmelnytsky's Uprising (1648–1654), the revolts of the haidamaks, and local Ukranian militia, led to violence and pogroms. Mysticism and the Jewish Enlightenment (the Haskalah) influenced Jewish identity.

Seventeenth-century Judaism was influenced by the mystical doctrine of the Kabbalah as developed a century before by Moshe Cordovero and Isaac Luria. The greatest interpreters of Cordoverian and Lurianic Kabbalah (Israel of Kozienice or Hayyim ben Joseph Vital) considered that the worldly divine fragmentation must be integrated into a whole through emotional and intellectual love. Understanding was a symbolic matrimony. God had created the world through ten "agencies" (*sephirots*) generating the masculine and the feminine principle. Their complex ontological/sexual game engenders the evil and the good in the world.

Kabbalists opposed exogamic marriages because Jewish souls would be confused. They were higher souls neither wholly deprived of original good nor totally free from original sin. Kabbalists believed this ambivalence and separation would cease when the Messiah comes.

Seventeenth-century Jewry were shattered by Sabbetai Zevi (1626–1676), a false prophet who claimed to be the Messiah, and who, finally, converted to **Islam**. He relied on Kabbalistic sources (the Zohar) and preached the necessity of asceticism in order to return to the world's initial harmony. At night he would sing psalms or coarse Spanish love songs to which he gave mystical interpretations. His marriage to Sarah, a woman of dubious reputation, reinforced his morally ambiguous attitude.

Jacob Frank (1726–1791), a Polish-Jew, pretended that he preached revelations communicated to him by Zevi. While expecting the Messianic moment, Frank organized meetings where participants worshipped Sion. During these meetings, in fits of passion and exaltation, sexual looseness was encouraged as mystic symbolism, and participants broke the sacred bonds of matrimony. In 1759 Frankists were excommunicated, and they accepted baptism.

One of the most influential opponents of Zevi and his followers was Rabbi Jacob Emden (c. 1697–1776), the author of a very popular siddur (prayer book), titled

Ammunde Shamayim. In this book, Emden discussed conjugal norms and sexuality. According to Emden, a child's intelligence depended on the intensity of his parents' amorous embrace at the moment of his conception. Emden saw sex within matrimony as a remedy for depression and mental disability. He also advised benevolently in situations where his advice as a rabbi was asked for. In 1723, in Lemberg, he was asked to give his opinion on a complicated case. A man had kidnapped a married woman. They went to Spain and converted to Catholicism. Then they returned to Lemberg. In the meantime, the husband had died of grief. The local rabbi imposed a very severe penitence on the couple, but afterward they were integrated into the community. Seven years later the dead man's brother returned and asked for further and more severe punishment of the couple. Emden advised kindness and forgiveness. In another case, in 1733, Emden approved of the matrimony of a man who had had one testicle ablated, as the man had the biological potential to fulfill his matrimonial duties.

Emden's attitude relied on the connection between sexuality and matrimony in Judaism. Sexual desire is inseparable from marriage. Love presupposes the partners' sexual fulfillment within matrimony. Unrequited love was not much of a topos in seventeenth- and eighteenth-century Judaism, nor has it ever been.

The importance of marriage for procreation and companionship also resides within Hasidism, the greatest mystical trend of the eighteenth century. Hasidism was founded by rabbi Israel ben Eliezar (c. 1698–1760), also called Baal Shem Tov or the Besht. He preached in Poland and Moldovia. He was against asceticism, considering the care of the **body** as necessary as the care of the soul. The most important activity of a pious Jew was prayer in joy. Hasidism relied on the charisma of the *zaddiks* whose magnetism created a real court around them. The *zaddik* and his apprentices formed a brotherly society whose utmost purpose was reaching a mystic union with God through love. The Hassidic wives were respected and honored and very influential. Such examples are Adel (Odel), the daughter of the Besht, or Feige, the daughter of Adel and mother of another Hassidic rabbi. The quest for mystic love did not exclude human affection and sexuality within Hassidic matrimony. A Hassid without a wife lived a sad life, without joy and blessing. He had to love and honor his wife. Neither should he impose his sexual desires upon his spouse.

Hasidism encountered great opposition since its birth. The most important personality among the *mitnagdim* (opponents) was Elijah ben Solomon Zalman (1720–1797), also called the Gaon of Vilna for his exceptional scholarship. The Gaon rejected the Hassidic emphasis on the love and service of God in joy. He recommended the study of the Torah and an ascetic life. He believed that girls, mothers-to-be, should also study because they have to know the Law and apply it in their families.

The Gaon was an opponent not only to Hassidism but also to Haskalah. The *Maskilim*, the adherents to the Jewish Enlightenment, supported a Jewish secular identity with a view to social and political integration and emancipation. The risk was acculturation, mixed marriages, and apostasy. The children of Moses Mendelssohn (1729–1786), philosopher and man of letters in Prussia, the great champion of the movement, are relevant examples in this respect.

Intermarriage between rich Jews eager to be socially accepted and Christians in need of capital became quite common in England after the resettlement of the Jews in this country, in 1655. Eliza Haywood gave such an example in her well-known novel *The History of Miss Betsy Thoughtless* (1751). *See also* Enlightenment Thought on Sexuality; Hinduism; Monasteries; Philosophy; Religion.

Further Reading: Buber, Martin. *Hasidism*. New York: Philosophical Library, 1948; Mann, Denese Berg. *The Woman in Judaism*. Hartford, CT: Jonathan Publications, 1979; Scholem, Gershon Gerhard. *Kabbalah*. New York: Quadrangle, Times Book, 1974.

Mihaela Mudure

LAWS.

MARRIAGE AND DIVORCE. Family law in early colonial America took its lead almost entirely from English courts. Men and women during this time chose to marry for a myriad of different reasons, including but not limited to love. Financial security, for example, usually figured heavily in a woman's decision to marry, since the union was generally understood to provide stability for her. Since **marriage** was viewed simultaneously as a religious, social, cultural, and legal union, the law attempted to encompass the social aspects and understandings of **gender roles**, as well as deal with the legal realities of marriage.

Marriage represented an interesting hybrid because it was at its essence a legal contract, but was more recognizable as a cultural and social construction. As such, marriage law codified common understandings of gender roles of the time. The husband was viewed as the head of the household and the law reflected this understanding. According to English common law, a principle called "coverture" governed legal rights of men and women in marriage. Coverture meant that a married woman's legal identity was "covered" by her husband's when they were married. A woman was subsumed by her husband upon marriage, so that the man was considered his family's representative in the eyes of the law. Therefore, by granting rights to vote and participate in the legal system to husbands, the legislature reasoned that it was effectively granting these rights to women, too, with their husbands acting as a proxy. However, since there was no requirement that women be consulted on these matters, the effect of the arrangement was simply that women had no legal rights in marriage.

This principle extended into almost all areas of law. Married women generally could not own property. All property that was obtained during the marriage was in the husband's name, and title to any property a woman inherited from her family automatically converted to her husband's name as well. If a woman's husband deserted her, which was during the seventeenth and eighteenth centuries the most common way of ending a marriage, she had no legal recourse to assert property rights against him. Scholars have pointed out that courts did grant some women limited property rights in certain situations, but it is worth noting that these rights were always limited in scope and affected only well-to-do women. For example, a husband could choose to leave marital property to his wife in a will, and she would then be considered the legal owner of the property. These women, though, encountered a problem when they wanted to remarry and had no way of protecting the property they had obtained through their first marriage from becoming the property of their new husbands. This problem only arose in cases of propertied individuals, which likely accounts for the willingness of some legislatures to make laws to remedy the situation. Massachusetts, for example, began enforcing prenuptial contracts in the eighteenth century to protect wealthy women in cases like this.

Married women further did not have the right to enter into contracts, to live alone, or to be parties in lawsuits. Husbands could sue on their wives' behalf and could also be held liable for their suits against their wives. Husbands could be sued for the cost of necessaries furnished to their wives in much the same way modern law allows parents to be sued to cover the cost of necessaries given to minor children. Husbands could also be punished for certain crimes committed by their wives and were therefore granted what courts called a "moderate right of correction." It was not described, but it typically granted husbands a legal right to "discipline" their wives in a reasonable manner. This legal right codified a defense of charges of brutality levied against husbands by their wives. While courts were sometimes known to convict a husband of wife-beating, in order to be successful, a wife would need to show that the beating rose to a level beyond this moderate correction, which was often difficult to do.

A woman's role as a domestic was likewise reflected in the law that governed marriage. According to English common law, in return for the security of marriage, and in exchange for her husband acting as head of the household and accepting all the duties that entailed, a wife was responsible for taking care of the home and the domestic needs of her husband and children. Interestingly, this was considered an understanding of the *law*; not just an understanding of the social contract, the principle was sometimes invoked in the courtroom. In this way marriage law was a legal anomaly, taking the language of law and applying it to nonlegal concepts.

Divorce, in both England and the colonies, was rare. In England, divorce became legal at the behest of Henry VIII in 1529. Henry broke with the Roman Catholic Church and made himself the head of the Church of England to divorce his first wife, Katherine of Aragon, and marry Anne Boleyn. However, until 1857 obtaining a divorce in England still required an act of Parliament, and it was usually only granted in special circumstances. From the mid-1600s until 1857, there were only 375 divorces granted. In colonial America, divorce was equally uncommon. Divorce laws in the colonies varied depending on region. The New England colonies completely legalized divorce in the 1600s, while the southern colonies flatly prohibited it. Most middle colonies had laws providing for divorce but limited it to grants by the governor. However, among all the colonies divorce remained rare. First, there were still strong religious sentiments that influenced people's reluctance to seek divorces. Second, since women had no legal rights in marriage, there was little incentive for them to seek divorce and a strong incentive for them to make sure their husbands did not try to obtain one as well. Finally, there were often external barriers. Many colonies granted divorces only in special cases, and they were sometimes hard to obtain. It was often easier to stay in an unhappy marriage than attempt to be granted a divorce. Many couples, specifically low-income couples, simply separated to end a marriage. There was no legal agreement; either the husband or wife would simply leave the home. When this happened, women would typically return home to live with their parents, and men, who retained the interest in marital property, would keep the couple's old home.

Child Custody. Ironically, while women were recognized as the caretakers of the domestic sphere, upon separation, men were understood to have supreme rights to children in child-custody battles. Courts in colonial America and England went as far as to say that maternal rights did not exist vis-à-vis paternal rights. Prior to 1839, the only cases that granted the right of custody of minor children to mothers were situations where fathers gave up their paternal rights by abandonment or excessive cruelty. Without this abandonment, mothers almost never successfully asserted their maternal rights over their ex-husbands' paternal rights, even in some cases, where it could be shown that the marriage dissolved because of cruelty to the mother. In fact, this presumption in favor of fathers was not limited to situations in which the marriage was dissolved. A father had the right to name a guardian of his children upon his death, and often he did not name their mother. A widow, then, could lose legal custody of her children if her husband appointed someone else guardian.

In England in 1839, the Custody of Infants Act passed, which allowed women a limited right to petition the courts for custody of children seven years old and younger. The rationale began to approach the more modern theory that young children belong to their mothers more than to their fathers. This thinking began to influence America as well, and courts began to shift to a default rule in favor of mothers' custody rights.

Marriage, Family, and Slavery. During the colonial period and into the antebellum era, it was illegal for two slaves to marry each other. Denied this basic right of self-determination, African slaves created their own traditions and means of creating a communally recognized union. The term "jumping the broom" originated during antebellum times and referred to the tradition created in slave communities of the bride and groom jumping over a broom together to symbolize the creation of a union. White slave owners sometimes allowed these unions, but seldom when they were not in the interest of the slave owner. The confines and duration of the unions were entirely dictated by the slaves' owners. When slaves of different owners married, they usually stayed with their separate owners and had to visit each other whenever they had the time. When slaves owned by the same owner married one another it made it easier logistically since they were able to stay with each other. However, a slave owner could still terminate those unions if either the husband or wife was sold to another owner. Sometimes slave owners sold spouses separately because they were worth more separately than as a pair. However, slave owners sometimes did this intentionally to keep families' members separated or as a form of punishment. Children from these unions also could be taken from their parents at the will of the slave owner.

The rationale for deprivation of the right to marry had three main prongs. The first reason was that giving slaves the right to marry would undermine the assumption that blacks were not fully human. The government reasoned that marriage was a legal status, and as such, had to be reserved for only those the law recognized as whole peoples.

The next reason was maintaining power. The law at the time dictated that slaves were the property of their owners. However, a marriage contract at that time made a wife and her children the legal property of the husband. Thus, the legal right to marry had to be denied to slaves for fear that black men would supplant slave owners as the legal owners of his wife and children.

The final rational for the denial of marriage to slaves was closely related to the previous reason. Not only was it true that marriage would complicate the question of ownership as a matter of law; slave owners also feared the moral impact it would have on the practice of slavery. It was extremely common for white slave owners to have sexual relationships with their female slaves. In fact, it was often one of the primary duties of a black woman slave to serve as a sexual partner for her owner. Slave owners feared the violent reaction of black men when confronted with the daily rapes of their wives and daughters.

SEX AND SEXUALITY. *Homosexuality.* In England, the Reformation Parliament of 1533 made illegal and punishable by death acts referred to as "buggery." Buggery referred to a number of offences that were traditionally regulated by the church. This statute marked the first time that secular law prohibited and punished these acts. The acts included **anal intercourse**, either between two men or between a man and a woman, and any act of **bestiality**. The statute did not explicitly mention sex between two women, but the understanding of the time is that it too was prohibited by this statute and carried the same penalty of death. Elizabeth I's second parliament reenacted this statute in 1562.

The American colonies adopted different forms of the statute. The southern and middle colonies adopted the statute and its death penalty for those convicted of engaging in any of these acts. The remaining colonies enacted similar statutes criminalizing the activities but did not authorize those convicted to be sentenced to death in all cases. Enforcement of these statutes proved difficult because they were, at their core, laws regulating consensual, albeit illicit, sex. Therefore it was extremely difficult to prove because there was often no one to report the wrongdoing, or there was no one who had witnessed the crime. This difficulty led authorities to conceptualize these statutes the same way as they did **rape**. **Sodomy** was generally understood to be a violent act, which could not be consented to, and one in which people only engaged when they were coerced. These statutes were most often enforced in cases where there was a power disparity between the two parties, typically where one man was much older or more established than the other man or woman. But sodomy was also generally understood, like rape, to be a penetrative act. If actual penetration did not take place, or could not be proven to have taken place, then usually a person could not be convicted of sodomy. In New Haven colony, however, the law made all nonprocreative sex acts between men and men, men and women, or men and children, whether they included penetration or not, a capital crime. There were reports of at least twenty sodomy prosecutions and four executions during the colonial period. By 1791, when the Bill of Rights was created, eleven of the thirteen colonies proscribed sodomy by criminal statute.

Prostitution. Prostitution held a unique position in colonial American and English law. On one hand, it was illegal and was often punished harshly. For example, there are accounts of women convicted of prostitution being punished by getting tied to carts topless and dragged through town while they were whipped. This punishment was also sometimes administered to women convicted of running brothels. However, on the other hand, prostitution was viewed as a necessary evil, and therefore, laws against it were not consistently enforced. There were several reasons for this willingness on the part of the law to look the other way. Prostitution existed from almost the beginning years of the American colonies. While laws were enacted in the colonies that prohibited prostitution, men who took advantage of their services were often not prosecuted. As cities grew and commerce developed, prostitution did, too.

Adultery. In addition to being one of the few accepted reasons for divorce in colonial America, adultery also represented an area of the law that created much debate between the colonies. Virginia, Massachusetts Bay, Plymouth, New Haven, and Connecticut all passed laws that declared sex with a married woman was punishable by death for both parties. Many people took issue with the decision to limit prosecution of adultery to situations when a woman was married. There was a sentiment that to protect the sanctity of marriage, adultery should include extramarital sex by either a husband or a wife. However, it was easier to convict women of adultery than it was to convict men because the telltale evidence was very often pregnancy. The statutes were also controversial because many of the other colonies considered the punishment too harsh. These statutes remained on the books until about 1670, but were sporadically enforced during this time. Typically, convictions of adultery were handled without resorting to the death penalty. Other punishments included public whippings and banishment. It was also common for wealthy men and women to pay a fine and be spared any punishment for engaging in adulterous affairs.

Abortion. English common law considered abortion a felony. The punishment associated with causing or procuring an **abortion** varied depending on the stage of the terminated pregnancy. The turning point was referred to as "quickening," which was the stage at which it is possible to detect fetal movement. Before "quickening" the punishment for an abortion was fourteen years in prison. After this stage, however, an abortion was considered **murder** and was punished by death without benefit of clergy.

The colonies adopted English common law and made illegal only abortions that took place after quickening. The law made no secret about the fact that the rationale was very strongly based on religious and moral sentiments that life began in the womb, not at birth. Doctors and moral reformers who were opposed to abortion began to aggressively lobby Congress for even stricter laws against abortion, arguing that it was in the best interest of the health of mothers to proscribe abortion at any stage of pregnancy. Finally, in 1887, they were successful in convincing Congress, and laws were changed so that abortion, regardless of the stage of pregnancy, was considered a felony. *See also* Bastardy; Bigamy; Child Rape; Consent; Domestic Violence; Fornication; Household Consumerism; Rape Law; Slavery.

Further Reading: Hartok, Hendrik. *Man and Wife in America: A History.* Cambridge, MA: Harvard University Press, 2000; Hughes, Cornelia. "'Taking the Trade': Abortion and Gender Relations in an Eighteenth-Century New England Village." *William and Mary Quarterly* (January 1991): 19–49; Minow, Martha. "'Forming underneath Everything That Grows': Toward a History of Family Law." *Wisconsin Law Review* (1985): 819–77; Wright, Danaya C. "The Crisis of Child Custody: A History of the Birth of Family Law in England." *Columbia Journal of Gender & Law* 11 (2002): 175–245.

Maya R. Rupert

LIBERTINE. Originally, the term *libertine* applied to a free thinker who questioned religious institutions and moral norms. However, by the mid to late seventeenth century, primarily in England and France, the term *libertine* had come to denote a person, usually male and aristocratic, whose purpose was to lead a life of sensual pleasure, both in and out of the bedroom.

The philosophy of libertinism valued the individual over the group, reveled in the relativism of social norms, and allowed an exploration of the concept of power. At its most extreme, libertinism took immorality as its moral code and was skeptical of humans' significance in the world and their power to order the world through reason.

The term *rake* became a synonym for "libertine," especially in England during the Restoration period (1660–1688), when the Stuart monarchy—which had been deposed by the **Puritan** Commonwealth in the 1640s—returned to the throne. The ascension of Charles II inaugurated a sexually charged milieu, especially in the court, the **theater**, and in verse. **John Wilmot**, the second Earl of Rochester, Sir Charles Sedley, and Charles Sackville, sixth Earl of Dorset were all highly visible courtiers of the King and notorious libertines of the period.

Libertinism thus became closely associated with the writings of the period, celebrated in the works of Thomas Shadwell, especially a play called *The Libertine*;

John Wilmot, 2nd Earl of Rochester and poet. © Mary Evans Picture Library.

by **Aphra Behn** with a poem titled "The Libertine" and many of her plays like *The Rover*; in George Etherege's *The Man of Mode*, William Wycherley's *The Country Wife*, and numerous others; and in John Wilmot's plays, verse, and life. Pierre Choderlos de Laclos's 1782 novel *Les Liaisons Dangereuses* describes the life and fall of Valmont, a libertine. Later, Amadeus Mozart's *Don Giovanni* and Lord Byron's *Don Juan* both celebrated the famous Spanish libertine.

The image of the libertine fell into disregard in England after the Glorious Revolution of 1688 exchanged the Stuarts for the stodgier William of Orange. Art, like **William Hogarth**'s painting series, *A Rake's Progress*, focused on the less appetizing aspects of the libertine, including the financial debts and **venereal disease**.

Of course, the best-known libertine, causing scandal even into the twenty-first century, was **Donatien Alphonse François de Sade** (1740–1814). More commonly known as the Marquis de Sade, his very name has come to mean sexual perversity with related terms *Sadean*, *sadistic*, and *sadomasochistic*. De Sade's work was banned during his lifetime as obscene with its graphic portrayals of **bestiality** and other perversities. Though De Sade was imprisoned for his writings, he continued to write. Hugh Hefner, *Playboy* founder, stands as the continuing example of this lifestyle in the twenty-first century. *See also* Literature; Pornography.

Further Reading: Adlard, John, ed. *The Debt to Pleasure: John Wilmot, Earl of Rochester, in the Eyes of His Contemporaries and in His Own Poetry and Prose*. Manchester: Manchester University Press, 1974; Foxon, David, ed. *Libertine Literature in England, 1660–1745*. New York: Lyle Stuart, 1965; Gillette, Paul J. *The Complete Marquis de Sade*. Los Angeles: Holloway House Publishing, 2005; McCormick, Ian, ed. *Secret Sexualities: A Sourcebook of 17th and 18th Century Writing*. London: Routledge, 1997; Schaeffer, Neil. *The Marquis de Sade: A Life*. Boston: Harvard University Press, 2001.

Samantha A. Morgan-Curtis

LITERACY.   *See* Education

LITERATURE.   Most scholars agree that Western literature of the colonial and revolutionary age could be roughly divided in two periods: first, the Neoclassical period, also known as the Age of Reason, between 1650 and 1760; second, the Romantic period, from 1760 until about 1850. Although Neoclassicism and Romanticism had a worldwide influence, the best literary examples of the two periods were written in English, French, and German. After the humanist Renaissance, the writers in the Neoclassical and Romantic periods show a renewed, though differently motivated, interest in man and his world.

The differences between Neoclassicism and Romanticism are in terms of **philosophy** and aesthetics of literary production, yet in broader terms these differences refer also to contrasting views on human existence, subjectivity, and sexuality. In literary terms, Neoclassicism and Romanticism are generally considered antithetical movements according to their respective approaches to the issues of order, nature, and emotion. In other words, Neoclassicism is about order and regularity in society and **art**, while Romanticism values the individual and the exceptional. Neoclassicism follows strict models of reasoning and formal precision, while Romanticism is about spontaneity and freedom of expression.

From a social point of view, Neoclassicism is a period of rules that aims at channeling aberrant behavior in every conceivable way and promoting civil conduct appropriate to the laws of the bourgeois structure. Romanticism, on the other hand, very often is connected to the ideas of excess, experimentation, and high individualism. To emphasize the difference between the two periods, it will be enough to mention just a few names of Romantic writers whose notorious lifestyles and idiosyncratic writings challenge the rigid ideas of Neoclassicism: **Marquis de Sade** in France, Lord Byron in England, and Edgar Allan Poe in the United States.

In philosophical terms, the French philosopher René Descartes is considered the father of Neoclassicism. His *Discourse on Method* (1637) clearly posits an admiration for reason and thinking over intuition and feeling, as expressed in the famous dictum "Cogito, ergo sum (I think, therefore I am)." One might argue that Descartes's philosophy is a direct negation of the violent spirit of the seventeenth century, with bloodsheds like the English civil wars in the 1640s and 1650s, the Restoration in 1660, and the Glorious Revolution in 1688–1689. The veneration for the human mind and its abilities is best illustrated in the well-structured domain of the sciences, and particularly in physics. Sir Isaac Newton's ground-breaking *Principia* (1687) formulates the laws of motion and gravity and, symbolically, puts the physical world in order, while the seventeenth-century world is marred by social unrest and disorder.

In literature, Neoclassicism flourishes especially in drama and poetry. Aristotle's *Poetics* is accepted as the measure of perfection by the seventeenth-century playwrights: they take his analysis of tragedy as the benchmark in the creation of powerful masterpieces. Racine's tragedy *Phaedra* (1677) is an impressive example of an exquisite literary technique and a significant message. Phaedra's obsession with her stepson Hippolytous cannot bring any sexual satisfaction or be resolved. It is rather a fixation which is the punishment of the gods for her ancestors' fallibility. Read from a naturalistic point of view, Phaedra is predestined from the start as the offspring of Pasiphae (another "indiscretion" of Pasiphae, an intercourse with a bull, gives birth to the monstrous Minotaur). Racine does not sentimentalize the destiny of Phaedra, but rather emphasizes the despair from the inherent weakness of the human nature. Once more the human flesh and mind are proven corrupt and fallible and, therefore, rightfully punished by uncompassionate gods, the rightful judges of man's destiny.

It will be wrong to assume that Neoclassicism promoted only dark, gloomy tragedy in literature. For example, Molière's comedy *Tartuffe* (1664) manages to impress even today with its virtuoso play of language combined with vibrantly comic situations and unforgettable characters. Tartuffe, the eponymous character of the play, is hypocritical and greedy for money and power, ready to use any means to satisfy his sexual appetite for the wife of his gullible benefactor.

Alexander Pope's *The Rape of the Lock* (1717) is an impressive long poem written with precision and utmost mastery of meter and rhyme. It is a mock epic which bemoans the stealing of a lock of hair from a young lady which causes a breach between two noble families. Although the poem formally abides to the strict rules of Neoclassic poetry, there is a strong underlying sexual reference which could not escape the caution of Pope's critics at the time.

In contrast to the strict canonical application of rules to literature in Neoclassicism, the Romantic period is marked by interest in the individual talent and the unbridled creativity of the writer and the poet. Thus Goethe's *The Sorrows of the Young Werter* (1774) is a reminder of the miseries and pain of unreciprocated love. Werter's passion for Lotte is only equal to his despair that she is already engaged to someone else, and thus could never be his. After many attempts to forget Lotte, Werter has no other choice but to take his own life, which is empty without love fulfillment.

The English poets William Wordsworth, Samuel Taylor Coleridge, and John Keats have written some of the best examples of Romantic lyricism: passionate and vigorous or subtle and tender poems that sing to the beauty of nature, of the beloved, or of the human body. Byron is another example of the flamboyant, gifted poet whose personal life reads like a legend of incestuous, prohibited love, of passions and obsession, yet, ultimately, a life of a literary genius.

As historical periods, both Neoclassicism and Romanticism left remarkable legacies in high literature, philosophy, and the sciences. The interest in man and his world is a common concern, although as ethics and execution of literary philosophies they represent two distinctive antitheses. *See also* Restoration Poetry; Seduction Literature; Theater.

Further Reading: De Laclos, Choderlos. *Les Liaisons Dangereuses*. Oxford: Oxford University Press, 1999; Hunter, J. Paul. *Before Novels: The Cultural Context of Eighteenth-Century English Fiction*. New York: Norton, 1990; Tanner, Tony. *Adultery in the Novel: Contract and Transgression*. Baltimore: Johns Hopkins University Press, 1979.

Rossitsa Terzieva-Artemis

MADNESS. Madness was the seventeenth-century term for mental illness, a behavioral dysfunction that expressed itself in many forms. Its association with sexuality, particularly women's, developed from beliefs about the uterus and **hysteria**, a term that had been coined in ancient Greece. A notch down from madness was the term *distraction*, used to describe mental agitation and excitement that was not quite equal to madness but equally abnormal. Doctors in England who treated madness were *alienists*, and until the latter part of the nineteenth century, institutions where the mad were incarcerated were called asylums. As perceptions of mental illness evolved from an etiology of moral inferiority to medical disability, so did the vocabulary. American doctors preferred the term *insanity*.

One of the most egregious events in history is the misinterpretation of aberrant behavior in women as proof of witchcraft. Unfortunately witchcraft had a high association with sexuality because witches were believed to be oversexed, seducing otherwise uninterested men, as well as having sexual relations with the Devil. Madness then was highly correlated with demonic possession and sexual relations outside one's own **marriage**. In 1648, there was a particularly dramatic series of events involving Sister Jeanne des Anges, the Prioress of a convent of Ursuline nuns. Initially, she fantasized erotic images with a very attractive priest, Father Urban Grandier. The fantasy grew to an obsession where she could not rid herself of sexual thoughts about him. Eventually the entire convent was acting out blatant sexual behavior, but it was only Sister Jeanne who was mentally ill. The church encouraged the expression of those behaviors as proof of demonic possession, even though the physicians could not find proof. In 1658, Sister Jeanne and her flock stated that they had undergone copulation with demons and lost their virginity. Again physicians were called in but diagnosed the nuns with *furor uterinus*, a disease characterized by "heat accompanied by an inextinguishable appetite for venery and an inability to think or talk about anything other than sex." However, the church superseded and eagerly performed exorcisms. One aspect of the test was to strip the women and subject their bodies to inspection in public, itself an erotic voyeuristic experience for the pious.

Up until this time, *furor uterinus* was considered a madness that resulted from the uterus being dissatisfied with its inability to be impregnated. Another way of describing the etiology of this madness was prolonged **celibacy**. In the seventeenth century, the uterus allegedly wandered throughout a woman's body in search of moisture in the form of semen. When it did not find satisfaction, it wreaked havoc wherever it went, causing all kinds of physical disorders.

Many of the Dutch artists of the seventeenth century painted sickroom portraits of depressed-looking women waiting for or being examined by the friendly doctor. Usually there is a peculiar-looking vessel in the room nearby. This was the pot or dish where herbs were burned as aromatherapy treatment for the uterus, which allegedly would lure it back into place, and thus provide a cure. The diagnosis of melancholy had already been defined in Robert Burton's 1621 work, "The Anatomy of Melancholy," a 450-page book with astute clinical descriptions of what is now called depression. But Burton considered *furor uterinus* a type of melancholia. Thus the disease characterized by heart palpitations, pain in various parts of the body, fainting, bad dreams, appetite disorders, and mood swings became gendered: melancholia for men, *furor uterinus* or hysteria for women.

Since psychiatry did not really become part of the medical world until the latter part of the nineteenth century, the reasons for madness remained a mystery. **Cotton Mather**, a Puritan minister and one of the most prolific medical writers in the American colonies, described his third wife's madness as "little short of a proper satanic possession." Mather's enthusiasm for finding sinful behavior or demonic possession in his parishioners, friends, and neighbors was extinguished after he himself was accused of being possessed. Soon afterward, his writings changed to reflect that there could be physical reasons behind the symptoms of mental aberrations. Unfortunately, he recommended the typical harsh treatments of the time: bleeding, purging, and herbal remedies. His book *Angel of Bethesda*, written in 1724, described these less supernatural, more normal causes of madness.

In the eighteenth century many reforms changed the way that madness was treated and defined, but certain beliefs regarding normality persisted. The idea that a woman could dress in man's clothing was tantamount to criminal behavior, and a woman who demonstrated any kind of boldness or independence was liable to be regarded as mad. Any sexual behavior exhibited by a woman was likely to be regarded as a transgression from the norm, and attempts to regulate her sexuality were present both legally and socially. The gradual shift of etiologies, from possession by demons to a punishment for sin, to an imbalance of the humors, eventually evolved to the medical. Then institutions were built, asylums where the insane were incarcerated. Punishment rather than treatment was society's way of dealing with aberrant behavior, and restraints such as cages, shackles, and irons were employed.

The close association of the moral with madness explains how guilt or exaggerated guilt could lead to mental illness. The work that Phillippe Pinel did in France to free the insane from their fetters and Benjamin Rush advocated in America changed the paradigm of madness. Rush did not accept hysteria as a form of mental illness, even though he wrote that extreme emotions whether they be positive or negative influence madness. But even Rush was biased in his analysis of gender and wrote that women, in particular, were subject to madness as a result of conscience or guilt. *See also* Cross-Dressing; Medicine and Science; Midwives and Physicians; Monasteries; Puritans; Witches and Witch Trials.

Further Reading: Dixon, Laurinda. *Perilous Chastity*. Ithaca, NY: Cornell University Press, 1995; Gamwell, Lynn, and Nancy Tomes. *Madness in America: Cultural and Medical Perceptions of Mental Illness before 1914*. Ithaca, NY: Cornell University Press, 1995; Huxley, Aldous. *The Devils of Loudun*. New York: Harper Brothers, 1953; Szasz, Thomas S. *The Manufacture of Madness*. New York: Harper and Row, 1970; Weyler, Karen A. "The Fruit of Unlawful Embraces." In *Sex and Sexuality in Early America*, edited by Merril Smith, 283–313. New York: New York University Press, 1998.

Lana Thompson

MARITIME CULTURE. Although life at sea has been conceptualized as a traditionally masculine sector, recent research suggests that women were surprisingly involved in early modern maritime culture. Sailors would sometimes sneak women on board ships, while captains were known to take female traveling companions. Seamen would regularly bring their wives on voyages, and the women would participate in activities like caring for the wounded after battles. These wives were almost never officially recognized by admiralty, however, and they are seldom included in ships' records. There were also several cases of women **cross-dressing** and attempting to pass for men, sometimes working as crewmembers for years before being discovered. The eighteenth-century-sailor Hannah Snell concealed her sex for over four years, during which time she served in both the British army and the navy.

While many sailors lived up to the naval reputation for a girl in every port, other seamen missed their wives and families; indeed, they would often write emotional letters to send back home, all the while finding souvenirs to give upon their return. And of the young sailors who did engage in sexual activities with the prostitutes of London, there is evidence to suggest that many of these crewmembers actually visited the same women on later trips, even asking the prostitutes to look after their wages earned at sea. Seventeenth-century London provided many opportunities for women to work in the sex trade or the taverns, both of which were always popular with young, unmarried sailors on leave. Bitter financial need demanded that some of these women enter prostitution; others chose the work over the grueling hours of seamstresses, well aware of the constant and large number of sailors who would pay for sex.

Recent research has uncovered the stories of a handful of women who dressed as men and spent extended lengths of time at sea. In the mid-eighteenth century, Mary Lacy apprenticed for seven years and spent six years as a crewmember on various ships, all the while dressing as a young man and using the name William Chandler. During her time as a crewmember, Lacy had several close, long-term relationships with women at port. She first concealed her sex in 1759 when she searched out work on the HMS *Sandwich* and was able to keep her secret until 1767. The two shipwrights who knew her real identity as a woman agreed to keep up the pretense, and Lacy did not leave the sea life until 1770, when severe arthritis made physical labor impossible. Lacy applied for and received disability pension that was equal to that of any superannuated shipwright. The Admiralty's records clearly note her practice of cross-dressing and that the pension was being given to a woman sailor.

More common were instances of sailors' wives living on the ships, usually with the approval of the captain. The American Navy, which formed after the Revolution of 1776, seems to have been more willing than the British Royal Navy to have women on board ships; however, women did live on British ships as well. The women who were given permission to sail with their husbands were usually married to standing officers—gunners, boatswains, or carpenters, for example. Wives could live below deck in their husbands' quarters and rarely came to the attention of more senior officers.

Women would also frequently accompany their sea-captain husbands on whaling ships. Indeed, whaling vessels would be at sea for more than a year at a time; couples would find such separations unbearable, and the women would choose to accompany their husbands rather than endure extended periods of loneliness on land. A captain's wife often led an isolated life on board a whaler. With few activities available to her and a limited number of tasks, a wife's time at sea could be quite dreary. In stark contrast to lonesome sea captains who would often write heartfelt letters to loved ones back home, the seamen aboard a whaler overwhelmingly presented themselves as strong and unfazed by time away from families, lest their sensitivity be mocked by fellow crewmembers.

While women were tolerated occasionally on vessels, the British Royal Navy was far less forgiving of any sexual relationships among men. Indeed, **sodomy** was listed among the crimes that could warrant execution. Officers with private quarters could more easily engage in sexual acts with other men; however, the Royal Navy was officially intolerant of homosexuality in all crew classes. Relatively few cases of homosexual relations resulted in naval court-martials, a point which implies that known cases were unreported, perhaps because of the brutal physical punishments that could result if a sailor was found guilty of behavior that was deemed lewd. *See also* Erauso, Catalina de; Gender Roles; Pirates; Prostitutes and Prostitution.

Further Reading: Cohen, Daniel A., ed. The Female Marine *and Related Works: Narratives of Cross-Dressing and Urban Vice in America's Early Republic*. Amherst: University of Massachusetts Press, 1997; Cordingly, David. *Women Sailors and Sailors' Women: An Untold Maritime History*. New York: Random House, 2001.

Laura Schechter

MARQUIS DE SADE. *See* Sade, Donatien Alphonse François de

MARRIAGE. The institution of marriage was an important foundation upon which familial, social, economic, and political organization rested in the colonial and revolutionary era. The marriage of a man and woman joined families and kin groups. It helped to define gender relations between men and women and frequently marked the emergence of adulthood and autonomy for males. It guided the production, utilization, and devolution of wealth and property within families and communities. In an age without government safety nets, marriage helped to ensure at least rudimentary care and support in old age. Marriage was also a key cultural lens through which most people understood their relations to neighbors, political authorities, and God. Marriage formation and expectations differed in different regions, and among different ethnic, religious, and social groups. Despite these differences, historians have argued that over the course of the colonial and revolutionary period, the perception of marriage as a primarily economic affair gradually shifted to a view that an ideal marriage should be based on love and companionship.

Perceptions of the institution of marriage were affected by social and economic circumstances and religious and legal traditions. In the European household formation system, men and women generally married late. Men frequently married around the age of twenty-seven or twenty-eight; women were generally two to three years younger than the men. In his 1755 treatise on commerce, Richard Cantillon remarked that "farmhands and artisans do not marry because they are waiting to save something to place themselves in a state of entering a household, or to find some girl who has some small savings for this." Historians estimate that the age of marriage generally increased from the seventeenth to the eighteenth centuries in all but the most comfortable social classes. Because adequate money for a new household was not an important issue, elite families tended to marry their children in their late teens and early twenties. The European household formation system was also distinguished by relatively high rates of unmarried or widowed single people. It is difficult to state with precision how long marriages lasted, but widowhood and frequent remarriage are important characteristics of colonial and revolutionary society.

In the seventeenth century, marriage was almost universally considered an affair of families rather than simply the joining of two individuals. Appropriate marriages joined two people from similar age, social-class, and religious groups. For many people, love was not a prerequisite for marriage. It was hoped that the couple would respect one another, find suitable and complementary characteristics, and eventually grow fond of one another as their years together increased. Even decades after marriage, couples frequently referred to one another as good friends or good companions, terms we would usually associate with modern conceptions of friendship.

Ideally, an opportunity for marriage commenced through the initiation of **courtship** activities by parents of the children, or by the prospective groom. Youth often met on the streets in urban areas, and in village activities, such as the spinning bee (or *veillée*) in smaller villages. Courtship rituals could be fraught with danger, especially for the men who risked dishonor upon refusal of their overtures to the women. Men engaged in courtship rituals in a very public manner that risked their good name and reputations. William Williams called courting the "Danger of Disappointment" in 1761. Men generally asked permission from their own parents as well as from those of the prospective bride. French men and women often used symbolic gestures to show their feelings on the matter. Upon the young man's arrival at the female's house, her parents might offer a small meal or stamp out the cinders in the fireplace, signaling an early exit for the potential spouse. On the other hand, parents who considered the prospective match attractive and respectable would maintain a strong fire in the hearth and offer their new guest wine and expensive meats as a sign of honor.

Once a marriage was approved, families negotiated the terms of the marriage contract. Like modern prenuptial agreements, colonial-era marriage contracts indicated which property would belong to the new household. In many colonial communities, the future bride's family offered a dowry, usually comprised of cash, animals, linens, and even rights to land. The groom offered property to the marriage as well. Marital property often had a distinct status. Part of the overall property was designated as ancestral or lineage property. Spouses could not alienate this property without permission of their families. If a spouse died without children, the property would be returned to his or her family line. The other part of the property was called community property and the couple had much more flexibility with this property. Any new wealth brought into the household was generally considered community property. Most European and colonial legal systems indicated that the husband had rights to all of the marital property. Women's legal identities and rights to property were often subsumed under the interests of the husband, a legal practice called coverture. Married women thus needed permission from their husbands to enter into contracts, ask for a loan, appear in court, or make a will.

After the families had agreed to and signed the marriage contract, a public declaration of the engagement followed. Legal restrictions on the process of forming a marriage first emerged in sixteenth-century France, and in the seventeenth and eighteenth centuries England and Spain followed suit. Most religious and civil regulations stipulated that the intention to marry (or marital banns) should be declared from the church pulpits or meetinghouses on three successive Sundays. In New England, families could also post their intentions on the meetinghouse door for two weeks. These declarations allowed the community to weigh in on the proposed marriage; they affirmed not only the public nature of the match, but also the guardian's right to halt a process begun by children without his or her **consent**. During this period, parents allowed and in some cases encouraged bundling, a ritual in which the future groom remained up all night with his future bride at her parents' house. The couple was to remain clothed in bed and they were not supposed to have sexual intercourse. Bundling encouraged the couple to feel comfortable and compatible with one another prior to the official marriage. The marriage ceremony was the next stage in the process. In rural society, marriages were celebrated around the peak work seasons. February was the most popular month for marriages in France, followed by January, June, July, and November. A feast followed the ceremony. Unlike contemporary marriage celebrations, the groom's family regularly paid for the festivities. The colonial and revolutionary marriage was not complete until it was consummated. A failure to have sexual relations was adequate grounds for the annulment of the marriage and the dissolution of the contract.

Colonists brought their ideas of marriage with them when they arrived in the Americas. Although the European marital system was not always carried over to the colonies in its entirety, the colonists often described their marriage practices as the lynchpin of civilization that distinguished them from the Native American peoples that they encountered. Many Native American groups practiced male-female groupings considerably different from those of the Europeans. Native American unions could be readily dissolved, for example, and elite men often took more than one wife, a practice called polygyny. In some communities, having more wives indicated social and political status, and the women helped both to produce important crops for the household and sustain village alliances between households. Anne Marie Plane has suggested that assigning the term "marriage" to Native American peoples is Eurocentric and misses the fact that Native relationships took place very slowly. "Rather than being 'married' or 'unmarried' people sometimes live[d] in relationships that only slowly, over many years or even a lifetime, evolve[d] into recognized 'marriages'" (Plane 6). Native American sexual relations were much more fluid, and European ministers, priests, and colonial officials often focused on marital practices as one main avenue toward the "civilization" and Christianization of the Native Americans. In Spain, King Charles III instituted regulations in 1778 for the Spanish American colonists that reinforced parental consent for marriages. The Spanish colonial administration became particularly concerned about unequal marriages between different social and ethnic groups.

The extent to which European marital practices were carried over to the colonies depended on the social, economic, and religious context in the Americas. Colonial marital practices differed from region to region. New England marriages most closely resembled the European pattern. Men and women in New England married late and through strict oversight of their parents. Many colonial marriages were not performed before a minister or priest. New England **Puritans**, for example, rejected marriage as a sacrament, and so the ceremonies were performed before a judge in a meetinghouse or at a family residence. In many cases, people simply got themselves married. Historians have argued that formal marriage celebrations in Maryland, for instance, were uncommon before 1700. In the Chesapeake region, a shortage of females and an unstable population meant that little parental control existed over marriages. Men were generally much older, sometimes even ten years older, than their brides. Informal marital arrangements meant that women were often pregnant upon their marriages. The high mortality rates within the difficult environment contributed to deaths of spouses and frequent second and third families. As a result, the Chesapeake colonists, especially in the seventeenth century, probably experienced much more sexual freedom and marital choice than did their northern counterparts.

Colonial and revolutionary society had clear expectations for marital relationships between men and women. Men and women were not considered equals in marriage, but both contributed to the economic well-being of the household. Authors of advice manuals argued that the family relationships were models of monarchical authority. The Englishman Richard Braithwait wrote that the family was a "domestic kingdom, a monarchy." The husband's and father's authority reflected that of the king over the kingdom. The husband's control over household property, and his ability to sign for the family in legal contracts, cemented him as the main representative of his family to the village and state representatives beyond the household. While the ideal marriage relationship reflected common beliefs about the legal and political hierarchies of the day, advice-book authors also spent considerable time reflecting on the economic partnerships created by the marriage. The colonial household was the center of production and consumption. For most of the families who made their living from the land, men were expected to work in the fields and tend the crops, while women were expected to produce and sell the products from the land. As Kathleen Brown has explained, women "made butter and cheese from cow's milk, they brewed and baked with grain products, and their manufactured linens and clothes from flax, hemp, and wool" (Brown 25). Women often sold these goods at markets in local villages and towns. While they were performing this work, women were also expected to care for the children and teach them the skills necessary to work in their own households as when they reached their adult years. Because of the important labor women provided for the household, colonial enterprises often encouraged women to settle in their communities.

While advice-book authors extolled husbands as kings within their households, historians have recently discovered that there were many avenues for women to express dissatisfaction with their spouses. The ability for women to express their grievances was often rooted in the social ideal of the economic partnership and the associated responsibilities that both spouses implicitly accepted upon marriage. In particular, women could use the law and the courts to provide checks on male behavior when their husbands failed to serve as good providers for their families. Men who failed to support their families with their labor were ridiculed by family and village alike. Spendthrifts and drunkards were particularly liable to court action and shaming. In an economy where access to credit rested on one's reputation, accusations against husbands could be very damaging to their future economic viability. Women could sue for separation of property if their husbands squandered the dowry or community property. In the worst cases, women could sue for a separation of persons in order to regain control over their family and children. Familial quarrels that turned public could devastate the man's reputation in his community. Husbands were ridiculed if their wives had sex outside marriage. Village men would shame their counterpart, forcing him to ride backward on a donkey as a symbol of his lack of control within his household. Thus historians have argued that the patriarchal social ideal created expectations for proper male behavior that allowed women to seek recourse in a number of venues.

Over the course of the colonial and revolutionary period, the perception of marriage as a primarily economic affair gradually shifted to a view that an ideal marriage should be based on love and companionship. Historians have introduced a number of factors that identify and explain these shifts. Illegitimacy rates rose in the eighteenth century, and one historian of eighteenth-century Britain has estimated that one-third of all brides were pregnant on their wedding day, and half of all children were born outside marriage. In New England, women began to outnumber men by the later eighteenth century, and land shortages reduced parental power. Higher rates of lifelong celibacy occurred among women, and women who married generally did so at a later age. Historians have suggested that these demographic and economic changes helped spur the ideal of mutual affection and love within marriage. While authors of seventeenth-century advice manuals stress the male desire for a virtuous domestic companion, their later eighteenth-century counterparts stressed attractiveness and intelligence. Eighteenth-century novels and plays emphasized the romantic qualities of a marriage, and young lovers often successfully engaged in marriage despite parental disapproval. New late-eighteenth-century Spanish laws that strictly regulated marriage were not uniformly applied in local colonial courts. By the late eighteenth century, French revolutionaries had attempted to demolish despotism at all levels of society. Accordingly, they reduced parental authority to block marriages of their children. A new, modern idea of marriage as a relationship based on love and mutual support had begun to emerge. *See also* Bastardy; Concubines; Divorce; Household Consumerism; Polyandry; Romantic Love; Widows and Widowhood.

Further Reading: Brown, Kathleen. *Good Wives, Nasty Wenches, and Anxious Patriarchs: Gender, Race, and Power in Colonial Virginia*. Chapel Hill: University of North Carolina Press, 1996; Hufton, Olwen. *The Prospect before Her: A History of Women in Western Europe, 1500–1800*. New York: Knopf, 1996; Plane, Anne Marie. *Colonial Intimacies: Indian Marriage in Colonial New England*. Ithaca, NY: Cornell University Press, 2000; Socolow, Susan M. "Acceptable Partners: Marriage Choice in Colonial Argentina, 1778–1810." In *Sexuality and Marriage in Colonial Latin America*, edited by Asuncion Lavrin, 209–51. Lincoln: University of Nebraska Press, 1989; Stone, Lawrence. *Uncertain Unions: Marriage in England, 1660–1753*. New York: Oxford University Press, 1992; Walsh, Lorena. "'Till Death Us Do Part': Marriage and Family in Seventeenth-Century Maryland." In *The Chesapeake in the Seventeenth Century: Essays on Anglo-American Society*, edited by Thad W. Tate and David L. Ammerman, 126–52. Chapel Hill: University of North Carolina Press, 1979; Wilson, Lisa. *Ye Heart of a Man: The Domestic Life of Men in Colonial New England*. New Haven, CT: Yale University Press, 1999.

Christopher R. Corley

MARVELL, ANDREW (1621–1678).   Andrew Marvell was a friend and disciple of **John Milton** and a metaphysical poet associated with John Donne and George Herbert. He graduated from Trinity College in Cambridge and left the town in 1640 after the death of his parents. In the following years he traveled to France, Holland, Switzerland, Spain, and Italy. In 1650 he became the tutor of Mary Fairfax, the future Duchess of Buckingham, and in 1653 he started his friendship with John Milton. Soon afterward he was elected a member of Parliament and continued the political activity throughout the rest of his life; he also wrote many political pamphlets and satires in which he expressed his strong criticism of, among other topics, the monarchy and censorship. His metaphors were often sexual, and he did not hesitate to use "**rape**" as one of them, the best proof for this being the poem "Last Instructions to a Painter" (1667).

The poem deals with the figures Marvell thought were responsible for the troubles of England at the time of Charles II's reign. Political abuse is described by Marvell as if it were sexual abuse, and the fact that the image presented in the poem becomes so powerful can be explained by adding that, first of all, Marvell wrote it when he was actively involved in politics himself, so he was aware of all the corruption and decay he would then criticize, and secondly, he wrote it just after the humiliating Second Dutch War. Marvell describes British statesmen of the time as indulging their sexual and political powers. Therefore, they are not able to defend their country against the foreign attack—one which is described here in the terms of a rape; what is more, it seems that the statesmen perform another rape on their country by following their greedy and disloyal ways, while their collaboration with the foreign powers also adds to the "violation from the outside." The poem begins with the critique of the king's court, but eventually it reveals the king himself as the main rapist of the country. The speaker in the poem identifies with the victim of the rape and tries to make a clear distinction between the victim and the rapists. All the shocking images Marvell uses in his poem were, obviously, common for the metaphysical poets, and it is worth noting that another poet who belonged to the same group, John Donne, once created a vision quite similar to that of Marvell's: in his "Holy Sonnet 14" Donne makes God a rapist and himself a besieged city.

Although Marvell repeatedly used similar metaphors to create the realm of psychosexual politics, his use of the metaphor of a rape was never quite as powerful as that used in "Last Instructions to a Painter." (It must be noted, however, that in "An Horatian Ode upon Cromwell's Return from England" [1681] he used a very similar technique to a good effect, this time playing with the metaphor of emasculation to describe the beheading of the king.) *See also* Literature; Restoration Poetry.

Further Reading: Craze, Michael. *The Life and Lyrics of Andrew Marvell*. London: Macmillan, 1979; Donno, Elizabeth S. *Andrew Marvell Complete Poems*. New York: Penguin Books, 1987; Patterson, Annabel M. *Marvell: The Writer in Public Life*. London: Longman Publishing Group, 1999.

Bartlomiej Paszylk

MASCULINITY. Masculinity is a set of behavioral characteristics associated with men and with being male. Although it overlaps with the property of biological maleness, it is not equivalent to it. Masculinity is the cultural counterpart—although not necessarily the opposite—of femininity. As a term that interconnects with gender, the body, and sexuality, masculinity is both complex and plural. Many have argued that it would be more accurate to talk of "masculinities" since a single term could never encompass the variety of men's identities, the changes in men's behavior, self-definition, and sexual practices across history. From 1600 to 1800, masculinity underwent a series of transformations that changed the forms of culturally dominant manliness, which affected both sexual relations and the nature of society itself.

Early modern masculinity reflected the religious and profoundly hierarchical society of the time. This society was inherently patriarchal, with superior civil and cultural status attached to maleness itself. Aristocratic masculinity had a clearly defined and highly codified form of amorous love, represented by the French courtly tradition. This tradition exalted the unapproachable female love object, vowing commitment and servitude to her. Chivalric masculinity was typified by its code of honor, emphasis on chastity, and religious piety. This culturally prestigious code was related to the elevation of ecclesiastical forms of masculinity that also stressed the importance of self-control and ascetic denial of sexuality.

Many forms of patriarchal manhood used the control and active subordination of women as the means of asserting and maintaining masculine status. Early modern ideas of sexuality saw women as sexually volatile and insatiate. In order to express masculine power, female sexuality had to be controlled, often through marriage. This form of masculinity has been seen as anxious, leading to a reconceptualizing of **gender roles** and new, more dominant forms of masculinity defined through relations between men, rather than between men and women. Men's participation in war and the military formed a strain of masculinity characterized by self-display and homosocial affiliations. Colonial expansion produced more muscular forms of maleness, again many dependent on fraternal bonding and religious motivation. Imperialism confronted both sides with versions of masculinity profoundly different, and riven with issues of nationality, politics, and race. Much of the discourse around empire is couched in terms of masculine sexual prowess. The self-sufficient colonial was promoted as an embodiment of the masculine ability to dominate, control, and subdue in the name of reason and civilization.

The use of sex and sexuality as power can be seen in libertinism, a creed based around the disregard of religious and social mores, and manifested in the promiscuous satisfaction of sexual desire. Libertinism had some precedent in the Renaissance sodomite, whose homosocial friendships and sexual practices transgressed the normative, heterosexual versions of masculinity. The rake, an individual who pursues sex indiscriminately for pure pleasure, became a popular masculine archetype in the mid to late seventeenth century. **John Wilmot, Earl of Rochester** (1647–1680), was the exemplary rake. Educated, intelligent, obscene, Rochester engaged in sexual acts with both men and women. His gleeful violation of moral codes expressed the power of his masculine identity. At the close of the eighteenth century the aristocratic French writer **Marquis de Sade** followed a more extreme and sexually violent version of libertinism in his writings. Both forms of **libertine** masculinity enact a cultural power, rather than a manifestation of an alternative form of nonheterosexual masculinity. Nonheterosexual masculinity was an object of fear and contempt in this period, although male nonsexual friendship along the Hellenic model continued to have civic respectability. Fear of same-sex masculinity was condensed in the figure of the "Molly," a man whose sexuality was directed toward the same sex. Such nonheterosexual desire transgressed the social order and was seen to threaten men's "natural" sexual and cultural roles as superior to, and unlike, women.

The early eighteenth century saw a reconception of the ideal gentleman as no longer necessarily aristocratic, but created through politeness and civil self-control. Again, this involved a normative stress on sexual self-restraint and a focus on the integrity of the masculine character. The polite gentleman conversed with women and was improved by his relationship with the opposite sex. Rather than socializing solely with other men, this form of masculinity drew power and legitimacy from its civil and proper relations with the feminine. Yet the connection to femininity compromised some forms of masculinity. Contemporary culture satirized male types such as the Fop, whose effeminacy was self-centered and ungentlemanly. By the end of the century, the Fop had been subsumed into the derided category of the nonheterosexual male.

The polite gentleman of the early eighteenth century was a theoretically sexless creature, whose energies were directed toward industry, colonial expansion, and the civil state. The popularity of sensibility in mid-eighteenth century novels and poetry represented a shift in the ideal of masculine morality. The man of sensibility was responsive and moral, but essentially passive. Yet both politeness and sensibility became theorized as feminine attributes. In the wake of the French Revolution (1789) and English philosopher Mary Wollstonecraft's critique of **patriarchy**, some forms of masculinity assumed reactionary forms. The conservative philosopher Edmund Burke called for a return to the chivalric code and governance by "strong" men. Yet the radical writers of the late 1700s, such as William Godwin, P. B. Shelley, and Samuel Taylor Coleridge, asserted their sexual liberation and sexual relations with women as part of a "strong" masculinity capable of actively intervening in politics and culture. Competition between conceptions of masculinity at the close of the eighteenth century demonstrates how contested the very terms of maleness have been throughout history. Masculinity's role in producing sexual conformity and practice is part of its ability to naturalize behavior, which is seen as natural. The very differences between masculinities shows how sociohistorical change affects both what is seen as masculine and what is seen as masculine sexuality. *See also* Byrd, William; Molly Houses; Sodomy and Anti-Sodomy Law; Women, Changing Images of.

Further Reading: Carter, Philip. *Men & the Emergence of Polite Society: Britain, 1660–1800.* Harlow: Longman, 2000; Cohen, Michel. *Fashioning Masculinity: National Identity and Language in the Eighteenth Century.* New York: Routledge, 1996; Fulford, Tim. *Romanticism and Masculinity: Gender, Politics and Poetics on the Writings of Burke, Coleridge, Cobbett, Wordsworth, De Quincey and Hazlitt.* New York: Macmillan, St. Martin's, 1999; Johnson, Claudia. *Equivocal Beings: Politics, Gender, and Sentimentality in the 1790s—Wollstonecraft, Radcliffe, Burney, Austen.* Chicago: University of Chicago Press, 1995; Sale, Maggie Montesinos. *The Slumbering Volcano: American Slave Ship Revolts and the Production of Rebellious Masculinity.* Durham, NC: Duke University Press, 1997.

Rebecca Barr

MASTURBATION. The great medical crusade against masturbation, which lasted into the twentieth century, began in the Enlightenment. Masturbation had long been considered a sin by the Christian Church as well as was forbidden by Jewish and Islamic law, but it had not been considered a matter of much consequence. During the Enlightenment, "solitary pleasure" moved to the forefront of medical and pedagogic concern. The creation of the medical antimasturbation discourse began with a pamphlet by an anonymous English quack, *Onania*, which probably first appeared in 1715, although the earliest surviving edition is the fourth, from 1718. The title is derived from the biblical character Onan. Although Onan was condemned for "spilling his seed upon the ground" as a contraceptive measure rather than masturbation, and featured as such in rabbinic writing on the passage, his story was increasingly commonly interpreted as divine condemnation of masturbation. The word "onanism" first appeared in 1719. The author of *Onania* blamed masturbation for ulcers, epilepsy, consumption, **impotence**, sterility, debilitation, and early death. As treatment, he recommended repentance, cold baths, and a drug available from the bookseller for a fee—a standard feature of quack pamphlets. *Onania*, which continued the focus on male activities, was a best seller, going through fifteen editions by 1730 and many more thereafter, in addition to a German translation in 1736. The editions swelled with letters purportedly sent by suffering masturbators begging the author's assistance. Such was the horror it produced that Bernard de Mandeville argued that it was better that young men visit brothels than masturbate.

The Swiss physician and medical popularizer Samuel-August Tissot (1728–1797) published the second major antimasturbation work, *Onanism*, in French in 1760. Influenced by *Onania* and his own clinical experience, Tissot painted a gruesome picture of the masturbator, male or female, as subject to hideous and crippling diseases. In addition to extending the attack on masturbation to female masturbators, Tissot provided it with medical legitimacy. He claimed that semen, or to a lesser degree an analogous fluid in women, was the highest perfection of bodily fluid, and a substance necessary to life. Masturbators wasted this substance, thereby weakening their constitutions and shortening their lives. This required some agility to explain why heterosexual intercourse, entailing a similar loss of fluid, was not debilitating, or why bloodletting, which Tissot recommended as a treatment for many diseases, actually strengthened the body. Tissot recommended cold baths and a restricted diet as a cure for masturbation.

Whatever its weaknesses, Tissot's thesis won general acceptance. Both the *Encyclopedie* and the *Encyclopedia Britannica* followed Tissot in their discussions of masturbation, and such leaders of European thought as Voltaire and Immanuel Kant found his arguments convincing. Physicians advised parents to closely supervise their children, and schoolmasters increased their surveillance of their charges. Specially designed nightclothes to prevent children from masturbating appeared by 1785, and by the end of the century some German surgeons were drawing and fixing the foreskin over the glans of the penis, a procedure called infibulation, and claimed to cure masturbation. Some masturbators internalized the Tissot thesis and expected their systems to collapse if they continued the practice. *See also* Ejaculation; Enlightenment Thought on Sexuality; Medicine and Science; Midwives and Physicians; orgasm; Pregnancy; Puritans.

Further Reading: Laqueur, Thomas. *Solitary Sex: A Cultural History of Masturbation.* New York: Zone Books, 2003; Stengers, Jean, and Anne van Neck. *Masturbation: The History of a Great Terror.* Translated by Kathryn A. Hoffman. New York: Palgrave, 2001.

William E. Burns

MATHER, COTTON (1663–1728). Cotton Mather was the penultimate New England Puritan minister. The grandson and son of two leading ministerial families, the Cottons and the Mathers, Mather combined intellectual ability, a strong work ethic, and an abiding faith laden with fear and respect for the Puritan God. He remains the youngest person admitted to Harvard (aged eleven and a half) and wrote 388 books, including his masterwork, *Magnalia Christi Americana* and *Ornaments for the Daughters of Zion* (in which he exhorted women and their daughters to display expected female virtues: chastity, modesty, silence, and diligence). He played a vital role in the Salem witch trials. Although he opposed the validity of spectral evidence, as did most prominent Puritan ministers, he believed that execution was the only appropriate punishment for a person convicted of witchcraft. He supported smallpox inoculations in 1721, much to the chagrin of his fellow Bostonians who feared that inoculations might spread rather than curtail the current epidemic.

Mather left diaries in which he chronicled his spiritual development, current events in Boston and Massachusetts Bay Colony, and, in heartfelt detail, his family life. As a young man he recorded his guilt about masturbatory impulses and his suitability for the ministry. He married thrice and had fifteen children, only two of whom survived him. He was an affective parent; even as he taught his children about his fearsome God and the fires of Hell, he preferred moral suasion to physical punishment. An impassioned diary entry, written after his scapegrace son, Creasy, had been accused of **paternity** by a "Harlot big with Bastard" and faced criminal prosecution for **fornication**, illustrates both his love for his son, Creasy, who tried his patience early and often, and his doctrinaire Puritan attitude to extramarital sexual intercourse. He wrote, "Oh! Dreadful Case! Oh, sorrow beyond any that I have met withal! What shall I do now for the foolish Youth! What for my afflicted and abased Family" (Silverman 309). Mather kept Creasy inside for the next few weeks, out of the reach of a constable, giving him sermons to read while reminding himself to maintain a Christian calm in the face of multiple provocations. If, unlike Creasy, one of his parishioners were prosecuted for fornication in the civil courts, he or she would have made a public confession in church, delivered, perhaps, while wrapped in a white sheet, to be forgiven, admonished, or excommunicated.

Undated portrait of Cotton Mather. Courtesy of the Library of Congress.

Cotton Mather contradicts the stereotypical Puritan he is presumed to embody. A strict Congregationalist, a loving father, a scientist, an indefatigable self-promoter, and author, he was endowed with capabilities far beyond the twenty-first-century caricature of a stern man who dressed in black, burned witches, and eschewed pleasure. His views on sexuality, as expressed in sermons, advice literature, and his diary, were in the Puritan mainstream. Coitus was the right and responsibility of all married couples. **Puritans** believed that sex was an essential component of **marriage**, not only to primarily fulfill God's command to be fruitful and to multiply, but also to promote marital harmony. Ideally, couples refrained from intercourse during **pregnancy** and while wives were **breastfeeding**. Premarital sexual intercourse was illegal. Couples whose first child arrived prior to thirty-two weeks of marriage and women who bore illegitimate children and their partners were prosecuted for fornication and whipped or fined. **Masturbation** was a moral offence; same-sex sexual activity a criminal offence, and **adultery** a capital crime. *See also* Bastardy; Medicine and Science; Religion; Witches and Witch Trials.

Further Reading: Silverman, Kenneth. *The Life and Times of Cotton Mather.* New York: Columbia University Press, 1985.

Else L. Hambleton

MEDICINE AND SCIENCE. During the seventeenth and eighteenth centuries in the West, medicine and science occupied a much more central role in defining sexual issues, in many ways beginning to displace **religion**. However this was not a revolutionary break, as the scientific revolution and Enlightenment inherited millennia of Western thought on sex and sexuality. The new medicine and natural philosophy dismantled some old ideas, but many continued, only expressed in a different language.

There were many early modern scientific theories on sex and the differences of the sexes. The two major groups of theories were those that emphasized the similarities of the sexes and those that emphasized their differences. The similarity, or "one-sex" school, drawing on ancient medicine and **philosophy**, found men's and women's organs analogous—the male nipples to the female breasts, for example. Women were incomplete men, whose primary sexual organs had not been fully pushed out due to insufficient "heat." Thus the vagina was an inside-out penis, and the ovaries were often referred to as female testes. (The increased attention given to the clitoris from its "discovery" in the late sixteenth century complicated this picture, as it competed with the vagina for the title of "female penis.") Biological processes as well as organs were claimed as common to males and females—hemorrhoidal bleeding was the male equivalent of **menstruation**. One consequence of one-sex thinking was the emphasis placed on the female **orgasm** in conception. Since a man must climax to beget a child, a woman must also climax to conceive one.

The difference school, with less ancient textual authority, conceived of men and women as radically different and complementary, at least in their sexual and reproductive roles. Difference thinkers minimized the importance of structural similarities. The difference thinkers, whose rejection of ancient thought had many parallels in the scientific revolution, became the scientific mainstream during the Enlightenment. The ancient similarity model disappeared from scientific discourse by the early nineteenth century, although it persisted in popular culture and medical handbooks aimed at a popular audience. The Dutch microscopist Anton van Leeuwenhoek's identification of the male spermatozoon, announced in 1676, and, his fellow countryman, the physician Reinier de Graaf's mistaken identification of the female egg in 1672 (the De Graafian follicle was thought to be the egg until Karl Ernst von Baer's discovery of the true female egg in 1827) showed that female and male contributions to conception were naturally different, rather than being simply a mingling of fluids. Menstruation was conceptually separated from male nosebleeds or hemorrhoidal bleeding. The ovaries gained that designation, based on the Latin *ova*, or egg, rather than being referred to as the "female testes." The idea that women needed to climax sexually to conceive was also abandoned by many learned physicians and scientists, although it remained a popular belief. Women were increasingly regarded as the less sexually passionate of the two genders, a startling inversion of traditional Western thinking, which had identified women's sexual lusts as much greater than those of men.

Embryology, the science of conception and fetal development, was highly contentious. The basic division in the eighteenth century was between epigenecists, who believed that the embryo was gradually formed out of preexisting materials, and preformationists, who believed that the embryo was already formed before conception. A further division ran between those preformationists who believed that the fetus was preformed in the male sperm, spermists, and those who believed that the fetus was preformed in the female egg, ovists. The sperm itself brought up the question whether the fertilizing principle resided in the spermatozoa, or whether it was located in the liquid semen and the sperm were parasitic worms. Most problems of conception and generation could not be resolved by empirical observation of fertilization and fetal development, as microscopes were not powerful enough.

During the Enlightenment, correct sexual behavior was increasingly defined in medical rather than moral terms. The great campaign against **masturbation**, which began in early eighteenth-century Europe, characterized the practice as a medical evil leading to weakness and debilitation rather than primarily as a sin. **Gender roles** in society were also "scientifically" determined. Women's functions in reproduction, identified with the uterus and ovaries, determined their proper social role as wives and mothers. The breast was also increasingly conceptualized primarily in the role of nursing children rather than as an adornment. Male medical practitioners employed the prestige of science to attempt to take over treatment of **pregnancy** and **childbirth** from midwives, although this effort was only beginning in the eighteenth century.

The growing importance of sex in eighteenth-century thought was not restricted to the human species. No one did more to promote sex and sexual difference as key organizing characteristics for all kinds of life than Carolus Linnaeus, the great botanical and zoological classifier of the eighteenth century. Linnaeus's "sexual system" of plant classification, building on the idea of plant sexual reproduction, relied on close analogies between plant and human sexes. Plant and human sexual organs were considered closely homologous, with, for example, the filaments of the stamens in plants homologous with the *vas deferens* in animal males. Linnaeus and his disciples proclaimed the social as well as the functional homology of plant and human sexes, referring to plants as "husbands" and "wives." Reproductive biology also played a central role in Linnaean animal classification. Linnaeus, a strong advocate of **breastfeeding**, made the female breast a sex-linked characteristic, rather than hair, the four-chambered heart, or other unique characteristics the defining attribute of the class *Mammalia*, the class to which humans belong. *See also* Enlightenment Thought on Sexuality; Midwives and Physicians.

Further Reading: Laqueur, Thomas. *Making Sex: Body and Gender from the Greeks to Freud.* Cambridge, MA: Harvard University Press, 1990; Roe, Shirley. *Matter, Life and Generation: Eighteenth-Century Embryology and the Haller-Wolff Debate.* Cambridge: Cambridge University Press, 1981; Schiebinger, Londa. *Nature's Body: Gender in the Making of Modern Science.*

Boston: Beacon Press, 1993; Schleiner, Winfried. "Early Modern Controversies about the One-Sex Model." *Renaissance Quarterly* 53 (Spring, 2000): 180–91.

William E. Burns

MEN. *See* Masculinity

MENSTRUATION. Prior to the relatively late discovery of ovulation (1870s) and sex hormones (1930s), the exact function of menstruation was uncertain. No single uniform definition of menstruation prevailed in premodern medicine, and ancient theories persisted well into the eighteenth century. Western and Chinese medical explanations of menstruation centered around the idea of balance and the flow of fluids in the body. This was explained through yin-yang dualism in Chinese medicine and the Greco-Roman humoral theory (based on an equilibrium of blood, phlegm, and yellow and black bile) in the West. Further Western theories ascribed menstruation to the phases of the moon, and from the late sixteenth century onward to the fermentation of corrupt and acrid blood in the uterus. In the seventeenth century the effects of mechanical forces were applied to female physiology, and a century later the idea of a uterine erection irritating the blood vessels and expelling the menses was developed.

The exact role of menses in procreation was also disputed. During **pregnancy**, menses were believed to nourish the fetus and to rise to the breasts after delivery, where they were transformed into milk. However, physicians were unsure whether menses were strictly necessary for conception, whether conception could actually occur during menstruation, when the optimum moment in the menstrual cycle was, and whether bleeding during pregnancy; was dangerous for fetal health. Medical practitioners observed girls who conceived without ever having menstruated and women who menstruated regularly, but were barren. It was generally believed that menstruation stopped during pregnancy; however, this was not a certain sign of conception since it was widely known that menstruation could be suppressed owing to famine, ill health, and overwork. The observation of women who continued to menstruate during pregnancy added to this uncertainty.

The menarche and menopause were significant stages in the female sexual and cultural life cycle. Regular menstruation was particularly important and late menarche provoked fears of the condition "green-sickness" (chlorosis) caused by suppressed menses in adolescent girls, which if untreated could lead to sterility. Such was the emphasis on regularity and periodicity of menstrual flows within the humoral conception of bodily health that periodic bleeding from other orifices including the ears, nose, and anus was also termed (vicarious) menstruation. Menopause signaled the end of a woman's fertile capacity and was believed to cause a decline in health. The symptoms of retained menstruation were likened to those of pregnancy (as were those of menopause) making it difficult for practitioners to distinguish between the different conditions and leading to fears that debauched women sought abortifacient remedies in the guise of stimulating their blocked menstrual flow.

This lack of medical consensus was reflected in wider attitudes toward menstruation, which were inherently paradoxical, oscillating between the polarities of polluting and purifying, sacred and defiling. Menstrual taboos, derived from Classical Antiquity and Jewish law, inscribed in the Old Testament (Leviticus 15, 20, 28), were subsequently reinterpreted by Christian scholars. Folkloric beliefs that menstruating women emitted poisonous vapors which could sour wine, turn milk, send dogs mad, cause pregnant women to miscarry, provoke thunder and hailstorms, and ruin harvests persisted into the nineteenth and twentieth centuries. Biblical taboos prohibited contact of any sort with a menstruating woman. Discussions of whether a menstruating woman could attend mass and receive communion were rife in premodern Europe. "Churching," a rite of purification following the lying-in period after **childbirth**, also related to menstrual taboos since postpartum bleeding was considered as unclean as menstrual blood.

Sex during menstruation was deemed a mortal sin by many premodern theologians, resulting in physical and spiritual defilement for both partners and the probability of leprosy (and other diseases) and malformations in any progeny conceived during such an act. Sex during menstruation was held responsible for red hair, freckles, and birthmarks. It was also cited as the cause of childhood illnesses such as measles and scarlet fever—the characteristic marking of which stemmed from an exposure to an excess of menses during gestation, which the body was now trying to expel. From the sixteenth century onward this fear transmuted into the danger of monstrous births, ranging from conjoined twins, infants with multiple limbs or lacking a limb, to demonic, animal-like creatures interpreted as evidence of divine wrath directed toward those who had indulged in an unnatural coupling and as a sign to the rest of the community.

The idea of menstrual blood as physically and spiritually polluting was incorporated into the Jewish Blood Libel. The premodern Catholic Church promulgated the belief that Jewish men were weak and effeminate and subject to a monthly hemorrhoidal flux, which was equated with menstrual bleeding. Scholars disagree over the implications of male menstruation; simultaneously portrayed as a convenient political and religious weapon at the seventeenth-century Spanish Court and as beneficial and therapeutic in seventeenth- and eighteenth-century medicine. Menstruation's purging properties were interpreted as both salutary and a sign of female weakness, emotionality, and inferiority in Eastern and Western medicine and culture. The pathologization of menstruation and the association of menstrual and psychiatric disorders, leading to the coining of the disorder "hysteria," did not begin in earnest until the nineteenth century. Prior to this, menstruation was generally treated with scientific curiosity as the key to the secrets of female sexual potency and fertility. Respect for the mysteries of procreation and the sacred role of the female and her menstrual fluid in this process coexisted with fear of female sexual potency, desire, and control over reproduction. The enigma of menstruation can be said to reflect the extent to which gendered and sexual hierarchies were culturally embedded in the profoundly pronatalist premodern world. *See also* Abortion; Baths; Breastfeeding; Gynecology Manuals; Judaism; Medicine and Science; Religion.

Further Reading: Beusterien, John. "Jewish Male Menstruation in Seventeenth-Century Spain." *Bulletin of the History of Medicine* 73, no. 3 (1999): 447–56; Crawford, Patricia. "Attitudes to Menstruation in Seventeenth-Century England." *Past and Present* 91 (1981): 47–73; Furth, Charlotte. "Blood, Body and Gender in Medical Images of the Female Condition in China 1600–1835." *Chinese Science* 7 (1986): 43–66; McClive, Cathy. "Menstrual Knowledge and Medical Practice in France, c. 1495–1761." In *Menstruation in History and Culture from Antiquity to Modernity*, edited by Andrew Shail and Gillian Howie. London: Palgrave, 2005; Niccoli, Ottavia. "'Menstruum Quasi Monstruum': Monstrous Births and Menstrual Taboo in the Sixteenth Century." In *Sex and Gender in Historical Perspective*, edited by Guido Ruggiero and Edward Muir, 1–25. Baltimore: John Hopkins University Press, 1990; Pomata, Gianna. "Menstruating Men: Similarity and Difference of the Sexes in Early Modern Medicine." In *Generation and Degeneration: Tropes of Reproduction in Literature and History from Antiquity to Early Modern Europe*, edited by Valeria Finucci and Kevin Brownlee, 109–52. Durham, NC: Duke University Press, 2001.

Cathy McClive

MEXICO, INDIGENOUS WOMEN OF. A variety of ethnicities are indigenous to Mexico, such as the well-known Aztec, Maya, and Lacandon peoples, as well as the lesser-known Pima, Yaquí, and many others. The brutal stories of conquest and colonization by the Spanish that are most widely known regard the two largest indigenous Mexican groups: the Aztec and the Maya. As a result of this conquest, indigenous women often endured **rape** by Spanish soldiers, as rape was frequently used as a tactic of war. During the conquest, indigenous women were both given to Spaniards by their own people and taken by force. In addition, indigenous women were often sexually abused. As a result, a new ethnic group was born: the children of indigenous women and Spanish conquistadors, called *mestizos*.

In the postconquest colonial years, **marriage** with indigenous women was rejected as socially unacceptable. However, Spaniards who were granted indigenous slaves would lose their slaves if they did not marry within three years, an attempt by both the Spanish crown and church to force their culture upon the indigenous populations. Therefore marriage between Spanish men and indigenous women increased, and the mestizo ethnic group continued growing.

Indigenous women slaves were powerless in the Spanish male-dominated society, yet still felt they had some rights, such as the right to married life. Marriage performed by the church was considered to bring certain rights to everyone, regardless of their ethnicity or their position in the caste society. In 1610, for instance, two slaves, Gerónima Negra and Luisa Negra, complained that their owners mistreated them by refusing to let them live with their husbands. Threatening excommunication, an ecclesiastic judge ordered their owners to allow them one night a week with their husbands.

Marriage brought additional rights, though more so for women than for men. When rape cases were brought to court, married women were favored over unmarried ones. However, colonial courts viewed any rape and sexual-assault accusations with suspicion. They often placed blame on the woman, agreeing with her attacker that she had provoked him.

In 1696, Catarina María, an indigenous woman, brought an indigenous man to court on charges of rape, suing for dowry money or marriage. She lost because the court could not be sure the unmarried woman was a virgin before the encounter. Her reputation was damaged by the loss of the suit. She would need to find a husband or live to a social standard of **virtue** to correct it.

Although the courts favored married women's claims, fewer cases of rape were reported for married women than unmarried ones. Penalties carried out against rapists of married women were rarely severe. Since they could neither expect retribution nor compensation, and since their communities would accuse them of being immodest, disreputable, or of shaky virtue, married women usually remained silent.

Rape meant a loss of honor to a Mexican woman. Marriage to one's rapist was considered a solution to regaining honor since it hid the rape and loss of virginity. Rape and sexual assault were often not only sexual acts against a woman, but also political acts of humiliation and domination of an entire family. Legally and socially, male relatives were understood to be the victims of a woman's rape. Families therefore accepted marriage to the rapist as a means of covering up their own dishonor. For example, when Leonarda Antonia, an indigenous woman, was raped by a man who wanted to marry her, she was whipped and threatened by her own sister who tried to force her to quickly marry the rapist. In another case, a man named Mariano Guadalupe was whipped because he refused to cover the honor of the cousin he had raped by marrying her.

Other sexually related crimes and behavior during this time period in Mexico were not documented very often. However, references to **adultery** and prostitution were used to discredit women. Neither the state nor church worked to eliminate prostitution, viewing it, perhaps, as a necessary evil, which should simply be kept hidden.

Although men dominated the medical profession, midwives were normally women. They relied mostly on traditional superstition and shamanism when caring for pregnant women and delivering babies. Even when pregnant, Indian women worked in the fields and performed hard physical labor daily. They frequently committed **infanticide** to cover up an illegitimate child. *See also* Interracial Sex; Mexico, Sexuality and Gender in; Mixed Marriages, New France; Native Americans; Slavery; Wartime Rape.

Further Reading: Johnson, Lyman L., and Sonya Lipsett-Rivera, eds. *The Faces of Honor: Sex, Shame, and Violence in Colonial Latin America*. Albuquerque: University of New Mexico Press, 1999; Stern, Steve J. *The Secret History of Gender: Women, Men, & Power in Late Colonial Mexico*. Chapel Hill: University of North Carolina Press, 1995.

Elizabeth Jenner

MEXICO, SEXUALITY AND GENDER IN. As the Spanish authorities asserted their influence over the many cultures that mingled in colonial Mexico, they imposed sexual and social ideals within the political and religious policies they enacted. However, the cultural negotiation and variation that characterized the colonial period was demonstrated in the debates surrounding questions of gender and sexuality.

Marriage was fundamental to understandings of gender and sexuality in colonial Mexico. According to the Catholic Church, sexual relations were to take place only within marriage and only for the purposes of reproduction. Thus, any nonprocreative sex was considered a sin. Even married couples were prohibited from "unnatural practices," which included excessive petting, sex talk, and nonvaginal **ejaculation**.

Spanish religious and social principles commended the patriarchal household as the key component of **gender roles** and relationships, and a gradual change from extended family households to nuclear family units affected the role and status of women. In association with the enforcement of Catholic expectations, Indians particularly were encouraged to marry. The limited evidence suggests that more Indian than Spanish men married, and usually at a younger age. A significant minority of men and women remained single; the largest proportion of this group were Spanish, probably as a result of reluctance to marry an inappropriate partner. Although religious law permitted men and women to wed from the ages of fourteen and twelve, respectively, marriage at such young ages was rare, although Indian women and daughters of the elite tended to marry younger than other groups. By the eighteenth century, the average age of marriage for women in Mexico varied between sixteen and eighteen.

The concern to guarantee family honor, which was closely associated with female chastity and the birth of legitimate children, went far beyond defensive measures such as early marriage, particularly amongst the elite. Women were rarely permitted to leave the home without chaperonage or to participate in dinner conversation. Betrothal brought a new sexual status, permitting chaste public affection and sometimes even tacitly condoned intercourse, provided that it did not threaten public propriety. A verifiable marriage promise could be a powerful weapon for a woman whose partner failed to fulfill his obligations; she might force a man to marry her or to provide financial remuneration for her loss of honor. This right was somewhat diminished in the eighteenth century as judges began to insist on written proofs of contract.

Legal rights often mirrored familial anxieties. Courts were permitted to commit a woman to a convent under suspicion of infidelity on the sole testimony of her husband or father. Ideologies that emphasized the potential vulnerability and inherent weakness of women resulted in their virtual seclusion during the sixteenth and seventeenth centuries. Such principles were applied more stringently at higher social levels, but the enshrining of such principles in law ensured that only women who conformed to social and sexual expectations were afforded protection. Reports of illicit affairs or a questionable reputation could rebut even a strenuous accusation of rape or assault.

The most common crimes against women in colonial Latin America were physical abuse and wife beating, followed by **rape**. Sexual offences tended to be committed by men from within the same social world as their female victims, who were often kin or acquaintances, and many crimes against women were a matter of male rather than female honor. By attacking a married woman, a rival could inflict a serious insult on her husband; this is reflected in the tendency for the husbands of victims to seek legal redress on their own behalf, rather than that of their wives. A large number of the recorded crimes appear to have been provoked by women's failure to conform to standards of gendered expectation, and, to a significant degree, the law was prepared to tolerate violence to enforce masculine "rights." **Domestic violence** cases often attest to prolonged periods of physical abuse. It was impossible for a woman to obtain a legal **divorce**, and only in extreme cases do families and acquaintances seem to have felt it necessary to intervene.

Women, especially Indian women, were frequently associated with trials for love magic. Even after indigenous people were removed from the Inquisition's jurisdiction, women continued to be accused of demonic sexual magic. In practical terms, however, female access to such informal sources of power could bring them tangible respect from a population convinced of the efficacy of supernatural forces. By the early eighteenth century, however, love magic had come to be regarded as a superstitious triviality, and this significant source of women's power was diminished.

Sodomy was strongly condemned by both religious and social standards and has frequently been omitted from the historical record. Recent work has suggested a significant male sexual subculture, although whether this should be termed **"homosexuality,"** implying a sociocultural dimension, or whether it should be examined as a purely sexual phenomenon has remained extremely contentious. Official condemnation of sodomy is clear, but the frequency of trial records concerning the *pecado nefando* (nefarious sin) attests to the existence of homosexual activity. The great purges of the later seventeenth century in Mexico City, the best known of which took place in 1656–1663, saw mass executions. Prosecuted by the Holy Office, sodomites shared the fate of heretics and Jews: they were strangled and then burnt at a special place reserved for their execution in an area of Mexico City known as San Lázaro.

The constant assertion of social and sexual normativity in colonial Mexico may be associated with key themes of colonial discourse, including the assertion of European ideals and the justification of foreign domination through the effeminization of their subjects. *See also* Erauso, Catalina de; Mexico, Indigenous Women of.

Further Reading: Lavrin, Asunción, ed. *Sexuality and Marriage in Colonial Latin America*. Lincoln: University of Nebraska Press, 1989; Pablos, Julia Tuñón. *Women in Mexico: A Past Unveiled*. Austin: University of Texas Press, 1999; Sigal, Pete, ed. *Infamous Desire: Male Homosexuality in Colonial Latin America*. Chicago: University of Chicago Press, 2003; Twinam, Ann. *Public Lives, Private Secrets: Gender, Honor, Sexuality, and Illegitimacy in Colonial Spanish America*. Stanford, CA: Stanford University Press, 1999.

Caroline Dodds

MIDWIVES AND PHYSICIANS. The occupation of the midwife—a woman who assists women in **pregnancy** and **childbirth**—has been a part of the human landscape since ancient times. Before the seventeenth century, and up until the twentieth century in many parts of the world, the rituals and events surrounding pregnancy and childbirth were exclusively a female domain. Men—even physicians, surgeons, priests, and husbands—rarely advised women on prenatal care and were only allowed into the birthing room under unusual circumstances. Instead, close female friends, relatives, and midwives gave emotional, spiritual, and medical assistance to one another during childbearing. In the West, the private world of pregnancy, childbirth, and care for women began to change in the seventeenth and eighteenth centuries, particularly in France and England. Physicians and surgeons, newly interested in anatomy and dissection, began to enter the birthing room and study women's bodies. In England, the addition of the word "man-midwife" to the English language in the early seventeenth century demonstrates that the occupation of midwifery no longer belonged to women only. While care for women changed first in France and England, other countries in Europe as well as England's American colonies eventually followed a similar course from the late eighteenth to the twentieth centuries. The private realm of birthing became the subject of public debates over whether men or women were more suited to care for women. The result was that traditional birthing rituals were gradually done away with in favor of a more medicalized and scientific approach to birthing. Once the sole providers for pregnant women, midwives had to compete for clients with medical men. Further, midwives were increasingly regulated by both the state and the medical profession.

It is difficult to describe midwives' practices in this period, as there are very few records from midwives themselves. In some sense, all women who assisted at births were thought of as "midwives." Because experience was so valued in the birthing room, midwives were generally married women or widows who had already had children. The practice of midwifery varied considerably depending upon where one practiced and whom one served. Rural areas and villages had different standards and regulations for midwives than cities did. For example, in rural areas in France, one or two women who were the most experienced in delivering babies were likely unofficially considered the local "midwives" and did not receive formal payment for their services. Yet midwives employed by towns and cities throughout western Europe usually apprenticed with another midwife before they were certified by either religious or municipal authorities, and were paid a modest fee for their services. While there were a few literate midwives who had access to birthing manuals, apprenticeship was the backbone of a midwife's training. Midwives often provided care beyond delivering babies and were considered important general health-care providers in their communities. Further, midwives were sometimes called upon to testify as experts in cases that involved illegitimate children, or in cases where examinations of women were necessary, such as **rape**, pregnancy, or **impotence**.

Physicians, who were at the top of the medical hierarchy, worked hard to differentiate themselves from their competition, including midwives, surgeons, and traditional healers. Physicians claimed superiority in medical theory since midwives, surgeons, and apothecaries were trained primarily through apprenticeship. In the eighteenth century, surgeons, who had always been considered manual practitioners rather than experts in medical theory, began to establish their own schools and to study anatomy through the use of dissections. As surgeons gained more authority as learned professionals, a long conflict between surgeons and physicians over clients and expertise developed, which had as one of its consequences the diminishing of the role of midwives.

Part of the reason for the erosion of the midwife's role in this period was that women were at a disadvantage concerning educational opportunities. Rather than improving **education** for midwives, many city ordinances throughout western Europe instructed midwives to call for a physician or a surgeon if there were any problems with a delivery. Because women were denied access to universities—except in Italy—since their inception, they were generally excluded from the new scientific study of childbirth. For example, they were not allowed to use new tools—such as the forceps—that had come into use by surgeons. The forceps, a tool that allows practitioners to deliver babies who would not be deliverable using the hands alone, was invented by Peter Chamberlen Sr. (1560–1631) in early seventeenth-century England. As surgeons' reputation for expertise in birthing grew, they began to establish their own practices and to have their own female clientele for both illnesses and birthing, encroaching on both physicians' and midwives' practices.

In eighteenth-century France, England, and colonial America, there were published debates over whether men or women made better birthing attendants. Many of the arguments in favor of female practitioners relied on norms about modesty—that it was improper for a man to examine a woman's body—and on the notion that women, because they were female, were inherently better at caring for other women. By contrast, the arguments in favor of medical men emphasized their education and their skills in using medical tools to assist women in labor. It was the issue of who could guarantee safe delivery of mother and child that eventually carried more weight than moral arguments, such as the notion that physicians and surgeons should never touch or see women's bodies. Thus, while medical men gained the experience that traditionally only midwives possessed, midwives did not in turn come to be regarded as medical practitioners. Further, midwives were no longer considered the final authorities in the birthing room, since their education and practices were regulated by both the state and medical men. By the beginning of the nineteenth century in parts of western Europe and the early Republic of the United States, midwives continued to care for women, but the private realm of pregnancy and birthing was forever changed. *See also* Gynecology Manuals; Medicine and Science.

Further Reading: Lindemann, Mary. *Medicine and Society in Early Modern Europe.* Cambridge: Cambridge University Press, 1999; Marland, Hilary, ed. *The Art of Midwifery: Early Modern Midwives in Europe.* London: Routledge, 1993; Ulrich, Laurel Thatcher. *A Midwife's Tale.* New York: Vintage Books, 1990; Wilson, Adrian. *The Making of Man-Midwifery: Childbirth in England, 1660–1770.* Cambridge, MA: Harvard University Press, 1995.

Bridgette A. Sheridan

MILTON, JOHN (1608–1674). John Milton was a famous English poet, author of *Paradise Lost* (1667) and *Paradise Regained* (1671), two works that are often referred to as the greatest epic poems in English **literature**. The subjects of sexuality, **rape**, and the role of a female in society appeared equally often in Milton's most famous poems and in his less-known works.

Milton was born in Cheapside, London, to a scrivener. At the age of sixteen he started learning at Christ's College in Cambridge, and when he received his MA he was proficient in Latin, Greek, French, Italian, and Hebrew. He decided against becoming a clergyman as he was put off by the "tyranny in the church." After his travel to Italy in 1638, Milton first thought of creating a work equal to those of Homer or Dante; he originally intended to base it on Arthurian legends, but soon started thinking about using the Bible's "Book of Genesis" instead, as this would enable him to ask all the many questions about the nature of God that he had in mind. However, he was to wait many more years before having his magnum opus published. In the meantime, he married thrice and, in 1652, became blind. When *Paradise Lost* finally came out in 1667, it was not received with unanimous awe. Some scholars deemed its re-visioning of the events first described in the Bible too controversial, and some others, plain inappropriate.

Milton's portrayal of a woman is that of an entity inferior to a man. It is often mentioned in *Paradise Lost* that Eve is "weaker" than Adam, which is the very reason why Satan turns to her and not to Adam in his attempt to convince humans to disobey God. Later, in Book 9, Adam famously admits that a man who had trusted a woman must then face all the consequences of the deed, while in Book 10, after they have both eaten from the Tree of Knowledge, he goes as far as to say that Eve is "nature's defect." In the end, however, Adam decides that he should forgive Eve for what she had done because she could not help but surrender to Satan's temptation, as it is in the nature of her sex to be vulnerable. His way of describing the difference between sexes is often a reason for labeling Milton a misogynous writer.

Sexuality itself has its place in *Paradise Lost*. In Book 4, before disobeying God, Adam and Eve are innocent and do not feel shame about their sexuality. In Book 9, after Eve and then Adam have eaten the forbidden fruit, their lust for each other becomes sinful; they suddenly feel they should cover their intimate parts, and they start blaming each other for having eaten the fruit. Eve argues that Adam could have surrendered to the temptation as easily as she did, while Adam cannot believe that his sacrifice, that of standing by his woman and accepting all the consequences of the mistake she had made, was not properly recognized by Eve. The distinction between love and lust seemed to be an important subject for Milton: while reimagining the episode of burning Sodom, he is telling us of a punishment that befell the city of lust; when he then juxtaposes it with the tale of a woman gang-raped to death (based on the Bible's Judges 19), it seems that Milton used both tales as a metaphor of rape. Also, the very scene of Eve being seduced by Satan has so much eroticism in it, that it could be easily interpreted as another thinly veiled rape scene—one after which the relationship of humans and God is broken, and which actually teaches Eve how to use her sexuality to manipulate Adam.

Incidentally, rape also features in the background story of *Paradise Lost*'s villain, Satan himself, as does **incest**. In the description of Satan's meeting with his lost daughter, Sin (a combination of a human and an animal that sprung out of Satan's head), it is explained that after bringing Sin into the world Satan had sexual intercourse with her, thus bringing to the world his son/grandson, Death, who soon raped his mother—in effect breeding the dogs that since then gnaw on her bowels. *See also* Puritans; Religion.

Further Reading: Corns, Thomas N. *John Milton: The Prose Works*. New York: Twayne Publishers, 1998; Lewalski, Barbara K. *The Life of John Milton: A Critical Biography*. Oxford: Blackwell Publishers, 2001; Ricks, Christopher B. *Paradise Lost and Paradise Regained*. New York: Signet Books, 2001.

Bartlomiej Paszylk

MISSIONARIES. *See* Explorers and Missionaries

MISTRESSES. *See* Royal Mistresses

MIXED MARRIAGES, NEW FRANCE. During the French regime in North America up to 1763, Euro-Indian mixed marriages in New France were a politico-military-commercial tool in the hands of the French state and church. These institutions pressed for Indian assimilation into French culture and Christianity and the augmentation of the colonial population. In 1633, King Louis XIV sent explorer Samuel de Champlain to Canada where he exclaimed to the Huron Indians: "Our sons will marry your daughters, and we shall be one people." Yet, in reality most Indians continued endogamous **marriage**, and the French started to complain that the Huron did not ally themselves to the French through mixed marriages. At the same time, French individuals entered into such marriages, mostly celebrated by **missionaries** or priests, and sometimes without state sponsorship or support, because they either simply fell in love with Indian women of various tribes or hoped for advantages to be gained for their trade with Indian nations. In 1644, Martin Prévost married Marie-Olivier Sylvestre Manitouabeouich. In 1649, Pierre Boucher, Governor of Trois-Rivières, married Marie Ouebadinskoue, later referred to as Marie-Madeleine Chrestienne. And in 1657, Pierre Couc dit Cafleur de Coignac celebrated his marriage with Marie Mitromigoucoué. In fact, most of these marriages were between French men and Indian women. Cases in which the bride was French were very rare and increased only after 1663 with the growing influx of French women from the metropolis.

In 1657, the Christian **religion** was made a precondition for mixed marriages: an edict of Louis XIV stated that marriages of French and Indians should be officially allowed, provided that the latter were Christians. Since the spreading of Christianity through missionaries was seen as vital, mixed marriage in New France was not a value in itself. Such marriages were seen as either being performed on the basis of Christian rules or being a means to assimilate Christian values. Consequently, in cases where French and Indians engaged in sexual relationships without marrying according to Christian customs, contemporaries commented on them in a rather denigrating tone: it was claimed that Frenchmen "took up with slave girls" and that New France was "a wifeless colony of mistresses." Therefore, authorities started to look for ways to remedy the chaotic situation, which they saw as anarchic, in contrast to the bourgeois Christian order in the metropolis. Growing libertinage and the lack of white women became a serious concern of colonial authorities, who were faced with the choice of either permitting fully legal marriages with Indian women in the colony or providing a sufficient number of white women from the metropolis to marry them to French colonists in New France.

Initially, authorities had favored the first option with the objective of creating one single French nation overseas through assimilation with Indian tribes. In this scheme, military marriages with Indian women were controlled with special regulations that made approval of authorities a precondition. However, such marriages constituted a perfect tool of integration, as they often happened at strategic points close to Indian villages. Therefore many officers married interculturally even without getting the necessary approval. Next to Tonty and Cadillac, other such examples were officers La Plante and La Chauvignerie. In the West, officer Paul Le Moyne de Maricourt married an Onondaga woman, and Louis-Thomas Chabert de Joncaire, who had a European wife in the colony, preferred to live with his Seneca concubine. It is difficult to judge if diplomatic considerations—such as aiming at an understanding with Indians—followed or preceded the French sexual activities with Indians. In any case, the diplomatic advantages to be obtained from good relations with Indians were an important factor in fostering politico-military-commercial alliances that secured French presence in the country.

While the military elite were subject to restrictions, ordinary settlers were enticed with financial incentives for marriage. Such was the second solution—the sending out of the so-called *filles du roi* from France at the expense of the royal treasury. This initiative was favored whenever the moral climate in the colony became libertine, that is, when Frenchmen increasingly started to live in concubinage with Indian women. The filles du roi received a présent du roi, a sum of money, as incentive to embark for the colony and marry French colonists there. The first contingent came from 1634 onward, and then again after 1713. This female migration was meant to counteract the increase in mixed unions, which authorities viewed with suspicion more and more.

At the end of the seventeenth century, racist views came to the fore, which saw assimilation through miscegenation and marriage as counterproductive to population growth. It was argued that skin color was altered through the biological mixing of blood, and that mixed children were dangerous to the colonial order. From 1735 onward, marriages of military personnel in Louisiana, where most of such scandalous cases were reported, were to be celebrated henceforth only with the approval of the governor and the commandant of the military post in question. Yet, in practice mixed marriages continued against the wishes of French authorities and Indian village chiefs throughout New France. However, in 1763, jurists at the Sorbonne decided that marriages celebrated in front of a Protestant minister—as opposed to a Catholic priest—should be regarded as concubinage. Furthermore, the Sorbonne professors held that in case a person wanted to enter into a prohibited marriage, he should do so without endangering his religious "well being." *See also* Concubines; Interracial Sex; Native Americans.

Further Reading: Aubert, Guillaume. "'The Blood of France': Race and Purity of Blood in the French Atlantic World." *William and Mary Quarterly* 61, no. 3 (July 2004): 439–78; Dickason, Olive P. "From 'One Nation' in the Northeast to 'New Nation' in the Northwest: A Look at the Emergence of the Métis." In *The New Peoples: Being and Becoming Metis in North America*, edited by Jacqueline Peterson and Jennifer Brown, 19–36. Reprint ed. Winnipeg: University of Manitoba Press, 1987; Jaenen, Cornelius. "Miscegenation in New France." In *New Papers in Ethnohistory*, edited by Barry Gough and Laird Christie. Hull: Canadian Museum of Civilization, 1983.

Devrim Karahasan

MOLLY HOUSES. Molly houses were symbolic of a growing subculture of homosexual activity in London that made **sodomy** more socially acceptable. These notorious sites, sometimes referred to as brothels, were safe meeting places for men. Many of the molly houses were located near the north side of the river Thames. Molly houses could be taverns, homes, coffeehouses, or public places that welcomed homosexual activity. Private rooms were sometimes available in molly houses enabling couples to have privacy.

Men who visited molly houses listened to music, danced, drank liquor, and had sex with each other. Originally the term "molly" referred to a female prostitute. However, in London during the early eighteenth century, men who engaged in intimate and sexual relationships often referred to themselves as mollies. While some of the mollies were married men with families, many of the mollies were unmarried, working-class men and boys. Cross-dressers also found comfort in molly houses.

The first author to write extensively about molly houses was Ned Ward, who published the *History of the London Clubs* in 1709. By the mid-1720s there were at least twenty molly houses in London. Mollies and other men who engaged in homosexual activity were subject to prosecution that could result in the death penalty; however, this rarely occurred. Some mollies who were charged with sodomy committed suicide to avoid prosecution.

Margaret Clap, also known as Mother Clap, owned the most prominent molly house. Margaret Clap's molly house was located in Field-Lane in Holborn. She opened her house as early as the fall of 1724. She welcomed mollies into her house and provided a pleasant atmosphere for them. On any given night, Clap would cater to thirty or forty guests. Several men, who may have been prostitutes, also lived at Mother Clap's house. She fully supported mollies who were charged with sodomy.

Clap's house was under surveillance from December 10, 1725, through February 1726, when it was raided. She was indicted for allowing disorderliness and acts of sodomy. Clap was found guilty and sentenced to two years imprisonment that included standing in the Smithfield market pillory and paying twenty marks. Citizens pelted Clap and other convicted criminals who stood in the pillory with various objects that sometimes included dung. Clap's molly house was shut down. Forty mollies were also arrested in the raid. They were taken to Newgate prison. Most of the men were eventually released; however, a few were convicted, fined, and punished. Unfortunately, three of the mollies were executed.

The campaign to close molly houses was led by groups such as the Christian Brethren and the Society for the Reformation of Manners. Molly houses, however, survived various attempts to eliminate them. The efforts of these antigay groups were unsuccessful because homosexual activity continued. Molly houses survived well into the late nineteenth century. *See also* Bisexuality; Cross-Dressing; Geisha; Homosexuality; Prostitutes and Prostitution; Sodomy and Anti-Sodomy Law; Yoshiwara.

Further Reading: Norton, Rictor. *Mother Clap's Molly House: The Gay Subculture in England, 1700–1830.* London: Gay Men's Press, 1992; Patterson, Craig. "The Rage of Caliban: Eighteenth-Century Molly Houses and the Twentieth Century Search for Sexual Identity." In *Illicit Sex,* edited by Thomas DiPiero and Pat Gill. Athens: University of Georgia Press, 1996; Senelick, Laurence. "Mollies or Men of Mode? Sodomy and the Eighteenth-Century London Stage." *Journal of the History of Sexuality* 1, no. 1 (1990): 33–67.

Claudette Tolson

MONASTERIES. Monastic life in continental Europe slowly revived following the upheavals of the Protestant Reformation and the Wars of Religion, only to be disrupted again by the French Revolution. Practice had become lax but not wildly scandalous, and notable efforts were made to reform monastic life at, among other places, Montmarte, Douai, and Holy Trinity at Caen. Despite the success of these reforms, there were nevertheless instances of same-sex activity in monasteries, as well as sex scandals involving men and women. Entrance into a convent often enabled women to escape **marriage**, but often this was not by choice, and even so, women achieved little in the way of spiritual autonomy despite noteworthy efforts by such gifted figures as Gertrude More and Mary Ward.

There was a rise in professions during this period, but some historians have suggested that Italian patriarchs, for example, forced their daughters into a convent to alleviate the demand for extravagant dowries, eventually resulting in the decline of their class as birth rates fell. Latin American women were also often forced into monasteries until they were old enough to marry, but by 1774 about one-half of the women who had entered as children were now past the age of marriage, and so remained nuns for life. Women forced into convents often retained deep desires for marriage and family, which may account for visionary experiences such as that of Marguerite du Saint-Sacrament, a seventeenth-century Carmelite in Beaune who fixated on the infant Jesus to the point of becoming like an infant herself. Others, like the seventeenth-century

French Ursuline nun Jeanne des Anges, experienced false pregnancies attributed to demonic possessions.

Despite forced entries into monastic communities, most European nuns who were offered a chance to renounce their vows during the French Revolution refused to do so. Monastic discipline reached a high point as the reform movement emphasized meditation and the cultivation of personal perfection. Renewed attention to the inner life resulted in a great flourishing of mystical **literature**, which often employed sexual imagery to describe mystical union. The Benedictine nuns of the Perpetual Adoration and the nuns of the Blessed Sacrament, both founded in this period, exhibited another form of personal devotion highly charged with physical imagery, as one was united physically as well as spiritually to the male Jesus through the adoration of the Eucharist. Emphasis on the human Christ may have allowed many women to transform carnal impulses into more spiritual forms of love, though some women, such as the seventeenth-century Castilian Franciscan Maria of Agreda, whose mother turned their home into a convent, continued to wrestle with sexual urges and channeled them into self-torture. Her case suggests that there may have been an element of truth in the Marquis de Sade's remark that self-flagellation had an element of eroticism.

The reform movement also emphasized the importance of the novitiate, and clothing rituals, such as at Nonnberg in Germany and at other places, often resembled a wedding with the novice wearing a white veil. She received a "bridegroom," in the form of a crucifix or a statue of the Infant of Prague and a wedding ring symbolizing her new status as a Bride of Christ. Nuns often kept the statues in their rooms and clothed them.

Nuns such as the seventeenth-century nun from Nantes, Marie-Alexis le Huédez, often described their monastic vocation as seductions by Jesus, and others, such as Benedetta Carlini, a seventeenth-century Italian abbess, reported ecstatic visions of mystical union with Christ. Christ took Benedetta's heart for three days and later gave her his own heart. During a mystical wedding to Christ, a "ring" mysteriously appeared on Benedetta's finger. She also claimed to be possessed by a male guardian angel, Splenditello, who showered flowers on her body when she behaved or, when she misbehaved, whipped her with thorns. It was later revealed that Benedetta had repeatedly persuaded or forced another nun to have sex with her while in the guise of Splenditello. While Splenditello gave Benedetta a more acceptable male identity in the context of her sexual escapades, it also enabled investigators to explain the whole series of events as a case of demonic possession, especially when she claimed not to be able to remember anything. Benedetta spent the last thirty-five years of her life imprisoned in her convent, while nevertheless still being widely venerated by the public.

Europeans of that day had limited awareness of lesbian sexuality, especially as they considered women inferior to men. Many agreed with the sixteenth-century writer Pierre de Brantôme in considering lesbian relationships mere trifles not on par with male/female sex. Others thought of lesbian relationships as misguided attempts by women to emulate men, and it was difficult for most to conceive that women might be more attracted to each other than they were to men. While earlier sources that dealt with sexual sins never mentioned lesbianism at all, there were **laws** in some areas that punished females engaging in same-sex relations by death. Although investigators were shocked by the details of Benedetta's lesbian affair, her punishment was relatively light and based more on her violation of vows as a nun than on her sexual relations with another woman. Her partner was never punished at all.

Though there are few references to cases involving lesbians in the legal records of the time, literature hints that such cases may have been more widespread in monastic communities. Denis Diderot's *La Religieuse*, originally intended as a joke on a friend, narrated the story of a nun harassed by a lesbian superior, whose details were remarkably similar to the life of Louise-Adelaïde of Orléans, abbess of Chelles. Andrew Marvell's poem, "Upon Appleton House," also touched on lesbian issues involving nuns, but both **Andrew Marvell** and **Denis Diderot** primarily intended their work to critique Catholic concepts of authority.

There were also numerous cases of homosexual behavior in male communities and rumors of affairs between nuns and men, as at the convent of Santa Chiara in Pescia. To be fair, monastic discipline seems to have been generally exemplary during the reform period. Sects such as the Jansenists in France even exhibited ultraascetic ideals that, when combined with troublesome doctrines about grace, eventually prompted Louis XIV to repress them. During the French Revolution many nuns were raped, while others were tried for treason as a result of their "persistent **chastity**."

There were also many enriching Platonic relationships between monastic women and men as, for example, between the English recusant Dame Gertrude More and her spiritual director, Augustine Baker. Gertrude More, however, suffered when she tried to break from traditional Ignatian patterns of meditation and create more suitable spiritual practices for women. Similarly Mary Ward, founder of the Institute of Mary, was persecuted when she attempted to form female communities governed by the same apostolic standards that applied to Jesuit male communities. Attitudes about male superiority colored monastic women's lives in this period, whether in the context of illicit sexual liaisons between women, women's entry into marriage or the convent, or women's spiritual autonomy. *See also* Bisexuality; Celibacy; Homosexuality; Religion; Revolution and Gender; Witches and Witch Trials; Women, Changing Images of.

Further Reading: Brown, Judith C. *Immodest Acts: The Life of a Lesbian Nun in Renaissance Italy*. Oxford: Oxford University Press, 1986; Guilday, Peter. *The English Catholic Refugees on the Continent 1558–1795*. Vol. I: *The English Colleges and Convents in the Catholic Low Countries*. London: Longman's, 1914; Hilpisch, Stephanus. *A History of Benedictine Nuns*. Translated by M. Joanne Muggli. Collegeville, MN: St. John's Abbey Press, 1958; McNamara, Jo Ann Kay. *Sisters in Arms: Catholic Nuns through Two Millennia*. Cambridge, MA: Harvard University Press, 1996; Sperling, Jutta Gisela. *Convents and the Body Politic in Late Renaissance Italy*. Chicago: University of Chicago Press, 2000.

Deborah L. Vess

MURDER. In the seventeenth century, larceny was considered the single most important crime. The bandit had replaced the medieval outlaw, and lonely country roads and city streets were seen as particularly unsafe, especially at nightfall. The criminals attracting the greatest attention were those whose deeds resulted in the death of their victims, the penalty for which carried with it almost invariably a death sentence.

Most early modern legal systems classified murders similarly to Old Regime France, where the gravity of the crime depended on the intention of the criminal. Deaths resulting from self-defense or accident were sometimes pardoned, while those declared to follow from intent to murder led to the execution of the culprit. One of the factors taken into consideration while deciding whether the killing was premeditated or not was the type of the weapon used. Similarly, suicide and **abortion** were also treated as murder, often resulting in confusing situations when a person who survived a suicide

Unattributed engraving of the death of Catherine Hayes, sentenced to burn for the death of her husband. © Mary Evans Picture Library.

attempt was punished by death, or a dead person was put on trial charged with the murder of his or her own self.

In the seventeenth and eighteenth centuries executions of criminals were a public business, and the audience they attracted represented a cross section of society. Many criminals were immortalized, thanks to their gallows speeches quoted in the press and sensational periodicals. In England, most executions were carried out at Tyburn, just outside London, where the majority of the condemned were put to death by hanging. Hanging at Tyburn stopped in 1784 because it was decided that the journey to the place of execution took too long, and gallows were put outside the prisons instead. In 1868 public hangings were stopped altogether in England, but executions continued to be carried out in private.

Due to the appearance of *The Newgate Calendar* comprising lives of notorious criminals, seen as the most significant publication alongside the Bible to instill principles of right living in children, we seem to know comparatively more about English murderers than their counterparts in other corners of the world. Among the best publicized cases were those of Richard (Dick) Turpin, a highwayman, horse thief, and murderer executed in 1739, or Matthew Clarke, who, surprised by a maid in an act of burglary, talked and flirted with her, reportedly, only to cut her throat for no apparent reason minutes later (executed in 1721). Publications devoted also much space to the once most famous Tyburn hangman, known as Jack Ketch (real name John Price), whose life also ended on the gallows, when he was executed in 1718 for attempted **rape** and beating of a girl resulting in her death.

Many seventeenth- and eighteenth-century murder cases can be seen as unpleasant consequences of aggravated marital disputes, frequently ensuing from a violent reaction of jealous husbands at the news of their wives' infidelity. Although, regardless of the sex of the culprit, the murderer was put to death, women fared an incomparably worse fate, since their crime was classified as petty treason and implied death by burning. Perhaps the most notorious was the case of Catherine Hayes, who convinced her neighbor, Thomas Wood, together with an alleged son of hers, Thomas Billings, that they should kill her husband. Having manipulated both men with fictitious tales of marital abuse and **infanticide**, Catherine Hayes served her husband a large quantity of wine, and when the latter was sufficiently intoxicated, Billings proceeded to hit him on the head with a hatchet, until the skull of the victim fractured. In an attempt to get rid of the body, the trio removed the man's head and contemplated boiling meat off his bones. The idea was soon discarded and the body was dumped into the Thames. When the head of the dead man was discovered a few days later, it was displayed for public viewing. Catherine Hayes confessed her crime and was burned at the stake in 1726. During her execution, the flames around her rose so high that it prevented the hangman from strangling her before her body caught fire, as was customary with a similar sentence. She is reported to have died in pain, surviving in the flames for a considerable time.

There were also several notable murder cases outside England. In seventeenth-century France, Marie de Brinvilliers, an aristocratic lady with an exceptional knowledge of undetectable poisons, practiced her skill. Marie experimented with her poisons on the sick in a local hospital, only to use them later on members of her family to obtain inheritance. In time, however, she came to poison people indiscriminately, and when arrested, her victims were supposed to have amounted to almost 100. Condemned in 1676, she was tortured to exact a confession and finally beheaded. Her body was then burned, and her charred bones picked by peasants as lucky charms.

In Germany, Anna Maria Zwanziger took advantage of her position as a cook and a housekeeper to poison household members with arsenic. Convinced that her subsequent employers harbored secret feelings for her, she tried to help them reach a decision by murdering their wives, and when her judgment proved to be in error, she attempted to right her wrongs by murdering the masters, as well. She was eventually tried and executed in 1811. Near the end of the eighteenth century, Bavaria witnessed the activity of Andreas Bichel, a serial killer and lust murderer. Introducing himself as a clairvoyant, Bichel took advantage of the naivety of young women, telling them their future could only be read once they were securely tied to a chair. Having immobilized his victims, he stabbed them with a knife, stripped their bodies, and buried them behind his house. When found guilty and sentenced to death in 1808, he was tied to a wheel and had his bones broken with a sledgehammer before he was eventually beheaded. Reportedly he remained defiant till the end. *See also* Torture; Wartime Rape.

Further Reading: Nash, Robert J. *Compendium of World Crime*. London: Harrap, 1983; Rayner, John L. *The Complete Newgate Calendar*. London: Navarre Society, 1926; Sharpe, J. A. *Crime in Early Modern England 1550–1750*. London: Longman, 1984; Weisser, Michael R. *Crime and Punishment in Early Modern Europe*. Brighton: Harvester Press, 1982.

Katarzyna Ancuta

MYTHS AND FOLKLORE. Certain myths about love and sexuality got new connotations between 1600 and 1800. Under the influence of the Enlightenment in western Europe, witch mythology faded, and witch trials eventually stopped. In eastern Europe, witches continued to be mythologized as salacious, promiscuous women who participated in orgies with the Devil and his assistants. However, their lubricity, taste for copulation, and **sodomy** were punished by ostracism and never with the stake. Ancient Greek and Roman erotic myths, especially those about Aphrodite, Eros, and Psyche, continued to be extremely popular, and they meshed with the neoclassical tastes of the time.

The myth of pastoral love also continued previous Renaissance traditions. People of quality disguised themselves as shepherds and shepherdesses to enjoy the slow pace of rural life and the lack of constraints. Sexuality lurked behind the lovers' affectionate gestures, but the consummation of love was not essential, rather the goal was sublimation and expectation.

The pleasure of amorous casuistries led to specific gallantry (*amour précieux*/affected love) where conversation was an expiatory exercise for the amorous tension. The myth of love as a disease, a torment, and a pain, the myth of the cruel and haughty woman and the submissive man led to a sophisticated cerebral game. Madelaine de Scudéry (1607–1701) mapped an initiating circuit for tender lovers that became a myth of the time (la Carte du Tendre/the Map of Tenderness).

As Europeans traveled to the New World, Africa, Asia, and the Middle East, they brought back their own versions of myths told in these places, as well as created their own myths about the people there. One eighteenth-century motif was the noble savage. After traveling to Tahiti (1766–1769), Louis Antoine de Bogainville published his *Voyage around the World*. The natives of the islands became the mythic noble savages who lived on a new Cythera. In 1772, **Denis Diderot** wrote a *Supplement to the Voyage of Bougainville* describing an ideal society instinctually promiscuous, free of any moral or sexual constraints, cautious, however, not to commit **incest**. In the eighteenth century, however, in his ship's logs Captain James Cook, who visited Tahiti and Hawaii denounced the noble savage as a projection of European erotic frustrations in his ship's logs.

Myths developed about "the Orient," and it was viewed as a place of enticing erotic attractions, mystery, lust, and sophisticated erotic techniques. Antoine Galland contributed much to this fantasy when he translated *Arabian Nights* between 1704 and 1714. Lady May Wortley Montagu, who spent two years in Istanbul (1716–1718) as the wife of the British ambassador, was the first Westerner to enter the Ottoman harem. In her *Turkish Embassy Letters* Lady Montagu unveiled the European fixation on Oriental eroticism and, in her view, revealed the veil as an empowerment device that allowed Oriental women freedom that Western women could not even think of.

In central and Southeast Europe, folklore created the myth of the *haiduk*, an outlaw and guerilla fighter against national and social oppressors. The mythical *haiduk* often grew from historic figures that had impressed the national imagination. Such were the Romanians Pintea the Brave (1670–1703) and Iancu Jianu (1787?–1842?); the Macedonian Petre Carpos, who fought against the Turks in 1689; or the Hungarian Iuraj Ianosik (1688–1713), who fought with Pintea the Brave against the Austrians. Sometimes the same *haiduk*, such as Gruia Novac, became a hero in Romanian, Serbian, and Bulgarian folklore.

The **masculinity** of the *haiduk* was enthralling. He was handsome, sexually attractive, just, and honorable with the underprivileged. If he was married, sometimes his wife also became a mythical figure of bravery and faith. This was the case with Sirma, a female *haiduk* leader in eighteenth-century Macedonia and Moscha, wife of Lambros Tsavelas, a guerilla fighter against the Turks in Greece. In other ballads, the *haiduk* was betrayed by his wife, who was jealous or tempted by the Turks. Occasionally, in these tales, the *haiduk* had a mistress, usually a female innkeeper, who betrayed him because she was not paid, or they were both betrayed by the wife. In no case was the *haiduk* put under any kind of moral blame for his gallantry.

There was also the myth that developed around this time of a girl kidnapped by the Turks somewhere in a port on the Danube (Ilincutza Sandrului, in Romanian folklore). In some versions, she committed suicide in order to save her honor; in other versions, she was rescued by her brothers, who afterward committed an honor killing because they were not sure she had resisted the Turks.

There were also many myths that circulated during this time about medicine and the **body**. Myths about **menstruation**, for example, existed in many cultures. In Europe, menstruating women were believed to be able to make wine or milk go sour, ruin harvests, and even cause another woman to miscarry. There were also myths about **food**, such as any food that resembled a sexual organ could work as an aphrodisiac when eaten. *See also* Harems; Medicine and Science; Ottoman Empire; Religion; Witches and Witch Trials.

Further Reading: Daniel, N. A. *Islam and the West: The Making of an Image*. Edinburgh: Edinburgh University Press, 1958; La Bossière, Camille R. *The Progress of Indolence: Readings in (Neo)Augustan Literary Culture*. Toronto: York Press, 1997.

Mihaela Mudure

NATIVE AMERICANS. Seventeenth- and eighteenth-century Native American cultures held diverse sexual views and practices. **Gender roles** were not confined to one's biological sex. Gender itself was often considered unstable, fluid, and unconfined to a dichotomous system. Usually, sexual and gender differences were accepted because those differences made unique contributions to society.

Among Native Americans, sexuality was believed to be guided or destined by supernatural forces. Therefore, all forms of sexual expression and identity were generally accepted. **Homosexuality** and various forms of gender bending were common.

Many Native American cultures honored androgynous people called **berdaches** who were seen as half-men, half-women. Berdaches were usually anatomically correct males with nonmasculine personalities. These revered people had a particular role and social status within the culture because they served a unifying function between women and men. They were not regarded as deviants. Instead, they were considered a nonthreatening, respectable third gender. They usually adopted asexual behavior or partnered with other men, sometimes becoming a man's wife. They adopted a combination of the dress, behavior, work, sexual, and social roles of both female and male genders. Variations in berdache customs were widespread: for instance, a Flathead male berdache might only occasionally wear men's clothing, whereas a Kutenai berdache would wear pants under a dress.

The Mohave of the Southwest had a transition rite for girls who wanted to be boys. These girls were called hwames. Once the hwames had undergone the rite, they were permitted to dress as boys and were taught the same skills that boys learned. The Mohave believed that hwames did not menstruate. While some hwames may indeed have had amenorrhea, others may simply have hidden their menses out of desire to be treated as men.

Hwames often married other women. If a pregnant woman married a hwame, the hwame was considered the true father of the child. Hwame sexual intercourse included **masturbation**, but did not include oral stimulation since the Mohave were repulsed by vaginal odor. Hwames participated when the tribesmen sat around describing their partners' genitals. In Alaska, the Ingalik people also recognized women who behaved like men as though they were indeed men, thus accepting their participation in all-male activities.

Native Americans also had myths in which lesbian behavior occurred. Lesbian relationships were documented far less than occurrences of male homosexuality. Generally, lesbians were not stigmatized and were allowed to marry. As well, they were

Dance to the "Berdashe" transvestite. Illustration by George Catlin, ca. 1830. © Mary Evans Picture Library.

able to return to heterosexuality and marry men later in life if their lesbian marriages ended.

Navajo lesbians and male homosexuals were highly valued people in the community. They were believed to bring and control wealth. Lumped together with **hermaphrodites** and transvestites, they were considered a separate sex category that was neither female nor male.

Attitudes toward homosexuality ranged, but there is much evidence of homosexual behavior among most tribes. Among the Southern Ute of the Great Basin and the Chiricahua Apaches of the Southwest, however, homosexuality was strictly forbidden, even in children's play. Chiricahua Apache individuals showing homosexual tendencies were killed.

Sexual and gender diversity generated many linguistic terms among Native American tribes. These terms translate into words and phrases such as one with rotten bones, one who acts like a woman, a boy-girl, one with split testicles, a hunting woman, a warrior woman, a supernatural female, one who changes time and again, woman pretenders, a would-be woman, one who is moon-instructed, an unmanly man, a boy whose sex changes at birth, one who dresses like the other sex, an anus copulator, and one who is awkward. Myths involving alternative genders often accompanied the presence of such people in a tribe.

Usually, women were highly regarded in Native American cultures. European **explorers** observed that Native American women generally acted independently, making choices without the **consent** of their husbands and other men. Many tribes, such as the Iroquois, Cherokee, and Navajo, were matrilineal. Navajo women had high societal status and equal rights as men. For instance, both sexes could inherit family land. Inheritance was based on matrilineal lineage. Navajo children were born into their mother's clan and born for their father's clan. The mother's clan was of primary importance, and the father's of secondary importance. Prior to the nineteenth century, Iroquois society was characterized by matrilineal descent, matriarchal power, and female political decision making. Iroquois women had an important role in deciding the fate of war captives, parenting children, and arranging marriages. Yet since reciprocity was an important cultural value, Iroquois women did not dominate men.

Many tribes, such as the Blackfoot peoples of the Plains and the Pomo from the West, recognized the important economic contribution of women. Blackfoot women were the main producers of essential goods, such as baskets, pottery, and tipi houses. Pomo women and men were equal in status since distinctions of gender had nothing to do with power. For a thriving community, everyone contributed, so everyone was valued.

Not only did Native American women play an economic role but they also contributed in wartime. Women frequently used sexual advances as a weapon of war. For instance, Algonquin women of the early 1600s would feign interest in invading English soldiers. They would then entice the soldiers into putting down arms and entering their houses, where rather than seducing them, the women would easily kill them.

Historians estimate that Native Americans took thousands of Europeans captive during the colonial period. Revenge was a common motive for taking male hostages. Men were often tortured with beatings, burnings, and amputations. But women enjoyed special protection. Native Americans rarely raped female captives, perhaps in part due to the practice of warrior abstinence. Young European girls who were taken hostage were easily transculturated. With Puritan upbringing that encouraged them to passively submit to authority, they usually came to embrace their new society after dealing with their initial trauma and culture shock. In 1758, for example, fifteen-year-old settler Mary Jemison was captured by a raiding party and given to the Seneca. She transculturated, married, had children, and eventually became a tribal matriarch. Similar accounts show many female Europeans refused to return to European colonial society when given the chance to do so.

Native American puberty rites were varied. An important goddess in Navajo mythology was Changing Woman who rid the world of monsters and represented Mother Earth. Since she underwent a puberty rite, it was Navajo girls, not boys, who underwent them as well. Both female and male offspring were equally desired by Navajo parents. Pomo men and boys who had been initiated into manhood lived in sweathouses, and only rarely stayed with women at their family homes.

Postmenopausal women sometimes shared the Pomo men's sweathouses. Next to family homes were separate menstrual quarters where menstruating women could stay away from their spouses and other men, a requirement of Pomo taboos. **Menstruation** was believed to cause illness in both women and men. In the American Great Basin, Paiute women also secluded themselves in menstruation huts. Navajo women breastfed their children for as long as possible in order to postpone their next pregnancies. Additionally, herbal forms of **contraception** were used.

Among Native American tribes, women had varying degrees of social and sexual freedom. Although the Muskogee peoples of the Southeast were organized in matrilineal, matrilocal communities, women were characterized as immature, overemotional, irresponsible, and immoral. They therefore had a subordinate status, were excluded from politics, and were ultimately blamed for the failures and crimes of men.

Unmarried Muskogee women had total sexual freedom, while married women were expected to be faithful to their husbands. A woman or man who committed **adultery** was usually severely beaten. Adulterous women also had their hair and ears cut off, and sometimes the tips of their noses. They were then usually divorced. Sexual assault and **rape** were considered the most serious sexual crimes. Polygyny was permitted.

In Navajo society, excessive sexual activity by either sex was scorned. Men often married sisters or the wives of their dead brothers. Women could join war parties but were forbidden to have sexual intercourse with any of its members.

Sexually and politically, Cherokee women had greater freedom than their Muskogee neighbors. Senior women held key political powers. They influenced wars and the fate of prisoners. Men who did not listen to the political opinions of these figures could receive public chastisement. Seniority, not gender, was the main determinant of one's value to society. While Muskogee men controlled land and produce, it was women who controlled land and produce in Cherokee society.

For the most part, Native American tribes found meaning in sexual variance and an honored position for people who did not fit into the sexual majority. They had a more equal view of women and men, and a more open view regarding sex and sexuality than the Europeans who conquered them. *See also* Marriage; Myths and Folklore; Patriarchy.

Further Reading: Gutiérrez, Ramón A. *When Jesus Came, the Corn Mothers Went Away: Marriage, Sexuality, and Power in New Mexico, 1500–1846.* Stanford, CA: Stanford University Press, 2004; Klein, Laura F., and Lillian A. Ackerman, eds. *Women and Power in Native North America.* Norman: University of Oklahoma Press, 1995; Roscoe, Will. *Changing Ones: Third and Fourth Genders in Native North America.* New York: St. Martin's Press, 1998; Williams, Walter L. *The Spirit and the Flesh: Sexual Diversity in American Indian Culture.* Boston: Beacon Press, 1988; Zabelle Derounian-Stodola, Kathryn, ed. *Women's Indian Captivity Narratives.* New York: Penguin Books, 1998.

Elizabeth Jenner

NEWSPAPERS. Eighteenth-century newspapers reported sexual scandals, circulated **gossip**, and dispensed moral advice, in addition to providing information on current political events and advertising goods and services. Per capita consumption of newspapers rose in London during the eighteenth century while more and more newspapers entered the market and competed for readers, but growth outside the London metropolitan area was insignificant except in urban pockets such as Bristol, Bath, and York. Country readership, though, remained consistently low compared to anything published in urban centers, and the bulk of English newspapers continued to be published, printed, distributed, sold, and read in London.

What did these early newspapers look like? Printed in black ink on white stock, they were two double-sided pages—that is, four pages in length, printed on both sides. They could be hard to read, as the dark ink tended to seep through to the other side and smear both pages. It was not easy to separate hard news from advertisements, and **theater** reviews were notoriously noncritical, heaping all London stage productions with praise. Copyright laws were difficult to enforce during the eighteenth century, as so many articles were pirated from one newspaper to another, actually taken whole, and reprinted without attribution.

The front page of a newspaper would often be three-quarters filled with advertisements for masquerade balls, auction houses, panaceas of all kinds, including cures for **venereal diseases**, new books, personal ads, and rooms for rent, while the second page would have news from the Court and Parliament, from abroad, reports of military engagements, and long columns of gossipy bits. Names were replete with dashes in poor attempts to disguise the persons involved, but it did not take much ingenuity to identify them. There was also widespread use of nicknames, but those in the know, knew.

The main thrust of the eighteenth-century press was not necessarily to alert and enlighten citizens on national and world events, though these were covered by newspapers published and circulated in urban areas, and wartime news, especially during the American Revolutionary War, took up a good amount of column inches. The economics of newspaper publishing, however, mandated that a large number of advertisements—as well as these paid articles—were sold, explaining the proliferation of ads in these early newspapers.

Unlike today, many newspaper columnists and contributors used assumed names. This was a way for them to avoid libel or the more serious charge of sedition, and it shielded those who moved in certain circles to remain anonymous while writing about those in their circles who might be friends or acquaintances, whether it was gossip or more substantive. Charges of libel against newspapers were primarily to do with criticisms of the government, the king, and his ministers, and were pursued by the state; personal libel was not usually pursued by individuals. Running afoul of the government was a constant problem for newspaper publishers; there was no real concept of freedom of the press.

In the urban press, the emphasis was clearly—especially from the period beginning in the 1780s—on nonpolitical news, social habits, fashion, and, above all, on London gossip. Gossip about one's social betters, the *ton*, was rife. The more titillating a story, the more copies a newspaper would sell; it was guaranteed. This could go to extremes in the eighteenth-century tabloids, but, unlike the government, private citizens did not usually go through the trouble to sue for libel.

In the British American colonies and later in the new republic, newspapers printed hundreds of notices of wives who had deserted their husbands, as well as ads for runaway servants and slaves. Both types of ads reflect the patriarchal and economic underpinnings of marriage and of households in early America. In their ads, husbands usually commented that they would not pay any debts incurred by their errant wives, but the ads also reveal ideas and expectations about **marriage** during this time.

In the latter part of the eighteenth century, American newspapers and magazines also printed cautionary tales, poems, and essays about young women who were seduced and abandoned by villainous men. This rise in **seduction literature** reflected anxieties about sexual freedom in young people and fears that towns would have to support unwed mothers and their offspring. *See also* Euphemisms and Slang; Literature.

Further Reading: "Concise History of the British Newspaper: The British Library Newspaper Library." See www.bl.uk/collections/britnews.html; Morsley, Clifford. *News from the English Countryside, 1750–1850*. London: Harrap, 1979; Sievens, Mary Beth. *Stray Wives: Marital Conflict in Early National New England*. New York: New York University Press, 2005.

Jo Manning and Merril D. Smith

NON-WESTERN ART. *See* Art, Non-Western

NUDITY. *See* The Body

ONANISM. *See* Masturbation

OPERA. Opera is a type of musical drama in which solo and choral singing and sung dialogue are accompanied by instrumental music, now usually orchestral. As an art form, opera became a prominent part of European culture from 1640 (the year in which the first public opera house opened in Venice, Italy) to 1800. The period saw great development and variety in the form, style, tone, and subject matter. The best opera singers became celebrities, enjoying fame, wealth, and growing prestige and social status. By the end of the eighteenth century, over fifty cities and courts had opera houses, a measure of the popularity and importance of opera.

The major European countries had some form of opera in their native languages by 1800, yet for the most part Italian opera dominated the stages, especially in the first half of the century. Early opera emerged from sixteenth- and early seventeenth-century Italian academies and courts, and its popularity spread to most European cities. In Paris, French opera appeared soon after Italian opera, and French audiences enjoyed both Italian and French opera. Elsewhere, Italian opera remained the predominant type even after the establishment of "national" operas in England and Germany.

The most important development of opera during the 1700s was the growing popularity of "opera buffa" or comic opera. Before that time, most thought of "opera seria" or serious opera as the only true form of opera. Composers, performers, and audiences, particularly aristocratic opera lovers, favored serious opera—with its serious subject matter, philosophical concerns, elevated musical style, and heroic characters (usually from myths and legends). Yet over time comic opera interested composers and attracted audiences first as "intermezzi," short scenes appearing between the acts of serious operas. Full-length comic operas appeared in the 1730s. These works focused on familiar characters and domestic conflicts from everyday life; many featured bantering male and female characters that fall in love by the final curtain. Comic opera had fewer traditions and conventions to limit composers, and they took full advantage, exploring new styles and incorporating popular tunes well known to audiences; as a result, many of these comic operas were easily translated into other languages. By the 1770s comic operas were produced throughout Europe—often to international acclaim.

The innovations in comic operas helped to bring about one of the most important changes in the history of opera—the declining status of castrated male singers known as castrati and the growing number of female performers. A castrato was an adult man who had been castrated as a young boy before his singing voice changed with the onset of puberty. The tone of young boys was long considered the purest, yet the voices of boys dropped before the necessary years of training and practice. **Castration** stopped the voice from deepening as the body matured. Thus, castrati had the sound of young boys with the wide range and vocal power of men possible only after years of rigorous instruction. Historians speculate that in the sixteenth century boys entering **monasteries** were first castrated for religious reasons, and because in Roman Catholic countries, women were forbidden to sing in church, castrati began to sing in services. Many listeners came to love their beautiful and distinctive, delicate but powerful sound. Eventually (but only in Italy it seems) young boys who showed promise as singers were sold by their parents and families to music teachers who oversaw their castration and subsequent training in the hopes of success as performers. Few were ever able to become professional singers, and as not regarded as "real" or "whole" men, castrati met with prejudice and scorn. Only those who were exceptional singers enjoyed status, wealth, influence, and fame. Nonetheless, the practice continued until the 1840s and 1850s.

Writing the first operas, composers most likely drew upon the styles and tones of church music, and they wrote songs that demanded the unique skill, physical abilities, and training of the castrati. In the early years of opera, music lovers and composers found tenors and basses unrefined, an attitude that helps to explain the partiality for the sweet, high voices of castrati for opera seria. As teenagers, castrati started their careers in operas by playing female roles, and if they continued to develop their craft and gained fame as they aged, they then played male roles.

The emergence of comic operas changed conventions and audience taste. Given the subject matter and "everyday" characters of comic opera, composers began to write fewer parts for castrati and more male parts for tenors and basses and more female roles for sopranos (the pitch natural to women). The cycle had begun: with fewer roles, fewer boys were "trained"; with fewer castrati, fewer roles were written. Finally, more opera lovers favored the "natural" voice and the castrati surely seemed to go against this new attitude. By 1830, with changing attitudes about castration in Italy and new styles in opera—now with tenors, basses, and sopranos—the reign of the castrati was soon over.

In short, opera was a major cultural and artistic institution in the eighteenth century, yet for the most part, it remained an art form favored by the very wealthy. Aristocrats were able to afford the high ticket prices and they frequented both serious and comic opera. As the century went on, however, more middle-class theater-goers were drawn to comic opera. *See also* Eunuchs; Theater, Chinese; Theater, Japanese.

Further Reading: Grout, Donald Jay, and Hermine Weigel Williams, eds. *A Short History of Opera*. 4th ed. New York: Columbia University Press, 2003; Heriot, Angus. *The Castrati in Opera*. London: Secker & Warburg, 1956.

Timothy J. Viator

ORAL SEX. Oral sex is absent almost completely from seventeenth- and eighteenth-century Western **literature**, while other similar nonpenetrative sexual practices, such as mutual **masturbation** between couples, are so mentioned, suggesting that fellatio and cunnilingus practiced on the penis and the vagina were simply not widely practiced. Ancient Roman moralists considered fellatio the most scandalous practice, because it was the most pleasurable sexual act. Roman and Greek literature is full of references to fellatio in this pejorative sense, since they were cultures of manliness and mastery. Passive **homosexuality** was more esteemed than performing fellatio, the basest form of self-humiliation. Likewise performing cunnilingus was considered demeaning to men. The master—a free man, not a servant, slave, woman, or boy—had to be in control of sexual activity, neither passively submitting to this pleasure nor abasing himself. It may be that later Western attitudes reflected the Roman attitude.

In seventeenth- and eighteenth-century England oral sex may have been contained in the catchall crime of sexual deviance known as **sodomy**, from the biblical towns of Sodom and Gomorrah. Nonprocreative sex acts, such as **anal intercourse**, oral sex, and **bestiality**, were liable to punishment. It was felt, generally, that perversion of God's law in this way would bring down a universal punishment on the country. There was in the seventeenth century, however, little interest in pursuing prosecutions for sodomy, and bestiality was the main area of interest for prosecutors in that respect.

In areas outside western Europe and its colonies, oral sex was viewed differently. For example, one Japanese Samurai, a man of honor and power of this time, boasted of the pleasure he could give women with his skill in performing oral sex on them. In the Chinese Tao view during the Ming period, oral sex was advised, so long as the male did not ejaculate, and thus lose, in the Chinese terms, any of his *yang* (active energy). Clitoral stimulation by oral sex was actively approved since it prepared the female and also gained *yin* (passive energy) for the man. Chinese manuals of Taoism, which Europeans came across at this time, describe oral sex (playing the flute) in great detail, along with other matters.

In the *Kama Sutra*, which governed the lives and imagination of the Indian people as a whole in this period, oral sex was practiced by male **eunuchs** dressed as females, or as males; for those who are obviously males, the *Kama Sutra* gives a great deal of instructions; presumably those dressed as females are imitating the relative passivity of the female sexual organs with their mouths. The practice of both partners performing oral sex on each other is known, says the *Kama Sutra*, as "congress of the crow." *See also* Ejaculation; Fornication.

Further Reading: Scruton, Roger. *Sexual Desire*. London: Weidenfeld and Nicholson, 1986; Tannahill, Reay. *Sex in History*. London: Hamish Hamilton, 1980.

Jason Powell

ORGASM. The history of orgasm in the seventeenth and eighteenth centuries is one of change, conflict, and a gendered split between male and female sexual pleasure. Although the necessity of male orgasm for **ejaculation** and conception was commonplace, the role of female sexual pleasure was far more contentious. The Catholic Church, suspicious of sexual pleasure in any form, condemned premarital, extramarital, nonprocreative sex, and excessive sexual passion within **marriage**. Seventeenth-century posttridentine casuists responding to the threat of Protestantism insisted on the separation of pleasure and procreation, as medieval scholars had before. Church doctrine prohibited sex during certain seasons and days of the week, and condemned overly frequent sex, as well as unnatural positions such as the "woman on top."

The one- and two-seed debate perpetuated by early modern Galenists and Aristotelians was a bastion of the legacy from Classical Antiquity. Roman physician Galen (131–201 CE) had reasoned that the heat of orgasm stimulated the emission of seeds from both male and female genitalia, which were used to form the embryo. Thus for Galenists, conception could not occur without both male and female seeds, and therefore orgasm was imperative for both sexes. Simultaneous, mutual orgasm ensured the optimum chance of a healthy progeny. Sixteenth-century French surgeon Ambroise Paré advocated a "philosophy of pleasure," advising the hotter male to cultivate a certain atmosphere of pleasure prior to the sexual act so that the cooler, slower-to-arouse female is properly prepared to release her seed. In contrast, natural philosopher

Aristotle (384–322 BCE) separated female sexual pleasure from conception, arguing that the male seed alone provided the form for conception and female menses the matter. Since females did not emit seeds upon orgasm, their sexual pleasure was secondary to conception.

In 1559, physician and Galenist Realdo Colombo rediscovered the clitoris, known as the focus of female sexual pleasure to the Greeks, but lost to medieval European medical authors, primarily as a result of the lack of appropriate vocabulary in Latin with which to translate the Arabic texts. Colombo was adamant that stimulation of the clitoris "the principal seat of women's enjoyment in intercourse … causes her seed to flow forth" (Park 177), but was imprisoned for his pains.

The new embryology of the late seventeenth century did little to resolve the conflict between one- and two-seed theories. The discovery of the ovaries by Regnier de Graaf (1641–1673) and of the spermatozoa by Anton von Leeuwenhoek (1632–1723) changed the terminology of the debate as ovists and animalculists argued over the predominance of egg and sperm in reproduction. However, the question of whether the female orgasm was necessary for reproduction or indeed the nature of the role of the female (seed) in conception remained unresolved. Both the one- and two-seed theories were disputed well into the eighteenth century and were resolved only with what Thomas Laqueur has termed "the demotion of female orgasm" as a result of a paradigmatic shift from a "one-sex model" of sexual difference to the "naturalization" of woman as an entirely separate sexual being with no propensity for sexual pleasure. *See also* Childbirth; Gynecology Manuals; Pregnancy.

Further Reading: Laqueur, Thomas. "Orgasm, Generation, and the Politics of Reproductive Biology." In *The Making of the Modern Body: Sexuality and Society in the Nineteenth Century*, edited by Catherine Gallagher and Laqueur, 1–41. Berkeley: University of California Press, 1987; Park, Katharine. "The Rediscovery of the Clitoris: French Medicine and the Tribade, 1570–1620." In *The Body in Parts: Fantasies of Corporeality in Early Modern Europe*, edited by David Hillman and Carlo Mazzio, 171–93. New York: Routledge, 1997.

Cathy McClive

ORPHANS.   Orphans are minor children who have lost a parent through death or abandonment. In the colonial and revolutionary era, children were very likely to be orphaned. High mortality rates meant that children could expect to lose at least one of their parents before the children became independent. In seventeenth-century Virginia, for example, over a third of children lost both parents before they reached their majority, and over 72 percent of the children lost at least one parent. Orphaned children were thus one of the main characteristics of the colonial and revolutionary demographic system.

Care for orphans was routinely handled within the family and extended kin group. When a parent died, family members gathered before a local magistrate to elect the guardian, most commonly the surviving spouse. The guardian agreed to care for the orphans until a specified age while protecting and managing any inheritance to which the children had rights. In southern Europe, the guardian's management was overseen by a family member elected from the deceased's side of the family called the trustee. When kin were scarce, families or courts found friends to care for the children, or they sometimes leased the children's services at an auction called a public vendue. Purchasers agreed to care for the children while hoping to use their labor on a farm or in a workshop. Courts also apprenticed the orphans and frequently sent them to colonies as **indentured servants**. Orphans comprised a significant percentage of British colonists sent to the Americas. In 1618, for example, 100 vagrant children were sent from London to Virginia.

Illegitimate births and frequent subsistence crises caused parents and kin to abandon children. In response, religious and civic leaders created orphanages to manage the increasing population of orphans. Orphans entered these institutions at numbers that far exceeded overall population growth. Historians have called the seventeenth and eighteenth centuries the golden age of orphanages in Europe and the Americas. Religious and civic leaders patronized orphanages as one form of charity for the urban poor. They also developed the institutions as a means to curtail the threat of **infanticide**, to reduce problems associated with vagrancy and begging, and to foster population growth. The first orphanages developed in southern Europe in the fifteenth century, and the institutions spread to the north in the seventeenth and eighteenth centuries. The first orphanage in colonial America was founded by Catholic Ursuline nuns in New Orleans in 1729. Two religiously affiliated orphanages opened in Georgia in the 1730s and 1740s. The first public orphanages in the Americas did not open until the 1790s.

Orphanage directors developed an intricate system of managing their charges. In many southern European cities, people could anonymously drop off newborn infants through small doors near the orphanage's entryways. Orphans would be nursed at the hospital, and then most would be shipped to the countryside to be nursed under contract by a farmer's wife. Survival rates for infants were appalling. Newborns, already weakened by dehydration, fatigue, and the chill of the night, were lucky to survive their next few years. In the western French city of Rennes in the late eighteenth century, for example, only 20 percent of the children survived their first two months following their abandonment. In Paris, the Hôtel Dieu had an even more abysmal record between 1772 and 1778, with a 17 percent survival rate. The lucky ones who did survive might return to the orphanage in later years, working in cloth factories and learning rudimentary survival skills needed to develop an independent lifestyle by their late teens.

The unstable demographic systems during the colonial and revolutionary era made the loss of a parent a normal, if still devastating, affair. Both familial and extrafamilial responses attempted to limit the difficulties orphaned children might experience and tried to prepare the children for their own path toward adulthood. *See also* Abortion; Bastardy; Childbirth; Childhood and Adolescence.

Further Reading: Ashby, Leroy. *Endangered Children: Dependency, Neglect, and Abuse in American History*. New York: Twayne Publishers, 1997; Corley, Christopher R. "Preindustrial Single-Parent Families: The *Tutelle* in Early Modern Dijon." *Journal of Family History* 29 (2004): 351–65; Tate, Thad W., and David L. Ammerman, eds. *The Chesapeake in the Seventeenth Century: Essays on Anglo-American Society*. Chapel Hill: University of North Carolina Press, 1979; Viazzo, Pier Paolo. "Mortality, Fertility, and Family." In *The History of the Family, Volume 1: Family Life in Early Modern Times*, edited by David I. Kertzer and Marzio Barbagli, 157–90. New Haven, CT: Yale University Press, 2001.

Christopher R. Corley

OTTOMAN EMPIRE. An Islamic empire centered in Istanbul, the Ottoman empire (1299–1923) extended its borders into Africa, the Middle East, Europe, and Russia by the seventeenth century. Founded by Osman I, the empire was the political and geographical unit governed by Ottoman Turks, a northwest Anatolian tribe of Muslims. In 1453, the Ottoman empire captured the city of Constantinople and renamed it Istanbul after the Greek phrase *eis ten polin*, which meant "in the city."

Ottoman sexual customs closely followed the laws and traditions of Islam; however, changes in the political structure of the seventeenth and eighteenth centuries emphasized the institution of slave concubinage and created significant changes in **gender roles**.

Ottomans mixed sex and politics. Similar to Romans and Persians, Ottoman rulers used gang **rape** as **torture** for enemy troops. Multiple Ottoman soldiers beat and raped enemy officers, quickly establishing dominance. Gang rape did not interfere with Islam's ban against **homosexuality**; as long as a sexual partner was inferior in status, a man was not guilty of homosexuality. Women, male prostitutes, inferior men, and boys were accepted sexual partners. In war, soldiers took boys along as sexual partners in lieu of women, thinking to protect women from battle. In bathhouses, segregated by gender, boys washed and provided sexual services to older men. In women's bathhouses, no such services were available, but reports of lesbianism exist. In the imperial palace, the Sultan's wives and **concubines** were secluded in the **harem**. Eunuch males, those castrated before puberty, guarded the women from young, virile men and carefully recorded when they had sexual intercourse with the sultan. This ensured that the **paternity** of any child born in the harem was without question. Teenage males, thought to be sexually aggressive, were kept away from women, girls, and boys.

In the seventeenth century, Ottomans practiced slave concubinage alongside legal **marriage** for sexual reproduction. Concubines were women who lived with a man who was not a husband, and with whom they had a sexual and usually reproductive relationship. As Muslims, Ottoman men were limited to four legal wives and as many concubines as they could support. While marriage was expected from an Ottoman male, concubines were desired. Slave concubines had no acknowledged heritage and could not exert any power over the male in the family. The Qur'an, Islam's holy book, does not explicitly condemn **slavery**. Any children born of the union between an Ottoman male and a concubine held the same status as those born to him in a legal marriage; they were free citizens and recognized as legitimate. After a concubine gave birth to a child fathered by her owner, she gained certain rights and protection. For instance, the concubine's owner had to support her and her children, he could not sell her to any other male, and she was instantly free if he died. Nearly all the offspring of sultans after Osman I and Orhan appear to have had concubine mothers.

In the sixteenth century, both male and female members of the imperial family used the title "sultan," including the favorite concubine. This eroded in the seventeenth century, a difficult century for the Ottomans, who experienced the rule of eleven sultans, political disorganization and major structural changes, and a failed military invasion of Vienna in 1683. By the late seventeenth century, only the mother of the sultan

An 18th century Ottoman miniature depicting childbirth in the Topkapi palace harem. © The Art Archive/University Library Istanbul/Dagli Orti.

used the term "sultan" in her title, Valide Sultan. Unlike males, females were not given sovereignty, but mothers of the sultan or his sons and brothers had the unique position of the custodians of sovereignty.

A woman's power was reliant on her sexuality; she did not have power until the cessation of her childbearing years, which in the imperial harem was the moment she gave birth to a son, often when a concubine was in her teen years. This shift in duties from bearing a royal son to ensuring his proper upbringing gave her strong influence over her son, who could later become sultan. As the son reached the age of maturity, the son and mother both entered into a public career. The son actively participated in the politics, while his mother participated in an advisory role. As sultan, when he greeted his mother, he knelt to her. Her stipend, the amount of spending money she received, was the highest in the empire, thrice as much as the sultan himself received. She was the guardian of the royal family and often chose the mothers of the sultan's heirs. Valide Sultans exercised their greatest political influence during the seventeenth century, the Sultanate of Women.

During the Sultanate of Women, the queen mothers served as regents to juvenile or mentally ill sultans, despite fertility. The Ottomans did not believe in primogeniture, the right of the eldest son to inherit the rule of the empire. Believing it unfair to younger sons who may be more capable, Ottoman princes battled for the throne. Fratricide, the killing of brothers, was common. After the age of expansion had ended, rulers did not need a proven record of battle success to win the throne. The Ottomans gradually adopted primogeniture and allowed the eldest son, regardless of ability, to rule the empire. Adopting primogeniture at this time caused political instability and allowed a string of underage and mentally incompetent sultans to rule; instead, the Valide Sultans reigned in their place. Younger sons and brothers of sultans were locked away in the palace. Although treated well, they often lived in isolation causing most to indulge in food and alcohol, and some went mad. Completely disengaged from running the government, they made unfit and uninterested sultans who, if and when their time came, allowed the Valide Sultans complete rule. *See also* Baths; Eunuchs; Religion.

Further Reading: Hourani, Albert. *A History of the Arab Peoples.* Cambridge, MA: Harvard University Press, 1991; Peirce, Leslie. *The Imperial Harem: Women and Sovereignty in the Ottoman Empire.* New York: Oxford University Press, 1993; Quataert, Donald. *The Ottoman Empire, 1700–1922.* Cambridge: Cambridge University Press, 2000; Robinson, Francis. *The Cambridge Illustrated History of the Islamic World.* New York: Cambridge University Press, 1996.

Melissa K. Benne

PATERNITY. Paternity refers to the social and legal acknowledgement of the parental relationship between a father and his child. The definitive contours of paternity law during the colonial and revolutionary age were laid out by Sir William Blackstone, an eighteenth-century English jurist and professor, in his historical treatise on the English common law. Both the English common law and American courts (which frequently quote Blackstone as the definitive pre–Revolutionary War source of common law) followed the marital presumption of paternity: "pater est quem nuptiae demonstrant"—the father is he whom the **marriage** points out—well into the twentieth century. Courts' reliance on such presumptions, based at least in part on social policy, were necessary, since objective proof of whose sperm fertilized the mother's egg was difficult to prove prior to the advent of DNA testing.

This presumption was refutable at common law only if the husband could demonstrate that he was "extra quatuor maria" (beyond the four seas) or otherwise similarly not in his wife's presence for the preceding nine months. Some English jurists refused to acknowledge even this limited defense to paternity, stating that the marital presumption was irrefutable. In the 1777 case of *Goodright v. Moss*, Lord Mansfield explained that the marital presumption "is a rule founded in decency, morality, and policy that they shall not be permitted to say after marriage, that they have had no connection, and therefore that the offspring is spurious." Maternity, on the other hand, was easily established from the moment the woman gave birth via the ancient maxim: "mater est quam gestation demonstrat"—by gestation the mother is demonstrated—since **pregnancy** could only occur through sexual intercourse between that woman and a man, resulting in the fetus carried by the woman.

Children who were born out of wedlock, on the other hand, had no such paternity presumptions working in their favor. These children were denied legal status and rights, such as inheritance, through the maxim "fillius nullius" (children of no one). They were, however, owed a duty of support which was first established in 1576 by the English Parliament as part of the British Poor Laws. These laws established a biological father's duty to support his children born outside marriage and allowed justices of the peace to obtain reimbursement from fathers whose biological children received public assistance. For the purposes of establishing paternity with respect to out-of-wedlock births, the sworn testimony of the mother was deemed sufficient proof for establishing paternity.

Thus, according to "An Act for the Setting of the Poor on Work and for the Avoiding of Idleness" (codified at 18 Eliz. 1, ch. 3, Section 2 (1576)) the following provisions were set forth:

> [C]oncerning Bastards begotten and born out of lawful Matrimony, (an Offence against God's Law and Man's Law) the said Bastards being now left to be kept at the Charges of the Parish where they be born, to the great Burden of the same Parish, and in defrauding of the Relief of the impotent and aged true Poor of the same Parish, and to the evil Example and Encouragement of lewd Life: It is ordained and enacted by the Authority aforesaid, That two Justices of the Peace, whereof one to be of the Quorum, in or next unto the Limits where the Parish Church is, within which Parish such Bastard shall be born, (upon Examination of the Cause and Circumstance,) shall and may by their Discretion take Order as well for the Punishment of the Mother and reputed Father of such Bastard Child, as also for the better Relief of every such Parish in Part or in all; and shall and may likewise by such Discretion take Order for the Keeping of every such Bastard Child, by charging such Mother or reputed Father with the Payment of Money weekly or other Sustentation for the Relief of such Child, in such wise as they shall think meet and convenient.

An unwed mother and her children who were not receiving public assistance were not, however, eligible to receive support from the biological father until 1844 when British unwed mothers acquired the right to sue biological fathers for support regardless of their welfare status. *See also* Bastardy; Fornication.

Further Reading: Baker, Katharine K. "Bargaining or Biology? The History and Future of Paternity Law and Parental Status." *Cornell Journal of Law and Public Policy* 14, no. 1 (Fall 2004): 1–69; Blackstone, William. *Commentaries on the Laws of England.* 4 vols. Oxford, 1765–1769. Available at: http://www.lonang.com/exlibris/blackstone/index.html. See specifically Vol. I, Book 1, Chapter 16: "Of Parent and Child."

Stephanie L. Schmid

PATRIARCHY. Patriarchy literally means "rule by the father"—hence, any social or political system that grants the privileged status to males and permits or encourages their domination over females. Patriarchy depicts men as the perfect norm against which women are measured and found lacking.

In the seventeenth and eighteenth centuries, women were socially and legally inferior: unable to vote, rarely educated, barely allowed to trade, persecuted as witches or prostitutes, and unable to control property unless single or widowed. The patriarchal pattern was reinforced by the cultural activity of the time. It was overtly manifested in the major religions, since monotheistic religions are patriarchal by definition. In the Western Christian world—especially after the Reformation—the Protestant emphasis was on the husband as the exponent of God's word to his household, while the Catholic symbol of womanhood, the **Virgin Mary**, was given less importance.

Literary manifestation of patriarchy can be seen in John Dryden's poem *Absalom and Achitophel*. The poem might be an apology for Charles II's sexual excesses, but first of all, it works as an argument favoring the patriarchal system of the Divine Right of Kings in the era of the restored Stuart monarchy. The theory of the Divine Right of Kings defines succession and the origin of power: the successor must be the legitimate offspring of the king; as the king derives his power from God, this power is then passed on to the succeeding generations through **virtue** of birth. In essence, *Absalom and Achitophel* attempts to show how a rebellion against the king is a rebellion against the patriarchal system, and hence a rebellion against God. Absalom, like the historical James, Duke of Monmouth, an illegitimate son, is doomed to fail as he questions the patriarchal system that depends on a proper line of descent. Still, Dryden's strategy is to feminize the enemy; the blame is put on the queen for her failure to give an eligible successor. Barrenness was seen as a sign of dissatisfaction or even rebellion against the husband; so here, the seeds of the rebellion were sown by a barren woman. Thus, the poem presents the patriarchal position through the feminization of the enemy and respectively through the masculinization and deification of the patriarchal system that Charles II represents.

In **philosophy**, the view of women as essentially emotional, weaker than men, requiring moral guidance from men, and necessarily subservient to men was virtually unchallenged. **Jean-Jacques Rousseau**'s general position was that men and women must play very different roles in society and marriage, and that woman's role requires her to take on a clearly subordinate position, which he claimed, was a law of nature. Although Jean-Jacques Rousseau was not uncritical toward the generally accepted view of women, he defended this perspective against any radical changes. John Locke's empiricism, on the other hand, underwrote the possibility of equal rationality in human beings, but it did not necessarily imply equal capacity that would require financial autonomy. As it was men who controlled property, woman's subjection to man was thus reinforced by the relations of property and inheritance. So, while women were capable of rationality, very few of them enjoyed the degree of autonomy needed to become fully rational; even the married woman had no title to money or right to litigation. Thus, Locke appeared radical for his time about women, but still, he combined it with elitism. Besides, in the sixteenth and seventeenth centuries, western Europe was moving from an agricultural economy to the industrial age. Locke recognized that the new relations of bourgeois society required a new definition of patriarchal rule to replace the equation of God, the father, and the king. The bourgeois system of property redefined the patriarchal basis of the society in bourgeois terms: woman's subordination to man is reinforced by the relations of property and inheritance. Woman's life was relegated to the "private sphere" by patriarchal ideology, and her exclusion from the market became a new tool of patriarchal control. *See also* Education; Enlightenment Thought on Sexuality; Marriage; Wollstonecraft Godwin, Mary.

Further Reading: Dolen, Frances E. *Whores of Babylon: Catholicism, Gender, and Seventeenth-Century Print Culture*. Ithaca, NY: Cornell University Publishing, 1999; Miller, Pavla. *Transformations of Patriarchy in the West, 1500–1900*. Bloomington: Indiana University Press, 1998; Murray, Mary. *The Law of the Father? Patriarchy in the Transition from Feudalism to Capitalism*. New York: Routledge, 1995.

Barbara Loranc

PERFECTIONISTS. Christian "Perfectionist" sects, seeking spiritual perfection on earth, have often practiced extreme sexual renunciation to the point of total **celibacy**. Perfectionist groups differ from monastic orders in that perfection is a requirement for every believer, not a religious elite. The two most important eighteenth-century perfectionist sects were the "United Society of Believers in Christ's Second Appearing," commonly known as the Shakers, in England and America, and the Skoptsi of Russia. Both associated perfectionism and sexual renunciation with the Second Coming of Christ, which they, like many of their contemporaries, believed imminent.

The Shakers originated in a religious revival among Quakers around the English town of Manchester in the 1740s. A young married woman named Ann Lee quickly emerged as the leader of the group. Shakers called her "Mother" Ann Lee and later developed the idea that she was the Second Coming of Christ, this time in female form to complement his original male appearance. Lee's renunciation of sex, which eventually caused her husband to leave her and the group, may have psychological roots in the deaths of her four children. She claimed that sexuality was properly used only for propagation, and the human inability to limit it to this purpose bound people to the carnal realm. Sexual renunciation brought people closer to God in the spiritual realm, partially reversing the Fall of Adam. The Shakers were persecuted in England and emigrated *en masse* to America in 1774.

The Skoptsi carried the renunciation of sexuality to an even greater extreme through self-castration of males, although this was not required for every male. (The earliest evidence for sexual mutilation of Skoptsi females dates from the early nineteenth century.) The term "Skoptsi" is derived from the Russian word for "eunuch." Skoptsi distinguished between the lesser and greater "seal," or **castration**, the first involving removal of the testicles, the second the penis as well. Castration was also called the "baptism of fire." Sexual desire was a distraction from God, and its removal by castration was preparation for a spiritual ascent to God in this life—the Skoptsi had little interest in life after death. The first evidence of the Skoptsi is an imperial decree ordering an investigation of their activities in 1772. Their founder, Kondrati Selivanov, claimed to be Christ and, like Mother Ann Lee, was revered by his followers and persecuted by the state. (Selivanov supposedly met the Czar Paul I and recommended that he castrate himself.) The sect was condemned as heretical by the holy synod of the Russian Orthodox Church in 1807. It was severely repressed but survived into the early twentieth century.

For the Skoptsi and the Shakers, sexual renunciation was part of a wider asceticism and a deliberate marginalization from mainstream society. Both groups were known for their plain clothing, hard work, and the Spartan quality of their daily lives. Celibacy also functioned to bring men and women closer to equality in the perfectionist sects than in mainstream churches. Both also engaged in ecstatic demonstrations, which gave the Shakers their name. *See also* Chastity; Eunuchs; Monasteries; Religion.

Further Reading: Engelstein, Laura. *Castration and the Heavenly Kingdom: A Russian Folktale*. Ithaca, NY: Cornell University Press, 1999; Stein, Stephen J. *The Shaker Experience in America: A History of the United Society of Believers*. New Haven, CT: Yale University Press, 1992.

William E. Burns

PERFUME. *See* Cosmetics and Perfume

PHILOSOPHY. The philosophical perspectives of the seventeenth and eighteenth centuries on sexuality range from sexual ethics of respect to sexual liberalism. The dominant legacy of the seventeenth century was Descartes's view, based on the rationalistic premise "I think, therefore I am." In his book *The Discourse on Method* (1637), Descartes (1596–1650) sought a method that would raise mankind to the highest possible perfection. His famous dualism was expressed by the thesis that reality of the physical world was entirely divorced from the mind, and the only connection between the two was the intervention of God. Descartes held that most bodily actions are determined by external material causes. In *The Discourse*, he also provided a provisional moral code exhibiting prudential conservatism, decisiveness, stoicism, and dedication; he advocated changing one's desires rather than the world. Still, Descartes's skeptical method and his egalitarianism about the faculty reason—a faculty distributed equally among all human beings—had liberating implications for women of his own period and great influence on the female thinkers of the seventeenth and eighteenth centuries.

This quest for perfecting nature, as something to be mastered, can also be found in the methodological writings of Sir Francis Bacon (1561–1626). Bacon's explanation of the means by which science will equip humans with power is given metaphorically through his frequent and graphic use of sexual imagery; he openly insisted on the virility and masculinity of the scientific mind.

Liberal conception of morality was manifested by Thomas Hobbes (1588–1679), an English philosopher who developed a materialist and highly pessimistic philosophy. His *Leviathan* (1651) was one of the most significant and highly controversial books of its time—it presented a bleak picture of human beings in the state of nature, where life is "nasty, brutish, and short." Fear of death is the principal motive that causes people to create a state, contracting to submit their natural rights to the absolute authority of a sovereign. For Hobbes, sexual pleasure was a valuable thing in its own right, the pursuit of which did not require external or nonsexual justification. And sexuality was a cardinal affirmation of the goodness of bodily existence. There was no contradiction in presuming that a virtuous person could seek sexual pleasure for its own sake, provided that in moderation. Therefore, reason cannot rule over the desires and passions; instead, reason is the instrument of the desires and passions. Hobbesian cynical view of humanity and reason, his liberal ethic along with disregard of **religion** as a source of enlightenment influenced the seventeenth-century libertinism. The libertines drew heavily on reinterpretation of those arguments found in *Leviathan* that emphasized satiating of the appetites, particularly the sexual ones, along with the ideas based around the writings of Epicures and Lucretius that promoted self-constraint: renewing appetites to allow their gratification again and again, rather than allowing them to be completely sated and thus destroyed.

Another philosopher who examined sexuality was David Hume (1711–1776). This Scottish philosopher, whose main work is *A Treatise of Human Nature*, provides a definition of "love" or the "amorous passion"; according to it, three elements are nearly always combined: sexual desire, kindness or benevolence, and the presence of and a response to beauty. Hume explains that love, or the amorous passion, might begin with lust, and spread into kindness and an appreciation of beauty; or it might begin with kindness and admiration, and spread into lust. For Hume sexual desire alone is "gross and vulgar," and by its nature opposed to benevolence. However, such disparate things can be joined together by appealing to the power of beauty: it can generate both lust and benevolence and can make both lust and benevolence coexist.

The most systematic elaboration on sexuality of the times was provided by Immanuel Kant, a German philosopher (1724–1804), one of the most influential philosophers in the history of Western philosophy, also the author of sexual ethics of respect. For Kant, human sexual interaction involves one person merely using another for the sake of pleasure: "Sexual love makes of the loved person an Object of appetite…. Taken by itself it is a degradation of human nature" (Lectures on Ethics 163). Since sexual desire objectifies, in the process of seeking pleasure without regard for partners and if sexual urges generate deception and manipulation, then sexuality is morally suspicious. However, not all sexual acts are objectifying and instrumental—Kant makes one exception for **marriage**, which is a reciprocal exchange of rights to possess the body, and marital sex can be justified by the ontological union of two persons married to each other, only in this case the possibility of instrumentality is excluded. Still, Kant condemns nonprocreative sexual activities—homosexual intercourse or **masturbation**—considering them unnatural, even if they are, in his own sense, noninstrumental.

In the eighteenth century, the philosophers rejected the seventeenth-century devaluation of the passions. **Jean-Jacques Rousseau** (1712–1788), a French philosopher, recognized that the human individual must transcend one's own needs and passions, by recourse to nature, if it is to discover the good. Still, Rousseau insists that sexuality was not the basis of society. His general position was that men and women must play very different roles in society and in marriage and that woman's role requires her to take on a clearly subservient position. And this, Rousseau claimed, was a law of nature. Rousseau studied man in the pure state of nature, prior to the development of human reason, language, and sociability. He discovered that the natural man is guided by the sweet sentiment of the goodness of his own existence: life itself is naturally good. This original and natural sentiment can be recovered by the civilized man through inner meditation. *See also* Diderot, Denis; Enlightenment Thought on Sexuality; Libertine; Puritans; Salons.

Further Reading: Baker, Robert, ed. *Philosophy and Sex.* New York: Prometheus Books, 1998; James, Susan. *Passion and Action: The Emotions in Seventeenth-Century Philosophy.* Oxford: Oxford University Press, 2000; Stewart, Robert M., ed. *Philosophical Perspectives on Sex and Love.* New York: Oxford University Press, 1995.

Barbara Loranc

PHYSICIANS. *See* Midwives and Physicians

PIRATES. Early modern pirates led lives that were often bound by strong ties of loyalty to their fellow crewmembers and other pirate ships, rather than any sense of connection to family members who remained on land. Indeed, pirates would often refuse to take on new crewmembers if they were married, so strong was the fear that a married pirate might choose his family and abandon the ship. The majority of pirates were men; however, several noteworthy women were members of pirate crews. The sixteenth-century Irish pirate Grace O'Malley was well known to authorities; indeed, her exploits were numerous enough that she was frequently mentioned in Elizabethan state papers and a 500-pound bounty was offered by Queen Elizabeth I for O'Malley's capture. During the eighteenth century, Mary Read and Anne Bonny were both active pirates in the Caribbean.

Piracy was on the whole, however, a masculine experience. In the first decades of the eighteenth century, the number of pirates who were active in the Atlantic numbered almost 5,000. Pirates were a cause of continual frustration and, at times, fear for administrators in the American colonies. They frequently attacked Anglo American merchants and absconded with great quantities of various goods. Early modern piracy had a changing and sometimes fraught relationship with authority. Sixteenth-century piracy often involved tacit approval from the English crown, as Elizabeth I knew the economic consequences for Spain, should Spanish ships be commandeered and their gold or silver diverted to English coffers. By the seventeenth century, violent North African pirates—often labeled Turks—had begun attacking ships in the North Atlantic, yet by the eighteenth century, Anglo American pirates operating in the Atlantic from Africa to Virginia had extensive codes for crew behavior and a deep-seated belief in alliances with other rogue crews.

Piracy was usually a career that one chose freely. It was a conscious attempt to live outside the bounds of social mores and authority figures. Most pirates had personal histories of legitimate naval service—as merchant seamen or as sailors for the Royal Navy, for example—and would decide to lead lives of buccaneering when their vessels were actually captured by pirates. In fact, the pirate's life was often a far less cruel and arduous option than that offered by either the merchant seamen service or the Royal Navy. Limited records suggest that the ages of pirates may have ranged from seventeen to fifty years, with twenty-seven years being the median. In addition to often having some experience with lawful maritime service, pirates were overwhelmingly from the lower economic classes.

An 18th century illustration of Anne Bonny and Mary Read, both convicted of piracy. Courtesy of the Library of Congress.

Pirate vessels maintained a sense of order through collective authority and written rules that had little variation among the different ships. The codes of behavior for the ship's company were negotiated and agreed upon by the crew before any new voyage or after a new captain had been chosen. Captains had complete authority when decisions had to be made that concerned giving chase or mounting a defense against authorities; however, captains could be dismissed by unhappy crew members, and provisions were made among the companies to protect against abuses of power.

When pirates failed to elude authorities, their subsequent trials often had fatal ends. Indeed, official bodies in the new American colonies often insisted on execution for the captured. This move only spurred pirates to wield a similar justice when authorities were taken by crewmembers. Pirates rarely attacked other ships that were sailing under the familiar Jolly Roger flag, and instead followed a nearly universal code of solidarity and support. Although pirates viewed their actions as part of an ethical framework that was directed against authority, their frequent attacks against these sites of authority seemed to confirm their status as veritable social threats who had to be brutally dealt with by the administrators of justice. The number of pirates who were active in the Atlantic peaked in the early eighteenth century. By 1726, government surveillance and frequent state executions for piracy had severely lowered the numbers of crews sailing under the black flag. *See also* Maritime Culture.

Further Reading: Paravisini-Gebert, Lizabeth. "Cross-Dressing on the Margins of Empire: Women Pirates and the Narrative of the Caribbean." In *Women at Sea: Travel Writing and the Margins of Caribbean Discourse*, 59–98. Edited by Lizabeth Paravisini-Gebert and Ivette Romero-Cesareo. New York: Palgrave, 2001; Rediker, Marcus. *Between the Devil and the Deep Blue Sea: Merchant Seamen, Pirates, and the Anglo-American Maritime World, 1700–1750*. Cambridge: Cambridge University Press, 1987; Sjoholm, Barbara. *The Pirate Queen: In Search of Grace O'Malley and Other Legendary Women of the Sea*. Emeryville, CA: Seal Press, 2004.

Laura Schechter

POLYANDRY. Polyandry refers to the form of polygamy in which a woman is married to more than one man at the same time. The two primary forms of polyandry are fraternal, in which a woman is married to a group of brothers, and nonfraternal, in which the husbands are not related. Fraternal forms have been common in Nepal and Tibet. Among the Nyinba of Tibet brothers live together, sharing domestic responsibilities within a patrilineally structured household. Each partner is expected to maintain a sexual relationship with the wife.

Polyandry is quite rare, its primary occurrences centered upon Himalayan areas in South Asia. Polyandry has been practiced, often over long historical periods, within several societies in a variety of places, including Tibet, Nepal, **India**, and Sri Lanka. It has also been observed in areas of China, among sub-Saharan African communities, and within indigenous communities in South America.

Many social-structural explanations have been put forward to explain the development of polyandry. Polyandry has been most commonly practiced in areas with forbidding environments in which large populations would place unsustainable burdens on agricultural systems. Polyandry works in such contexts to limit population growth.

Others focus on economic consequences of polyandry. In this view polyandry allows families to keep estates, relatively small to begin with, intact across generations rather than see land divided into ever smaller parcels, as would occur if land were allotted to each conjugal unit.

During the colonial period, polyandry, along with other traditional aspects of indigenous societies, was targeted for prohibition. As a result it is difficult to know more fully the extent of the practice in the past. Christianity, **Judaism**, and **Islam** all have prohibitions against polyandry.

The practice certainly did not escape the often excited attention of European commentators during the colonial period. This is clear from the many vivid accounts they provided, including two centuries of writing by Europeans about polyandry among the Sinhalese. Perhaps not surprisingly these accounts are often quite focused on sexual relations.

As early as 1672 the Dutch missionary Philip Baldaeus noted in his *Description of Ceylon* that the Sinhalese suggest that conjugal duties be performed by their own brothers. The English author, Robert Knox, provides a seemingly surprised account of the practice in his work of 1681, the *Historical Relation of Ceylon*. Knox exclaims: "In this country, each man, even the greatest, hath but one wife; but a woman often has two husbands. For it is lawful and common with them for two brothers to keep house together with one wife, and the children do acknowledge and call both fathers" (quoted in Hussein 2003). The Portuguese historian, Joao Ribeiro, even provides details of the ranking orders of consummation following the **marriage** ceremonies.

> These first days being past, the husband has no greater claim on his wife than his brothers have; if he finds her alone, he takes her to himself, but if one of his brothers be with her, he cannot disturb them. Thus one wife is sufficient for a whole family and all their property is in common among them. They bring their earnings into one common stock, and the children call all the brothers indifferently their fathers. (Quoted in Hussein 2003)

During the English Revolution there were significant Christian departures from monogamous marriage. These alternative approaches to marriage were most commonly advocated and practiced among the left-wing sects, including especially the Diggers and Ranters. **John Milton**, the poet and author of *Paradise Lost*, himself a supporter of the far left wing of the Revolution, wrote a tract during the Revolution in which he defends all forms of polygamy. For Milton, all marriage is honorable, thus polyandry, as a form of marriage "leaves the bed undefiled."

Interestingly, Christian polygynists have tended to view polyandry as a form of **adultery**. While accepting men marrying multiple wives, Christian polygynists refer to a scriptural definition of adultery as "women that breaketh wedlock" to prohibit polyandry.

Societies in which polyandry is practiced typically do not exhibit the sorts of hierarchies reflected in societies that practice polygyny, since women do not gain status according to the number of men to whom they are married. In many societies people have practiced polyandry outside formal sanction by the state or law.

If there were any possibility of a broader expansion of polyandry within revolutionary Europe it was finally closed with the strict family clauses of the Napoleonic Code. The development of industrial capitalism and its reinforcement of monogamous family form further closed the possibilities for polyandrous marriage. *See also* Bigamy; Concubines; Harems; Revolution and Gender.

Further Reading: Cairncross, John. *After Polygamy Became a Sin: The Social History of Christian Polygamy*. London: Routledge, 1974; Childs, Geoff. "Polyandry and Population Growth in a Historical Tibetan Society." *History of the Family* 8 (2003): 423–44; Hussein, Asiff. "Etage-kema: Fraternal Polyandry among the Olden-Day Sinhalese." *Sunday Observer*, July 27, 2003, see also http://www.sundayobserver.lk/2003/07/27/fea24.html; Levine, Nancy E., and Joan B. Silk. "Differential Child Care in Three Tibetan Communities: beyond Son Preference." *Current Anthropology* 38, no. 3 (1997): 375–98.

J. Shantz

PORNOGRAPHY. Definitions of pornography vary dramatically, but most historians agree that it involves graphic descriptions of sexual activities or genitalia and carries a recognizable breaking of a shared taboo. Although the term "pornography" was first mentioned in the Oxford English Dictionary only in 1857, modern pornographic works were flourishing from the sixteenth century. Pornography came in all forms and found a market throughout Europe—ribald poems, salacious prints, sensational trial reports, medical advice manuals, attacks on religion and the aristocracy, scandal sheets, and obscene fictional tales were all part of a trend related to the new print culture.

Italy took the lead in the publication of pornography during the sixteenth century, followed by France in the seventeenth, and England in the eighteenth century. The earliest erotic Italian works were by Pietro Aretino (1492–1556); his *Sonetti lussurioso* (1534) was accompanied by erotic illustrations by Guilo Romano, engraved by Marcantonio Raimondi. This led to a genre of engravings known in eighteenth-century England as *Aretino's Postures*. Pornographic texts and images were imported and exported, often in the form of reprints, translations, and emulations from other countries. Aretino's *Ragionamenti* (1536) was first seen in London in 1584, and English writers were inspired to produce their own versions such as *The Crafty Whore* (1658). Further renditions of whores' stories include *La Puttana Errante* (1660), translated as *The Accomplished Whore*, and Ferrante Pallavicino's *La Retorica delle Puttane* (1642) translated as *The Whore's Rhetorick* (1683). The latter incorporated common elements of pornography using the story of a whore's life to satirize the Jesuits and religious hypocrisy. Sex manuals such as Nicolas Venette's *Tableau de l'amour conjugal* (1686) and the anonymous **Aristotle's Masterpiece** (1684) were both popular and full of advice on copulation, supplemented with amorous illustrations derived from earlier works.

Erotic French classics such as Michel Millot's *L'Escole des Filles* (1655), Nicolas Chorier's *L'Académie des Dames* (1680), originally published in Latin as *Satyra Sotadica* in 1659 or 1660, and Jean Barrin's *Venus dans la Cloître* (1683) carried popular themes of sexual initiation, defloration, and interest in body parts and bodily fluids which were to become essential elements in English pornography. Early texts consisted of dialogues between an experienced woman and a virgin, a technique inherited from Aretino. In addition, the anti-Catholic theme with its mockery of the cloistered existence of the nunneries and attacks on the priesthood was easily accepted by the contemporary Protestant British and French pornography and translations, as seen in *Venus in the Cloister* would become popular.

In France, *Histoire de Dom B* (c. 1742), attributed to Jacques Charles Gervaise de Latouche, and *Thérèse Philosophe* (1748), attributed to Jean-Baptiste Argens, were two major pornographic novels, a new development of the eighteenth century. *Histoire de Dom B* had a huge impact in Britain, the translation being available as early as 1743. The book was frequently reprinted under various titles, including *Dom Bougre, Portier des Chartreux, Mémoires de Saturnin,* and *Histoire de Gouberdom.* In England, although plenty of ribald erotica was published, little new pornographic fiction emerged at the beginning of the eighteenth century until publication of John Cleland's *Memoirs of a Woman of Pleasure* (1749).

Publishers, such as Edward Rich, Edmund Curll, and George Cannon, responded to public demand for more suggestive and explicit sexual material and increased production to incorporate a wide range of tastes, and to suit all pockets. New printing methods increased supply and lowered costs of all printed materials—pornographic material could now be bought in penny sheets and sixpenny chapbooks. In revolutionary France, buyers had a choice between anti-Royalist attacks decrying Queen Marie Antoinette as a lesbian as found in cheap scandal sheets and anti-Catholic pornographic scenarios depicting bawdy Jesuits in leather-bound books costing up to six guineas. In England, more ribald humor was found in two-penny poem sheets and in expensive calf-bound **flagellation** novellas.

Some historians have suggested that erotica was mainly written for, and read by, elite gentlemen, yet evidence points to a broader readership. Robert Darnton states that French Enlightenment pornography such as *Thérèse Philosophe* was read mainly by a "Champagne-and-oyster" readership of the elite, but has pointed to cheap widespread pornographic sheets read by lower classes. Jean Goulemot comments that erotica could be found everywhere in France, "from the apartments of the highest nobility to the little room of a preacher's servant," indicating a readership which stretched from the upper to the lower classes.

Women such as libertines' mistresses and gentlemen's wives, as well as schoolgirls, were readers of pornography; playwright Edward Ravencroft (*The London Cuckolds*, 1682) remarked, "the other day I caught two young wenches, the eldest not above twelve, reading the beastly, bawdy translated book called the *Schoole of Women*." Obscene prints were even sold in girls' schools. George Cannon, infamous pornographic bookseller, even employed people to throw pornography over the walls of girls' boarding schools as an enticement to later sales. Women were also, to a lesser degree than men, involved in publishing and selling pornography; London wholesaler, Bridget Lynch, "own'd she had sold several of the School of Venus'." A female bookbinder was found by the

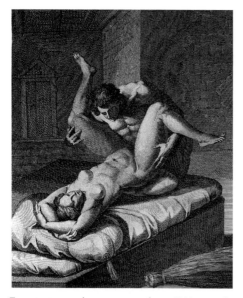

Frontispice and engravings from "L'Aretin by Agostino Carracci, or erotic postures" after Carracci's paintings by J.J. Coigny. © Erich Lessing/Art Resource, NY.

Parisian police in 1800 with 200 unbound copies of Piron's *Oeuvres badines*, a book illustrated with erotic engravings.

By mid-seventeenth century, France's Louis XIV's crackdown on the press drove many of the French pamphleteers underground, many fleeing to Holland. In England, at the beginning of the eighteenth century, the amount of small fines involved for selling "obscene and lascivious books" showed the lack of regard which the authorities gave this material, yet by the last quarter of the eighteenth century, a demand for tighter moral controls was evident, with the foundation of the William Wilberforce's Proclamation Society in 1787 which aimed to suppress, "all loose and licentious Prints, Books, and Publications, dispersing Poison to the Minds of the Young and Unwary, and to punish the Publishers and Vendors thereof." A wave of prosecutions indicated a new crackdown on publishers and sellers of obscene books. *See also* Gossip; Newspapers; Seduction Literature.

Further Reading: Darnton, Robert. *The Forbidden Best-Sellers of Pre-Revolutionary France.* London: HarperCollins, 1997; Foxon, David. *Libertine Literature in England 1660–1745.* New York: University Books, 1965; Goulemot, Jean Marie. *Forbidden Texts. Erotic Literature and Its Readers in Eighteenth-Century France.* Cambridge: Polity Press, 1994; Hunt, Lynn, ed. *The Invention of Pornography: Obscenity and the Origins of Modernity, 1500–1800.* New York: Zone Books, 1993; Kearney, Patrick. *The History of Erotica.* London: Macmillan, 1982; Peakman, Julie. *Mighty Lewd Books. The Development of Pornography in Eighteenth-Century England.* London: Palgrave, 2003; Wagner, Peter. *Eros Revived. Erotica of the Enlightenment in England and America.* London: Secker & Warburg, 1988.

Julie Peakman

PREGNANCY. In the seventeenth and eighteenth centuries, women were expected to become pregnant throughout their childbearing years, which might last from their twenties well into their forties. The average span between pregnancies was often dependent upon when a nursing infant was weaned, with pregnancy generally occurring at fifteen- to twenty-month intervals. Even though pregnancy was viewed as natural, some women were often afraid of becoming pregnant because they feared the pain of the birth process and the possibility that they or the child, or both, might not survive the birth.

Estimates of those who did not survive **childbirth** range from 1 to 15 percent, depending on demographics and the mother's general health. For instance, American women who were generally better fed and who benefited from knowledge of basic sanitation were more likely to survive pregnancy than European women living in crowded, unsanitary conditions. Women who survived initial births might later develop what was inaccurately called "milk fever" but which was likely some other type of infection that resulted in death. Because of scanty knowledge of how germs were spread, **midwives and physicians** sometimes infected women with diseases. The bodies of some women were unable to bear the strain of repeated pregnancies and births, causing them to suffer chronically poor health and early death.

It was not uncommon for women of the seventeenth century who thought they were pregnant to take a wait-and-see attitude in the early days of pregnancy. Midwives who made initial diagnoses often made mistakes, identifying pregnancies where none existed. Other women who were told they were not pregnant discovered misdiagnoses only after signs of pregnancies became unmistakable. There was little agreement on the length of human gestation, and predictions varied from twenty to forty weeks.

The practice of misdiagnosing pregnancies continued into the eighteenth century, since physicians possessed only limited knowledge of women's anatomy, and no infallible pregnancy tests existed. In 1674, Cosme Viardel's *Observations on the Practice of Childbirth* suggested that women who were pregnant were likely to experience a "shiver" at the time of conception, which was followed by the closing of the womb. Based on observations of pregnant women, Viardel also identified suspended menstrual periods and swollen breasts as signs of pregnancy.

In addition to what is commonly known as morning sickness, other physicians stated that loss of appetite, irritability, dull and listless eyes, and changes in the shape and color of a woman's breasts were signs of pregnancy. Quickening, the point at which a mother first feels the fetus move, was accepted as positive proof of a pregnancy, but some women were unable to identify these butterfly movements in the early stages of pregnancy.

Pregnant women of the seventeenth and eighteenth centuries received little or no prenatal care other than word-of-mouth warnings and advice, and superstitions concerning pregnancy were plentiful. It was commonly believed that pregnant women should remain inside and refrain from being startled or frightened because such occurrences were thought to mark unborn children. Pregnant women were also warned against cats, touching their abdomens for fear of causing birthmarks on unborn children, and rolling washtubs in certain directions. In Estonia, women changed shoes weekly to mask their scents from the Devil. In the United States, the Reverend **Cotton Mather** recommended that pregnant women wear a lodestone to "hold" the fetus in place in the womb.

The prenatal care that did exist was often based on the desire to restore the true balance of a woman's body because it was believed that pregnancy had created imbalance. Some midwives and physicians believed that balance could be restored through bleeding, leeching, or purging. Various herbs or properties might be offered to pregnant woman who experienced problems. Neither physicians nor midwives were aware of the need for a balanced diet or vitamin and mineral supplements. Pregnant women were encouraged to drink water and refrain from eating meat, and it was understood that drinking tea and coffee could result in heartburn. Ingesting spearmint, rose or cinnamon water, or drops of opium was offered as cures for excessive vomiting.

Although common morality dictated that pregnancies should occur within the confines of **marriage**, they did, in fact, often occur before marriage or among those who had no desire to marry. In New England, for example, between 1690 and 1699, percentages of women who remained single after they became pregnant ranged from 45.1 percent in Plymouth to 94.1 percent in New Hampshire, according to a study by Lyle Koehler.

When unmarried women became pregnant, local community leaders usually demanded that they name the father, who was subsequently ordered to marry the expectant mother; or, failing marriage, to support his offspring. If the father was not named or could not be found, and no other means of support was forthcoming, local communities provided relief.

Some pregnant women were unwilling to face a life of single motherhood and attempted to abort fetuses through ingesting herbs or applying certain ointments and oils to their skins. Others sought help from outside sources that included midwives, friends and family members, apothecaries, and later physicians. In addition to herbs and ointments, outside sources might engage in vigorous internal or external massage to cause a pregnant woman to abort. Other activities that were thought to cause a woman to miscarry included binding, falling, running, lifting, leaping, excessive exercise, starving, bleeding, blistering, hot and cold baths, emotional distress, fretting, excessive laughing, purging, and vomiting. Reluctant mothers who did not abort sometimes committed **infanticide**, killing their infants after birth, even though they could be executed if they were convicted of this crime.

For women in the seventeenth and eighteenth centuries, pregnancy was often a time of apprehension and fear rather than expectation and joy. Existing knowledge about women's anatomy, pregnancy, and fetal development was sketchy and often inaccurate. This lack of information, combined with the lack of prenatal and postnatal care and limited access to contraception that would have controlled the number of pregnancies a woman experienced, often created chronic health problems and lower life expectancy. *See also* Abortion; Bastardy; Fornication; Menstruation.

Further Reading: Gélis, Jacques. *History of Childbirth, Pregnancy, and Birth in Early Modern Europe.* Boston: Northeastern University Press, 1991; Hanson, Clare. *A Cultural History of Pregnancy: Pregnancy, Medicine, and Culture, 1752–2000.* New York: Palgrave, 2004; Koehler, Lyle. *A Search for Power: The "Weaker Sex" in Seventeenth-Century New England.* Urbana: University of Illinois Press, 1980; Shorter, Edward. *A History of Women's Bodies.* New York: Basic Books, 1982; Sterk, Helen M., et al. *Who's Having This Baby? Perspectives on Birthing.* East Lansing: Michigan State University Press, 2002.

Elizabeth R. Purdy

PREMARITAL SEX. Views about premarital sexuality varied throughout the seventeenth and eighteenth centuries, as did the practice. In Early Modern Europe, most people married in their mid to late twenties, thus most men and women were sexually mature for quite a few years before marriage. Because this was a period in which many brothels were closed and the rate of illegitimate births was very low, historians differ in their opinions as to whether young men and women of this time internalized their sexual desires and kept themselves chaste until marriage, or whether they engaged in other forms of sexual gratification, such as **masturbation**, and perhaps relied upon basic forms of birth control. All seem to agree, however, that despite the condemnation by church and state officials, young couples routinely engaged in forms of sexual experimentation with potential marital partners with the approval of their parents and the community.

In England and the English colonies, the practice was called "bundling," but it was practiced throughout much of Europe under various names and forms. In general, it involved a young man and woman spending the night together in bed, usually in a room apart from the woman's parents, with the understanding that they would not engage in sexual intercourse. Sometimes the young woman's legs were symbolically tied together, or other physical barriers were put up to guard her **virtue**, but in general, there was an understanding that although this was a time when couples might kiss and fondle one another in private, it was also an opportunity for the couple to talk and get to learn about one another to see if they wished to wed.

Throughout the seventeenth and eighteenth centuries, many couples who considered themselves engaged did not believe it was wrong to have sexual relations. However, both Catholic and Protestant authorities spoke out against this practice, and in some cases, the offending men and women were punished. Because church and state were so closely tied together during this period, and many states were trying to regulate **laws** about **marriage**, premarital sex was usually against the law—not just a violation of religious beliefs. In his play *Measure for Measure*, **William Shakespeare** explores this issue. Claudio and Juliet are betrothed, and they do not believe it is wrong for them to have had sexual relations. After Juliet becomes pregnant, Claudio is arrested by Angelo, a man put in place by the duke to clean the city of vice. Angelo intends to make an example of Claudio, however, after Angelo meets Isabella, Claudio's beautiful, virginal sister, he makes a bargain: he will spare Claudio's life, if he can have sex with Isabella. Angelo's scurrilous behavior leads to his downfall.

In this play, Shakespeare is commenting on the politics and behavior of his time. The Church of England had been trying to regulate marital law for decades. With couples required to wed within the church, all sex outside marriage, including that between engaged couples, was illegal. However, as religious reformers tried to combat what they considered immoral behavior, they were coming up against the notion held by many people that sexual relations between a man and woman who intended to marry was acceptable. This battle between the two groups grew more heated after the death of Elizabeth I in 1601, and the accession of James I.

Even in Puritan New England, many couples believed that having sexual relations was acceptable if they planned to marry. In the Puritan colonies of the seventeenth century, marriage was a civil contract, and a judge or other government official performed the ceremony, after the couple made public their intention to marry. Still, some Puritan couples believed that having sex with their betrothed was not a sin, since they considered themselves under a contract to marry. Nevertheless, those who were discovered, usually due to a baby that arrived too soon after the nuptials, were subjected to fines, whipping, and public shaming designed to persuade others not to engage in such sinful behavior.

In the Chesapeake colonies of Virginia and Maryland, the situation was somewhat different. In the early years of settlement, most Anglo Americans in these colonies were young men and women who arrived as **indentured servants**, and therefore could not marry until the years of their service had been completed. However, since there were many more men than women, nearly all women who did complete the terms of their indentures married. For women who had completed their service, **pregnancy** was not a problem, since they were likely to find a marriage partner quickly, but female servants who became pregnant usually had additional time added to their indentures, to make up to their masters for lost time due to the pregnancy. Still, because most young men and women did not have parents living in the Chesapeake, either because they had not emigrated or because they had died from illnesses endemic to the unhealthy environment, they enjoyed more sexual freedom than did their New England counterparts, at least in the early years of the colonies.

By the late eighteenth century, in both England and America, young people were engaging in more sexual freedom, especially within urban areas, such as Philadelphia and London. Prosecutions for **fornication** fell, but those for **bastardy** rose, as towns did not want to have to pay for the raising of illegitimate children. Growing fears about young women being seduced and abandoned—along with the growth of literacy—led to the widespread publication and reading of **seduction literature**, which reflected these fears. *See also* The Body; Chastity; Childbirth; Contraception; Courtship; Education; Romantic Love.

Further Reading: Godbeer, Richard. *Sexual Revolution in Early America*. Baltimore: Johns Hopkins University Press, 2002; Grieco, Sara F. "The Body, Apperance, and Sexuality." In *A History of Women: Renaissance and Enlightenment Paradoxes*, edited by Natalie Zemon Davis and Arlette Farge, 46–84. Cambridge, MA: Belknap Press of Harvard University Press, 1993; Hambleton, Else L. *Daughters of Eve: Pregnant Brides and Unwed Mothers in Seventeenth-Century Essex County, Massachusetts*. New York: Routledge, 2004.

Merril D. Smith

PROSTITUTES AND PROSTITUTION.   Worldwide, sexual commerce was in a state of flux between 1600 and 1800. Prostitution was introduced in some regions and institutionalized in others. Prostitutes received adulation in some quarters and

PROSTITUTES AND PROSTITUTION

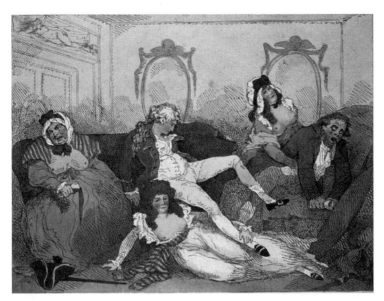

Scene in a bordello where the Prince of Wales lounges on a sofa next to a large, bare-breasted woman, probably representing Charles James Fox. Courtesy of the Library of Congress.

condemnation in others. Some women prospered by commodifying their sexuality, most did not.

Courtesans made a certain type of prostitution eminently respectable in Rome, northern Italy, France, and England. The beautiful and accomplished women who served as companions to men of the royal court were not conventional prostitutes. They could be selective in their choice of partners, never trolled the streets as public women, and never received money for their services. In exchange for the sexual fulfillment, entertainment, and political advice offered by courtesans, their royal paramours rewarded them with jewelry, estates, and royal titles for themselves and their families. Women like Nell Gwynn and Jeanne-Antoinette Poisson (Madame Pompadour) were celebrated by European artists and poets.

Also profiting from sexual commerce were the madams who controlled the prostitution business in the seventeenth and eighteenth centuries. If she could manage a household and a staff of borders, a madam stood a good chance in one of the few lucrative professions available to women. Madams succeeded because men preferred them to pimps. Women could provide a more comfortable, domesticated setting for prostitution. In addition to sex, they were shrewd enough to offer their customers a variety of other services. Men went to brothels to eat, drink, play cards, talk business, and deepen the bonds of camaraderie between men. Madams facilitated these purposes. They also gave men advice, supervised the gambling, and lent money at attractive rates. In addition to the brothel, a good madam also had a network of seemingly respectable independent prostitutes (gallant girls) who she could call on in a rush or send to customers' homes. Madams made additional money by procuring boys and girls for other madams or for wealthy men. Brothel keeping was an illegal and risky business, but, unlike prostitutes, a madam with luck on her side could count on a comfortable retirement.

Many women dreamed of becoming a madam, but for most this dream remained unfulfilled. They lived in a world where urban growth, industrialization, and exchanges with the wider world had, in just a few decades, created a new and much more open urban society. For one reason or another, prostitutes had been unable to find a place for themselves in that new society. These young men and women were usually illiterate and unskilled, lacked stable family support, and were often pregnant or emotionally troubled. Through sexual commerce they created a tenuous community that offered them a small measure of comfort and support. Still, brothel life was far from a perfect situation. They had a sure source of food and protection, but these came at a high cost. Brothels restricted their freedom, they were obligated to bed undesirable men and (for some male prostitutes) women, and most of their earnings went to madams, pimps, and tavern owners. **Venereal disease** and, for women, **pregnancy** were occupational hazards with profound consequences. For most of this period, prostitution was a transitory life stage. They either left prostitution for **marriage**—something that became much more difficult when the French police began registering prostitutes in 1796—or stayed on the fringes of the sex industry as maids, procurers, or tavern servers.

While the lives of most European prostitutes were bleak and grim, the *tayu* of Edo (Tokyo), Japan, had other worries. The city, at this time, was overwhelmingly male. To limit **homosexuality** among the samurai, the government praised and sanctioned heterosexuality in special sex districts. The largest and most important district, **Yoshiwara**, was founded in 1618. Sex was ritualized and very expensive, but little of that money went to the *tayu*. Most women ended up in debt, if they survived at all. Although the district glorified romance and love between the sexes, women who fell in love with a customer were never allowed to see the man again. He might lose his position and inheritance. To secretly prove their love, *tayu* mutilated themselves. When a couple could no longer hide their emotions, mutual suicide, hara-kiri, was the only option. Such deaths were epidemic in Yoshiwara by the 1700s.

While real prostitutes seemed to end their lives in despair, in the mid-1700s a literature emerged which portrayed sexual commerce as an attractive option for women. John Cleland's **Fanny Hill** (1749) prostitutes all over London, saves her money, finances a business for her true love, marries, and raises beautiful children. Daniel DeFoe's *Moll Flanders* (1722) was born in prison, prostituted for twelve years, married five times, lived as a thief for a dozen years, and was transported to America as a felon. There, she became a wealthy plantation owner. Ten years later, Abbe Prevost's novel, *Manon Lescaut*, presented prostitution as the best way for the main characters to maintain the indolent pleasure-filled lifestyle on which their love was based. Books, like *Satan's Harvest Home, or The Present State of Whorecraft, Adultery, Fornication, Procuring, Pimping, and Sodomy* (1749), gave prurient readers shocking glimpses of brothel life. Prostitutes also figured prominently in hardcore **pornography**, such as Charles de Granval's *Le Bordel, Le Jean-Foutre Puni* (1732).

At the same time, other cultures were introduced to prostitution in a different way. When European traders arrived in the East Indies and Indochina, they found women freely offering their love. The men refused. They preferred to purchase sex. This demand led local rulers to sell the sexual labors of their slaves and wives. Eventually, local men began to visit prostitutes because it was easier and cheaper than taking the traditional second wife. Because the women received no profit from the sale of their bodies, this was not prostitution in the strictest sense. However, this began a culture of sexual commerce in the region that was controlled by the royal families of Thailand and Cambodia well into the twentieth century.

Similarly, in Africa, Europeans refused the offers of the women and insisted on sexual commerce. About 1700, the Dutch East India Company built a large compound of African sex slaves near Cape Town. Originally intended for company employees, when times were slow local men were allowed to purchase sex. Thus, Europeans introduced prostitution to Africa.

In the British North American colonies, prostitution was uncovered as early as 1633, but ministers noted its rapid increase in the second half of the eighteenth century. During the American Revolution, Continental Army officers tried in vain to keep prostitutes away from the camps, and parents tried to keep their sons from enlisting because of the reputed loose morals of the women who followed the troops. After the war, prostitutes were highly visible in seaport cities. Urban life allowed a greater personal autonomy as young people were freed from the tight sexual surveillance of their families and small towns. At the same time, a cash economy was replacing indentured servitude. This meant young men had money to spend on their pleasure. It also meant young women who became pregnant would be discharged, not sheltered, by their employers. This combination of male pleasure seeking and female desperation gave rise to a vibrant sexual commerce.

In the new nation, the family was considered the repository of the **virtue** and order the republic needed to survive. Prostitution appeared as the most potent threat to the family, and prostitutes symbolized the calamity that would result if citizens pursued licentiousness and pleasure. Nonetheless, unless the neighbors made strenuous complaint, cities did nothing to curb sexual commerce. Many believed prostitution was necessary to protect respectable women and girls from **rape**. Also, many influential men and government leaders patronized the brothels.

When action was taken against brothels, no attempts were made to investigate the reasons women prostituted or to help them find a better means of earning a living. It was assumed that prostitutes were naturally immoral and beyond redemption. Finally, in 1800, the Philadelphia Magdalen Society was organized by Quakers to redeem women and return them to respectability through hard work, **religion**, and rigorous discipline. The mission floundered on prostitutes' resistance to reform, but it paved the way for the extensive American moral-reform organizations of the nineteenth century. *See also* Adultery; Concubines; Fornication; Geisha; Molly Houses; Royal Mistresses; Sodomy and Anti-Sodomy Law.

Further Reading: Elias, James E., Vern L. Bullough, Veronica Elias, and Gwen Brewer, eds. *Prostitution: On Whores, Hustlers, and Johns*. Amherst, NY: Prometheus, 1998; Godbeer, Richard. *Sexual Revolution in Early America*. Baltimore: Johns Hopkins University Press, 2002; Ringdal, Johan Nils. *Love for Sale: A World History of Prostitution*. Translated by Richard Daly. New York: Grove Press, 2002.

Mary Linehan

PUEBLO INDIANS. The Pueblo have lived in the New Mexico and Arizona area for around 11,000 years. They belonged to many different tribes and spoke seven languages. Their origin stories told of life's unchanging events: **marriage**, sex, birth, fighting, migration, and death. During the seventeenth and eighteenth centuries, Spanish conquistadors and colonialists came to Pueblo territory determined to dominate the indigenous people.

Many Pueblo tribes had traditional myths that sanctioned alternative **gender roles** for males (though not for females), such as those of the **berdache**. Berdaches were generally men who lived as women and were considered to belong to a third gender category.

They existed in a majority of Pueblo communities. Ceremonies displayed and celebrated alternative gender roles. Western Pueblos also performed dances in which they dressed up as half-man/half-woman gods called kachinas.

Some Pueblo tribes were matrilineal societies in which women were autonomous and made major economic contributions to their communities. Women generally had a high position in Pueblo societies. Therefore, men who became berdaches did not feel they were lowering their status or giving up any privileges that might be associated with men in other cultures. The Keres Pueblo believed masculine qualities included only half of human characteristics, whereas feminine qualities comprised all of what it means to be human, including masculine qualities. Keres Pueblo men who became berdaches were viewed as fully manifesting all human characteristics, having risen above masculine limits.

Pueblo women prepared food, tanned hides, made pottery and baskets, and built all houses. Before girls could be considered adults, they needed to learn these skills and gain a husband. Pueblo men hunted, tended crops, conjured rain, wove cloth, and were trained in warfare to protect the community. To become men, boys needed to master these skills and obtain a wife.

Spaniards reached New Mexico in 1598 and immediately demanded total subjugation. Pueblo men sought sexual intercourse not only with the Spanish women who were with the soldiers, but with the soldiers as well. Pueblo women also sought intercourse with the soldiers, in an attempt to pacify what they considered the wicked conquistador psyche and the malice of their gods, thereby stealing their power.

The Spanish, however, saw sexual intercourse with Pueblo women simply as their right due to their superior masculinity. They considered **rape** acceptable both to assuage their sexual needs and to conquer the population. Many Pueblo men were murdered when Spanish soldiers entered their houses to rape their wives. A record from 1601, however, tells of confusion, as the Pueblo men seemed not to care if their wives were faithful or not. The Spaniards were shocked that Pueblo men did not punish their wives for unfaithfulness. Furthermore, they were bewildered to find that Pueblo women did not show distress during the rape encounters.

Pueblo men abstained from sex while practicing ritual magic, but did not understand why Spanish friars would voluntarily abstain from sex for life. To the Pueblo, sex was a guilt-free activity of great value. There were no restrictions upon sexual intercourse because it kept the cosmos in order.

The Pueblo practiced both serial monogamy and serial polygamy. They had a positive **body** image and often walked around naked. Their songs and myths celebrated sexual activity, and their dances ended in sexual intercourse. According to the Spanish, **incest** was common at public dances between all members of a family. Women routinely placed themselves on all fours as men penetrated them from behind. Variance to the norms was not considered deviant: the half-women, half-men berdaches were symbolic of cosmic balance.

The Catholic Spaniards tried in vain to stop the unbridled sexual behavior of the Pueblo, which they considered bestial. One method of forcing obedience was through humiliation. The Spanish tried to switch the gender roles of the Pueblos. The Spanish forced Pueblo men to build houses, a role distinct to women. The women would often laugh, causing the men to cower or run away in embarrassment.

Another method of imposing sexual repression was punishment. Friars whipped the Pueblo publicly, placed them in stocks, and cut off their hair. They would also grab a sexually promiscuous Pueblo man by the testicles and twist until he collapsed. This was done in front of a man's children to humiliate and emasculate him. In one case, in 1638, Fray Nicolas Hidalgo twisted the penis of Pedro Acomilla of Taos so much that the penis head was ripped completely off. *See also* Celibacy; Explorers and Missionaries; Native Americans; Religion; Torture.

Further Reading: Gutiérrez, Ramón A. *When Jesus Came, the Corn Mothers Went Away: Marriage, Sexuality, and Power in New Mexico, 1500–1846.* Stanford, CA: Stanford University Press, 2004.

Elizabeth Jenner

PURITANS. Puritans sought to reform the Church of England through the adoption of a set of rigorous Protestant beliefs. They gained political control of England (1640–1660) and established the New England colonies of Massachusetts and Connecticut in the seventeenth century. Puritans believed that only persons who were married to each other should engage in sexual intercourse. Unmarried persons, or married persons who engaged in coitus outside **marriage**, were prosecuted for **fornication** in ecclesiastical courts in England, and, later, secular courts in England and New England. Terms used to describe out-of-wedlock sexual intercourse, "uncleanness," "filthiness," and "incontinence," illustrate the distaste Puritans felt for sexual activity that lacked the imprimatur of marriage.

Ambivalence toward sexual intercourse was rooted in Puritan theology. First, Puritans believed that life on earth was merely the temporal precursor to eternal life in Heaven. God had placed human beings on earth not to enjoy its pleasures but to improve upon His creation. Coitus was necessary for procreation and to the creation of an affective bond between husband and wife, but excessive enjoyment of sensual pleasures brought with it the potential to divert one's focus from his or her primary relationship with God. Second, the doctrine of original sin, predicated on the biblical expulsion of Adam and Eve from the Garden of Eden, convinced Puritans of the importance of self-control. From infancy, Puritans were taught submission that they might gain the strength to resist their natural inclination to sin. Sexual arousal and **orgasm** represented the ultimate loss of self-control and as such were regarded with suspicion. A third factor prevailed in New England. The colonists believed that New England had been founded upon a covenant. Puritans promised to refrain from sin; in return God would see that their new-world enterprise prospered.

Marriage provided Puritan men and women with a legal and necessary sexual outlet. Continence was as reprehensible to the Puritans as excessive sexual activity, as ministerial dismissals of Roman Catholic paeans to abstinence indicate. Indeed, in New England, mutually satisfying sexual intercourse was considered the right and responsibility of both partners to a marriage, and **impotence** was a ground for **divorce**. Sexual intercourse was an important factor in the creation of the marriage bond. It knit together disparate persons for whom status appropriateness and parental approval were necessary criteria for marriage formation.

Procreation and sexual pleasure were mutually compatible to Puritans. Sexual pleasure, however, was construed as an instrument of procreation because it was believed that conception would not occur unless both partners reached orgasm. The primary purpose, officially, then, of orgasm, was procreation, not pleasure. Married couples endured a long sexual drought if they followed the prohibitions of the church against sexual intercourse from the moment that conception was known until the wife had finished **breastfeeding**, which could be prolonged for twenty months. That this custom may have been adhered to, at least in the final months of **pregnancy**, is suggested by the number of married men prosecuted for fornication in seventeenth-century Puritan New England whose wives were pregnant when they had sex with another woman. A married woman, however, who engaged in extramarital sexual intercourse with a man other than her husband, committed **adultery**, technically a capital crime, although customarily pled down to a misdemeanor. It was not unusual to sentence the erring wife and her lover to public whippings and some time on the scaffold with nooses around their necks as shame punishments. Married men who were convicted of fornication faced merely a fine and a temporary loss of status.

It is possible to find positive affirmations of the role of sexuality within Puritan marriage. Puritan letters, diaries, and wills depict strong emotional and physical relationships, but the ambivalence inherent in marital sexual attitudes foreshadows the difficulties couples faced reconciling natural sexual desires and their hope of salvation. If sex raised troubling issues of conscience for married couples, it was even more fraught for a single woman in New England who faced a fornication conviction with the concomitant whipping or fine and loss of marriageability; for the poor, single woman in England who was prosecuted for **bastardy**, or for the married couple in New England, the birth of whose first child before thirty-two weeks of marriage had elapsed, led to a fornication prosecution. *See also* Childbirth; Laws; Religion.

Further Reading: Hambleton, Else L. *Daughters of Eve: Pregnant Brides and Unwed Mothers in Seventeenth-Century Essex County, Massachusetts.* New York: Routledge, 2004; Ingram, Martin. *Church Courts, Sex and Marriage in England, 1570–1640.* New York: Cambridge University Press, 1987; Verduin, Kathleen. "'Our Cursed Natures': Sexuality and the Puritan Conscience." *New England Quarterly* LVI (1983): 220–37.

Else L. Hambleton

RAPE/COERCED SEX. Rape did not exist in all societies, but in those in which it did happen, there were **laws** that attempted to prevent and/or punish its occurrence. These laws varied in complexity, with many societies distinguishing between victims of the crime on the basis of age, gender, marital and social status, while some also distinguished according to the status of the accused rapist. According to the laws of some states, it was not possible to rape certain people (even though in actuality these people were sometimes forced to engage in sexual intercourse against their will). The evidence required to prove a case of rape also varied.

Age was one variable that was often identified in early modern **rape laws** and legal practices. In *ancien regime* France, the rape of a child was punished by death, a slow, torturous death on the wheel, if the victim was a really young child. The rape of young girls was particularly common in eighteenth-century England because of a belief that sex with a virgin would cure **venereal disease**. Such assaults were rarely severely punished. In England, as in many societies, sexual intercourse with a minor was considered a crime, regardless of whether the victim had consented or not. However, who was considered a minor varied: a 1576 English statute defined a minor as a girl ten years of age or under; an Irish statute of 1710 set the age at twelve and under.

Nearly all medieval and early modern societies had laws against the rape of an adult woman. Holland was an exception, having no known law against rape prior to the seventeenth century. The majority of early modern law codes listed death as the penalty for rape. In practice, however, this punishment was rarely applied and then only in cases considered particularly heinous, for example, if the rape had been particularly brutal or the victim was a child assaulted by her father. In the American colonies, the death penalty was generally reserved for cases involving a white victim and a black rapist.

The laws and legal practices regarding the rape of an adult woman were frequently quite complex, with attitudes varying according to the social and marital status of the victim and the accused rapist. For example, in Ottoman Egypt, the compensation due to the victim of a sexual assault was determined according to the age, religion, gender, and social and marital status of the victim, whereas a 1715 Russian military law applied the death penalty to all rapists, regardless of the social status of the victim.

Furthermore, not all acts of coercive sex were considered criminal. Many early modern societies, including England and France, did not recognize coerced sex with a prostitute as a crime. Prostitutes were common women and could not legally deny their sexual favors to any man. A man who caught a woman committing an illicit sexual act in China could rape her with impunity, as the law considered her as no longer having any honor to defend. Another type of coercive sexual relations not punishable by law was that inflicted by a husband upon his wife. The reasoning for this in the Christian states of western Europe was that a woman gave her body to her husband upon marriage, and he had the right to use it whenever he so desired. Thus, in eighteenth-century Ireland, it was not illegal for a husband to force his wife to engage in sexual relations, but to force her to perform "unnatural acts," such as anal intercourse or to infect her with a venereal disease, were against the law. In Chinese society, while the effect remained the same, the reasoning was different: Chinese social order was based upon the premise of submission to one's superiors; marriages were arranged by parents for the purpose of continuing the lineage—women were expected to submit to their husbands' sexual demands.

The social status of the accused rapist also affected the handling and outcome of a case. Prior to the early modern period, many Catholic countries had distinguished between rape by a cleric and rape by a layman. Clerics were originally defined as men who had taken at least minor vows. Clerics accused of rape were tried in the ecclesiastical, rather than secular, courts. The penalties applied by the ecclesiastical courts were generally more lenient than those of the secular courts and did not include the death penalty. However, such clerical privileges were becoming more restricted in some countries in the early modern period: in 1576, an English statute denied benefit of clergy to men accused of raping a minor, while in 1613, such privileges were denied to all accused rapists in Ireland.

Many rapes were committed by soldiers during war, though few were ever punished. A debate raged across early modern Europe as to whether **wartime rape** was a crime or a right won by the victorious army. In Muslim society, the issue of rape during war was also being debated. The issue there was whether Muslim rape law applied or not to Muslim soldiers fighting in non-Muslim territories, with the Maliki and Shafi'i schools arguing that it did, while the Hanafi argued that it did not.

According to the laws of some states, men and boys could also be sexually attacked. The Maliki school of Islamic Sunni jurisprudence acknowledged that either a man or a woman could be the victim of a sexual assault. Most European law codes listed any sexual interaction between two men, whether consensual or not, as a crime. Sodomitical rape was recognized as a crime in China in 1740, while in France, forced **sodomy** was not distinguished from consensual homosexual relations until 1804.

The evidence required to prove a charge of rape varied according to place and time, but was almost universal such that it made it very difficult for a conviction to occur. In some countries, such as Qing China and Ottoman Egypt, failure to prove an accusation of rape resulted in the punishment of the accuser, and in most, it meant an admission of a loss of honor and chastity and thus also of social worth.

In Qing China, three types of evidence were necessary to prove a charge of rape: witnesses, bodily harm, and torn clothing. In eighteenth-century Massachusetts, a woman needed two witnesses or one witness and physical evidence in order for a rape charge to proceed to trial. In Ottoman Egypt, both the accused and the accuser had to supply character witnesses, as well as character witnesses for the character witnesses. The prompt reporting of a rape increased the likelihood of a conviction everywhere, though the time allowed to lapse between assault and report varied: Scotland and Aragon gave only one day whereas in England forty days could elapse before charges were made.

The Puritan magistrates of seventeenth-century colonial Connecticut were more inclined than many of their contemporaries to accept a woman's claims of rape.

They believed that people were ethically obligated to both God and their neighbors to tell the truth. Some societies did not allow a woman to bring forward a charge of rape, but left this up to the discretion of her closest male kin. This was because it was the man against whom the crime had been committed, the woman being his property.

The eighteenth century was a period that witnessed the extreme idealization of female purity and **virtue** in cultures as geographically, religiously, and culturally disparate as France, China, Ireland, and Muscovy. In short, a woman's worth was in direct proportion to her sexual purity: loss of that purity was equivalent to a social death and was thus deserving of capital punishment in numerous law codes.

In Muscovy, the dishonoring of a woman was punished twice as harshly as the dishonoring of a man. This was because without honor (i.e., sexual purity) a woman had nothing, whereas a man had his wealth, physical strength, and education or job skills. In many places, rape settlements were made out of court to avoid public humiliation and loss of reputation. Sometimes a woman was advised to keep the assault a secret in order to avoid losing all marital prospects or being repudiated by a husband. In Qing China, the extreme valuation of female **chastity** and the high honors accorded the woman and her family who maintained this standard made it difficult for a woman to successfully prosecute a man for rape. A woman's sexual history and her actions during the assault were examined very carefully. If her behavior was found lacking in any way, no matter how small, then her assailant was exonerated and the woman's reputation was ruined. Virtually the only way for a woman to prove her innocence was to commit suicide: in other words, to choose an honorable death over a dishonored future. The family of the woman who chose death over dishonor would have her funeral paid for by the state and would receive a plaque attesting her virtuous status. *See also* Abduction; Adultery; Consent; Interracial Sex; Marriage; Prostitutes and Prostitution; Puritans; Sex Crimes.

Further Reading: Block, Sharon. "Rape and Race in Colonial Newspapers, 1728–1776." *Journalism History* 27, no. 4 (Winter 2001): 146–55; Kaiser, Daniel. "'He Said, She Said': Rape and Gender Discourse in Early Modern Russia." *Kritika: Explorations in Russian and Eurasian History* 3, no. 2 (Spring 2002): 197–216; Walker, Garthine. "Rereading Rape and Sexual Violence in Early Modern England." *Gender and History* 10, no. 1 (April 1998): 1–25.

Tonya Marie Lambert

RAPE LAW. Historically, most societies have construed **rape** as a crime, a public wrong against the assaulted woman and the general welfare of the community, but what was necessary to constitute the crime has varied from society to society and has changed over time. In the seventeenth and eighteenth centuries, most Western cultures defined rape as the unlawful carnal knowledge of a woman by a man, forcibly and against her will. Despite rhetorical assertions about protecting females, women who brought a rape charge faced numerous obstacles to successful prosecution. Courts typically required proof that the man's penis had penetrated the woman's vagina. Some jurisdictions went so far as to require proof of full penetration, and many even demanded evidence that the accused had ejaculated semen inside the woman, before a conviction could be secured. Most courts commonly adhered to the folkloric notion that a woman who became pregnant could not have been raped because conventional wisdom held that conception required **orgasm**. A woman compelled to have sex could never become so aroused as to have an orgasm, thus making it impossible for a pregnant woman to secure a rape conviction against her assailant.

Men tended to be highly suspicious of women who accused men of rape, and the exceptional legal precepts and doctrines that courts implemented in rape trials reflected that suspicion. Seventeenth- and eighteenth-century stereotypes of women depicted them as manipulative and diabolic on the one hand and aggressive and oversexed on the other. For this reason, courts gave most men the broadest latitude possible when defending themselves against a rape charge. Defendants could claim that their accusers had consented, and many jurisdictions even allowed them to assert that the woman had consented *after* the rape. Both claims established a bar to conviction.

Women were competent witnesses in rape trials, but judges typically admonished all-male juries to consider women's testimonies carefully. They instructed jurors to take into account the circumstances in which the rape allegedly occurred. The law required women to make an immediate complaint, or else it deemed the charge false and malicious. This requirement was rooted in the notion that a woman who had been so brutally injured would "naturally" tell the first person she encountered. If the alleged act occurred at a time or in a place where the woman could have cried out for help and she did not, that suggested she had not been coerced. On the witness stand, defense attorneys commonly assailed the complainant's character. In "ordinary" criminal cases, ones not involving women testifying against men, character impeachment was limited to attacking a witness's general reputation to show that he was known to be untrustworthy and should not be believed, even under oath. In some jurisdictions, judges made an exception and allowed defendants in rape trials to impeach the complainant's character by giving examples of her unchaste behavior, and to do so for the express purpose of demonstrating the likeliness that she had consented to the act. This exception to the general rule of law stemmed in part from the common belief that an unchaste woman would be more likely to **consent** to illicit sexual intercourse and then accuse a man of rape, and in part from the popular convention that if a woman had consented to illicit sexual relations at one time with one man then she would accede to any man who solicited her.

The issue of the woman's consent goes to the very essence of a rape charge. If she consented, then she could not have been raped. Women who made a rape accusation had to prove that they had physically resisted. Rape was the only crime that allowed a consent defense but mandated proof of actual resistance to show that the act was against the complainant's will. Rape cases were complicated by the popular notion that some violence was natural in the course of a consensual sexual encounter. Judges devised the "utmost resistance standard," which stipulated that a woman had to resist to the utmost of her ability, to help them determine at what point an act of sexual intercourse exceeded acceptable and expected norms of violence. It was not enough for a woman merely to state verbally that she did not wish to have sexual relations with a man. If he persisted in obtaining sex from her, she had to fight him until she literally no longer had any strength. In the eyes of the law, the "weaker sex" should always somehow be able to muster the strength to fend off her assailant in defense of her chastity. If he succeeded in raping her, the law presumed it was because she had consented. Consummation meant consent, or at least strongly suggested it. To cover more ambiguous cases, courts also crafted the "half-consent rule." Defendants could assert that the woman's resistance was so weak, irresolute, and halfhearted that it could reasonably have been mistaken for consent. The law deemed a half consent as equivalent to a whole one.

Courts tended to reject women's assertions that they did not resist to the utmost of their ability because the defendant had threatened them with a gun or a knife. Rape is the fate worse than death, and the law presumed that a woman would rather die in defense of her **virtue** than submit to sexual dishonor. For this reason, courts tended to hold that unless the defendant actually shot or stabbed the woman, or in some other way maimed her, she had not resisted to the utmost of her ability and thus had not been raped. If she consented through fear, she still had consented and that nullified a rape charge.

In law, a rape occurs only where there is forced sexual penetration, but there was one exception to this rule. Men who had sexual relations with a minor female, one younger than a stipulated age of consent, were guilty of a crime akin to rape and could be convicted even in the absence of force or the presence of consent. The law deemed females under a specified age too immature of mind and body to be able to render a valid consent to sexual relations. The age varied from culture to culture and changed over time, but most seventeenth- and eighteenth-century nations had ages of consent set between ten and thirteen years. Female children had their own difficulties in achieving rape convictions when they could not prove penetration. Legal and medical wisdom held that a mature male's sexual organ was too large to penetrate an immature female, and where there was no penetration, there could be no rape. A number of jurisdictions rejected the charge of criminal assault with intent to rape an infant female, holding that a man could not attempt an impossible act. The requirement of penetration also meant that intercrural sex, sex between the legs, did not constitute the rape of a child either.

Some women who brought a rape charge were less likely to be believed than others. The seventeenth and eighteenth centuries mark an era where the notion of equality before the law was at best in its infancy and certainly not accepted by most nations. Even nation-states that rhetorically acknowledged this radical concept did not really practice it. Most countries of the world were hierarchically structured, and persons of status and privilege controlled the mechanisms of law such as legislation, interpretation, and enforcement. They were not inclined to turn against one another in matters of sexual transgressions with women, especially if those women were of the lower orders. With regard to women of the same socioeconomic status, whether a woman was to be believed depended on many factors, but rested primarily on her personal and familial reputation in the community and secondarily on community perceptions of the accused.

Some women could not be raped at all. The law defined slave women as the chattel property of their masters, and stipulated that a man could do whatever he wished with his own property. The historical record is less clear about a man who was not the bondswoman's master. The weight of the evidence suggests that a master could prosecute someone who coerced sex from his slave, but the charge would be for trespass not for rape. Indigenous women who lived under colonial regimes suffered from a status very much akin to that of slave women, even if they were not actually slaves, and neither the law nor the courts of the dominant culture were inclined to protect them. Also, under the law a husband could not be prosecuted for the rape of his wife, unless he aided and abetted another man in perpetrating the crime. Under the legal fiction of coverture, a wife owed her husband obedience and that included acquiescence to his marital right. *See also* Child Rape; Ejaculation; Laws; Marriage; Native Americans; Slavery.

Further Reading: Blackstone, William. *Commentaries on the Laws of England*. Vol. 4. Oxford: Clarendon Press, 1769. Reprint, Chicago: University of Chicago Press, 1979; Hale, Matthew. *The History of the Pleas of the Crown*, vol. I, edited by George Wilson. London: E. Rider, 1800.

Mary Block

RELIGION. In the Western world, during the early modern period, the various churches controlled and developed sexuality by the institution or sacrament of **marriage**. The recognized reasons for marriage in the West, particularly in England in this time, were all broadly religious. According to the Prayer Book, the first was to bring up children with the fear of God; the second, to avoid **fornication** and the use of prostitutes; and the third, to bring comfort and mutual society. In general most Christians accepted these priorities. As a result of the Reformation, the newly formed Protestant sects modified and restructured many of the beliefs and practices of the Catholic Church. Thus, marriage was no longer a sacrament. The Church of England, for example, considered marriage "an honourable estate," which only "signified" the mystical union of Christ and his church. Under Catholicism, however, marriage remained a sacrament in which God's love was mirrored and worked amongst men and women, while remaining the best remedy against fornication.

In Muslim countries, such as Turkey, with which the West was coming into contact then, there was an enormous emphasis on the necessity of marriage. **Islam** considers marriage a civil arrangement, not a religious significance, and so couples were permitted sexual practices with few restrictions, so long as their marriage was legal. By the seventeenth century, due to the rise of the **Ottoman empire**, Islam reached into Poland, Hungary, and the Balkans, as well as the Near East and North Africa and elsewhere. Islam permitted polygamy, and men were permitted up to four wives and as many **concubines** as they could support.

In the Ottoman empire, ruling Turkey and the Middle East at this time, women had become mere sexual luxury items. Due to the wars waged, the female population increased significantly, as women were often captured as spoils of war. The Qur'an advised that no woman must remain single due to shortage of males or the death of her husband. The Ottoman **harem**, in which up to a thousand women were kept as the sultan's concubines, was the center of the government toward the end of the early modern period.

Muslims are prompted by the Qur'an to seek women for sexual union and marriage during this life, and a man will be blinded by the beauty of the great quantity of virgins who confront him in the afterlife. Sex is prohibited during the daylight hours during the month of Ramadan. As in Pauline Christianity, which begrudgingly accepted sexual congress, the union of man and woman was part of the loving relationship of Allah to the soul. It is more of an offence to avoid sexual union than undertake it for Muslims.

The Ottoman Turks took the harem to the highest level, especially with the extreme segregation of the sultan from his people. Exaggerated contradictions emerged, such as a celibate military elite (the janissaries) and the eunuch civil administrators. Extreme sexuality and sexual repression went hand in hand. The Grand Turk's lifestyle in his court with his mythical women was not fully known then, as it was kept a secret. The Grand Turk's mother ruled the harem, while his up to 1,200 women resided alone with him. Children born to the Grand Turk were never "legitimate," and yet it was customary for such children to have a chance of ruling after his death. Indeed, there was no concern over legitimacy in the Western sense. There was no law of primogeniture. By 1603 Achmet I decided to put an end to the battles that had to be fought by any sultan for his right as the ruler, by locking up all his brothers for as long as he himself lived. When the succeeding sultan emerged, he would be completely out of touch with the world and would proceed straight to the harem. It was left to the sultan's mother to see that his subjects obeyed him.

Sexual mores in Islamic countries were modeled on those of the ruler of the Muslim world, the Grand Turk. *The Perfumed Garden*, a book that resembles the *Kama Sutra* in its intentions and teachings, is a highly practical and humorous book that is thought to have been written around the sixteenth century. The author added twenty-five new positions to the eleven he believed to be in use in the Near East, taking his sources from **India** and China.

Sexuality varies in importance across the religions. The Buddha began to seek enlightenment after seeing poverty, disease, and death outside his palace, but it was waking amongst "his pleasure girls" who lay in unbecoming postures about his feet, which revolted him from his sensual pleasures and awoke him to compassion. But Buddhism advised, as in much else, a middle path, neither of excess nor too much of unnecessary restraint. Then again, Buddist monks are prohibited from sexual union. There were also Chinese style Tantric practices in Tibetan Buddhism.

In **Judaism**, there is suggestion in the first books of the Torah that sexuality was the instigator of the Fall, that is "knowing" another person is the knowledge which Adam and Eve gained, and which lost them eternal life. But there is no regulation prohibiting family life for Jewish rabbis, and family life is part of the religion.

Hindus believed that they took their wives with them to the afterlife, and their women were burnt on their dead husband's funeral pyre to that end. The *Kama Sutra* attests to the injunction on men and women of the correct age to procreate and enjoy their bodies as part of the way of Brahma's creation. In order for a member of any caste to ascend to the next caste in his next life, the member of the caste had to be a perfect specimen of that caste, and do his duty. It was therefore a religious injunction for most men to marry and to give themselves and their wives, pleasure. It is traditional for an older member of a family, depending upon his caste, to enter a life of **celibacy** once his duty to his family, the duty to *have* a family, has been done. But the aim of loving in the *Kama Sutra* is the attainment of sensual pleasure. Sex, it is said in this book, is a religious duty. It would not put him in touch with the infinite, but it would improve his *karma*, or his credit in this life.

Aryan Vedic-Hinduism had more or less died out by the year 1000, and the popular worship of female deities, fertility goddesses, had resurfaced in the south of India, where, indeed, worship of the Aryan, male gods had never taken root. In the north, the religion of the Vedas, a religion that required the Brahman as the intermediary for the sacrifices, had been under attack from popular forms of worship in which the god and the worshipper are face to face. This brought about a sexualization of Indian religion. Indians saw a god with a female consort who did things, while the male sat back and simply *was*. This female enjoyed sexual activity with her husband in popular imagination. The major god was Siva; his wife was Parvati. The god was seen in the shape with which he was most like his worshipper, in the throes of love, and also as a great phallus. With greater contact with other cultures, such as the Tantric and the Taoist, the vision of the gods became homely, natural, and sculpted into more sexy, and seductive forms. The *Kama Sutra* influenced devotion, a way of seeing the gods that was very popular to the ordinary Indian.

Hinduism and Buddhism both had their Tantric schools; they were apparently revolutionary faiths aimed at breaking class distinctions and using drugs, magic, and sexual intercourse as part of religious ritual. The aim was, by these means to merge the soul with the world soul. To this end, the focus of the person had to be shifted from the body to the greater truth. Magic and sex could be used for this. Bodily energy would be channeled into this task. The female in an act of physical union would become the emanation of Siva, or a sakti, and by becoming one with sakti, the practitioner would be one with the World Soul. It is an ancient practice apparently; there is speculation that Buddhism incorporated the native religion into itself as it spread north into Tibet. Originally it would have, perhaps concerned itself with pleasure alone, rather than with this mysticism.

For Christians, the physical, worldly nature of sex and the fleshly union is associated with physical death and the corruption of the immortal soul, the decay that the body will suffer. Sexual **chastity** is demanded of priests in the Church of England and the other nonconformist churches; in Catholicism the priest must remain completely celibate. The eighteenth century waged a war against ecclesiastical obscurantism—which it won—turning the West into a liberal and state-based society, while retaining the overall Christian impulses which had given rise to the Enlightenment in the first place.

When Europeans arrived in the Americas, they encountered groups of people who worshipped many different gods. The religion of the Aztecs in Mexico required human sacrifices. Some anthropologists suggest a reasonable figure for Aztec sacrifices of human life at about 700 per day, over a number of temples. The victims were taken from the surrounding populations. War was organized so as to select victims; so war was a cosmic duty to the sun. The victims were usually adult males. The Aztec population is estimated to have been 25 million. The reason for the sacrifices was that the Sun god would wipe the world out if they were not done. There is indication that this preoccupation with killing the body in this way, and even eating it, was part of a denial of other forms of bodily activity and worship, such as ritual orgies or private sexual devotion.

In South America, Inca harems were formed by regular visits of officials to population centers, wherefrom the prettiest ten-year-old girls were selected. After about five years the girls were ready, and were sifted by the Inca ruler; some kept for himself, others given as gifts, and the rest dedicated to perpetual chastity, for the Sun god.

When Westerners came to China in the seventeenth century, they found a Confucian way of life, which was that of the gentleman on the surface, but underneath existed Taoism, which was the adverse of Christianity, and very sexualized. Westerners did not readily see this, since the Confucian bureaucracy had recently removed Taoist writings, including Taoist manuals on sex. Illustrated poems and **pornography**, as well as scatology, were also removed. These manuals and the freedom they expressed collapsed with the Ming dynasty (1641). The new Ch'ing dynasty imposed strict censorship. So private life turned obsessively inward. Thus 2,000 years of sexual freedom were lost overnight.

So deep was this private turn that all trace of it was lost for the Europeans. Enlightenment, rational, non-religion-based thinking about sex gained its inspiration from Jesuit writings about China. This was seen as "natural morality." By the time Westerners discovered China, Taoism, as it was practiced in private undercover of state Confucianism, was similar, and similar to the Tantrism of Indian Buddhism. Taoism was a religion of different types of energy. It posited centers and lines of the two brands of female and masculine energy in any person; to make these energies flow into a perfect and higher level which is usually only potential, obscure physical positions had to be adopted by the couple. Since the energy was located in the bodies of men and women, to force them to flow required particular and intricate positions of the body in lovemaking. The aim was to release this force up, from the spinal cord and the breast, up into the brain and the mind, and to deliver the personality into the onefold World unity of Being. The idea was bound up with redirecting the semen, not from the penis, but up through the body. The tradition resulted in a great many poetic manuals.

In general, then, religion has far more interest and positive contribution to sexual life than would at first suggest itself from the Christian perspective. Indeed, religious morality often demanded sexual practices as part of religious observance. *See also* Explorers and Missionaries; Mexico; Native Americans; Perfectionists; Puritans; Taj Mahal.

Further Reading: Kakar, Sudhir. *Intimate Relations, Exploring Indian Sexuality*. Chicago: University of Chicago Press, 1990; Robinson, Francis. *The Cambridge Illustrated History of the Islamic World*. New York: Cambridge University Press, 1996; Tannahill, Reay. *Sex in History*. London: Hamish Hamilton, 1980; Weber, Max. *The Sociology of Religion*. Translated by E. Fischoff. London: Methuen, 1956.

Jason Powell and Merril D. Smith

RESTORATION POETRY (1660–1700). The vigorous period of the Restoration in England is best known for a pleasure-loving and libertine court where keeping mistresses was common and regarded as concubinage rather than **adultery**; King Charles II himself was known to have a number of mistresses. His enthroning in 1660 initiated an era of acceptance and enjoyment of sexual and verbal freedom, which contrasted with the Restoration's literary predecessors: the intellectual school of Donne and the severe and moral Puritan writing. This new atmosphere consequently prompted a change in style toward greater clarity and natural wit, along with increasing popularity of coarse satires and pamphlets.

Sexuality abounds in Restoration poetry—the works of this period are infused with explicitly sensual and physical qualities and themes: Adam and Eve in their "bower of bliss" in John Milton's *Paradise Lost*, idealized lovers in Aphra Behn's pastoral "On a Juniper Tree," the sanctified polygamy in John Dryden's *Absalom and Achitophel*, or **John Wilmot**, the second Earl of Rochester's preoccupation with the obscene. Moreover, satires—the major genre in the Restoration—discover and use sexualized bodies as a way of questioning the political status quo. Rochester's "A Satyr on Charles II" pictures a monarch whose "sceptre and … prick are of a length." Andrew Marvell's "Last Instructions to a Painter" presents the king as a rapist and hedonist.

John Milton (1608–1674) in *Paradise Lost* links sexuality with morality—Adam and Eve blissfully enjoy physical love until they commit the original sin, and from then on sex between them becomes lustful, degrading, and shameful.

For John Wilmot, the second Earl of Rochester (1647–1680), a courtier and notorious libertine, sexuality could not entail artifice. His literary offensiveness and personal sexual recklessness brought him into disfavor even with the oversexed and tolerant king. But still, sexual honesty is essential in Rochester's works. In the exemplary "A Ramble in St. James's Park" a woman is attacked for engaging in sexual intercourse without either physical or emotional motivation. Her flaw is to have sex with men for the sole reason that they desire her. The ideal advocated by Rochester is to have a sexual liaison only when stirred by lust, and to simply give in to others' demands for sex when one does not feel attracted to them would be an unnatural and disgusting act.

The female voice in Restoration poetry, **Aphra Behn** (1640–1689) also imbues her writing with erotic content. Although Behn's poetry is groundbreaking for its examination of the male-centered society during the Restoration, she does not offer an alternative to other works of her times, presenting women as passive and submissive, the ones who are supposed to be taken by men. "On a Juniper Tree" pictures a passionate couple in a pastoral countryside. The intimacy is presented in terms of a battle: the lovers behave like enemies; the male character is a sexual aggressor, while the mild woman is tamed, persuaded to give in to his desire. Female passivity and weakness seem to be entirely natural; the woman in "On a Juniper Tree" is not depicted as a real victim of a sexual attack, she just needs some encouragement to go all the way.

Sexuality in Restoration poetry stays interlinked with politics. **Andrew Marvell** (1621–1678) accused the king of political abuse upon England, comparing his misruling to acts of sexual violence. John Dryden (1631–1700), a prominent poet and dramatist of the Restoration, also connected sexuality with political cause. His satitirical poem *Absalom and Architophel* aims at ridiculing political opponents who attempted to enthrone the king's favorite but illegitimate son and exclude the legitimate one. An analogy is made between the conflicts surrounding the reign of Charles II and that of the biblical King David, as both rulers led sexually libertine lifestyles and suffered crises regarding illegitimate heirs. The poem works as an apology for Charles II's sexual hedonism. The king's polygamy and excess are compared to God's ability to create the universe. Furthermore, Dryden supports the king by putting the blame for the lack of a legitimate heir upon the queen's barrenness and not Charles's libertine lifestyle. Dryden even creates an imaginary age "In pious times … before Polygamy was made a sin" that could account for the faults of Charles II (or David) in such a way that almost made them seem virtues. *See also* Actors; Concubines; Libertine; Literature; Puritans; Royal Mistresses.

Further Reading: Chernaik, Warren. *Restoration Literature: An Anthology*. Oxford World's Classics. Oxford: Oxford University Press, 2002; Chernaik, Warren. *Sexual Freedom in Restoration Literature*. Cambridge: Cambridge University Press, 1995; Dolan, Frances E. *Whores of Babylon: Catholicism, Gender, and Seventeenth-Century Print Culture*. Ithaca, NY: Cornell University Press, 1999.

Barbara Loranc

REVOLUTION AND GENDER. The eighteenth century, a time of political upheaval, is generally regarded as a period during which a significant transition occurred in the understanding of gender and sexuality. During this period biology became destiny, as gender categories were given a basis in nature. Medical science during the eighteenth century purported to have discovered an underlying incommensurability between male and female bodies. These medical arguments, which posited a gender as an expression of biology, would provide the basis for the rigid binary system of gender that would be instituted in the West by the end of the nineteenth century. Indeed it has been suggested that sex and many of the stereotypes of gender behavior that have persisted in the contemporary period have their origins in eighteenth-century formulations.

Within this dualist system of gender division men and women became mirror images of each other. Men were presented as aggressive leaders, charged with sexual energy, while women were constructed as passive and unmotivated in matters of sexual expression. The adoption of gender categories over this period did not occur in a straightforward or unproblematic manner, however. There were often quite visible displays of counter or alternative understandings of gender.

As diverse bodies of work, ranging from E. P. Thompson through Bakhtin to Terry Castle, suggest, the popular festivals, carnivals, and masquerades of the seventeenth and eighteen centuries reveal the creativity and playfulness of, and resistance to, gender categories. Contested spaces, in which gender categories were socially disrupted through public rituals, ceremonies, and performances, suggest that such categories were viewed as situational or creative rather than natural.

Indeed these were periods of revolutionary potential and experimentation in which notions of gender were highly contested, challenged, and revised. The outcomes were by no means certain. Notions of gender were interlinked with a variety of issues including class, ethnicity, nationhood, and imperialism.

During the English Revolution of the seventeenth century, there emerged new demands for individual rights and freedom. A variety of quite radical perspectives were developed within the numerous millenarian sects that came to prominence during the Revolution. Among the squatters, vagabonds and travelers, master-less women and men asserted the desire for independence above security or comfort.

Of the various groups to emerge in the English Revolution, it was the Ranters, an anarchic fraction within the Digger colony at George's Hill, that presented the most libertarian vision of social relations, including gender. As antinomians and heirs of the Heresy of the Free Spirit, the Ranters advocated complete emancipation from all **laws** and rules. They rejected private property and all forms of government, whether religious or civil, calling for the abolition of these and other structures of authority. The Ranters argued that the power of love would suffice to usher in a new era of peace and freedom, and they advocated free love.

The Ranters went furthest in moving beyond the sexual revolution of the **Puritans**, which sought only to install monogamous partnership in place of property **marriage**. Gerrard Winstanley, the most prominent Digger, insisted that "every man and woman shall have the free liberty to marry whom they love." The Ranters went beyond this to question the desirability of marriage itself.

For the Ranters, the soul knows no difference of sex. According to Ranter beliefs, "natural people" should act naturally, as their desires and consciences informed them. The Ranters, in practice as well as in ideology, offered some space for women to develop as independent and voluntary beings with rights to pursue their own sensual pleasures. As advocates of a form of voluntary communism and the abolition of all property, the Ranters promoted and practiced free love and refused possessiveness in relationships. Ranters argued that sexual relations, including **adultery**, were not sinful and suggested an open community of participants, including women, in festivals and revelries of music, drink, and sex.

The following excerpt from the anti-Ranter tract, *The Routing of the Ranters* (1650), provides a description, intended to be negative, of a prototypical woman Ranter:

> She speaks highly in commendation of those husbands that give liberty to their wives, and will freely give consent that she should associate her self with any other of her fellow creatures, which she shall make choice of; she commends the Organ, Viol, Symbal, and Tonges in Charterhouse Lane to be heavenly musick; she tosseth her glasses freely, and concludeth there is no heaven but the pleasures she injoyeth on earth, she is very familiar at the first sight, and danceth the Canaries at the sound of a hornpipe. (Quoted in Cohn 1984, 297)

Here the Ranter women are condemned largely because the litany of activities in which the author accuses them of being involved are understood to transgress the bounds of gender appropriateness as the author views them. The Ranter women are dangerous not only because of their libertarian attitudes, but also because they enjoy activities that are perceived by the tract's author to be the activities of men. Still, many women were attracted to the Ranter communities and their teachings, which offered a playful and joyous celebration of freedom unencumbered by the more rigid gender classifications of either the broader society or the other radical sects.

While early American notions of gender are typically portrayed as dominated in a straightforward manner by Puritan morality, recent scholarship presents a more complex picture. Through a detailed examination of multiple sources, including letters, publications, court depositions, and government documents, Richard Godbeer has contributed to a reconceptualization of early American sexual attitudes, values, and customs prior to 1800. His research suggests that the Puritan roots of American sexual behavior are surprisingly complex. Godbeer's research uncovers a wide range of sexual discussion and debate revealing a variety of excesses and anxieties. Adultery and experimentation were more widespread than generally believed given the context of moral surveillance and public shaming.

Popular views of Puritanical abstinence are countered by the numerous examples of alternative practices and relationships. Premarital cohabitation and sex, as well as polygamy, were common. Clergy of the day felt the need to comment on the extent of such practices, as well as the fact that many sectors of the population viewed such relationships as without sin. As in the English Revolution there was a shift in sexual culture away from authoritarian rules and toward more individual notions of sexual expression and fulfillment.

The American Revolution played a great part in the reconceptualization of women's roles, even if this reconceptualization was complex and often contradictory. While some cultural and social venues were opened, the Revolutionary period reinforced many of the political and economic disparities between men and women, notably in terms of employment and access to government.

During the Revolution women assumed a variety of atypical responsibilities. They took on roles as carpenters, shipbuilders, and blacksmiths. Some developed home-based industries.

Following the Revolution some roles assigned to women achieved new emphasis. Republican mothers were viewed as largely responsible for shaping the moral character of the new nation. The view that **education** was necessary for this task led to an increase in literacy among women. At the same time women were denied access to higher education and employment in most professions.

From the flux of the French Revolution there emerged numerous calls for the liberation of women along with experimentation of social roles. During the early periods of the Revolution, between 1789 and 1791, women formed clubs to educate themselves on their changing roles as citizens rather than subjects and to develop and advocate for specific acts of legislation. Among the key issues discussed and debated were the equality of rights, publicly guaranteed access to education, including vocational training and licensing, rights to employment outside the home, the right to **divorce**, and the rights of widows to raise their children and maintain property.

As early reforms failed to address the concerns of the poor and working classes (*sansculottes*), more women mobilized to assert their demands collectively. More clubs were formed, and mass marches were organized by women to support their demands and petition the government. Clearly governments, even revolutionary ones, came to fear the organized power developed by women.

In 1793, the Society of Revolutionary Republican Women, initiated by poor and working-class women, was abolished after only six months. Among the issues they advocated were penal reform, occupational training, and economic reforms to benefit poor women. Notably the Society was critical of all parties that failed to address their concerns, and they found themselves opposing first the Girondins and then the Jacobins who followed in power. The Jacobin Council responded by disbanding the Society and outlawing all women's clubs and associations. Women were harassed and encouraged to return to the home in order to provide the increased numbers of children deemed necessary for proper defense of the newly born nation. Women identified as leaders, such as Olympe de Gouges, author of the *Declaration of the Rights of Women and the Citizeness* (1791), were imprisoned, tortured, and guillotined.

Interestingly the outlawing of the clubs was accompanied by an explosion of state-sanctioned images of women. Joan B. Landes suggests that images of women during the Revolution served as consolation for women for their expulsion from the public sphere. She proposes that visual production during the Revolutionary period worked both to contest and maintain traditional conceptions of gender roles and the roles of women within private and public realms.

These images also reflected a pervasive social anxiety regarding the evolving roles of men and women. At the same time, they expressed an attempt to navigate tentative or shifting gender boundaries. As revolutionary movements rose and fell, new definitions of the state, society, family, and gender disrupted traditional as well as newly emerging conceptions of identity, belonging, and status.

Many of the most aggressive images were directed at the queen. Notably many images called into question her gender or sexuality. These portrayals were directed toward undermining royal authority. If the monarchs were incapable of running their own families, they could not expect obedience from the people.

One of the significant theoretical attempts to extend Enlightenment values of liberty and equality to women came in the form of **Mary Wollstonecraft**'s *A Vindication of the Rights of Women* (1792). In this important work Wollstonecraft argued that the mind has no gender. She also attacked hereditary distinctions and economic inequality and suggested women become independent beings, in part through access to education. Against popular views of women as passive mistresses, Wollstonecraft counterpoised an image of women as rational actors. Wollstonecraft was no revolutionary, however, and she advocated the reformation of government to protect "natural rights" for all.

Still her ideas positioned her as radical, certainly from the perspective of English authorities, who viewed her work as too closely associated with the revolutionary notions coming from France. Thus ideas of women's liberation and gender freedom were strongly linked with issues of politics, imperialism, and nationhood. The association with French radicalism, in addition to the material transformation suggested by calls for women's liberation, a political concern of elites in many nations, contributed to the dismissal of these early works. *See also* Consent; Enlightenment Thought on Sexuality; Gender Roles; Masculinity; Medicine and Science; Religion; Salons; Women, Changing Images of.

Further Reading: Cohn, Norman. *The Pursuit of the Millenium: Revolutionary Millenarians and Mystical Anarchists of the Middle Ages*. London: Paladin, 1984; Godbeer, Richard. *Sexual Revolution in Early America*. Baltimore: Johns Hopkins University Press, 2002; Landes, Joan B. *Visualizing the Nation: Gender, Representation, and Revolution in Eighteenth Century France*. Ithaca, NY: Cornell University Press, 2001; Marshall, Peter. *Demanding the Impossible: A History of Anarchism*. London: Fontana, 1993; Winstanley, Gerrard. *The Law of Freedom and Other Writings*. Cambridge: Cambridge University Press, 1983.

J. Shantz

ROMANTIC LOVE. Romantic love signifies a complex range of emotions between two people, a construct that combines in particular companionate affection and sexual desire (often regarded as opposites) into a single attraction. The idealization of romantic love posits it as a true source of both personal fulfillment and happiness.

The emergence of this construct in the West reflects the fundamental changes from the Renaissance to Romanticism. It may be said to be one of the most significant cultural developments of that period, pointing to changing attitudes toward women, growing acceptance of individualism, and the burgeoning notion of personal happiness.

In the spirit of humanism associated with the Renaissance, **education** of women became more prevalent. Europe remained clearly a **patriarchy**, and most men considered women's roles in society primarily as child-bearers. Even the most liberal thinkers regarded women as physically and intellectually inferior to men, but gradually more Protestants began to see women as spiritual equals. Protestant challenges to Roman Catholic views on **marriage** and celibacy play key roles in the development of romantic love. In particular, Martin Luther argued that marriage should be seen as a secular institution—outside the control of the clergy—and as an idealized and spiritual outlet for a man's sexual urges. Protestants also argued against arranged marriages, instead emphasizing "love marriages" and personal choice. John Calvin and his followers influenced views in England and then in America, holding that romantic love was a controlling factor to help men lead virtuous lives. Nonetheless these early calls for change point to the new attitudes toward women. The dichotomous view of women common in the Middle Ages held that women were either Mary-like figures who inspire good men to **virtue** or Eve-like figures who seduce men to vice.

During the Renaissance more men began to hold women as worthy of their love and to consider marriage as meaningful and spiritual. Yet most contemporary accounts maintain that the strongest intimate relationships were found in friendships of heterosexual men because they lack sexual desire. Romantic love was most likely more celebrated in **literature** and plays—for example in the love sonnet sequences that were the rage throughout much of Europe—than practiced in real life, yet that literature helped to encourage, define, and promote romantic love as worthwhile, valuable, and true.

Sensing new attitudes about love, many late seventeenth- and eighteenth-century writers and theologians questioned the validity of romantic love, especially as a reason for marriage. Writing during what has been called The Age of Reason or The Enlightenment, these rationalist thinkers privileged reason or rationality, and as such, they were quick to dismiss romantic love as an immature, short-lived, and rash emotion. The French satirist Francois de La Rochefoucauld rebuffs love by noting, "True love is like ghosts, which everyone talks about and few have seen." Many maintained that love was nothing more than a fantasy created in and promoted by novels written by and for women; Jonathan Swift, for example, complained that love is "a ridiculous passion which hath no being but in plays and romances." Female writers warned the women reading their works to reject love as fiction single men use to trap women into marrying. Mary Lady Chudleigh in "To the Ladies" equates marriage with servitude and warns single women to hate men professing love as "fawning flatters" determined to entrap them into marriage. At best most still regarded love in the way medieval and renaissance thinkers did: as an emotion of the young, an infatuation, and an intense but short-lived attraction.

These attacks upon romantic love point to growing acceptance of romantic love; often conservative thinkers speak out when they sense changes in their culture, and the fervor of their denunciations of love suggests more and more of their contemporaries accepted romantic love as genuine. A contemporary of Swift, Elizabeth Rowe described her husband in an elegy for him she wrote in 1715 as "The husband—lover—and the friend I mourn." By the start of the nineteenth century romantic love was widely accepted. The romantic poet Samuel Taylor Coleridge is credited in the *Oxford English Dictionary* with the word "soulmate" for the first time, advising a friend in 1822 that romantic love is key to happiness in marriage as one "must have a soulmate as well as" a spouse.

Soon after, most accepted romantic love as something real and natural. Most maintained that it lasts forever and grows deeper over time, and it is so central to one's life that it is the true source of personal happiness. In the West the expected consequence for a couple "in love" was to marry and have children that they see as an expression of that love. Romantic love became the key reason to marry, more important than age, class, religion, and other social and family reasons. *See also* Courtship.

Further Reading: Murstein, Bernard. *Love, Sex, and Marriage through the Ages*. New York: Springer Publishing, 1974; Stone, Lawrence. *The Family, Sex and Marriage*. New York: Harper & Row, 1977.

Timothy J. Viator

ROUSSEAU, JEAN-JACQUES (1712–1788).

Jean-Jacques Rousseau was a Swiss political philosopher of the Enlightenment, best known for his views on equality expressed in *The Social Contract* (1762) and his views on women and sex presented in the novel *Julie, or The New Heloise* (1761) and in his educational manifesto *Emile* (1762).

Frequently identified as the "Father of the French Revolution," the works of Jean-Jacques Rousseau have been a major influence on the development of democracy and on interpretations of women's sexual and societal roles. Unlike most philosophers of his time, Rousseau was unabashedly a sexual being and recognized the importance of sex in other individuals. His openness about sex was particularly surprising in eighteenth-century Switzerland where the government attempted to regulate morality by making illicit sexual acts punishable by law. Both *The Social Contract* and *Emile* were seen as threatening to organized government and **religion**, and Rousseau was forced to flee his native Geneva.

Like other contract theorists, Rousseau theorized about a state of nature wherein both men and women were politically free. Rousseau believed that both sexes were also sexually free in such a state and were free to follow their passions and appetites. Because the state of nature is inherently insecure, contract theorists hypothesized that individuals traded total freedom for security under organized government. Rousseau contended that individuals lost their sexual autonomy along with political freedom when governments were formed. The loss of autonomy was more noticeable among women, who were more susceptible to the dictates of society.

While Rousseau accepted theoretical equality for males and females, in practice he believed that women by their very natures were restricted by their reproductive functions and their sexuality, which, contrarily, gave them enormous power over men. Rousseau believed that men, who were known to be easily aroused, became victims of women who aroused desire without offering satisfaction. Since **rape** was not an option to Rousseau under any circumstances, sexually powerless men were forced to woo, flatter, and placate woman in order to obtain sexual satisfaction. Because Rousseau saw women as naturally sexual beings who were conditioned by society to appear modest and prudish, while men were free to act on sexual inclinations, the conflict between the sexes was inevitable.

In *Emile*, Rousseau created Sophie, designed as the ideal mate for Emile. Sophie's **education** is targeted toward preparing her for her role as Emile's wife and sexual partner, which includes instilling in her a desire to please Emile in all ways. Julie, or the new Heloise, is much more openly sexual than Sophie. She is also contemptuous of social mores, becoming pregnant by her tutor. However, like Sophie, Julie chooses a traditional **marriage** partner. Rousseau's novel does not, however, follow a traditional course, and he allows Julie to die tragically.

Scholars have looked to Rousseau's personal background to explain his well-documented masochist tendencies and the sexual fear and guilt that are evident in his writings, particularly in the autobiographical *Confessions*. Rousseau's mother died a few days after his birth and Rousseau's upbringing was filled with alienation and conflict. He admitted that, while working as her secretary, he had a sexual relationship with Mme. Louise De Warens, whom he called "Maman," and confessed becoming aroused while being punished by Mlle. Lambercier, the sister of a minister with whom he lived briefly. While Rousseau equated punishment by females with sexual arousal, he perceived punishment by males as physical **torture**.

In *Confessions*, Rousseau also describes masochistic acts practiced with his wife Therese Levasseur, who was of dubious intelligence and who was socially and educationally unequal to him. The couple abandoned five children on the steps of foundling homes immediately after their births. Ironically, Rousseau argued that the issue of **paternity** gave males a major stake in the consequences of sex, while women were generally only concerned with guarding their reputations.

Even though feminist scholars have viewed Rousseau's works as detrimental to women, it is clear that he was fascinated by women both as individuals and sexual beings. His inherent feelings of inferiority coupled with his passionate nature led to masochistic practices in his personal life, exhibiting his recognition of women's sexual power. Rousseau's portrayal of sexual, complex women has certain commonalities with the modern woman who surfaced after the Sexual Revolution. *See also* Enlightenment Thought on Sexuality; Philosophy; Sade, Donatien Alphonse François de; Salons; Wollstonecraft Godwin, Mary.

Further Reading: Janata, Jaromír. *Masochism: The Mystery of Jean-Jacques Rousseau*. Danbury: Rutledge, 2001; Mortensen, Peter. "Rousseau's English Daughters: Female Desire and Male Guardianship." *English Studies* (August 2002): 356–70; Rousseau, Jean-Jacques. *The Confessions of Jean-Jacques Rousseau*. New York: Heritage, 1955; Rousseau, Jean-Jacques. *Emile*. London: Dent, 1974; Rousseau, Jean-Jacques. *Julie, or the New Heloise*. Hanover, NH: Dartmouth College Press, 1990; Schwartz, Joel. *The Sexual Politics of Jean-Jacques Rousseau*. Chicago: University of Chicago Press, 1984.

Elizabeth R. Purdy

ROYAL MISTRESSES. A woman involved in a sexual relationship with a man of rank or wealth not legally married to her, a European royal mistress, is not synonymous with a concubine, who is more properly associated with Asian cultures. Although by all practical standards, a mistress and a concubine were equally intimate and fairly common extramarital companions, their legal statuses and the moral perceptions about them were very different. Whereas **concubines**, kept in Asian or Muslim **harems**, often in staggering numbers, were considered the birthright and company both essential and suitable for powerful men, in Western courts, a mistress was officially regarded as an illicit companion. European royal courts were traditionally constrained by Christian beliefs about **chastity** and **adultery**, which complicated the violation of **marriage** vows. **Divorce** was unusual and generally illegal. In theory, both ecclesiastical and secular laws demanded that men, even kings, do not take mistresses. In practice, many European nobles ignored these prohibitions.

Such unions also brought forth children, some of whose fathers were not always willing to recognize them as their offspring. Some monarchs fathered more illegitimate children than rightful heirs to the throne. In perhaps the most extreme case, King

Charles II of England is believed to have fathered twenty illegitimate children, but no legitimate children at all, and as a result, his brother, James II ascended the throne of England after Charles's death.

Apart from their mere existence being a flagrant disregard for the teachings of the church, many royal mistresses were an affront to social decorum because they were not of noble birth. Instead, they were most often prostitutes, street sellers, servants, or actresses; these were not socially privileged or respected groups back then either. An important exception to the rule of humble origins of royal mistresses was Arabella Churchill, the daughter of Sir Winston Churchill, who was a direct ancestor of Britain's World Wart II prime minister. She was the mistress of King James II of England.

In addition to an evidently alluring physique, an important factor securing their social ascension was their ability to adjust to challenging situations or to outwit their rivals. Despite humble upbringings (and in some cases even illiteracy), the women proved remarkably deft manipulators, and on account of their intimate relations with European monarchs, many women amassed considerable wealth, privileges, and power. One of King Charles II's mistresses, Nell Gwynne, described in Samuel Pepys's diaries as "Pretty witty Nell," is said to have been endowed with a rare, often self-deprecating sense of humor, which she used to win the king's favors, such as royal titles for her children, or to extricate herself from uncomfortable or dangerous situations. Her original quick wit is reported to have saved her from a furious mob that mistook her for one Catholic mistress of the king. Having understood her predicament, Nell corrected the irate masses saying that she was "the *Protestant* whore."

The social ascension of many mistresses was a gradual progression. For a woman of a lower social station to immediately catch the attention of a king would have simply been implausible. Instead, many were first romantically linked with wealthy prominent men, and from that they built their way into higher circles, some of them eventually reaching royal courts. Such were the careers of Nell Gwynne or **Grace Dalrymple Elliott**, a Scottish prostitute who, after a number of affairs in Britain, moved to France and became mistress of the Duke of Orléans, the cousin of King Louis XVI. Similarly, Dorothy Jordan was King William IV's mistress and she gave birth to at least ten of his children after first being involved with a police magistrate and later a theater manager. Among social-climber mistresses was one of the most powerful mistresses of all time, Marta Skowronska. Originally a peasant woman from Lithuania, Marta was taken prisoner by the Russian army, and after an affair with a friend of Tsar Peter the Great's, she later became the mistress of the Tsar himself. He had been separated from his first wife and married Marta; she survived her husband and, as Tsarina Catherine I, became the empress of Russia.

By romancing their way into royal courts, mistresses often joined directly the political events that engulfed the elites. Grace Elliott was entangled in the turbulent events triggered by the French Revolution and she escaped the guillotine by a hair's breadth. Less fortunate was Madame du Barry, the mistress of Louis XV of France, who was beheaded after a hasty prearranged trial. *See also* Actors; Bigamy; Geisha; Gossip; Prostitutes and Prostitution.

Further Reading: Manning, Jo. *My Lady Scandalous*. New York: Simon & Schuster, 2005; Parker, Derek. *Nell Gwyn*. London: Sutton, 2000.

Konrad Szczesniak

SADE, DONATIEN ALPHONSE FRANÇOIS DE (1740–1814). The Marquis de Sade, or Comte Donatien Alphonse François de Sade, was born on June 2, 1740, in Paris. What little is known of his childhood and early years, leading up to his brief military career (1754–1763), seems singularly uneventful in the light of his later notoriety. Sade's biographers describe his life as filled with sexual excess and debauchery, and his proverbial penchant for cruelty inspired a nineteenth-century sexopathologist, Richard von Krafft-Ebing, to coin the term *sadist* to denote a person deriving sexual satisfaction from inflicting pain on others.

Sade's **libertine** activities with actresses and prostitutes, which he paid for with ill fame and frequent periods of incarceration, continued throughout most of his adult life, despite his keeping up the pretence of a family life and fathering three children with his wife. The first in a series of arrests on the grounds of Sade's outrageous behavior came only several months after his demobilization, even if at that stage Jeanne Testard, the prostitute whose complaint brought about his successive imprisonment, claimed to have been assaulted only verbally. Released a few weeks later, Sade remained under the surveillance of Inspector Louis Marais, the head of the Vice Squad. Consequently, he was reported to have resumed his former lifestyle, and proprietors of brothels were warned of his abusive tendencies and advised not to allow the girls to follow Sade to his private quarters.

Sade's life of excess continued unabated, irrespective of the death of his father and the birth of his first son, Louis-Marie, in 1767. In 1768 Rose Keller, a prostitute who had escaped a whipping at Sade's house in Arcueil, pressed charges, leading to Sade's repeated imprisonment and exile at his chateau of La Coste. The third period of incarceration, on the orders obtained by Sade's mother-in-law Mme de Montreuil, coincided with the charges of poisoning and **sodomy** brought against him in relation to a series of orgies at Marseilles. Imprisoned in the chateau of Vincennes, he was transferred to the Bastille in 1784 when Vincennes closed.

When in prison, Sade occupied himself with writing, noting down his observations on life, art, and sex, and giving vent to fantasy in sexually explicit erotic novels. In 1785 he finished his final draught of *120 Days of Sodom*, a story of four libertines who kidnap people for the sake of transgressing the limits of perversion. The manuscript, hidden in the cell, was rescued by a guard before the sacking of the Bastille. The Bastille was also the place of origin of perhaps the best-known de Sade novel *Justine, or The Misfortunes of Virtue*, written in 1787, in which the pointless, as it transpires, sufferings of Justine were to disprove the existence of God and reality devoid of desire.

Transferred to the insane asylum at Charenton with the start of the riots in 1789, Sade did not see the fall of the Bastille. After his release, however, he returned to Paris and embraced the Revolution, despite his aristocratic origin, enthusing about the possibility of political liberation. Calling himself Citizen Louis Sade, he joined one of the most radical Paris sections (section des Piques) and began publishing political pamphlets. Arrested as "suspect" during the Great Terror, under the death sentence, he was spared only because of the overthrowing of Robespierre.

Regardless of his political activity, Sade continued to publish his works of fiction, some of them anonymously. The subsequent years saw in print *Justine, or The Misfortunes of Virtue* (1790), *The Philosophy in the Bedroom* (1795), *Aline and Valcour* (1795), and *The Crimes of Love* (1800). The performance of Sade's play *Oxtiern* was causing riots in Paris in 1801, when the author was arrested, again in connection with his anonymous writing. Sent to Sainte-Pélagie prison, Sade remained in isolation for nearly fourteen years without charge. In 1803, to avoid further scandal and a public trial of his allegedly pornographic works, Sade was once again transferred to the insane asylum at Charenton, where he died in his sleep on December 2, 1814, after a brief illness at the age of seventy-four. According to his diary, he engaged in affairs with asylum workers and remained sexually active till the day he died. *See also* Flagellation; Literature; Madness; Prostitutes and Prostitution; Revolution and Gender.

Undated portrait of Donatien Alphonse François de Sade, from an engraving by Eustache L'Orsay. © Mary Evans Picture Library.

Further Reading: Du Plessix Gray, Francine. *At Home with the Marquis de Sade*. London: Pimlico, 2000; Hayman, Ronald. *Marquis de Sade: The Genius of Passion*. London: Tauris Parke Paperbacks, 2003; Laws, Robert Anthony. *The Marquis de Sade: Madman or Martyr?* Nottingham: Paupers' Press, 2002; Schaeffer, Neil. *The Marquis de Sade: A Life*. London: Picador, 2001.

Katarzyna Ancuta

SALONS. In the twenty-first century, French salons of the seventeenth and eighteenth centuries conjure up visions of luxury and decadence. While many salons were luxurious, most salons could not be accurately described as decadent. Hosted by women, most salons were designed to bring together the greatest minds of the period to discuss politics, **literature**, science, **philosophy**, and society. Celebrated writers, artists, musicians, clerics, historians, orators, and civil servants frequented French salons, where *salonnieres* brought them together with French aristocrats. The salonnieres also taught scores of young men how to behave properly in society. While salons also existed in England and the United States, they were more limited in scope and never obtained the societal impact of French salons.

Roles of French women of the seventeenth and eighteenth centuries were less rigid than those of either English or American women, and salonnieres were free to take leadership roles in determining the mores of French society. At the same time that all-male literary clubs provided gathering places for Frenchmen, the French salon brought males and females together to interact intellectually and socially.

Each salon had its own personality, and the lavish décor of the salon was easily associated with the name and style of its hostess. Such was the case with the "blue chamber" of the Marquise de Rambouillet, who established the first salon by turning an inherited town house into the Hôtel de Rambouillet with small, intimate rooms. Subsequently, salonnieres such as Mademoiselle de Scudéry, the Marquise de Lambert, and Mademoiselle de Sable further refined the concept of the salon by widening the debate of social and political issues and expanding the influence of the salon.

During the early seventeenth century, the emergence of Neoplatonism with its emphasis on love and the quest for beauty and perfection freed its proponents, many of them regular visitors to salons, to pursue love outside the bonds of holy matrimony. In this atmosphere, sexual promiscuity and infidelity were common in some salons.

The celebrated salonnieres of the seventeenth century were succeeded by salonnieres such as Claudine-Aléxandrine Guérin de Tencin and Anne-Thérése de Marquenat de Courecelles who provided fertile ground for eighteenth-century progressivism. In this atmosphere, French salons became instrumental in articulating the rebellion against the monarchy that led to the French Revolution in 1789, partly by erasing social barriers within the salon. During the Enlightenment, Marie-Therésè Geoffrin, Julie de Lespinasse, and Suzanne Necker used the salons of Paris to introduce the Enlightenment ideas of the French *philosophes*, leading to challenges of the status quo.

In England, the first salons appeared in the mid-sixteenth century but did not attain their heyday until the late seventeenth century. In 1675, Hortense Mancini moved to London and established a Parisian-style salon. Enchanted with Mancini, Charles I established an annuity of 4,000 pounds and gave her a suite at St. James Palace. In Mancini's salon and those patterned after hers, sexual liaisons were often brief and intense, and rivalries were frequent and violent. By the late 1770s, the levee had become the most popular salon-type event, occurring any time from eight in the morning to three in the afternoon, bringing individuals together for entertainment and debate.

English literary salons of the eighteenth century provided avenues for discussing the place of women in literature and society. These salons were generally run by bluestockings, so named after the bluestockings worn by naturalist Benjamin Stillingfleet, a salon habitué. Bluestocking salon hostesses included Elizabeth Vesey, Hannah More, Elizabeth Montagu, and Elizabeth Carter. Of all English eighteenth-century salons, that of Elizabeth Vesey was considered the most promiscuous. While Vesey refrained from engaging in sexual liaisons, she allowed her guests to express themselves freely.

In America, the atmosphere of salons was distinctly different from those in England and France. A number of women writers, such as Anne Bradstreet, Mercy Otis Warren, Abigail Adams, Annis Boudinot Stockton, and Elizabeth Graeme, held court to discuss literature and the issues of the day. Perhaps the most illustrious and distinguished salon circle gathered around First Lady Martha Washington who held drawing rooms on Friday evenings. Sarah Livingston Jay and Lady Kitty Duer also gathered the political elite in particularly American-style salons.

While salons have the reputation as places conducive to promiscuity and decadence, most salons were, in fact, designed to promote the interchange of ideas and to celebrate the arts and sciences. Salons were instrumental in expanding definitions of women's roles in society and in tearing down social barriers based on wealth and family lineage. *See also* Gender Roles; Rousseau, Jean-Jacques; Wollstonecraft Godwin, Mary.

Further Reading: Kale, Steven. *French Salons: High Society and Political Sociability from the Old Regime to the Revolution of 1848*. Baltimore: Johns Hopkins University Press, 2004; Quennell, Peter, ed. *Affairs of the Mind: The Salon in Europe and America: From the Eighteenth to the Twentieth Century*. Washington, DC: New Republic Books, 1980; Tinker, Chauncey Brewster. *The Salon* *and English Letters: Chapters on the Interrelations of Literature and Society in the Age of Johnson.* New York: Gordian Press, 1967; Wharton, Anne Hollingsworth. *Salons: Colonial and Republican.* New York: Benjamin Bloom, 1971.

Elizabeth R. Purdy

SCIENCE. See Medicine and Science

SEDUCTION LITERATURE. The seduction novel as a subgenre is probably one of the most notorious and celebrated developments of eighteenth-century Western **literature**. While the romance at the time was seen as unsatisfyingly fictional, the novel claimed a greater lifelike representation that enthralled the reader with its combination of didactic and sensational elements, convincing narration, and realistic characters.

An unlikely follower of the conduct book, the seduction novel proved a more successful and creative offspring of the literary imagination, which successfully addressed the audience's growing interest in sexuality and its social importance. Originally, the purpose of the conduct book was the instruction on the proper ways of social behavior for young ladies aiming at **marriage** and ultimate domesticity. The conduct book, however, sounded prescriptively dull and unimaginative most of the time. The seduction novel, on the other hand, made use of an array of literary devices to convey a message, yet entertain.

Samuel Richardson published *Pamela or Virtue Rewarded* (1740), which immediately grabbed the audience with its narrative power and subject matter. Planned originally as a conduct book, *Pamela* was finally rewritten as an epistolary novel composed of a series of letters and journal entries. In the first part of the book, *Pamela*, tells a story of rewarded **virtue**, which easily connects to the yearning of many readers for respect and stability. She is a maid pursued by her master, Mr. B, who is trying to seduce her after the death of his mother, Pamela's former employer. The seducer, however, has to face the strong-willed and virtuous Pamela, who manages to reject his advances until Mr. B is ready to propose an honest marriage, and thus acknowledge her socially. In the second part of the novel, Pamela tries to build a successful relationship with her husband based on mutual respect, and to prove adequate to the demands of the upper-class society she has joined.

Another well-known novel by Richardson is *Clarissa: Or the History of a Young Lady* (1748). Again, it tells the story of virtue under attack, yet this time Clarissa is not spared but raped by the male character Lovelace. She dies tragically, although completely aware of her own innocence.

Despite the acknowledged popularity of *Pamela*, the novel inspired a number of parodies, the most well known of which are *Shamela* (1742) and *Joseph Andrews* (1742) by Henry Fielding. In *Shamela*, the main character is a calculating social climber who uses her sexual appeal to achieve a higher social status. In *Joseph Andrews*, the roles of a seducer and seduced are switched, thus leading to a virtuous male character desperately trying to resist the sexual advances of ever so persistent rich women.

Susanna Rowson published *Charlotte Temple: Or a Tale of Truth* (1790), and it immediately became a sensation in the publishing word in both America and England. The book sold thousands of copies in numerous editions and was celebrated as one of the most popular novels of the century. Rowson claimed the novel was based on a real story that had been narrated to her by a woman who appears in the book under a fictional name. The destiny of Charlotte, who elopes with Montraville, only to be left by him and to die in despair, reflects the sad story of a social phenomenon of the times: eloping as a means of "liberation" and an outlet for sexual passion.

The seduction novel easily probed into the questions of virtue and **seduction**, domesticity versus promiscuity, and sex as a tool used equally by men and women, thus touching upon some social taboos and clichés of the times. The seduction novel, while undoubtedly following the instructive tradition, delved into some sensitive issues of the turbulent eighteenth-century society—the issues of sexuality and gender identity. The subject of sexual conduct, it seems, had been popular with a growing number of female readers who directed their attention to stories that dealt with the topics of sex, love, and marriage beyond the purely didactic rhetoric. Female readers, who had grown wary of mere advice, actively engaged with stories about female characters who made the best of their lives without compromising their sexuality. *See also* Gender Roles; Romantic Love.

Further Reading: Armstrong, Nancy. *Desire and Domestic Fiction: A Political History of the Novel.* New York: Oxford University Press, 1987; Roussel, Roy. *The Conversation of the Sexes: Seduction and Equality in Selected Seventeenth- and Eighteenth-Century Texts.* Oxford: Oxford University Press, 1986; Watt, Ian. *The Rise of the Novel: Studies in Defoe, Richardson and Fielding.* London: Penguin Harmondsworth, 1976.

Rossitsa Terzieva-Artemis

SEX CRIMES. Actions considered to be sex crimes varied between cultures and throughout time, as did the degree of unacceptability. Sex crimes in the early modern period can be divided into two categories: those believed to go against nature and those deemed disruptive of the social order.

CRIMES AGAINST NATURE. Crimes against nature were sexual activities that cannot result in procreation. Particularly in Catholic cultures, reproduction was seen to be the only legitimate reason to engage in sexual relations. In Protestant cultures, sex within marriage for the purposes of pleasure was also accepted.

Sodomy was the term used by the Catholic Church to encompass all nonprocreative sexual acts. **Masturbation, bestiality, anal intercourse** (whether between two men or a man and a woman), as well as any type of sexual relations between two members of the same sex, were all acts of sodomy.

Masturbation is an action that often happens unbeknownst to others. Thus, in those cultures where it was considered a crime, it was almost never punished. In early modern western Europe, however, masturbation was increasingly condemned as the cause of numerous physical and mental problems. Consequently, though it was not illegal, parents went to great lengths to prevent their children from masturbating.

Unlike masturbation, sexual relations between men were legally banned in Christian societies. This prohibition was based upon biblical passages. The punishment was often burning at the stake. In Austria, this was changed to life imprisonment in 1787. In France (1791), consensual male homosexual relations were decriminalized if enacted in private, while China introduced its first laws against sex between consenting men in 1740.

Lesbianism, or sexual relations between two women, was condemned in most European countries, England being an exception. However, it was a practice that rarely came to the attention of the authorities. Convents, prime locations for such relationships, generally dealt with such matters internally. Secular cases that attracted attention usually involved women whose activities undermined the social order in other ways, as well—for example, in instances in which two women lived together with one adopting the role of the husband in dress, **marriage**, or work.

Sex with animals was not unheard of in this period when most people lived in rural areas where they interacted with animals on a regular basis, sometimes living alone with them for extended periods of time, as in the case of shepherds. The early modern period saw many Swedish men and boys prosecuted for bestiality. Jonas Liliequist has suggested that in areas with pronounced gender roles, such as Mediterranean cultures, actions such as sodomy, which crosses or blurs boundaries between male and female, were harshly punished, while in areas without such pronounced gender roles, such as Sweden, actions such as bestiality, which blurs the prominent age differentials between boys and men, were more troubling.

A final form of unnatural intercourse was sex with a spiritual being. The early modern period was the heyday of European witchcraft trials, and the majority of continental cases involved allegations of demonic sex, that is, sex with the Devil or his minions.

CRIMES AGAINST THE SOCIAL ORDER. Sex within marriage, especially for women, was the ideal in most societies at this time. Sex outside marriage was disruptive, as it could result in children with no obvious means of maintenance. Nonetheless, both **premarital sex** and extramarital sex occurred frequently. In many European societies, premarital sexual relations that resulted in **pregnancy** often led to marriage and the reestablishment of social order, but not before the couple had been publicly punished. In northern Europe where the average marriage age was high, many marriages resulted from a premarital pregnancy.

Not all premarital pregnancies ended in marriage. Sometimes the woman faced the difficult task of supporting both herself and her child. Other members of their society often treated unwed mothers poorly; often the women were viewed as disruptive, sinners, and economic burdens. In early modern England and many Protestant areas of Germany, people forced unwed pregnant women from their communities to avoid having to pay for the upkeep of the child. As a result, some women tried to induce an **abortion** or committed **infanticide**.

Both single and married men consorted with prostitutes. The legality of prostitution varied, but existed almost everywhere. The career of a prostitute varied in its duration. Some had very short careers, being forced out after contracting a **venereal disease**. Others practiced their trade for life. Some managed to find husbands or wealthy protectors. Some switched to other service jobs. Many women only sold sex occasionally to supplement the family income. Though prostitutes themselves rarely became rich, some bawds and brothel owners did.

Not all women engaged in illicit sexual relations willingly. Some were forced to do so. **Rape** occurred in most early modern cultures. It was also severely condemned in those cultures. However, while rape laws often carried harsh penalties, few rapes were ever successfully prosecuted. In Qing China (1644–1912), the standard of evidence required was almost impossible to meet. Thus, in many cases, the woman committed suicide to prove her innocence.

The rape of a girl was often dealt with differently. Many countries had a legal age of **consent**. Sexual contact with a girl under that age, whether consensual or not, was considered rape. Proving such a crime could be difficult, however, as some believed it was physically impossible to penetrate one so young. However, in cases where it was proven, the punishment was often harsh and swift.

Most societies prohibited incest, though exactly which relations were included varied widely. In Catholic countries, people related by blood, affinity, or spiritual kinship up to the fourth degree were unacceptable partners. Punishment for incest was often severe and included both parties, whether both had consented or not. In Iceland, those convicted of incest were executed.

Polygamy, or the practice of multiple marriage, is one which was more common than monogamy during the early modern period. Many cultures allowed the taking of more than one wife, and a few allowed the taking of more than one husband. Islamic law allowed a man to have up to four wives, if he was able to provide for them. Christian communities, on the other hand, rarely allowed multiple marriages. A brief exception occurred in Nuremberg in 1650: men were allowed to take two wives, as women greatly outnumbered men following the Thirty Years War.

Christianity also condemned the keeping of **concubines**. Nonetheless, in Catholic areas, where priests were not allowed to marry, it was not uncommon to find them living with concubines. In China, on the other hand, concubinage was common. The legal rights of concubines (or second wives) were less than those of a (first) wife: a concubine could be discarded at will, but her children were legitimate. In areas where concubinage and polygamy were legal, fewer women remained single.

Adultery was a crime that was defined differently for a man than for a woman. If a married woman had sexual relations with any man other than her husband, it was adultery. However, if a married man had extramarital sexual relations, it was only considered adultery if the woman involved was married. The reason for this difference was to prevent the foisting of another man's child upon the woman's husband. *See also* Bastardy; Bigamy; Child Rape; Fornication; Homosexuality; Laws; Prostitutes and Prostitution; Witches and Witch Trials.

Further Reading: Farr, James R. *Authority and Sexuality in Early Modern Burgundy (1550–1730)*. New York: Oxford University Press, 1995; Gerard, Kent, and Gert Hekma, eds. *The Pursuit of Sodomy: Male Homosexuality in Renaissance and Enlightenment Europe*. New York: Harrington Park Press, 1989; Liliequist, Jonas. "Peasants against Nature: Crossing the Boundaries between Man and Animal in Seventeenth- and Eighteenth-Century Sweden." *Journal of the History of Sexuality* 1, no. 3 (1991): 393–424; Sommer, Matthew H. *Sex, Law and Society in Late Imperial China*. Stanford, CA: Stanford University Press, 2000.

Tonya Marie Lambert

SHAKESPEARE, WILLIAM (1564–1616). William Shakespeare redefined the image of the playwright, the nature of drama, the voice of love poetry, and the human psyche. Psychoanalyst Sigmund Freud cited many of Shakespeare's characters as models. Shakespeare's plays were not formally collected and published until after his death, in the 1623 edition known as *The First Folio*, wherein contemporary poet-playwright-critic Ben Jonson extolled him as "not of an age, but for all time!" Though issues of authorship remain open to debate and speculation, the texts attributed to the man called Shakespeare resound throughout Western culture.

Creating tragedies, comedies, histories, and romances, Shakespeare recorded the full spectrum of human emotions and conditions. From respectable but by no means noble beginnings, Shakespeare apparently gained the full benefit of the standard **education**—Latin grammar, reading, and writing—available at the Stratford-on-Avon Grammar School. He married, while relatively young, a slightly older woman, Anne Hathaway, possibly due to an impending birth. Sometime between 1582 and 1592, Shakespeare moved to London and became active in the **theater**, initially as an actor/player but with aspirations to write.

Shakespeare's later works resonate with the seventeenth century's cultural discussions of **gender roles** and sexuality. His comedies of this period focus on women with strong voices who are active in the selection of well-matched men of wit as their spouses. The sharp-tongued Beatrice in *Much Ado about Nothing*, published in 1600, refuses Don Pedro's noble advances, but is "tricked" into an appreciation of her male-equivalent Benedick (the trick hinges on self-love—we love that which loves us). The so-called "problem plays" *Measure for Measure* (1603–1604) and *All's Well That Ends Well* (written between 1601 and 1606) feature active heroines who perch on the edge of tragedy and chaos. With the framing story of **premarital sex**, chastity becomes the central issue for Measure's Isabella. In a gender reversal of romance stories, All's Helen goes on a quest to seduce her reluctant husband, via a traditional "bed trick," and earn his love.

The women in Shakespeare's tragedies of this period (Hamlet, Othello, Antony and Cleopatra, King Lear, and Macbeth), while facing similar issues, fare far less well than his comic heroines. Hamlet's mother Gertrude, for example, unintentionally commits suicide after partaking in a possibly incestuous **marriage** with her husband's brother and murderer. Ophelia is driven to madness and suicide by Hamlet's dismissal of her. Each character is chastised by Hamlet in frankly sexual terms. The eroticized nature of these relationships led Sir Laurence Olivier (influenced by literary critic Ernest Jones) in his 1948 cinematic version of the play to focus on the possible Oedipal Complex reverberations in Hamlet and Gertrude's relationship. In his 1996 film based on the play, Kenneth Branagh hints at Ophelia's possible **pregnancy** as being the motivating factor in her suicide.

Macbeth, meanwhile, revolves around the evil of three witches and a conniving, manipulative woman, playing upon King James's own fear of witches, whom he believed had tried to kill him, and against whom he had written and persecuted in his native Scotland. Though James did not pursue the same type of burnings in England, the cultural representations of women suffered. Shakespeare's weird sisters prophesy Macbeth's rise and fall, but leave their speeches open to misinterpretation which leads to Macbeth's agency in causing his own downfall, and Lady Macbeth "desexes" herself in order to be more effective in pushing her lord toward power.

Besides the representations of women and heterosexual relationships, homosocial issues gain central stage in Shakespeare's seventeenth century. **Homosexuality**, referred to as "the detestable and abominable vice of buggery," had been formally outlawed in 1533 in England. However, the passionate attachment of James I to many of his male courtiers gave rise to rumors of homosexuality. Likewise, the "Fair Young Man" sonnets, which make up the majority of Shakespeare's collection (126 of 154) and which he revised until their publication in 1609, have created discussions of the possibility of Shakespeare's own **bisexuality**. The Fair Youth is immortalized in the line, "Shall I compare thee to a summer's day?"

The wide range and enduring popular appeal of Shakespearean texts combined with the cultural capital accruing to those familiar with these works all contribute to the formidable influence they continue to exert on contemporary notions of gender and sexuality. See also Literature; Romantic Love; Seduction Literature; Witches and Witch Trials.

Further Reading: Garber, Marjorie. Shakespeare after All. New York: Pantheon, 2004; Greenblatt, Stephen. Will in the World: How Shakespeare Became Shakespeare. New York: W. W. Norton, 2004; Wells, Stanley, et al. William Shakespeare: The Complete Works. 2nd ed. London: Oxford University Press, 2005.

Samantha A. Morgan-Curtis

SLANDER/DEFAMATION OF CHARACTER. See Gossip, Eighteenth-Century England; Gossip, Seventeenth-Century America

SLANG. See Euphemisms and Slang

SLAVERY. Slavery is a social stratification system in which several groups may exist; however, a slave society is characterized by the ownership of a group of persons by another group under their control. Many forms of slavery can exist, but they all have in common the security of service from the slave. The most prevalent form of slavery that existed throughout history is chattel slavery. Chattel slavery involves the complete ownership of a person, including the legal right to buy, sell, or trade humans. Because slaves were considered the property of their masters, they were subject to sexual, emotional, and physical abuse without legal recourse.

During the American Revolutionary period, as colonists began to agitate England for their own freedom, many of the founding fathers became aware of the contradictions of slaveholding. This inconsistency and blatant hypocrisy is embedded in the symbolic imagery of the death of Crispus Attucks, a former mulatto slave who escaped his master in the Massachusetts colony in 1750. Ironically, the first person to die for freedom of the colonies was himself in jeopardy of reintroduction into slavery—had he been caught. Many of the founding fathers who owned slaves as British citizens released them in the years following the separation of the colonies from England (e.g., George Washington, John Dickinson, Ceasar Rodney, William Livingston, George Wythe, and John Randolph of Roanoke). Furthermore, many of the founders had never owned slaves. In contrast, other founding fathers, such as Thomas Jefferson, did own slaves. Jefferson owned an expansive plantation that employed both slaves and indentured labor until his death.

Slaves and the condition of slavery existed across many societies where humans oppressed members of their own group, as well as those of different races and ethnicities, and of either sex. African slaves brought to the Americas during the sixteenth, seventeenth, and eighteenth centuries were typically taken as prisoners of war, sold as children by their parents, or exchanged as labor for a debt. Also, in times of dire economic distress and lack of **food**, people have been known to sell themselves into slavery. Slavery was common in Africa, as a part of the structure of everyday life. The system of slavery and slaves came in different guises in different societies: there were court slaves, slaves incorporated in national armies, freedom fighters, domestic slaves, farmhand slaves, highly skilled artisans, couriers, intermediaries, and even traders. In many cases, the living conditions were not the best. The diets of slaves were often inadequate or minimally adequate to meet the needs of the laboring conditions, which tended to be from sunup to sundown. Slaves lived in crude, barely heated quarters with minimal clothing and bedding, leading to unsanitary conditions, making them susceptible to many diseases, especially malaria.

The worth of a slave in the seventeenth and eighteenth centuries was based on their health, stamina, and skills. Men were employed as farm laborers of all sorts, stablemen, coachmen, stage drivers, sailors, boatmen, miners, ironworkers, sawmill hands, house and ship carpenters, wheelwrights, coopers, tanners, shoemakers, millers, cooks, bakers, and in a variety of other skilled and manual-labor tasks. Likewise, slave women were employed in all kinds of household service, including cooking, serving, spinning and knitting, farmhands, field hands, dressing maids, midwives, and labor nurses. Slave women with children were viewed as less valuable and were often sold because they had children. Slaves were under the constant threat of sale. Even in the best of times, a slave could be sold; however, any form of financial loss, setback, or personal crises of the master could lead to a sale as well. The value of a slave was also a form of social control. Since slave marriages were not legal, husbands and wives could be separated at the whim of their masters. Slaves were often threatened with family separation if they did not "behave." Mothers, children, fathers, grandparents, and other immediate family members could be scattered across several plantations without seeing other members of the family again.

In the thirteen colonies, and then in the new republic, slavery was met with a series of double standards. Slave owners, overseers, and taskmasters took sexual liberties with female slaves, and others had long-term concubine relationships. These relationships were not hidden from the public, even though the men might be civilly married to white women. Farther still against the social norms, and more rare, was the freeing of a slave. However, the intimate relations between slave and master were not normally consensual; they were "overlooked," coercive interrace liaisons between black slaves and members of the white elite society. Slaves knew that the power of life and death was firm in the hands of the white planter/owner class, and they were in no position to elect to engage or not engage in sexual relationships—there was very little choice in intimate relationships. The relationship between master and slave typically manifested itself in three main ways: the most common of which was **rape** and concubinage because the slave had very little, if any, say in the interaction; the next type was concubinage *via* privileged arrangements; and finally, true relationships between men and women. It is important to note that not all relationships were initiated by white men of the seventeenth and eighteenth centuries. White women initiated some relationships with their male slaves, and some slaves presented themselves in such a way as to gain the favor of their master to gain more for their own families or to keep from being sold to another owner and never seeing their children again.

SLAVERY AND INTERRACIAL RELATIONS. A part of the ideology of the time compelled owners, in many ways, to exert extreme power and control over the social world, in every aspect of the slave's life, bringing maximum economic and social returns for the investment the owner made. This meant the owner had the right to extract a wide variety of nonprofit oriented sociosexual benefits as a legitimate return on the investment made in the purchase of the slave. In some respects, this meant that the slave owners had a right to unrestricted sexual access as a product of ownership. With respect to an enslaved woman who also worked in the fields or household, not only was she expected to tend to the normal labor of her regular responsibilities, but also the household responsibilities which included sexual services and the production of children. Thus reproduction served as a measure of the marginal product of the slave, which fueled the capitalization process. Moreover, in some parts of North America, a culture emerged where young white boys were given a sexual apprenticeship with domestic slaves and prostitutes brought into the house solely and explicitly for the purpose of sex.

Plantation owners consistently denied that slave women were raped. Because slaves were considered property, without feelings or reputation, slave women fell outside the protection of the law, and few formal actions were brought against masters for the rape of slaves. Since a master's **consent** was needed to file a charge of rape, few masters sought to render the preservation of their "property's" **virtue** and reputation, both these concepts thought not to be a part of the slave's social status. In essence, and by many legal definitions, a slave could not be raped. Indeed, owners maintained that black slave women were generally promiscuous and pursued sexual relations with white men for their own social and material gain and betterment. Some slave women did gain their legal freedom through manumission or by purchasing freedom from their masters after periods of concubinage, but in fact, many of the rapes actually benefited the master.

However, in both the northern and southern states, male slaves were charged with rape, if the rape involved a white woman. In most cases, the rape of a white woman assured the accused the death penalty, whereas white men accused of the same offence would have a range of penalties.

SLAVE CONCUBINES. Concubinage in North America refers to an ongoing sexual relationship between a female slave and a male member of a slaveholding class. Often these relationships were socially accepted. This type of arrangement emerged because many communities in seventeenth- and eighteenth-century America forbade some types of sexual and marital relationships, so concubinage emerged as a quasi-legitimate state of socially shunned activities. In some regions, concubinage was considered a legal relationship, where privileges were offered to the children resulting from the intimate relationships. In the former French colony of Louisiana, the law did not initially prevent European settlers in the colony from intermarrying or cohabitating with non-Europeans, specifically Native Americans. French authorities attempted to stop the practice in the colony by promoting the immigration of French women to Louisiana, but this had no significant impact. By the late seventeenth century, King Louis XIV decreed the conditions under which slavery was to take place. The *Code Noir* or *Black Codes* referred to all slaves in the French colonial empire and delineated laws governing slavery and intimate relations between masters and slaves. Specifically, the *Black Codes* fined married men for maintaining mistresses and **concubines**. In an attempt to discourage master-slave concubinage, King Louis XIV decreed that if a married man engaged in concubinage, then the slave and any children would be freed; however, if the man was not married, he should then marry the woman, thus freeing the woman and any children from the said relationship and granting them free French citizenship as freed people living in the colony.

Once the Americans purchased the colony from France, concubinage continued, even in the face of laws designed to maintain America's racial purity. In as much as interracial unions were common, the French and Spanish settlers recognized three distinct populations in the colony, Europeans, free people of color, and slaves, and the American attempt to maintain "racial purity" by establishing two groups only served to maintain a racial caste system and white superiority. However, concubinage took a new form in Louisiana with women of mixed race, especially those known as quadroons (a person with at least one white ancestor), becoming an elite group of desirable mistresses for white men. *See also* Atlantic Slave Trade; Byrd, William; Interracial Sex; Laws; Rape Law; Thistlewood, Thomas.

Further Reading: Clinton, Catherine, and Michele Gillespie. *The Devil's Lane: Sex and Race in the Early South*. New York: Oxford University Press, 1997; Davis, David. *The Problem of Slavery in the Age of Revolution, 1770–1823*. 2nd ed. Oxford: Oxford University Press, 1999; Robinson, Donald. *Slavery in the Structure of American Politics 1765–1820*. New York: Harcourt Brace and Jovanovich, 1971.

DeMond S. Miller

SODOMY AND ANTI-SODOMY LAW. The settlers of early Colonial America brought their viewpoints on sexuality with them across the Atlantic, including what they considered a particular perversion—sodomy. From the "sodomy courts" of fifteenth-century Florence, to public executions for sodomy and buggery in early modern England, the crime was considered particularly deviant in most Western civilizations. The sodomite committed an act that muddied the roles of masculinity and femininity, an unforgivable sin in rigidly defined early modern society. The punishments and stigma associated with sodomy, therefore, were worse than any other sexual crime, perhaps save **bestiality**, and exposed the accused not only to official and clerical punishment, but also to private scorn, banishment, and blackmail. The first statutory reference to sodomy in English law was a 1533 act passed during the reign of

The Spanish Captain Valboa orders Natives, who have been accused of sodomy, to be torn apart by dogs. Colored engraving by Theodore de Bry, 1595. © Bildarchiv Preussischer Kulturbesitz/Art Resource, NY.

Henry VIII. At this time, sodomy was defined as **anal intercourse** between two men, a man and a woman, or between a man and an animal. The penalty was death. This statute remained in effect until 1861.

Laws enacted in Jamestown in 1607 followed English precedent, bestowing the death penalty for sodomy, and the early colonies enacted similarly harsh codes. Even when the capital crime could not be definitively proven, suspected sodomites faced cruel penalties, including whippings and rituals of public shaming. Even if consensual, sodomy was considered far worse than infidelity or promiscuity; it ranked as one of the lowest levels in Puritan minister **Cotton Mather**'s downward steps of unclean acts. Several thousand New Englanders appeared before seventeenth-century church congregations and courts, and five teenaged boys who confessed to sodomy aboard the ship *Talbot* in 1629 were considered so detestable that the General Court in Boston shipped them back to London.

Statutes in Massachusetts, Connecticut, and New Hampshire all contained the same piece of biblical scripture, Leviticus 20:13: "If any man lyeth with mankind, as he lyeth with a woman, both of them have committed abomination; they shall both surely be put to death." Others noted similar scripture. The laws themselves were vague, reflecting a difficulty faced by colonial officials—how exactly to define an act they did not want to discuss in detail. In 1642 a Massachusetts Court sought advice from ministers throughout the colonies, asking whether acts such as **masturbation** and partial anal penetration should be considered sodomitical acts. Ultimately, a strict interpretation was adopted which defined the act as necessarily including penetration, even though that meant fewer chances for prosecution and removed somewhat the catchall nature of the crime in regulating sexual acts. Sexual laws tended to increase in their degree of punishment for transgression as the colonists moved south and west.

However, very few convictions of sodomy are found in colonial and revolutionary court records, indicating that few defendants were brought to trial, and those who were proved extremely difficult to convict. Only two individuals—William Plaine and John Knight—are known to have been executed for sodomy in seventeenth-century New England. The contradiction of rhetorical damnation with legal lenience was due to a number of factors, including the difficulty of the mechanics of prosecution (an accuser could have the tables turned, and himself charged with the same crime), power dynamics between men (a servant would have a difficult time bringing action against his master), and the tendency to turn a blind eye toward such unspeakable misdeeds in a small community. The day-to-day hardships of the early colonies could take precedence over moral absolutes.

The case of Nicholas Sension is an example. Sension was a prosperous seventeenth-century Connecticut businessman with one weakness—he made repeated unwanted sexual advances toward other men, many of whom accused him of attempts at sodomy. Yet for almost two decades no charges were brought against him. Sension's prominent position in the town clearly had influence, as even the men who accused him of attempted sodomy spoke out in favor of his overall character. Finally, in 1677, a criminal court found him guilty of attempted sodomy, and he was whipped and his estate put into bond on promise of good behavior. Actual prosecutions for sodomy were rare in the colonial era, as the rigorous legal standards of the day meant that evidence that did not withstand strict scrutiny did not result in convictions. Accusers who asserted that defendants had a certain proclivity to sexual acts found that such accusations, without definite proof (difficult to obtain in private sexual matters), carried no legal weight.

The modern perception of "sexual orientation" was unknown in the seventeenth and eighteenth centuries. The act of sodomy, like masturbation or bestiality, was considered a disobedience, through weakness, of God's will. The law against sodomy was intended to vilify the act, not necessarily the person, as if the desire for sodomy was present in all creatures and needed to be suppressed by threat, rather than being a particular trait of a homosexual person.

In general, laws against sodomy were eased through the end of the eighteenth century, or at least the crime itself was brought underground—recognized still as a crime against nature, but perhaps more forgivable than before. A sexual lapse could be dealt with privately before a justice of the peace, rather than in a public criminal trial. While anti-sodomy laws continue on the books of certain U.S. states even in the twenty-first century, and some parts of the world still consider sodomy a capital crime, changing sexual mores and definitions of popular morality recognized that sodomy was far from being a capital crime. *See also* Homosexuality; Laws.

Further Reading: Bullough, Vern L. *Sexual Variance in Society and History*. London: Wiley, 1976; Godbeer, Richard. *Sexual Revolution in Early America*. Baltimore: Johns Hopkins, 2002; Weeks, Jeffrey. *Sex, Politics and Society*. London: Longman, 1981.

Doug Krehbiel

SOUTHEASTERN INDIANS. Sex was a defining aspect of Native American life in the early American southeast. Although European colonists frequently concluded that Indian sexuality went unbridled, the sexuality of southeastern Indians was carefully regulated by rules and expectations that crossed national boundaries. Some differences existed between Cherokees, Choctaws, Chickasaws, Seminoles, and Creeks, but the cultural regulations that structured their sexual behavior united them.

Colonial Europeans frequently misread or failed to see the sexual rules that shaped southeastern Indian society, and as a result they frequently thought that Indian women were licentious. "Naked" Natives seemed to wear less clothing, bare their breasts, and otherwise be less concerned with **chastity** and modesty than European colonists. Colonists observed that Native women could participate in sexual behavior before and outside **marriage** without the condemnation of their community. Family members encouraged the women in their families to engage in sexual relations with Europeans, often to obtain access to desired trade goods. Native women acted in rather forward ways when it came to sex and their sexuality. They openly initiated sexual encounters with Indian men and colonists, sexually teased many colonists, and used their sexuality to their advantage in intercolonial interaction. These sexual practices all helped lead European colonists to see unbridled sexual freedom in Indian society.

Despite vast differences between European and Native rules and behavior, sex was carefully regulated in southeastern Indian society. A series of rules and taboos which went unnoticed by most colonists shaped the sex lives of all Indians. For starters, southeastern Indians had very strict rules about who could have sex with whom. Matrilineal clans divided and structured all southeastern communities. All southeastern Indians were members of a clan and all members of a clan were considered relatives. Thus they considered sex or marriage between two members of the same clan incestuous. Clans often contained hundreds or thousands of individuals, and thus relations with a large percentage of a village or nation was automatically taboo.

Because sex was deemed a dangerous yet necessary form of power, Native custom also regulated when and where sexual relations could take place. Men abstained from sex when they prepared for battle, while they engaged in the hunt, and when they returned home. Young men avoided sex when they were training to become hunters. At the same time, menstruating women and pregnant women similarly could not have sex. Pregnant women faced many other restrictions involving food preparation, travel, and participation in sacred ceremonies. Even after giving birth, the sexual activity of women remained taboo. Husbands also lived restricted lives while their wives were pregnant. They could not participate in stickball, dig graves, or dance alongside other men in communal ceremonies. Southeastern Indians also punished those who had sex in agricultural fields. **Adultery** was severely punished, and among the Creeks it could result in death.

In addition, divorces and polygamous relationships between one man and multiple wives were both rather common in the Southeast. Women and men could both ask for and obtain a **divorce** in Indian society. Divorces became final at the Green Corn Ceremony, a summertime ritual of communal renewal that took place once a year. When marriages ended, the children and the property of the marriage remained in the hands of the woman, and the divorced man returned to the home of his mother or sister. Because biological fathers belonged to a different clan from their children, they were not considered part of the same family.

Polygynous relationships, between one man and multiple wives, were also rather common in the Southeast. Many of these relationships were the results of sororal polygyny, where sisters married the same man often at the same time. In these instances, the sisters/wives all lived in the same household, and thus the husband became a member of only a single household. Some Indian men married women of different villages and clans. These husbands became members of and obtained the obligations of multiple households.

Southeastern Indians defined most of their lives according to gender. Traditionally, men hunted and women farmed. Communities were built around matrilineal networks of related women, while men from the same clans gathered together to form hunting parties. Although men and women obviously interacted, gender divided Indian society to the extent that they practically lived separate lives. At the same time, biology did not always determine one's gender roles. Some southeastern Indians crossed gender lines by living as transvestites. Some men practiced **sodomy** and performed female tasks such as farming. A few southeastern women earned the exalted title of a "War Woman" for their acts on the battlefield. Male transvestites normally abandoned their biological identities when they chose to pass for women; female warriors did not.

None of the European powers in the Southeast ever formally sanctioned intermarriages with Native Americans. Throughout the region, though, intermarriages and cross-cultural sexual relations were common and public. Usually initiated by Native women or their families, these relationships occurred in various forms. Some lasted for decades and until the death of one of the participants; others lasted for a much shorter duration. Most relationships occurred between Indian women and European men. Relationships also connected Indian women with African American men, usually fugitive slaves from the region. These families almost always lived within the wife's village and according to the rules of village leaders and expectations of native society. Native women raised their children and maternal uncles played the central socialization roles for male children. *See also* Berdache; Celibacy; Gender Roles; Incest; Interracial Sex; Menstruation; Native Americans.

Further Reading: Frank, Andrew K. *Creeks and Southerners: Biculturalism on the Early American Frontier*. Lincoln: University of Nebraska Press, 2005; Perdue, Theda. *Cherokee Women: Gender and Culture Change, 1700–1835*. Lincoln: University of Nebraska Press, 1999; Perdue, Theda. "Columbus Meets Pocahontas in the American South." *Southern Cultures* 3, no. 1 (1997): 4–21.

Andrew K. Frank

SWIFT, JONATHAN (1667–1745). Jonathan Swift was a poet, satirist, and clergyman, most famous for his satirical novel *Gulliver's Travels*. Born in Dublin, Swift was brought up by his nurse and his uncle as his father died soon before Jonathan was born, and his mother left for England soon after that. He studied at Trinity College in Dublin and then started work as a secretary in the home of William Temple in Surrey. There he met a young woman, Esther, who became his friend and, most probably, also his wife. During the last years of his life he was in ill health and stopped writing. Swift's interest in human sexuality can be noted in many of his works, but it seems that *Gulliver's Travels* may be the best one to illustrate the author's attitude toward the subject.

Often mistaken for a children's book, *Gulliver's Travels* is anything but it; Swift uses all the fantasy worlds his character encounters to criticize the vices of the world he himself lived in—human sexuality among them. However, this way of writing about sex in a constantly disgusted manner might well be a sign of Swift's repressed interest in the subject. The most striking example of it is a scene in Book 3 of *Gulliver's Travels*: while visiting the world of Houyhnhnms and Yahoos (the first ones being very reasonable entities, the second ones, their uncivilized servants), Gulliver decides at some point to take a bath, and, knowing very little of the Yahoo ways, makes the mistake of undressing completely. When an eleven-year-old girl sees Gulliver naked, she rushes to him in an attempt to **rape** him. Although lucky enough to avoid the rape by the lascivious Yahoo girl, Gulliver is deeply shocked after the event, and, quite surprisingly, decides that he is, in fact, a Yahoo rather than a reasonable Houyhnhnm. Both races described by Swift in this part of the book serve to show how difficult it is for human entities to find the right balance between their primitive needs and reason.

There are other important passages in *Gulliver's Travels* that help us understand Swift's attitude toward sexuality and, especially, toward the female sex. In Book 2, when Gulliver is traveling to the land of the giants, he complains about how difficult it is for him to look at the giant women when they undress before his eyes, which they do rather often, thus unspeakably tormenting Gulliver. Another problem for him is the smell: he can't stand the stench of an unwashed body, but the smell of the perfume the giant ladies use makes him even more dizzy. This is all too similar to the image of Celia in Swift's *The Progress of Beauty*, where the main character is shown as "the mingled mass of dirt and sweat." This image, together with the negative portrayal of females in *Gulliver's Travels*, suggests that the author did not hold women in high esteem. *See also* Baths; Cosmetics and Perfume; Enlightenment Thought on Sexuality; Literature; Women, Changing Images of.

Further Reading: Swift, Jonathan. *Gulliver's Travels: An Authoritative Text, the Correspondence of Swift, Pope's Verses on Gulliver's Travels and Critical Essays.* New York: W. W. Norton, 1971; Swift, Jonathan. *Major Works.* New York: Oxford University Press, 1984.

Bartlomiej Paszylk

TABOOS. In England and the West in general, the **laws** were set out and upheld in three ways: the church law with its own courts, the canon law, and the civil law. But a taboo is a social, not legal prohibition of behavior, which is considered unacceptable within a particular society. Its essence is the disgust or fear of a certain object or act associated with an object. For example, **incest** is a taboo of more or less universal acceptance. What matters is that each and every person accepts that the taboo will be observed.

Western society had many taboos involving the **body** and bodily functions. For example, nudity in children was generally accepted, but taboos on nudity in public were widespread for those who had reached puberty. The exposure of the genitals and female breasts was usually restricted by social taboo, except in the privacy of the bedroom, during **breastfeeding**, and during particular fashion trends when women's gowns revealed their breasts. Both Christians and Jews had taboos against **menstruation**, menstruating women, and menstrual blood, as did many Native American tribes. **Pregnancy** and **childbirth** were also the source of taboos.

The taboo on extramarital sex was enforced in much of the world, as children fathered by other men might not be accepted into male-dominated households. The anger and disgust felt by the Islamic Arabic man when he finds one of his wives being unfaithful is a common theme of the *Arabian Nights* cycle of stories. However, married men could visit prostitutes, sexually coerce female servants and slaves, and take mistresses or **concubines**. In general then, the taboo on sexual freedom offered a double standard: males committing this crime were accepted, but a woman could be ostracized or subject to punishment, or even death.

When Europeans came into contact with civilizations on the other side of the Atlantic, they were exposed to taboos that were strange to them. For example, the Aztecs murdered great numbers of slaves in ritual sacrifices. They even asked for volunteers, who would enjoy several weeks of the utmost leisure and happiness, before their ritual murder. **Sodomy**, incest, **adultery**, **rape**, **murder**, and theft were just as illegal in the dominions of the Aztecs and Incas as they were in the West. The Spanish attempted to make the **Native Americans** they encountered look less human by repeatedly sending messages home accusing the Aztecs of sodomy, and other such "taboo" things. *See also* Cross-Dressing; Gender Roles.

Further Reading: Bataille, Georges. *The Accursed Share*. 2 vols. Translated by R. Hurley. New York: Zone Books, 1991; Frazer, James. *The Golden Bough, Part II: Taboo, and the Perils of the Soul*. London: MacMillan, 1936; Freud, Sigmund. *Totem and Taboo*. Translated by A. A. Brill. London: Routledge, 1919.

Jason Powell

TAJ MAHAL. Located in Agra, **India**, southeast of New Delhi, the Taj Mahal is a tomb built by the order of the Mughal emperor Shah Jahan as a tribute to his deceased wife, Arjumand Banu Begum also known as Mumtaz Mahal, who died of labor complications in 1631. Built in white marble, it is an example of the finest Mughal architecture blending Indian, Persian, and Islamic styles. Perhaps the most celebrated tomb in the world, the Taj Mahal is a large complex consisting of five main elements, including gardens and a mausoleum, completed after over seventeen years of construction, and involving more than 20,000 workers from India, Persia, the **Ottoman empire**, and Europe. Although there have been coined various translations of the monument's name such as "the Crown of the Palace," it is probably an abbreviated version of the queen's name, Mumtaz Mahal, given to her after she was married to Shah Jahan.

Apart from being an obviously significant architectural piece inscribed on the UNESCO World Heritage List of sites with outstanding universal value to mankind, the Taj Mahal is also a curious illustration of the hierarchical relations in polygamous societies of the time. The Taj Mahal is often described as a monument erected in memory of the emperor's "favorite wife." By the time he married her, the Muslim emperor had already been married and had a **harem** of countless **concubines**. Yet in plural marriages, unequal relations commonly develop, where some wives enjoy privileges far greater than those granted to the remaining women. While his other wives barely even receive a mention in the documents about Shah Jahan's court, Mumtaz Mahal, whose name tellingly translates as the "Chosen One of the Palace," is now commonly recognized as the epitome of a ruler's consort of captivating beauty, wit, and generosity. Adored and admired by the emperor and the subjects alike, she was Jahan's trusted adviser and the most powerful woman at the court, who accompanied Jahan even when he embarked on military campaigns against rebels in the Mughal territory.

The early loss of a wife so dear to the emperor inspired thousands of subjects to join foreign workers in the plan to build a tomb of unparalleled greatness, which was to testify to the queen's unlimited virtues; the sheer size and the architectural resplendence of the edifice shows the distraught ruler's obsessive desire to surpass all limits to honor the memory of his wife. Legend has it that the construction of the tomb was one of a number of promises that Mumtaz extracted from the emperor at her deathbed. Whether that is a fact or an apocryphal story, the emperor's resolve to undertake a task of these dimensions cannot but be taken as an expression of his genuine grief.

Nowadays, the Taj Mahal is popularly recognized as "the seventh wonder of the world" and is India's most important tourist site, attracting thousands

The Taj Mahal, India. Courtesy of the Library of Congress.

of tourists per day. It has recently become a source of controversy over property rights to its grounds. Prince Yaqub Habeebuddin Tucy, who traces his family's lineage to Shah Jahan himself, demanded formal custodianship of the monument, protesting against claims to the ownership of the Taj Mahal by either Muslim or Hindu communities. *See also* Marriage; Polyandry; Royal Mistresses.

Further Reading: Rai, Raghu, and Usha Rai. *Taj Mahal*. New York: Vendome Press, 1997.

Konrad Szczesniak

TENORIO, DON JUAN. The legendary, fictitious sexual trickster, Don Juan Tenorio was introduced into **literature** in 1630. This literary character, an obsessive seducer of women, was regarded as a symbol of libertinism.

Originally, Don (*Mister*) Juan Tenorio (J.T.) was the character in a famous legend from the Middle Ages. Using the pseudonym Tirso de Molina, Spanish dramatist Fray (*Friar*) Gabriel Téllez (1571–1641) gave literary form to the Don Juan character for the first time. His tragic drama *El Burlador de Sevilla y Convidado de Piedra* (*The Seducer of Seville and the Stone Guest*) was published in 1630. In it, Tenorio is the same handsome Sevillan nobleman of the legend who obsessively seduces women.

Tenorio is considered a prototypical **libertine**; an immoral, indulgent, sensual being unrestrained by conscience or moral conventions. He led a sexual career of unrepentant serial promiscuity. Tenorio was unconcerned by his social deviance, even when confronted by his shamed father. He was addicted to sexual gratification and conquering women, especially unavailable ones. However, the moment his sexual conquests were complete, he guiltlessly lost interest and abandoned them.

The gallant womanizer used tricks, lies, and disguises to try to seduce as many women as possible. De Molina's play is made up of several *burlas*, or tricks, whereby Tenorio is able to seduce both commoners and noblewomen.

In the first trick, Tenorio is in the palace of the King of Naples, obscured by darkness, where he pretends to be Duchess Isabella's fiancé. She screams upon discovering the real identity of her seducer. The king puts the Spanish ambassador in charge of arresting Tenorio, not realizing the ambassador is Tenorio's uncle. The trickster then manipulates his uncle into allowing an escape.

Fleeing Naples, Tenorio is shipwrecked on the Spanish coast. There he charms a notoriously hard-to-get young beauty, Tisbea, and turns her into an enchanted lover. He then immediately abandons her.

In Seville, Tenorio runs into his oldest friend, the Marquis de la Mota, who admires him for his libertinism and tries to emulate him. But loyal only to pleasure, Tenorio disguises himself as la Mota, and goes after his friend's lover, Ana de Ulloa. She discovers the deception too late and shouts for help. Her father, Don Gonzalo, responds, but Tenorio kills him. This trick indicates Tenorio was unable to form meaningful relationships with either sex.

Next, arriving uninvited at a wedding, Tenorio desires the just-married bride, Aminta. Mocking the husband Batricio, a simple peasant, Tenorio drives him from his own wedding feast. He usurps the new husband's position, then he disappears.

De Molina's charming but ruthless, romantic but heartless Tenorio has inspired literary and musical masterpieces for centuries. Celebrating Tenorio's sexual prowess, Italian theatrical troupes of the 1700s brought the story to France. Mozart's 1787 **opera** *Don Giovanni* transformed Tenorio again. Many others have given their own versions of the character, each with a slightly different twist to his personality and motivations.

The hero-villain glories in his immoral behavior. Through Tenorio's actions and arrogance, the ghost of the murdered Don Gonzalo is finally able to drag him to the Hell. This punishment is likely part of a moral lesson the religious friar de Molina wanted to teach society about libertinism. *See also* Casanova, Giacomo Girolamo; Seduction Literature; Theater; Wilmot, John, Earl of Rochester.

Further Reading: De Molina, Tirso. *Trickster of Seville and the Stone Guest.* Translated by Gwynne Edwards. Warminster, England: Aris & Phillips, 1986.

Elizabeth Jenner

THEATER, CHINESE. The theatrical arts in China have been traced back to as early as 200 BCE, and though originally attributed to Shamanic dance rituals they slowly adapted themselves into a form of high culture during Imperial rule. Ancient Chinese court records provide evidence that the emperor enjoyed and actively encouraged dramatizations as part of rituals and religious ceremonies. The sheer size of China, coupled with the diverse ethnic minorities and their rich verbal and written traditions meant that Chinese theater often absorbed aspects of cultural difference—thus creating a wide variety of theater that appealed to different segments of Chinese society at the time. It is believed that over 300 different regional forms of theater existed throughout the early historical periods of China and these were systematically absorbed into the dominant theatrical art form commonly referred to as Chinese or "Peking" Opera. Chinese theater employs the use of males in female roles who mimic all aspects of a gendered performance. In fact, it was considered highly unusual for an actual female to perform a female role. The male **actors** in Chinese theater used makeup, costume, and speech to assume the female role quite convincingly.

Theatrical performances usually consisted of spoken or sung prose by actors amid a background of highly stylized instrumentation. The score would function to heighten the effect of specific words, or phrases and was played at once. During the early fourteenth century, as theater gained popularity amongst the elite, the costumes and scenery became more elaborate and performances became increasingly stylized and verbose. Intelligent interplay between the sexes became more obvious and the story line often stretched for days. This was clearly a departure from the early theatrical performances made most often of simple regional (folk) songs and stories.

The most widely known theater was the Imperial theater—with plays given to and enjoyed by royal patronage and royal courts throughout Chinese history. The foundations of exclusivity in Imperial theater started during the Tang dynasty (618–907) where it enjoyed royal patronage and a following amongst the Chinese elite. Due to its increase in popularity within the royal court, schools and training centers were set up to ensure actors were abundant. The theatrical tradition was further improved upon throughout the Sung dynasty (960–1279) and the Yuan dynasty (1280–1368). The foundations of Chinese theater were established during these periods and successively built upon by the Yuan and Ming Dynasties. The Yuan dynasty is believed to be responsible for the flourishing of literary forms of expression (poems and songs) throughout greater China. This period witnessed an amalgamation of southern (*ch'uan-ch'i*) and northern (*tsa-chu* or *nan-hsi*) theatrical forms. The commonality lay in the portrayal of the lead individuals/groups within the plays, which did not deviate, no matter what the geographical location or theatrical setting. Familial and social relationships were often explored, albeit rather tamely and usually without obvious sexual references. Most however focused upon communal responsibilities and various folk stories.

The Ming dynasty (1368–1644) also witnessed a further explosion in theatrical performance, in particular the growth of three distinct dramas—*Yiyan Chiang* (Tunes of Yiyang), *Pang-tze Chiang* (Clapper Opera), and *Kun-chu* (Drama of Kunshan). Each was adapted and performed locally by wandering theater troupes that succeeded in spreading the various forms throughout China. Eventually the *Yiyan Chiang* and the *Pang-tze Chiang* became the most popular cultural forms of Chinese theater, especially during the late sixteenth century as they focused upon local and national Chinese history and culture, in particular, upon female vixens and their escapades against enemies. *Kun-chu* on the other hand appealed to the elite in Chinese society through its presentation of love and **marriage**. Despite the difference in presentation between the popular modes of expression, Chinese theater actively represented forbidden love (which alludes to forbidden sexual relations). The topic became a popular choice of traveling troupes and commonly related to both male-and-female and male-and-male relationships.

Chinese theater is often viewed as a vehicle for the promotion of transgendered and homosexual relationships within a socially acceptable framework of entertainment. The increase in emphasis on sexual relationships occurred at a time when China was undergoing political, social, and economic changes. The once-popular topics of familial love and celestial infatuation were considered somewhat common by the late nineteenth century when Chinese theater returned to a more historical style and period dramas. Chinese theater enjoyed a renaissance amongst the elite of society from the nineteenth century onward. *See also* Dance; Opera; Theater, European; Theater, Japanese.

Further Reading: Birch, Cyril, ed. "To the Reader as Fellow Mandarin." In *Scenes for Mandarins*. New York: Columbia University Press, 1995; Mackerras, Colin. *The Chinese Theatre in Modern Times: From 1840 to the Present Day*. London: Thames and Hudson, 1975; Ramet, Sabrina Petra. *Gender Reversals and Gender Cultures: Anthropological and Historical Perspectives*. London: Taylor and Francis, 1996; Shih, Chung-Wen. *The Golden Age of Chinese Drama: Yuan Tsa-chu*. Princeton, NJ: Princeton University Press, 1976.

Samaya Lea Sukha

THEATER, EUROPEAN. Theater in eighteenth-century Europe was dominated by the French and the English. Breaking from the rigid conventions of classical drama, they experimented with character and plot; these developments reflect emerging attitudes about class and gender. While the theaters remained controlled by men, women were afforded some opportunities, especially as performers.

Serious drama changed after French and English playwrights attempted to write serious plays focusing on the concerns and misfortunes of the common people of their day, not of kings and mythological figures of classical drama. These plays became known as domestic tragedies. The philosopher and author **Denis Diderot** (1713–1784) argued that plays that relate to middle-class audiences might serve to instruct, a view of the function of theater that continued into the late nineteenth century. The most important of these domestic tragedies is probably *The London Merchant* by George Lillo (1693–1739) which premièred in London in 1731 and was soon after translated and produced in France and Germany.

France and England also produced the most significant developments in comedies as well. Like domestic tragedies do, the *comédies larmoyante* or sentimental comedies center on middle-class characters. Often very serious in tone and rarely humorous, these plays were thought of as comedies because they end happily. Eighteenth-century audiences enjoyed these new comedies very much, and contemporary accounts describe audience members in tears at the outcomes. The best French playwright writing *comédie larmoyante* was Pierre Carlet de Chamblain de Marivaux (1688–1763). He emphasized characters and their emotions in his plays, for which his plays remain well regarded. From England a fitting example is *The Conscious Lovers* (1723) by Richard Steele (1672–1729), an influential and popular play throughout the century.

Thus the plays reflect, celebrate, and help to promote budding middle-class values and ideologies, especially unselfish consideration, the supremacy of family, and **romantic love**. Grounded in the middle-class morals and ethics, poetic justice prevails as the good are rewarded and villains punished by the play's end. On the whole, strong, decent, and genuine men are the heroes, and virtuous, passive, and proper women are the heroines. Men who are too interested in "female pursuits," such as fashion and gossip, and women who are too independent are depicted as selfish, vain, and ultimately foolish.

The eighteenth century marks changing views of **actors** and actresses. Nearly a century after they first appeared on French, Spanish, and Italian stages, women were permitted to act in England by 1660. Their impact upon the types of plays and characters companies selected was immediate and long-lasting. At that time actresses were perhaps the most visible professional women throughout Europe, yet because of the emphasis on their physical attractiveness and sexuality, many critics regarded actresses as no different from prostitutes. Over time, performers earned more respect as some of the period's biggest stars altered perceptions. In France, Adrienne Lecouvreur (1692–1730) helped to establish a simple, natural acting style. Rumors speculated that she was poisoned by a rival, and indicative of the status of actresses, she was refused a Christian burial, and the leading French writer of the time, Voltaire (1694–1778), wrote a bitter poem questioning the indignity of such a refusal for a genius of the French stage. In England, Sarah Siddons (1755–1831) excelled in tragedies, and her talent changed views of actresses. Generally regarded as the best actor of his time, David Garrick (1717–1779) attracted crowds with a new "realistic" acting style. His gentle and pleasing demeanor helped bring new respectability and professionalism to acting.

Drama as a type of literature was held in high regard at the time, and most plays accepted for performances at the commercial theaters were written by men, yet despite those obstacles, women saw their plays staged in France and in England. During times of theatrical competition, when theater companies needed new plays to attract audiences, female playwrights had the best chances to have plays produced. In France, Marie-Anne Barbier (1670–1745) wrote a popular tragedy, *Arrie et P'etus* (1702), and Stéphanie Félicité Ducrest de St-Aubin, comtesse de Genlis (1746–1830), wrote an important, influential sentimental comedy, *Cenie* (1750). In England, **Aphra Behn** (1640–1689), one of the century's first professional female writers, and Susanna Centlivre (1667–1723) wrote comedies that remained on English stages throughout the century, and Elizabeth Inchbald (1753–1821) had several popular plays and wrote theatrical criticism as well. *See also* Opera; Shakespeare, William; Theater, Chinese; Theater, Japanese.

Further Reading: Brockett, Oscar G. *History of the Theatre.* 5th ed. Boston: Allyn and Bacon, 1987.

Timothy J. Viator

THEATER, JAPANESE. Japan has a rich tradition of theatrical arts. Most early theatrical performances originated from religious rituals, which, as time passed, solidified into a type of performance art in its own right. Later, **dance** became entertainment, and theatrical performance was considered commonplace throughout Japan. The increase of popular theater throughout Japan saw the strict religious rituals and religious, moral, and ethical sensibilities in performance slowly making way for social and political commentary that included references to relationships and love.

Before the nineteenth century, Japanese theater was referred to as *Shibai* (theater). The collective term did not however extend to Noh performances or other stage-based performances. Kagura (first mentioned in 885 CE) was considered Japan's first performance art form and is literally translated as "entertainment for the kami." It was thus highly religious in its tones and was meant as an expression of devotion to the kami spirits of indigenous Japanese religion. Kagura was found mostly in shrines and temples and was really only accessible during specified ritual days, or when otherwise required. In this sense, Japanese theater had a strong foundation in **religion** and ritual, which, for the most part, focused upon the relationship of the person to the divine (kami). Despite this, Japanese culture encouraged generalized performance and theatrical arts so that from the sixteenth century to the modern historical period it has flourished remarkably.

Noh theater is thought to have shared the same origins of Kagura—that of ritual, which later turned into entertainment. During the Edo era, Noh was the official theater of Japan and hence was tightly controlled to ensure political and social stability. Noh, therefore, is considered highly stylized. It is believed that most Noh traditions were stable by the mid-1650s, and it slowly became the theater of choice for the wealthy. Noh actors were even anointed to Samurai class and thus acquired a whole new world of opportunity for homosexual relationships outside the theatrical circles. It is interesting that Noh theater employs the use of face masks (around thirty different characters and styles), and as such the actors' faces are unseen and do not produce an emotional response to the theatrical content. There is a sense of dislocation, and stories often revolve around the loss of a child, parent, or other family member. Demons and struggles between various embodiments of good and evil inevitably occur, and the use of sexual tension between characters was often observed.

The popularity of Noh ran parallel with Kabuki theater. Kabuki developed during the early sixteenth century and was regarded as quite avant-garde in nature. It is believed to have been created by Izumo no Okuni at Shijogawara in Kyoto, who incorporated the sound of a gong in her folk dances. Okuni's style of performance became popular and spread throughout Japan by troupes mainly made up of various types of women. Some troupes were made up entirely of prostitutes who saw the opportunity to leave the profession. Originally Kabuki moved away from the regimented male-dominated Noh theater, as it consisted mainly of female performers delivering lively social (sexually and politically orientated) anecdotes. In 1629 women troupes were made illegal by the Tokugawa shogunate, and only male Kabuki performers (consisting mainly of young teens to early adult members) became the norm. They too were considered lewd, and their sexualized performances were also banned; in fact they were considered immoral by the Shogun. Adult male Kabuki performances were allowed as long as they did not challenge the social fabric of society at the time, and only as long as they performed within the social etiquette of Japanese society. It slowly became the norm that male actors portrayed women characters.

Ukiyo-e triptych showing scenes from a Kabuki play. Right section: Actress Sadato no Tsuma (Abe no Sadato's wife) with another unidentified actor dressed as an elephant. Courtesy of the Library of Congress.

Kabuki's historical plays (from 1603 to 1867) relied heavily upon the romanticized presentation of the Samurai and noble classes. It was forbidden to base performance on current events and people of the day (with the exception of the underprivileged classes). However this was frequently circumvented by situating the play in a time period other than the one they were in. Another genre of performance that was considered extremely popular was the type that featured "love-suicides." Public displays of affection could be realized upon the stage in a most dramatic manner, and these always drew in a sizable viewing audience. From the late nineteenth century, the majority of Kabuki plays then became focused upon the everyday rituals and folk stories associated with Japanese life, such as weddings and funerals, and also incorporated current events in the theater.

Japanese theater offered a unique perspective on relationships and familial and social responsibility. It appears that all forms of theater (popular and high cultural theater) attempted to provide a forum for theatrical commentary on issues (or ideals) that would have otherwise been too controversial to discuss openly. *See also* Actors; Prostitutes and Prostitution; Theater, Chinese; Theater, European; Yoshiwara.

Further Reading: Ernst, Earle. *The Kabuki Theatre*. New York: Grove Press, 1956; Gunji, Masakatsu. *The Kabuki Guide*. Tokyo: Kodansha International, 1987; Nakamura, Yasuo. *Noh: The Classical Theater*. Tokyo: Walker/Weatherhill, 1971; Pflugfelder, Gregory. *Cartographies of Desire: Male-Male Sexuality in Japanese Discourse, 1600–1950*. Berkeley: University of California Press, 1999; Watanabe, Tsuneo, and Junichi Iwata. *The Love of the Samurai: A Thousand Years of Japanese Homosexuality*. Translated by D. R. Roberts. London: Gay Men's Press, 1989.

Samaya Lea Sukha

THISTLEWOOD, THOMAS (1721–1786). Thomas Thistlewood, an English immigrant to Jamaica, served as a slave overseer and owned about thirty slaves. He habitually raped slave women because a white man could do so without fear of any consequences and because he needed to demonstrate his domination over slaves. Thistlewood's actions were typical of eighteenth-century white male Jamaicans. He is only unique in that he left a diary detailing his sexual activities.

Thistlewood, born in Tupholme, Lincolnshire, was a fatherless second son with few prospects of obtaining land in Great Britain. After apprenticing as a farmer and spending two years in the service of the East India Company, he boarded a ship bound for the West Indies on February 1, 1750. He disembarked in Jamaica, the most productive of the British sugar colonies, on April 24, 1750. The overwhelming proportion of slaves to whites in Jamaica meant that white men had their pick of overseeing jobs, and that brutality toward slaves was commonplace as a means to avoid a slave uprising.

Thistlewood settled in western Jamaica. He found a job as an overseer on a cattle ranch almost immediately. He had his first sexual experience with a slave on August 10, 1750, and recorded the episode in schoolboy Latin in his diary. In 1751, he became overseer on a sugar estate just west of the town of Savanna la Mar. In 1767, he acquired his own property, Breadnut Island, and raised livestock, vegetables, and flowers. Thistlewood was well respected among Jamaican whites for his agricultural skills, his industry, and his heavily stocked library.

During his thirty-seven years in Jamaica, Thistlewood noted 3,852 acts of sexual intercourse with 138 women. A majority of his sexual encounters were with a principal slave partner who served as his wife. The remaining acts were with other female slaves and the occasional white prostitute. He never showed any interest in privileged white women, perhaps because he would have to court them and black women made easy sexual targets.

None of Thistlewood's female slaves escaped having sex with him. He had sex with slave women from early in the morning to late in the evening, and in places that ranged from his home to sugarcane fields to curing houses to slave houses. Thistlewood had sex with his slaves when they were either in puberty or not long afterward. He made them have sex even when they were heavily pregnant. One pregnant slave, forced to engage in sex with Thistlewood, miscarried eight days later.

It is not always clear whether Thistlewood's sexual activities with slave women were sometimes consensual. However, it is apparent that refusing to have sex with Thistlewood was not a realistic option. He typically had sex with slave women under his care and made it clear to slaves who were caught transgressing that they could avoid punishment by having sex with him. He also used **rape** as a weapon against a female slave at least once.

Slave owners in Jamaica needed to emphasize the powerlessness of blacks against whites. Rape demonstrated that they were strong, violent, virile men who ruled as they pleased. Thistlewood, willing to subject his slaves to creatively sadistic punishments, was undoubtedly a brutal sociopath. It is probable that all of his slaves feared him. He died of natural causes on November 30, 1786. *See also* Byrd, William; Interracial Sex; Slavery.

Further Reading: Burnard, Trevor. *Mastery, Tyranny, and Desire: Thomas Thistlewood and His Slaves in the Anglo-Jamaican World.* Chapel Hill: University of North Carolina Press, 2004; Hall, Douglas. *In Miserable Slavery: Thomas Thistlewood in Jamaica, 1750–86.* London: Macmillan, 1989.

Caryn E. Neumann

TOBACCO. Tobacco was a cultural staple in the seventeenth and eighteenth centuries in America, grown on both continents of the New World. **Native Americans** ritually used tobacco, which they called *cohiba*, long before Columbus arrived. It was smoked, chewed, used as a medicine to kill intestinal worms and applied topically as a counterirritant. Its active ingredient, nicotine, is a substance that can be therapeutic in tiny amounts, but when taken in larger amounts it is a poison that can cause convulsions and death.

In the South American Andes, men burned tobacco and blew the smoke over women prior to sex. Some tribes associated tobacco with fertility, and Indian maidens were given tobacco on their wedding night. The substance received the name, tobacco, from Tobago, where in 1498, its use was documented by the Spanish. In 1560, Jean Nicot, an ambassador to France, reported that tobacco, no matter where applied, cured whatever was wrong, including **venereal disease**. Nicot sent some seeds from Lisbon to Carl Linnaeus, the French scientist who named the plant, *Nicotiana rustica*, in honor of the ambassador.

Western Europeans enjoyed tobacco, particularly in Spain, where the Inquisition eagerly used revenues to pay for its dungeons, cloaks, and regalia. Both men and women of the upper classes smoked cigars. Tobacco was so addictive that many clergy members were expelled because of their habit. Tobacco production began in South America, where tobacco was grown and packed by slaves. After packing it was shipped either to Seville or to a factory in Cadiz. In Seville, at the Fabrica del Tobacos, female workers ground it into snuff because men were found to be too clumsy. In Seville, the birthplace of tobacco's association with sex, it was rolled into cigars by scantily clad women. This connection of cigars with seductive women lasted for centuries, and the image of a dark-haired factory worker who wore a short red skirt, white silk stockings, red shoes, and a mantilla parted to expose her shoulders inspired the character *Carmen*, immortalized by Bizet's **opera** of the same name in 1875.

However, not all Europeans endorsed the use of tobacco. In 1602, Philaretes wrote that smoking was a pestiferous vice, even though it had value as a drug. Allegedly it was proven to cure gonorrhea by drying up the discharge. But, continued use of tobacco would act in an unwanted manner and dry up the necessary moisture for sperm to grow, thus rendering a man sterile. This idea remained in British culture as late as 1674, where it can be seen in a document called *The Women's Petition against Coffee*, which addresses not only coffee, but tobacco as well. This complaint by "several thousands of buxome [sic] good women languishing in extremity of want" proclaims that when a married woman approaches the marital bed expecting that her husband will be a vigorous lover, instead, she finds "A Bedful of Bones" and "a meager useless Corpse … dryer than a Pumice-Stone, by the perpetual Fumes of Tobacco, and bewitching effects of this most pernitious [sic] COFFEE," causing offspring to be weakened and descendents "dwindled" into apes and pygmies.

Although some Europeans looked down on smokers because of the residual smell and allegedly demonstrated lack of self-control in its users, they welcomed snuff, at least initially. Snuff did not assault the senses the way tobacco did, and if unattended, could not cause fires. At first only men used snuff, but soon women adopted the habit. The merits were likened to an **orgasm** because it was inhaled and then provoked a sneeze.

By 1750, tobacco accounted for half the goods exported by America and was responsible for bringing first thousands of **indentured servants** and then slaves to the British American colonies. And although hemp was grown as a cash crop for fiber, its psychedelic properties and association with sex were not yet appreciated by Anglo America, whose citizens preferred tobacco and **alcohol**. *See also* Food; Slavery.

Further Reading: Anonymous. *The Women's Petition against Coffee Representing to Publick Consideration the Grand Inconveniencies Accruing to Their Sex from the Excessive Use of That Drying, Enfeebling Liquor*. London. See http://www.staff.uni-marburg.de; Bettmann, Otto. *A Pictorial History of Medicine*. Springfield, IL: Charles C. Thomas, 1956; Gateley, Iain. *Tobacco*. New York: Grove Press, 2001; Inglis, Brian. *The Forbidden Game*. New York: Charles Scribner's Sons, 1975.

Lana Thompson

TOM JONES (FIELDING, 1749). *Tom Jones*, a novel by Henry Fielding, was published in 1749 and is usually regarded as the writer's masterpiece. The book's main character, Tom Jones, is a likeable rogue and womanizer—a fact that caused much controversy at the time of the first publication, as it stood in stark contrast with other influential novels of the eighteenth century, which were commonly praising virtuous characters. Most notably, it clashed with Samuel Richardson's *Pamela: or, Virtue Rewarded* (1740). In fact, Henry Fielding's main aim while writing his novel was to oppose the preaching of authors such as Richardson and to create a story that would be much more daring and much more true to life. Not only was *Tom Jones* an attack on Fielding's contemporaries, but it was also a biting critique of the piousness, morals, and high society in the eighteenth century, and it still remains one of the most vivid and interesting documents describing this period.

Tom Jones, supposedly the illegitimate son of a prostitute Jenny Jones, is found by Squire Allworthy on the day of his birth; when he grows up he falls in love with Sophia, the daughter of his neighbor. Unfortunately, even though the feeling of love is mutual it cannot lead to **marriage**, as Sophia's father has already decided that his daughter should marry Tom's cousin. Soon both Tom and Sophia are forced to head for London: Tom to escape the charges of a crime, and Sophia to avoid marrying a man she despises.

Rape, or attempted rape, is a key to the plan of one of Tom's lovers, Lady Bellaston, who is trying to get rid of Sophia. She tries to convince Lord Fellamar, a nobleman in love with Sophia, that if the girl tries to resist him he should take her by force. At the beginning Lord Fellamar does not believe that it is really the right thing to do, and he also does not wish to separate Sophia from Tom after he sees how much she loves him. However, the wicked Lady Bellaston finally manages to make the man believe that raping Sophia would only turn out for the best: Sophia would be forced to marry him then and in effect would be leading a life much more satisfying than she would have had otherwise. The final argument of Lady Bellaston's, the one that pushes Lord Fellamar to do the deed, is that women sometimes like it when their men are violent. When Fellamar enters Sophia's room he proposes to her; when she harshly refuses, he grabs her violently. Sophia screams, but there is no one in earshot, just as Lady Bellaston had planned it, and the girl is only saved by her father accidentally entering the room. The rape did not happen, but Sophia was once again reminded that she should marry Tom's cousin, which prospect made her eventually leave her home for London.

The meaning of Fielding's use of the scene of the attempted rape is rather clear here—he wishes to point out that whatever moral flaws his main character may have, some women, like Lady Bellaston, for instance, are even more morally corrupted. They, rather than the good-hearted Tom, should be condemned. *See also* Courtship; Fanny Hill; Fornication; Romantic Love; Seduction Literature.

Further Reading: Battestin, Martin C., and Ruth R. Battestin. *Henry Fielding: A Life*. New York: Routledge, 1993; Fielding, Henry. *Tom Jones*. New York: Oxford University Press, 1998.

Bartlomiej Paszylk

TORTURE.   No time period has a premium on torture. During the seventeenth and eighteenth centuries, Europeans frequently attempted to convert people they considered heathens, heretics, or pagans by using the most inhumane methods of persuasion.

Power differentials often determined punishments in early America. Those with political or religious power, higher status, or social standing, such as landowners or slave owners, were in better positions for both making judgments and gaining immunity if accused. Thus, those who were tortured most often were women, servants, slaves, Native Americans, and the poor of both sexes.

During the colonial period, most Europeans perceived **Native Americans** as savages. Although some lived commensally with Puritan families, they were labeled as heathens or worse yet, heretics, because they were not Christian. However, their indigenous tortures and mutilation had religious significance, just as human sacrifice did to the Aztec and Maya in Middle America. In one ritual, an enemy captive was forced to run in front of assembled men. As he passed each one, they reached out with a piece of burning bark and burned a part of him. Some grabbed a hand and broke the bones of his fingers. Some used sharp sticks to pierce his ears. There is little documentation of torture specifically to sexual organs other than use of the term "loin" with regard to applying a hot brand to that area.

Accusations of witchcraft were common in New England and much of Europe, and torture to obtain a confession usually preceded execution. Most accused witches were female, and many accusations against them related to their sexuality and **gender roles**. Women were expected to be subservient and answerable to their husbands. They were not allowed agency in church or politics, and married women were denied property rights. Young women were accused of being seductresses; married women of making their husbands impotent; and old women, spoilers of crops and capable of putting curses on livestock and agriculture.

One torture was called "swimming the witch," an ordeal by water. The accused's thumbs were bound to her toes, and she was lowered into a body of water by men who were holding ropes. If she floated, it proved she was a witch because water rejected witches; if she drowned, she was proven innocent. Grace Sherwood, in North Carolina, underwent such a trial. Her right thumb was tied to her left foot and her left thumb to her right foot. She was then thrown into the water. However, she floated. Five women examined her body and found two things like teats on her private parts. Sometimes an enlarged clitoris and its hood were mistaken as "witch's tits," the place where the Devil allegedly sucked. Luckily Sherwood escaped from jail after her incarceration.

Another water torture was the dunking chair. In this ordeal, the accused was restrained in a chair, immersed in water, and held there for periods of time that tested her ability to hold her breath. If she survived, that proved she was a witch and she was subsequently executed. If she drowned, she was proven mortal, and therefore innocent. Another torture, a method of execution, was called *peine et fort*. The accused was suffocated by having a series of heavy planks and iron tools pressed on top of him or her so heavily that it prevented the person from breathing.

Tortures for alleged witchcraft were probably the most severe, but some of the punishments ordered by the courts for premarital, extramarital, and nonprocreative sex would be considered torture by many societies today. Although legal and religious authorities believed sinners would be punished in the hereafter eternally, they also believed it was necessary to address the crimes in this life as an example and deterrent to others. Ostracism and peer pressure worked well to force conformity to a strict moral code, however, when a sinner was discovered, punishment sometimes escalated to torture or mutilation. Both women and men were whipped in public or branded, as well as banished, assessed fines, or sometimes even executed for moral infractions. If the woman was pregnant, execution was delayed until the child was born. Women were sometimes punished more severely than men. Although both were stripped to the waist, there was no shame in a man's chest being exposed, but when a woman's breasts were bared; this doubly violated her privacy, giving spectators voyeuristic pleasure.

There were some torture devices meant to be used only on women. Bilboes, for example, were torture devices used to restrain women and force them into an unnatural position. The woman's ankles were placed in sliding shackles, similar to handcuffs. Her legs were spread, and she would be forced to the ground on her back, the bilboes raised so that her legs were positioned high in the air. The brank, or scold's bridle, looked like a birdcage with a tongue depressor, and it was put over the woman's head so that the blade went into her mouth, forcing her to utter guttural or undecipherable sounds and preventing her from eating. It was attached to a leash, and she could be led through the town to demonstrate the consequences of talking back to her husband or expressing her opinion too often.

In contrast to these court-ordered punishments, the power that came with slave ownership permitted masters to torture slaves of both sexes as they wished. Female slaves were always subject to **rape** and sexual abuse, and male and female slaves could be whipped at any time, but some slave owners devised more sadistic tortures simply to assert their power. For example, **Thomas Thistlewood**, a Jamaican slave overseer, created some horrific methods of torture to show his dominance and control over his slaves. *See also* Castration; Laws; Rape Law; Slavery; Witches and Witch Trials.

Further Reading: Friedman, Lawrence. *Crime and Punishment in American History*. New York: Basic Books, 1993; Lowe, Ben. "Body Images and the Politics of Beauty." In *Connecting Spheres: European Women in a Globalizing World, 1500 to the Present*, edited by Marilyn J. Boxer and Jean H. Quataert. Oxford: Oxford University Press, 1999; Rugoff, Milton. *Prudery and Passion*. New York: G. P. Putman's Sons, 1971; Walker, Barbara. "Torture." In *The Woman's Encyclopedia of Myths and Secrets*. New Jersey: Castle Books, 1996; Wood, Stephanie. "Sexual Violation in the Conquest of the Americas." In *Sex and Sexuality in Colonial America, 1492–1800*, edited by Merril D. Smith. New York: New York University Press, 1998.

Lana Thompson

TOUCHET, MERVYN, EARL OF CASTLEHAVEN (1593–1631). Mervyn Touchet, the Second Earl of Castlehaven, was executed in 1631 for arranging the **rape** of his wife and committing **sodomy**. The rape and sodomy, along with Castlehaven's efforts to cuckold and disinherit his son, created the greatest scandal of the early Stuart era. Castlehaven denied his guilt to the very end, but he had virtually no supporters.

The Castlehaven affair began when the **marriage** of Castlehaven's heir, Lord Audley, collapsed. The teenage Lady Audley, both Castlehaven's daughter-in-law and his stepdaughter, wanted a **divorce**. Castlehaven counseled her patiently, but either with his help or his **consent**, Lady Audley soon entered into a sexual relationship with a servant. This servant, Henry Skipwith, was known as Castlehaven's favorite. It would later be alleged that Castlehaven hoped the relationship would result in the birth of a child who would inherit the Castlehaven properties and titles. Castlehaven's indulgence of Skipwith enraged his son. In October 1630, nineteen-year-old Lord Audley complained about his father to the Privy Council. He stated that Castlehaven intended to disinherit him by giving money, a furnished townhouse, a farm, and significant personal property to Skipwith. Audley claimed that Castlehaven encouraged Skipwith and other servants to cuckold Audley and that Skipwith was excessively familiar with the Countess of Castlehaven.

After a brief formal investigation, the Privy Council ordered the arrest and imprisonment of Castlehaven and Skipwith in December 1630. At the April 1631 trial, Lady Audley claimed that Castlehaven had forced her to have sex with servants by threatening her with the loss of her home and income. In addition to the claims made by her daughter, Lady Audley, the Countess of Castlehaven also made accusations about the Earl. She stated that the Earl had shunned her from the first days of their marriage in favor of prostitutes and male servants. Further, she alleged that Castlehaven not only humiliated her with lewd words and lewd suggestions but also attempted to pair her sexually with various servants. The Earl supposedly claimed that he owned her body and could do what he wanted with it. Describing her marriage as a war over her honor, the Countess stated that rape was the price of her resistance. Several members of the Castlehaven household, including her daughter Lady Audley, believed that the Countess was promiscuous and sought to legally **murder** the Earl. However, Skipwith testified that the Earl had ordered him to have sex with the Countess and had even held her down to aid Skipwith's attack.

The trial was only a formality. King Charles I had already determined the outcome. A trial of a peer was a public spectacle designed to be educational. The Castlehaven case offered lessons about the obligations of privilege. An aristocrat was supposed to behave morally and enforce morality throughout his household. Castlehaven failed to do this. Additionally, he may have died because he was an outsider. Castlehaven held an Irish earldom, preferred his Irish properties, had Irish relatives, and hired Irish servants. He was also widely suspected of being a Catholic and had no friends at court to argue on his behalf.

On April 25, 1631, Castlehaven was formally condemned for rape and buggery. He was beheaded at the Tower of London. In July 1631, his co-conspirators and servants, Giles Broadway and Florence Fitzpatrick, were hanged for rape and sodomy. Skipwith escaped punishment for reasons that have been lost. *See also* Laws; Masculinity; Rape Law.

Further Reading: Herrup, Cynthia B. *A House in Gross Disorder: Sex, Law and the Second Earl of Castlehaven*. New York: Oxford University Press, 1999; McCormick, Ian, ed. *Secret Sexualities: A Sourcebook of Seventeenth and Eighteenth Century Writing*. New York: Routledge, 1997.

Caryn E. Neumann

VENEREAL DISEASES. A venereal disease is a sexually transmitted disease so named in mocking tribute to the Roman goddess of love, Venus. The major venereal diseases of the seventeenth and eighteenth centuries, syphilis and gonorrhea, were believed to be the same disease for many years because they were frequently contracted together. Most likely, syphilis first appeared during the Renaissance, but whether it began in Europe and was then transmitted to the New World or vice versa is still a bone of contention among medical anthropologists and historians of medicine. In Europe, the French called it the Neapolitan disease, and the Italians called it the French disease; the Portuguese called it the Castillian disease, and the Japanese and Indians (from India) called it the Portuguese disease. It was referred to as the great pox by Renaissance physicians and *lues venerum* or *lues* in medical writings in America.

During the colonial period in America, the progress of medicine was excruciatingly slow. In the colonies, medical practitioners were usually ministers such as **Cotton Mather**, itinerant physicians, or barber surgeons. Midwives also provided medical care. There was very little formalized medical education. Even though the first medical school in America was opened in 1765 in Pennsylvania, it took over a century to establish requirement standards, and many medical practitioners had only empirical knowledge. It was not until 1837 that Phillipe Ricord, in France, proposed three separate stages of syphilis: primary, secondary, and tertiary. Forty-two years later, Albert Neisser identified the bacterium that caused gonorrhea, and named it *Gonococcus neisseria* in 1879. But the causative agent of syphilis, *Treponema pallidum*, a spirochete, was not identified until Schaudinn and Hoffmann isolated the microbe in 1905. Hence much chronic suffering, deformity, and pain as a result of syphilis and gonorrhea were present in early America. Unfortunately since there was a moral judgment attached to a person who presented with a sexually transmitted disease, people prayed rather than sought what medical help was available. A common belief was that disease, any disease, was God's punishment for sin, particularly sins of a sexual nature, and humans should not interfere with divine pronouncement.

Because the natural history of syphilis consists of an initial skin lesion that goes away, people were not aware of the insidious and long-lasting nature of the disease. Syphilis mimicked so many other diseases that it was frequently confused with tuberculosis, leprosy, and treponemal skin diseases in times where few writings were available, and many people could not read. In the seventeenth century, the microscope was a curiosity, a toy; it and barely gained respect as a useful diagnostic tool by the eighteenth century. It took another 100 years until dark field microscopy, a technique where light hits bacteria and bounces off them, identified the causative spirochete of syphilis.

In Europe, mercury was used to treat syphilis, but often the treatment caused more problems than the illness. The preparation used in America, known as Calomel, was mercurous chloride, a highly toxic substance. When used too much, it caused irreversible neurological damage, gum disease, and skin lesions.

During the American Revolution, it is estimated that 75 percent of the British soldiers fighting against the Americans, suffered from venereal disease, sometimes getting new infections twice or thrice in a year. Since they were incapacitated from three weeks to four months (or forever), they could not perform their duties. And, because infected soldiers were charged "venereal money" that was deducted from their pay, many did not report to the medical authorities for treatment. It is possible that the lower rate of infection among Americans is due to more of them being involved in monogamous relationships, since they were fighting on their home turf and closer to their wives and sweethearts.

Perhaps the best advertised treatment prior to the war is from 1742, a document in testimonial form by John Watson, an apothecary whose alternative medicine, Mr. Hauksbee's purging pills, could only be purchased from him. He describes one patient's venereal disease as cordee (a painful erection), shankers (chancres), swelled testicles, blotches, or breaking out in the head or body, and nocturnal pains.

After the revolution, one well-known book on domestic medicine written by William Buchan (1785) describes treatment for gonorrhea using a cooling regime: bathing the parts in warm milk and water, injecting the urethra with sweet oil or linseed tea, and bleeding, a common remedy for almost everything. Most of this document refers to men's symptoms and treatments. What is written for women describes "a suppression or overflowing of the menses, hysteric affections, an inflammation, abscess, scirrhus, gangrene, cancer, or ulcer of the womb."

Throughout the eighteenth century, Calomel remained the standard treatment for syphilis because it was endorsed by one of the most prestigious and well-known early American doctors, Benjamin Rush. It continued to be used despite its horrible side effects. The journals of Lewis and Clark (c. 1804) refer to "Louis Veneri" contracted from a Chinook woman and treated with mercury. Chippewa Native Americans used lobelia and sumac.

The evidence of venereal disease in the New World consists of bones that have been excavated from plantations and African American cemeteries—writings by apothecaries and physicians, such as Benjamin Rush, and the second edition of a 1769 book on domestic medicine because the first did not contain information on venereal disease. Perhaps the punishments for premarital and extramarital sex were so severe in Puritan New England that venereal disease was rare or unmentionable. Conditions were different in the southern colonies and the Caribbean islands. There, wealthy plantation owners demonstrated their power by using sex to exploit slaves and servants. **William Byrd** is one such person who had frequent sexual encounters with prostitutes (when he went to London) as well as social inferiors. His diaries give adequate proof that promiscuity would assure the ongoing transmission of the microbes responsible for syphilis and gonorrhea. See also Baths; The Body; Medicine and Science; Midwives and Physicians; Prostitutes and Prostitution.

Further Reading: Buchan, William. "Domestic Medicine: Of the Venereal Disease." See http://www.americanrevolution.org/medicine.html; DeVoto, Bernard, ed. *The Journals of Lewis and Clark*. Boston: Houghton Mifflin, 1953; Godbeer, Richard. "William Byrd's Flourish: The

Sexual Cosmos of a Southern Planter." In *Sex and Sexuality in Early America*, edited by Merril Smith. New York: New York University Press, 1998; Stacy, Kim R. "Venereal Disease in the 84th Regiment of Foot during the American Revolution." *Journal of the Society for Army Historical Research* 77, no. 312 (1999): 237–39.

Lana Thompson

VIRGIN MARY. The Virgin Mary, the mother of Jesus Christ, was born in Nazareth as the child of Joachim and Anne. In the Christian tradition, Mary is the perpetual virgin and the new Eve, the woman who was given the chance to bear the Savior. Her exceptional dual nature, virgin and mother, shows the eschatological nature of Christian virginity. Modern researchers consider Mary a manifestation of the archetypal mother. The valorization of Mary relies on ancient beliefs that **chastity** and virginity gave one special powers.

Between 1600 and 1800, in the Christian world, the worship and the representation of the Virgin Mary were deeply affected by the Counter-Reformation, the intensification of Catholic proselytism in eastern Europe through the appearance of the Greek-Catholic Churches in Ukraine and Transylvania, on the one hand, and by the defensive strategies of Eastern Christianity against Protestantism and Catholicism, on the other hand. During all this period, the Roman Catholic Church stubbornly tried to remove the Virgin Mary as much as possible from any possible connection with human sexuality and love. In 1616 Pope Paul V forbade any argument about Mary's purity in the pulpit. This ban was reenforced by Pope Gregory XV in 1622. During his pontificate (1655–1667), Pope Alexander VII declared Mary exempt from the original sin in a Bull, which foreshadowed the 1854 dogma of Mary's Immaculate Conception. In 1677 Pope Innocent XI banned the representation of any embrace of Anne and Joachim. The multiplication of minor feasts connected to the Virgin Mary and established or extended during this period turned her into a perfect focus of sublimated desires. Pope Paul V (1605–1621) ordered the spread of the cult of the seven sorrows/griefs of the Virgin. In 1644 the Feast of the Purest Heart of Mary was established. Among the earliest worshippers of the Heart was Jean Eudes, who formed a congregation with this view and even declared himself the public defender of Mary's honor. In 1683 the Feast of the Holy Name of Mary was extended to the whole Roman Catholic Church. It marked the grateful love of Christianity for the Virgin Mary interceding during the siege of Vienna by the Turks. In 1716 after the victory of Prince Eugen of Savoy, also over the Turks, the Feast of the Rosary (an arrangement of 150 Hail Marys in fifteen decades) was also extended to the whole church.

St. Alphonsus de Liguori, who published *The Glories of Mary* in 1715, felt the tension between the subtle eroticism contained in the worship of Mary and the erotic edge in the relationship between God and Mary. In order to diminish this potential promiscuity and divert attention from it, he introduced into the text a Joseph who was exceedingly happy that Mary entered the Heavens.

The ribald potential in the relationship between God and Mary, as well as the exaggerations of Mary's cult, became food for thought during the Enlightenment. In his *Traité sur la tolerance* (1763), Voltaire worked hard upon rooting out the false ideas that praying to the Virgin for thirty days gave people impunity for whatever they did during the rest of the year.

In Eastern Christianity, the 1600–1800 period witnessed the forcible affirmation of the Orthodox opinion that Mary was exempt from original sin because of her impeccable behavior and because Jesus was conceived within her. However, in

Orthodoxy her exceptional status did not include her own "immaculate conception." Two of the most influential Orthodox theologians of the time, Petru Movila (Petro Mohyla), the Metropolitan of Kiev, and Dositei, the patriarch of Jerusalem, reinforced these ideas. Mary must be loved and worshipped because she was human and her nature was human. Movila's 1642 *The Orthodox Confession* (translated into Latin as *Confessio fidei orthodoxae* and published in Amsterdam in 1643) and the 1672 *Confession of Dositei* of Jerusalem are emblematic for the Orthodox refusal to de-corporalize Mary. Negotiation with the Catholic dogmas exists in other respects, but full resistance to Catholic proselytism is seen in the worship of Mary.

On the other hand, the Orthodox worshipped objects connected to Mary's bodily use and worshipped her face as represented in icons. An interesting sample, in this respect, is the Virgin's girdle. The Virgin herself had woven this personal object to cover her body and she presented it to St. Thomas. At present, a fragment of the girdle is preserved at the monastery of Vatopedi, at Mount Athos. In 1794, a Paraclis of the Holy Girdle of the Virgin was built at Vatopedi with Romanian assistance. In the same century, the silver casket where the girdle was kept was also repaired with assistance from Wallachia. The love of the Virgin was also expressed in worshipping the icons, which are regarded by Orthodoxy as visual communication of the reality of the invisible divine. This particularly suited Mary with her complex double status as virgin and mother. Famous in the eighteenth century was the icon of the Virgin painted in 1681 by Father Luca of Iclod (Romania). In 1694, the icon, apparently, cried for the misery of humanity for twenty-six days.

Protestantism was extremely cautious about worshipping Mary. An interesting case is the cult of Gloriana (Elizabeth I) who came to hover on the cult of the Virgin. To love and worship the Virginal English Queen became an element of public order and stability.

In **Islam**, the clash of the **Ottoman empire** with the Christian world did not affect the cult of the Virgin Mary, who continued to be worshipped as a prophet's mother. *See also* Monasteries; Religion; Virgins/Virginity.

Further Reading: Cunneen, Sally. *In Search of Mary: The Woman and the Symbol*. New York: Ballantine Books, 1996; Pelikan, Jaroslav. *Mary through the Centuries: Her Place in the History of Culture*. New Haven, CT: Yale University Press, 1996; Spidlik, Tomas. *The Spirituality of the Christian East: A Systematic Handbook*. Translated by Anthony P. Gythiel. Kalamazoo, MI: Cistercian Publications, 1986; Warner, Marina. *Alone of Her Sex. The Myth and the Cult of Virgin Mary*. New York: Pocket Books, 1976.

Mihaela Mudure

VIRGIN OF GUADALUPE. The Virgin of Guadalupe is a Mexican religious icon with origins in the early 1500s, and around whom a popular cult grew in the early 1600s. She is a symbol of a representative who could help the Nahua people (Aztecs) escape from the dynamics of Spanish colonialism. The Spaniards feminized the Nahua in their writings, calling them passive and weak. But as the Mother of God, Guadalupe trumped the standard gender dynamic of male over female. Furthermore, seen as both a goddess and a being with direct access to God, she had the power to change the domination of the Spaniard over the Nahua.

The Virgin of Guadalupe is known by many additional names, such as the Queen of Virgins and Our Lady of Guadalupe. She is also known as the Dark Virgin, since she has the same skin tone as the indigenous Mexicans. She is said to have originally appeared in a vision to a poor indigenous man at the hill of Tepeyacac in 1531.

VIRGIN OF GUADALUPE

Our Lady of Guadalupe, 1746. At the National Palace in Mexico City. © The Art Archive/National Palace Mexico City/Dagli Orti.

Guadalupe began as an ancient Aztec divinity, a mother of the Aztec gods named Tonantzin (Tonan is a reverential suffix meaning Our Mother in Nahuatl, language of the Aztecs). Tonantzin was worshipped in a temple on a hill called Tepeyacac (now known as Tepeyac). Spanish conquistadors, however, called it the hill of Guadalupe. With evangelistic intentions, the Christian conquistadors suppressed the Nahua's **religion** and reformed the identity of Our Mother Tonantzin to their likings, renaming her Our Lady of Guadalupe. Her identity was now that of Mary, the mother of Jesus. The Nahua, however, did not understand the intended identity difference. To them, she was just Tonantzin renamed.

The colonial system degraded Nahua women's position in society just as it degraded their important female deities. As the Spanish conquerors forced a new religion upon them, the Nahua were willing to accept the one important female offered to them.

Guadalupe as a virgin mother did not seem extraordinary to the Nahua people, since two of their own gods were conceived without sexual intercourse: Huitzilopochtli was conceived with a tuft of feathers, and Quetzalcóatl by a precious stone. The mothers of these Aztec gods were also termed virgins. However, a goddess' virginity or lack of it was irrelevant when considering her holiness and importance. Indeed, in Mexico, it was only the Spaniards to whom female virginity was an important cultural norm before **marriage**. Abstinence from sexual intercourse before marriage was not a focus for the Nahua. Many Nahua couples who were engaged had sex without consideration.

Nahuas viewed abstinence before marriage as a required state for the successful completion of religious rituals, rather than as a **virtue** or an avoidance of sin. It made sense to them that Guadalupe should maintain her virginity since she had intimate and ongoing contact with a powerful god. But the meaning of her story as portrayed by the Spaniards began to influence colonial Nahua priests. The priests began to encourage their people to marry younger in order to maintain their virginity before marriage.

By the early 1600s, Spaniards were attributing miracles to Guadalupe. The legend of Guadalupe was first published in 1648 in Spanish, then in 1649 in Nahuatl. With the Nahuatl publication came Guadalupe's widespread popularity throughout Mexico. With the upsurge in fervor, a new church dedicated to Guadalupe was constructed at Tepeyacac between 1695 and 1709. It rivaled the grandeur of other Mexican cathedrals of the day.

The Nahua believed Guadalupe was literate. Her literacy indicated that she was highly educated, an opportunity unheard of for Nahua women. She acted on her own volition, appearing to followers as she pleased. Furthermore, Guadalupe had direct communication with God. All these characteristics made her a natural symbol for women's independence and empowerment. She was the only part of the Spaniard's religion and cultural worldview that upheld the Nahua's social status of women. *See also* Mexico, Indigenous Women of; Mexico, Sexuality and Gender in; Native Americans; Virgin Mary; Virgins/Virginity.

Further Reading: Brading, D. A. *Mexican Phoenix: Our Lady of Guadalupe: Image and Tradition Across Five Centuries.* Cambridge: Cambridge University Press, 2002; Lafaye, Jacques.

Quetzalcóatl and Guadalupe: The Formation of Mexican National Consciousness. Translated by Benjamin Keen. Chicago: University of Chicago Press, 1974; Laso de la Vega, Luis. *The Story of Guadalupe: Luis Laso de la Vega's Huei Tlamahuiçoltica of 1649.* Translated by Lisa Sousa, Stafford Poole, C.M., and James Lockhart. Stanford, CA: Stanford University Press, 1998; Poole, Stafford, C.M. *Our Lady of Guadalupe: The Origins and Sources of a Mexican National Symbol, 1531–1797.* Tucson: University of Arizona Press, 1997.

Elizabeth Jenner

VIRGINS/VIRGINITY. In European Christian societies, control of female sexuality had long been a concern of the patriarchal church and patrilineal inheritance system. During the seventeenth century, this concern intensified with the focus shifting more directly onto a woman's virginal status rather than her longer-term **chastity**.

With the increasing value placed on premarital virginity, men began to seek definitive means of determining whether a woman was a virgin or not. Virginity was seen less as a state of mind denoting sexual innocence and lack of desire and more as a physical state. Thus, women who had fallen prey to a seducer or rapist were no longer considered virginal and were therefore seen as worthless; many resorted to prostitution in order to survive. The high value placed on virginity is evidenced in the English slang term "money" for a prepubescent girl's genitals and in the French phrase for hymen, "le petit capital."

English medical texts of the period provide evidence that doctors were divided over the existence of this vaginal membrane. Some cautioned that its lack of existence did not indicate previous sexual activity, as any number of things, from sneezing to scratching, could rupture it. Some women resorted to trickery to ensure that the necessary drops of blood appeared on their wedding night, either to confirm their actual virginity or fool their new spouse. There were countless methods of inserting blood from an alternate source into the vagina, methods that had been around for centuries. Some younger prostitutes used these methods to enable them to sell their "virginity" to the highest bidder over and over again.

The importance of virginity and the physical conceptualization of it at this time can be seen in contemporary paintings. In this artwork, the womb was depicted as a clay or glass vessel; if broken, it meant that the woman was no longer a virgin. It can also be found in the **rape laws** of many countries, for example Ottoman Egypt and early modern Spain. In these places, rape was perceived as a property crime that deprived a woman and her family of her virginity/hymen/honor. In Egypt, only a virgin was entitled to compensation.

In eighteenth-century England, there was a high incidence of rape of young girls. It was a common myth that sex with a virgin could relieve the pain of syphilis by transferring the disease to the girl and curing the ailing man. While such actions undoubtedly infected many children, it did nothing to relieve their assailants.

There was also an increase in penetrative sex in later-eighteenth-century England, with the **bastardy** rates and premarital pregnancies increasing dramatically. It is not clear why this happened. It is likely linked to a number of changing attitudes. The growing condemnation of **masturbation** during the early modern era deprived couples of a form of mutual sexual satisfaction that avoided **pregnancy**. In addition, the social characterization of men and women underwent a change during this time. Women, who in 1600, were largely seen as sexually voracious, were, in 1800, viewed as asexual. Thus, whereas formerly some women may have eagerly sought sexual, but nonpenetrative sex during **courtship**, they now began to internalize these newer feminine ideals. Some men, however, became more sexually demanding, and they demanded penetrative sex more often. Also, the increased urbanization that occurred with industrialization, along with growing literacy rates, meant that people were learning about sex through more impersonal methods such as the growing number of sex manuals being printed. All these forces and perhaps others combined to make it more difficult for a woman to reach her wedding night a virgin.

This changing conception of women from sexually demanding to asexual during this period can also be seen in the medical understanding of a rather mysterious ailment known as **hysteria**. Lethargy, melancholy, and fainting were all symptoms of hysteria. Dutch and English doctors of the seventeenth century believed that it was caused by the buildup of vapors and menstrual blood in the womb of a woman. As sexual intercourse was needed to release these substances, **marriage** was usually recommended. Until then, masturbation was advised as a temporary form of partial release. Not surprisingly, it was thought to be most common in young, unmarried women and became also known as "morbus virgineus," the disease of virgins. Exposure to a man was thought to exacerbate the disease as his presence caused the womb to act up, attempting to seek him out.

However, as women came to be increasingly seen as asexual, medical understanding of this disease was also altered. Whereas virgins were once thought the most susceptible women, now they were considered the only women immune to the illness. A woman was asexual until her desire was released through penetrative sex. Hysteria was the result of too much sexual activity, not too little.

The Protestant doctors of seventeenth-century England and the Netherlands strongly condemned the Catholic belief that lifelong **celibacy** was the most desirable state. Protestants thought lifelong celibacy was unnatural and rarely attainable. They mocked nuns, telling tales of the sexual escapades they engaged in.

Not all cultures valued virginity. In traditional Filipino societies, there was no word for virginity; the concept did not exist. Filipino society was much more sexually expressive than the Christian societies of Europe. At about age six, girls had their hymens broken by an elder man, so that once the girls became sexually active, intercourse would not be painful. Youths were sexually promiscuous, and even married people could engage in sexual relations outside marriage. All this changed once the Spanish missionaries arrived in the late sixteenth century, but these practices fell out of favor only gradually during the course of the early modern period. *See also* Gynecology Manuals; Midwives and Physicians; Monasteries; Prostitutes and Prostitution; Venereal Diseases.

Further Reading: Bouce, Paul-Gabriel, ed. "Some Sexual Beliefs and Myths in Eighteenth-Century Britain." In *Sexuality in Eighteenth-Century Britain*, 28–46. Manchester: Manchester University Press, and Totowa, NJ: Barnes & Noble Books, 1982; Brewer, Carolyn. *Shamanism, Catholicism and Gender Relations in Colonial Philippines, 1521–1685*. Women and Gender in the Early Modern World Series. Aldershot: Ashgate Publishing, 2004; Dixon, Laurinda S. *Perilous Chastity: Women and Illness in Pre-Enlightenment Art and Medicine*. Ithaca, NY: Cornell University Press, 1995.

Tonya Marie Lambert

VIRTUE. Virtue is the moral excellence, or value, of an individual. The concept of such excellence, of human goodness, was profoundly important throughout the colonial and revolutionary age. Moral philosophers, poets, and politicians contested whether virtue was an innate human characteristic or it was inculcated through society and the family. Contemporary writers repeatedly drew the connection between individual morality and social stability in this period. As a result, personal virtue became a crucial constituent of social morality: an indicator of the moral state of the community.

In religious terms, human virtues reflected the attributes and wisdom of the divinity. Christianity's emphasis on the importance of sexual continence led to virtue becoming largely associated with its sexual ramifications in the course of the period.

Such stress on the sexual characteristics of virtue also led to a gendered divide in what virtue meant for men and women's moral excellence. Ironically, the word "virtue" itself derived from the Latin for "the male function" or manliness, but became predominantly associated with female qualities. For women, individual virtue became increasingly synonymous with personal **chastity** or fidelity, and deracinated from other forms of personal value. For men, virtue was a more diffuse and varied term, which did not generally involve sexual abstinence. The early eighteenth-century shift from the sexually permissive attitudes embodied in restoration drama and the traditional bawdy folk-ballad, saw a reemphasis on female sexuality as the prime site for staging trials of virtue. Such emphasis on female chastity can be seen in the slew of sentimental and romantic European novels of the mid-century, which represented "virtue in distress" (R. F. Brissenden). Works such as Samuel Richardson's monumental *Clarissa* (1747–1748) depicted women of moral excellence subjected to sustained sexual aggression by male predators, and usually culminated in the violation and subsequent death of the heroine. The negative outcome found in such sentimental novels of virtue implies a moral pessimism, which sets sexuality at odds with virtue and yet which acknowledges the force (and triumph) of sex.

While female virtue became increasingly conflated with sexlessness, male, or masculine, virtue was often defined without reference to the sexual arena. Male sexuality was "natural," unlike female sexual desire. The participation of women in the French Revolution (1789) was seen by many Tory commentators as signs of the ruination of female virtue, the revolution itself as symptomatic of an insatiate female sexuality that had destroyed ordered, male civilization. Male virtue was active, unlike its female counterpart. It manifested itself in acts of benevolence, charity, and civic responsibility. Male virtue could often coexist with sexual license and appetite, seemingly without conflict. Virtue, far from being a static moral concept, reflects the changing desires and values of the period. *See also* Libertine; Masculinity; Religion; Revolution and Gender; Seduction Literature; Virgins/Virginity; Women, Changing Images of.

Further Reading: Bloch, Ruth H. "The Gendered Meanings of Virtue in Revolutionary America." *Signs: Journal of Women in Culture and Society* 13, no. 1 (1987): 37–58; Brissenden, R. F. *Virtue in Distress: Studies in the Novel of Sentiment from Richardson to Sade*. London: Harper & Row, 1974; Smith, Merril D., ed. *Sex and Sexuality in Early America*. New York: New York University Press, 1998.

Rebecca Barr

VOYEURISM. The term *voyeur* is derived from the French verb "voir," which means "to see," and is used to describe a person deriving sexual gratification from observing other people (with or without their **consent**), objects, and activities. The word itself begins to be used specifically in relation to sexual behavior from the nineteenth century onward, mainly in the works of sexopathologists and psychiatrists of the time, who classified voyeurism as one of the sexual disorders, or paraphilias. For these reasons, it may be difficult to talk about voyeurism in the seventeenth and eighteenth centuries, although it would be impossible to deny that the times in question abounded in many an opportunity for voyeuristic enjoyment.

Historical accounts of early modern households (both in Europe and America) describe them as large in size and consisting of immediate family members, as well as distant relatives, servants, and apprentices. Since remarrying of widows and widowers was commonplace, often households comprised children of different parents. As a unit, the household was seen as more important than a single family, as a result of which it was difficult to talk of any special intimacy among blood relatives, including the spouses. The spatial arrangement of early modern houses put a serious strain on marital privacy, since even the more socially advanced families put several beds into one room, and often several people into one bed. Among the poor it was common to see a dwelling being shared by many families, and as many as five to six people sharing a bed.

Although in early modern times sexuality was controlled by authorities, sex as such was not seen as a secret activity. Lack of privacy meant that children or servants were sometimes present when the couple consummated their **marriage**; sleeping arrangements sometimes meant that unrelated persons of opposite sexes had to share a bed. When a woman gave birth to a child, her female relatives and neighbors frequently moved in with the family for several days, helping with the nursing, and even sharing breast milk when necessary. Any illicit, extramarital sexual activity was most likely spied on by the culprit's housemates or neighbors, and resulted in trials, in which the explicit description of the committed offences was made public. It was only in larger urban areas, such as London, that the size of the city offered its inhabitants some opportunities for anonymity, allowing unfaithful, or bigamous wives and husbands to live for years without being discovered.

The seventeenth- and eighteenth-century voyeurism, however, did not concern merely acts of spying on someone else's sexual activities. In accordance with the requirements of the times, women and men were educated to fit the roles of objects of scrutiny and judges and arbiters, respectively. The changing position of women affected customs connected with the marriage market, demanding that young women of the upper classes display their eroticized and aestheticized bodies through their accomplishments, that is, posing while painting or playing a musical instrument. While playing their parts as the connoisseurs of art, men could gaze at the **body** of the artist while pretending they were admiring her painting, or listening to her play. Such behavior resulted in further fetishizing the body of a woman, observed particularly at the end of the eighteenth century and later.

One of the earliest references to a figure of voyeur in **literature** comes from a 1634 version of the legend of the Lady Godiva of Coventry. The medieval Godiva (historically recorded as the eleventh-century Godigfu, wife of the earl of Mercia, Leofric) was supposed to have ridden across the town naked to ease the taxes imposed on the town by her husband. In original accounts of the legend she succeeded in her mission unseen by anyone, perhaps because her naked body was covered at all time by her long locks of hair. Later editions add the figure of Peeping Tom, construed to stand in opposition to Godiva, and punished for his transgression. Beginning with 1678, the reenactment of Godiva's ride replaced *Corpus Christi* processions in Coventry, where Godiva is considered a local saint, and her body gradually replaced the body of Christ in the procession. Although boys initially performed the role, later actresses, who were seen as already compromised in erotic displays, took over playing the part of Lady Godiva. *See also* Actors; Gossip; Indentured Servants; Laws.

Further Reading: Abate, Corinne S., ed. *Privacy, Domesticity, and Women in Early Modern England.* Aldershot: Ashgate Publishing, 2003; Bermingham, Ann, ed. *The Consumption of Culture, 1600–1800.* London: Routledge, 1995; Donoghue, Daniel. *Lady Godiva: A Literary History of the Legend.* Oxford: Blackwell, 2003; Gowing, Laura. *Domestic Dangers—Women, Words and Sex in Early Modern London.* Oxford: Clarendon Press, 1996.

Katarzyna Ancuta

WARTIME RAPE. "Rape of enemy warfare" has a long history in many parts of the world. Contrary to the claims of numerous authors, wartime rape on a massive scale is not a development of the twentieth century. Ancient, medieval, and early modern accounts of warfare frequently report the occurrence of **rape**, both individual and *en masse*.

Rape occurs during war for a variety of reasons. During the early modern period, rape of enemy women was generally thought of as one of the rewards accruing to the victorious soldier. After the defeat of an enemy, soldiers were often allowed to pillage and plunder, seizing booty in the form of goods and women as compensation for the hardships which they had endured while fighting the war. Such activities were so commonplace in European warfare that repeated prohibitions against them by kings and commanders were ignored. French soldiers turned against their colonel, Benedict-Louis de Pontis, in 1635, when he attempted to prevent them from raping the nuns of the convent of Tourlement in Flanders.

Mercenaries were foreign men hired to fight. Often they had few, if any, reservations about raping women, having no real connections with the people on either side. These men were sometimes encouraged to plunder when a lack of funds made it impossible to pay them for their services. The lawlessness of mercenary soldiers was well known and feared. German mercenaries known as *Landsknecht* had a reputation for sexually abusing women.

Women and girls were frequently raped in the presence of family members, usually parents or husbands. This was done to further humiliate the woman and embarrass her male kin by highlighting their inability to protect their family or property. Nathan Hanover tells of Ukrainian Cossacks raping the wives and daughters of their Jewish and Polish enemies in the presence of the woman's husband or father during the uprisings of 1648. English soldiers did likewise after the defeat of the Scottish Jacobites at the battle of Culloden in 1745 and during the American Revolution twenty years later.

Rape was also utilized as a form of punishment and as a warning not to cause any problems for the victor. That rape was a form of punishment inflicted upon the defeated is evidenced by its frequent occurrence after the defeat of a besieged city, while in cases where a city quickly surrendered, attempts were made to minimize the amount of plundering and raping that occurred. The brutality exhibited by French soldiers after the fall of the Dutch town Bergen-op-Zoom in 1747 was such that even one of their leaders was appalled.

Wartime rape can be either opportunistic or systematic. Many people believe that the latter is a modern phenomenon. However, it is not. For example, in 1776, the women of the American colony of New Jersey were systematically raped by English soldiers. The violence was widespread and sometimes repetitive, with the same woman being raped on more than one occasion. Some women and girls were taken to the soldiers' camps and gang-raped, sometimes being held captive for days.

Rape is a violent crime, but rape in war is often especially so since there is little, if any, external restraint to curtail the extent of the violence. Gang rapes occur more frequently in times of war. Repetitive assaults can result in severe physical injury and even death. Some women are murdered after being raped. A few are raped even after they have died.

The seriousness of the crime was minimized by the prevalent belief that women, as the heirs of Eve, were sexually insatiable. It was only false modesty that prevented them from readily agreeing to engage in sexual intercourse with any man. As a result, many men believed that women enjoyed being forced to have intercourse. This was further complicated in the case of a resultant **pregnancy** by the belief still common at the beginning of the early modern era: that a woman could not conceive unless she enjoyed the experience, which in turn required her to have consented to it. Many German women, pregnant as a result of such rapes, found themselves banished from their communities and forced into a life of dire poverty (and frequently, beginning with **infanticide**) after the area had been devastated by enemy soldiers during the Thirty Years War (1618–1648). The social hierarchy and power structure of the new Protestant states was built upon a marital foundation that had no place for such women and their offspring. Tales have come down to us, however, of Scottish women and their husbands after the battle of Culloden (1745) agreeing not to engage in sexual intercourse for nine months after a rape so they could be sure of the **paternity** of any offspring.

Few soldiers were (or are) ever punished for the crime of rape. The women who were assaulted had no authority to appeal to any one other than the commander of the opposing army. In an age which valued a woman's **chastity** so highly, many women would not have told anyone about being raped for fear of being socially ostracized and scorned. Thus, as historian, Mary Beth Norton reports in her book, *Liberty's Daughters*, an American man wrote of the women raped during the War of Independence, "Against both Justice and Reason We Despise these poor Innocent Sufferers ... Many honest virtuous women have suffered in this Manner and kept it Secret for fear of making their lives miserable." Rape of enemy women during warfare was not, however, a universal practice during the early modern period. For example, it was not practiced by the native peoples of northeastern North America.

While the vast majority of sexual assaults were perpetrated by men against women or children, assaults by men against other men or boys also occur during war. Through anal penetration, male victims of sexual assault are gendered female. In other words, sodomitic rape is a means whereby the rapist indicates his social superiority by physically and sexually dominating the other man. Such rapes can happen during war but are more common following defeat or capture. The Tumucua of southeastern North America sodomized or castrated defeated enemies on the battlefield before killing them, while both the Winnebago and Osago to the north raped captured enemy warriors.

There is even the occasional report of sexual assault by women against men, though these are rare. In the journal of Dr. John Rae, there is an account of an attack upon Rae and a group of other men, including Robert Clive, the English commander, by a group of Bengali women in **India** in 1752. The women held the men down and rubbed a substance on the men's penises, which caused them to be irritated, itchy, and erect. Then, the women left them in agony.

A few voices, however, did begin to be raised against wartime rape during the early modern period. Diane Wolfthal has detected a definite shift in the depiction of sexual conquest in European art, from its glorification in medieval **art** to its increasing denigration throughout the early modern era. In the late sixteenth century, Alberic Gentili (1558–1602), an Italian lecturing at Oxford, advised soldiers not to rape enemy women so as not to give the other nation cause to launch a just war in retaliation. Hugo Grotius (1583–1645), a Dutch jurist, argued against rape in times of war, as well as in times of peace in his 1623 publication *Law of War and Peace*, while noting that most authorities did not agree with him. For example, the Spaniard Francisco de Vitoria (1492–1546) had written a century earlier that the possibility of raping enemy women was a necessary incentive to get soldiers to fight.

Muslim legal theorists also debated whether rape laws applied during times of war. They also further pondered over whether the **laws** could be applied in the case of rapes perpetrated in enemy territory. The Maliki and Shafi'i schools of Islamic Sunni jurisprudence argued affirmatively in both instances, while the Hanafi disagreed in both.

The topic of rape was also employed as a rhetorical tool, both then and now. Tales of women being raped by enemy soldiers were used to garner support by depicting the enemy as cruel and inhuman. An example is the book *Advis Fidelle aux Veritables Hollandois* written by Abraham de Wicquefort and illustrated by Romeyn de Hooghe describing the horrendous crimes, including rape, committed by French soldiers in the Dutch villages of Swammerdam and Bodegrave in 1672. The more often that rape is employed as a rhetorical tool to demonize the enemy, the less impact the actual occurrence of the crime has: rape during war becomes naturalized as the audience itself becomes desensitized. *See also* Atlantic Slave Trade; Child Rape; Consent; Ottoman Empire; Women, Changing Images of.

Further Reading: Norton, Mary Beth. *Liberty's Daughters: The Revolutionary Experience of American Women, 1750–1800*. Boston: Little, Brown, 1980; Trexler, Richard. *Sex and Conquest: Gendered Violence, Political Order, and the European Conquest of the Americas*. Ithaca, NY: Cornell University Press, 1995; Wolfthal, Diane. *Images of Rape: The "Heroic" Tradition and Its Alternatives*. Cambridge: Cambridge University Press, 1999.

Tonya Marie Lambert

WIDOWS AND WIDOWHOOD. Widows are women whose husbands have died. Most marriages during the colonial and revolutionary era did not last more than twenty years, and, as today, women were more likely to outlive their spouses. Between 6 and 12 percent of eighteenth-century households were headed by widows, but some port and seafaring communities had as many as 20 percent of their households headed by widows whose husbands had been lost at sea or died in military expeditions. After the Seven Years' War (1756–1763; also known as the French and Indian War, 1754–1763), 25 percent of households in Boston were headed by widows. Remarriage rates for widows varied; younger women who lost their husbands were much more likely to remarry than widows who were over forty years old. Remarriages also were much more likely in a dynamic urban environment with portable property. Overall, however, widows were half as likely to remarry than widowers.

Widowhood was a new stage in a woman's life and an important development within a family's life cycle. To commemorate these changes and reinforce the widow's status, seventeenth- and eighteenth-century social mores dictated specific forms of personal deportment and public gestures following the death of a husband. Newly widowed women had to carefully balance their behavior while grieving. For example, they had to show proper respect for the life of their husbands as they continued to care for their family members, but they were also advised to avoid ostentation. Although they planned wakes and funeral services, new widows were also expected to remain inside their homes in the month following the death of their husbands. Widows were advised to reject any offer of new relationships for a period of time, generally ten months to one year, and they wore shades of black and gray clothing with veils over their faces so that everyone in the community could see their status. These social mores were often rooted in fears about the unabated sexuality of new widows. Theologians and medical experts warned that since widows had already experienced sex, their husbands' deaths and subsequent lack of male oversight would create uncontrollable sexual urges for the women. Widows were encouraged to live private and chaste lives, and Catholic moralists advised the women to give up public life, and any hope of remarriage, by entering a convent. Early modern society articulated these fears about female sexuality in witchcraft prosecutions, for example, in which widows were frequently accused of using the Devil's powers to fulfill sexual urges.

Household economies in the colonial and revolutionary era depended on the labor of both husbands and wives, and life could become precarious with the loss of a partner. A widow's economic position depended on many variables, including the settling of the estate, the economic status and type of work the family performed, and the number and ages of her minor children. Most European and colonial inheritance law stipulated that in estates without a will (*ab intestate*) the widow had rights to her original dowry that she had brought to the marriage, plus a percentage of the overall property. In common law regions, women generally had rights to at least one-third of the total property in the estate. The drawing up of a last will and testament frequently adjusted common law in the women's favor. In most wills, husbands stipulated that the widows would retain usufruct of all of the husbands' property until their minor children married or came of age, or until the widows remarried. Second **marriage** contracts frequently included clauses specifying that the minor children would be cared for from the overall community property of the second marriage, and not merely from the widows' property. Creditors had interest in all estate settlements, and if there were not enough funds to pay off the debts of the estate, widows had to liquidate portions of the property before they retained their rights over the estate or distributed it to heirs.

Economic status and familial situation determined many options for widows. Widows from comfortable social classes, whose wealth was based on land, rents, and annuities, usually had little trouble maintaining their lifestyles. The poorest widows had always worked to augment their family incomes, and the death of their spouses only aggravated their precarious situations. Many recent historical analyses have stressed the uncanny abilities of these poor women to avoid utter poverty and destitution, especially in the urban economy, by arranging living arrangements with other single or widowed women, performing day work, or reselling clothing and other items on the streets of seventeenth- and eighteenth-century cities. The women who faced the most difficult challenges by the loss of their partners were the middling urban and rural widows of artisans and small landholding farmers. Upon the deaths of their husbands, these women were immediately faced with the question of whether they could carry on the family business. If widows were fortunate enough to have healthy teenage sons, they could use the children to replicate their husbands' labor in the shop or on the farm.

Urban artisan widows had to receive permission to continue the family business from their husband's guild. Most guildsmen allowed the woman to continue previously contracted work with the help of her journeymen, but without a son to carry on the business, the guilds would have likely encouraged the widow to remarry or stop production altogether. Rural women with children could use them to help work on the land, and the widows frequently handed over the farm to their older children in return for care. Many of these women supplemented their income with cottage industry textile work. Rural and urban widows with particularly young children would have faced much more dire situations. *See also* Gender Roles; Household Consumerism; Witches and Witch Trials; Women, Changing Images of.

Further Reading: Hufton, Olwen. *The Prospect before Her: A History of Women in Western Europe, 1500–1800*. New York: Alfred A. Knopf, 1996; Wilson, Lisa. *Life after Death: Widows in Pennsylvania, 1750–1850*. Philadelphia: Temple University Press, 1992; Wulf, Karin. *Not All Wives: Women of Colonial Philadelphia*. Ithaca, NY: Cornell University Press, 2000.

Christopher R. Corley

WILMOT, JOHN, EARL OF ROCHESTER (1647–1680). John Wilmot, Earl of Rochester, stands as one of the most controversial English poets and playwrights of the Restoration period (1660–1688). Wilmot, also commonly referred to as Rochester, was one of the most infamous "**libertines**" or "rakes" (short for "rake-hell") during a period marked by the reopening of the theaters that had been closed under Puritan rule and a maelstrom of sexually charged revelry. Wilmot pushed the bounds of morality at every level: sexual, religious, and political. Many scholars contend that he was so renowned for his sexual exploits that he served as the model for the character Dorimant in George Etherege's 1676 play *The Man of Mode*.

Besides writing and producing plays for the Restoration stage, Wilmot is best known for his poetry, including *Satyr against Mankind*, his oft-anthologized response to Enlightenment visions of humanity, which defends the worth of our animal nature in marked contrast to his age's veneration of reason. Though condemned as merely "common" and lacking any "particular character" by Dr. Samuel Johnson in his *Lives of the English Poets*, Rochester's poetry has enjoyed increased appreciation from various critics since the latter half of the twentieth century. They read Rochester's poetry as simultaneously very much of his own time and yet very modern in its themes of sexual liberation.

Wilmot's infamy rests not only with his "free" lifestyle but also with his sexually explicit poetry, including his "Imperfect Enjoyment," a contribution to the poetic subgenre known as the "Premature **Ejaculation**" poem, which details the circumstances and emotions leading up to and immediately following the failed act of coitus (the male speaker addresses his member more than his companion).

Wilmot lived to his end the same sexual/sensual debauchery that permeates his writing, having claimed at one point to have been drunk for "five years together." Dying a slow, debilitating death, apparently from syphilis, Wilmot made (according to many sources) a deathbed retraction of his atheism. Numerous tracts ostensibly reproducing his conversion became quite popular as Wilmot became an exemplum of the "reformed rake."

Even in the twenty-first century, Wilmot's life and work has continued to excite critics, scholars, and students alike, even having inspired the play *The Libertine* by Stephen Jeffreys (the basis for the 2004 film of the same name starring Johnny Depp in the title role). Even a rare copy of his posthumously published play *Sodom, or the*

Quintessence of Debauchery, which had been ordered to be burned for its obscenity, caused a stir when it was sold for 45,600 pounds (approximately 83,000 U.S. dollars) in December 2004 at a Sotheby's auction. This published play is considered by many to be the first professionally published piece of **pornography**. With the U.S. release of the film, Wilmot's place on the cultural landscape should remain constant. *See also* Hogarth, William; Literature; Restoration Poetry; **Theater**; Venereal Diseases.

Further Reading: Adlard, John, ed. *The Debt to Pleasure: John Wilmot, Earl of Rochester: In the Eyes of His Contemporaries and in His Own Poetry and Prose.* New York: Routledge, 2002; Johnson, James William. *A Profane Wit: The Life of John Wilmot, Earl of Rochester.* Rochester, NY: University of Rochester Press, 2004.

Samantha A. Morgan-Curtis

WITCHES AND WITCH TRIALS. Many witch trials that occurred in early modern Europe, particularly those in continental Europe, had a distinct sexual component to them. Early modern people might not have recognized the sadistic sexual aspect of the practice involved in poking the genitals of accused women with pins to see if they felt any pain or not, a practice carried out in front of a male audience. Nonetheless, they would have agreed that most witches did engage in irregular sexual practices. There were four main types of sexual perversion for which a witch could be accused: (1) unsanctioned sexual acts with other people, such as **adultery**, **sodomy**, or **incest**; (2) **bestiality**; (3) sex with demons; and (4) sex with the Devil himself. Witches were also accused of interfering with the sexual functioning of other people, especially men, by stealing their penises or making them sterile.

Nonetheless, it was the sexual pact with the Devil that labeled one a witch in many areas of Europe, such as the German southwest; the performance of *maleficia* or evil deeds being of a much lesser, secondary importance (and in many cases not even necessary for a conviction). This emphasis on sexual relations between witches, particularly female ones, and the Devil or his minions can be explained. The first humans (that is, Adam and Eve) as well as the Devil and other rebel angels had fallen from grace with God. A primary consequence of this fall for humans was sexual desire, which in turn led to sexual sins. Since the demons were in theory fallen angels, it is not surprising that sexual deviance would also have been thought to be prevalent among them. Since the demons' offence against God had been greater than that of humans, their sexual desires were more abominable—a parallel that likely did not escape early modern theologians who were becoming increasingly interested in the Devil. Thus, the tales of demonic sex, which inquisitors forced from accused witches, became more and more degraded and torturous.

The most horrid of these tales were elicited from women accused of witchcraft. Women frequently confessed to great pain during intercourse with the Devil and demons, due to the strange nature of the penis (icy cold, very hard, covered in scale or barbs) and the types of acts that they were required to perform. For example, some women told of a penis with two or even three prongs, each of which was inserted into a different orifice of their body—vagina, anus, and mouth. Such detailed and disgusting stories were rarely extracted from men accused of witchcraft. Male suspects usually mentioned sex with a succubus only in passing, and then it was stated (or assumed) to have been quite ordinary, aside from the type of partner, of course.

The idea that witches had sexual intercourse with demons became popularized before tales of sexual orgies involving witches, demons, and the Devil at sabbats became widespread. There were two types of demons, incubi and succubi. The succubus was a

A 17th century German woodcut depicting Walpurgis Night. © The Granger Collection, New York.

demon in female form that mated with a man in order to acquire his "seed." The incubus was a demon in male form. There was a debate in the early modern period over whether incubi slept with women or not in order to impregnate them with the "seed" taken from a man by a succubus, or whether they might also do so to pleasure the woman and thus win her over to the Devil.

Most tales of witches having sexual intercourse with the Devil involved female witches, though a few did involve men. In these tales, the Devil often adopted a female form. However, sometimes he took the shape of an animal, often a goat, ram, or black cat, and would copulate with the witch as such. Witches were also believed to engage in sexual relations with their animal familiars, who were really demons in disguise, and to have a teat with which to suckle them.

Witches were often depicted in a highly eroticized manner in the visual arts of the period: nude, voluptuous female bodies in suggestive and inviting positions; naked witches straddling goats, a symbol of the Devil; or sometimes even scenes of women witches engaged in sexual activities with the Devil or a demon familiar. It should be noted that these eroticized portrayals of witches almost always depict the witch as female.

The preoccupation on the part of the male magistrates with the sexual escapades of female witches with the Devil can be explained by the greater threat that these women posed to gender relations. Witches who were women were a threat to their male superiors because of the inordinate power they were believed to possess; power which they were said to lose upon being captured. It was through interrogation that it was revealed that these women had actually only been the tools of another male—the Devil—who through stories of lewd sex was shown to have dominated them. In this way, the gender hierarchy was revealed to be secure.

The period of the witch hunts coincided with a period of history in which women were seen as sexually insatiable. Hence, because of the long association of women with sexual sin and the Devil, most of the confessions, demonological treatises, and other works of art and literature of the period that examined the connection between sexual sin, the Devil, and witches did so through the female, and not male, body.

Women's ability to access power in early modern society was through their bodies and sexuality. The Devil was viewed as a very powerful being, as well as a sinful one. Thus, a woman seeking power could obtain it from the Devil by engaging in sinful sexual relations with him. Women believed to ingest the power of the Devil or demon by literally taking him within (that is, by taking his manhood/power within) during the sexual act and retaining that power in the form of his seed. Conversely, tales of men having demonic sex are fewer because many people at this time believed that men lost their strength and power through sexual intercourse. When perceptions of women and femininity changed in the latter half of the seventeenth century and women were no longer believed to be sexually insatiable, perceptions about the Devil changed, as well. Since sex is linked with power as a means of either achieving or losing it, then the loss of sexuality necessitated a corresponding loss of power, both for the witch and the Devil. By denying that women felt desire, Enlightenment thinkers also denied them agency, without which they could not engage in *maleficia*, and hence the very idea of the witch became preposterous. Thus, with the severing of this connection between women and sexual sin also went the most immediate link tying female witches with the Devil. It can hardly be a coincidence that it was at this very time that the great European witch hunts came to an end. *See also* The Body; Enlightenment Thought on Sexuality; Gender Roles; Laws; Madness; Religion; Torture; Women, Changing Images of.

Further Reading: Roper, Lyndal. *Oedipus and the Devil: Witchcraft, Sexuality and Religion in Early Modern Europe*. London: Routledge, 1994; Stephens, Walter. *Demon Lovers: Witchcraft, Sex and the Crisis of Belief*. Chicago: University of Chicago Press, 2000; Zika, Charles. "Durer's Witch, Riding Women and Moral Order." In *Durer and His Culture*, edited by Dagmar Eichberger and Charles Zika, 118–40. Cambridge: Cambridge University Press, 1998; Zika, Charles, ed. "Fears of Flying: Representations of Witchcraft and Sexuality in Early Sixteenth-Century Germany." In *Exorcising Our Demons: Magic, Witchcraft and Visual Culture in Early Modern Europe*, 237–67. Boston: Brill, 2003; Zika, Charles, ed. "She-Man: Visual Representations of Witchcraft and Sexuality." In *Exorcising Our Demons: Magic, Witchcraft and Visual Culture in Early Modern Europe*, 269–304. Boston: Brill, 2003.

Tonya Marie Lambert

WOLLSTONECRAFT GODWIN, MARY (1759–1797). Mary Wollstonecraft, considered by many as the Mother of Modern Feminism, was an Enlightenment thinker and philosopher involved in the debate over the French Revolution, of which she was a supporter. Wollstonecraft grew up in a household plagued by debt and **domestic violence**. Leaving home to avoid both, she began as a paid companion and governess, becoming a professional educator before finding her calling as a writer, where her reason-based rhetoric redefined the accepted voice of female authors. Raised in the Anglican Church, Wollstonecraft became a radical in her religious, political, and social beliefs due to her friendships with various social anarchists, like Henry Fuseli. Wollstonecraft's primary goal was to include women in the ongoing social discussions by dealing directly with their sexuality, the justification for their exclusion. Her experiences with her mother, her sister Eliza, and her female friend Fanny Blood, all of whom suffered mental, emotional, and physical abuse at the hands of their husbands, provided much of Wollstonecraft's impetus for her work.

Wollstonecraft's *Vindication of the Rights of Man* (1790) preceded Thomas Paine's *The Rights of Man* by more than a year. Her best-known book, *A Vindication of the Rights of*

Woman (1792), which she wrote in six weeks, argues for the **education** of women to prevent their moral and mental decay, and decries society's misogynistic images of women. The most controversial portion of the text remains her condemnation of **marriage** as "legal prostitution," wherein women "may be convenient slaves, but slavery will have its constant effect, degrading the master and the abject dependent." Furthermore, Wollstonecraft blames society for forcing women into prostitution because of their lack of education and legitimate employment. Her final, incomplete novel, *Maria or The Wrongs of Woman* (1798), deals with the complexity of sexual desires, features characters including a prostitute and a seduced woman, and closes with Maria retreating to an all-female community.

Wollstonecraft's own sexual exploits eventually overshadowed her work and led to its near erasure for nearly 100 years. Her attraction to a married man, her affair with the "shady" American, Gilbert Imlay (whose child she had), and her suicide attempt after Imlay's infidelity bear witness to her passionate nature and disdain for the social mores of her eighteenth-century world. Her subsequent marriage to social philosopher/anarchist William Godwin occurred after she discovered she was pregnant and lasted only for a year. Wollstonecraft died as a result of **childbirth**, a fever taking her life eleven days after delivery. Godwin contributed to Wollstonecraft's posthumous negative reputation with his *Memoirs of the Author of A Vindication of the Rights of Woman* and *Posthumous Works* which include her torrid love letters to Imlay and led to her portrayal as a "hyena in petticoats."

Her daughter Mary Wollstonecraft Godwin Shelley later helped found science fiction with her writings, including the Romantic classic *Frankenstein*. Beginning in the 1970s, Wollstonecraft's writings regained their deserved status as significant texts in the development of Feminist Thought and the Women's Movement. *See also* Enlightenment Thought on Sexuality; Philosophy; Prostitutes and Prostitution.

Further Reading: Gordon, Lyndall. *Vindication: A Life of Mary Wollstonecraft*. New York: HarperCollins, 2005; Johnson, Claudia L., ed. *The Cambridge Companion to Mary Wollstonecraft*. Cambridge: Cambridge University Press, 2002; Todd, Janet. *Mary Wollstonecraft, a Revolutionary Life*. New York: Columbia University Press, 2002; Wollstonecraft, Mary. *A Vindication of the Rights of Woman: An Authoritative Text; Backgrounds; the Wollstonecraft Debate; Criticism*. New York: W. W. Norton, 1988.

Samantha A. Morgan-Curtis

WOMEN, CHANGING IMAGES OF. White women in Europe and the American colonies were generally measured against their recognized roles as wives and mothers. If they lived up to this ideal, they were usually respected. If they deviated from these roles in England and North America, they were criticized and most likely ridiculed, though in France, where they enjoyed more freedom, they might be celebrated.

The most prevalent image of women in the seventeenth and eighteenth centuries is undoubtedly that of the "notable housewife," a wife, mother, and housekeeper. According to *The Oxford English Dictionary*, at that time *notable* denoted "capable, managing, bustling, clever or industrious in household management." A good wife had to serve her husband, be his friend, raise their children, tend to household choices, and do so economically, efficiently, pleasingly, and happily. She assured the comfort, security, and happiness of the home for her husband and children. This image of the notable housewife continued into the twentieth century, becoming the ideal to which Victorian wives had to live up. Affluent middle-class and wealthy families were able to hire servants, thereby freeing the wives of daily household chores. The criticism of these "idle" women was that they wasted their days reading novels, gossiping, and playing games—and thus neglecting their duties and responsibilities.

In North America, the image of the dutiful wife and mother was transformed by the American Revolution into the cult of republican motherhood. While calls for political rights went unfulfilled, women were now given the task of teaching the ideals of the republic to the next generation, allowing them at least the opportunity to discuss politics without criticism. This change is nonetheless conservative, because despite this slight increase in freedom, the image of the republican mother was designed to maintain order.

Because they felt that wife and mother were the only roles for women, many disapproved of women who remained single. In England and in the United States, women outnumbered men; as a result, women went unmarried, and these unmarried women were called spinsters. They posed a problem to societies that held **marriage** as the true, appropriate role for women. In Catholic countries, many entered nunneries, a solution that Protestants lacked. Poor girls found work as domestic servants or prostitutes. Girls from the middle and upper class were not trained for work, and there were few professions for them anyhow. Most lived with their parents and siblings as part family members and part servants. Those with some **education** served as governesses, an occupation with low pay and no respect. Instead of earning sympathy, these women were scorned and criticized for not serving their proper roles in society, that is, being a man's wife. The "old maid" became a comic figure in stage comedies and novels, depicted often as unpleasant, foolish, and shrewish. Nonetheless, diaries and letters from that time, particularly in the United States, indicate some women chose to remain unmarried and remained happy with that decision.

As was the spinster, the coquette and the learned lady were also objects of ridicule in literature. The word *coquette* means a young, attractive woman who flirts with men with no regard for their feelings; she merely craves their attention to please her vanity. In a period in which women were supposed to marry, young women who seemed to make a game of **courtship** for amusement upset the order. Coquettes were seen as foolish, immature, vain, and cruel. Predictably, poems and stage plays satirized coquettes as self-centered girls alluring men, enhancing their beauty with cosmetics, and attracting men only to reject their attention.

Serious women ambitious for education were likewise condemned. A majority of people believed that men and women are different naturally, and they widely accepted that men were physically and intellectually superior to women. For this reason, even though more and more people felt that middle-class and wealthy women should be educated, they did not see a reason for women to receive an education equal to one given to men. For girls from wealthy families which primarily wanted a good match for them, this education was intended to help girls attract a suitable husband, so they were taught to play a musical instrument, sing, or to entertain their husbands with pleasant "small talk." Middle-class girls were also taught practical skills as a way to earn extra income by sewing and embroidering. Women who pursued the type of learning associated with that appropriate for men, usually studying Latin and Greek to read classical literature, were criticized for overstepping boundaries. French women were especially held by the other European cultures in contempt for their ambition, yet these French women inspired other women to want more. Very quickly, however, the learned lady became a stereotype, mocked by male writers for being bold and independent.

Arguably the most positive image emerging at that time was the "lady author." In England and France, more women began publishing their writing, a "public role" long considered only for men. Their work was largely dismissed, harshly criticized, and mocked, yet they inspired more women in England and the United States to write, in particular to write novels. The rise of the novel in the eighteenth century is an important part of women's history. Regarded then by most men as an inferior literary form, the novel was left to women. They were at that time an inexpensive form of entertainment, and the forms and conventions make novels more accessible than other types of **literature** to a wider range of readers, and working and middle-class women hungry for literature favored them. Written for women and by women, these works focused on the lives of women, and they helped their readers reflect on being women. Female novelists, poets, and playwrights became some of the very first women to step out in very public, professional roles. *See also* Gender Roles; Household Consumerism; Virgins/Virginity; Widows and Widowhood.

Further Reading: Norton, Mary Beth. *Liberty's Daughters*. Ithaca, NY: Cornell University Press, 1980. New edition, 1996; Spencer, Samia I., ed. *French Women and the Age of Enlightenment*. Bloomington: Indiana University Press, 1984.

Martha Graham Viator

YORÙBÁ ORAL POETRY, SEXUALITY IN. The Yorùbá occupy the southwestern part of Nigeria, and they number about 20–25 million (figures projected from the Nigeria Fertility Survey, 1984). According to oral tradition, the Yorùbá migrated from the Northeast between the seventh and tenth centuries, establishing Ile-Ife as their city of origin and spiritual capital, from which the sons of their mythic founder, Odùduwà, were sent forth to found their own cities and kingdoms. The family unit is a key part of everyday life within the society. Culture structures the behavioral patterns of the people, and sexuality cannot be separated from culture. Sexuality is a central aspect of being human throughout life and encompasses sex, gender, identities and roles, sexual orientation, eroticism, pleasure, intimacy, and reproduction. To the Yorùbá, sexuality governs the harmony and continuity of the community, and this was true in the seventeenth century. An Ifá poem showed that the Yorùbá despise extramarital sexual intercourse, and the ills associated with it are revealed in that Ifá poetry, as follows:

> Ó palé oko, ó palé ọkọ—She destroyed her husband's house (Twice),
> Ó palé àlè, ó palé àlè—She destroyed her concubine's house (Twice),
> Ó poko tán, ó pàlè tán—Having killed her husband and the concubine,
> Ó wá lo rèé para rè sógbun jìngbun jìngbun—She terminated her life in a far-flung deep hell,
> A díá fún panságà obìnrin—Divination was made for an adulteress,
> Tíí ṣeni ikú—The one who is a deadly person.

This poem reveals that the Yorùbá traditional community detests **adultery** and **fornication** and holds the ethical principles that **death** in various forms is associated with illicit sexual intercourse in the seventeenth century. That view is also applicable at any time. The hunters' guild also warns against frivolous sexual intercourse. In recent times this warning has focused on HIV/AIDS. One of the chants before the campaign against HIV can be seen below:

> Bèbò wò—Examine the vagina
> Kí o tó wò ó—Before you enter it
> Nítorí ohun tó ń bẹ lóbò obìnrin—Because of things inside vagina
> Tí ń ṣekú pani—That causes death.

This ethical appeal in the above hunters' genre connotes that an individual must restrict himself or herself to a single sexual partner or else such erring can contract any form of sexually transmitted diseases. It is also a warning that it is unethical for a married woman to have illicit sexual intercourse. It is not only harmful to her husband

and **concubines**, but she will also enjoy its fruit, which is untimely death. That is why there is social control of sexuality mainly in the traditional society through measures such as Mágùn (literally, do not climb) and Tésòó (literally, disgrace apparel/appearance) and others. The essence of these magical acts that are giving way to modernism is to enhance continence.

Chastity before marriage and fidelity after marriage have always ranked high in the hierarchy of merit for women among the Yorùbá. Contrary to the erroneous impression of some, sex **education** was part of the social curriculum in traditional Yorùbá society in the past, even in the seventeenth and eighteenth centuries. However, the purpose of sex education in Yorùbá society was to instil the values of premarital chastity. Sex education for young women usually begins with **menstruation**. When the young woman first notices her menstrual flow, it is a thing of joy and pride to the parents, particularly the mother. This is because the commencement of menstruation is considered a sign of fruitfulness and sexual fertility in the young woman that used to be celebrated with pounded yam and a cock and melon soup in the distant past.

Chastity was the subject of poetry, serving as a form of sex education to young men and women and promoting traditional values. A promiscuous person is lampooned in certain nuptial poetry such as the following:

Lílé: Ìbálé kìí fò—Solo: Virginity does not fly
       Kín lo mú tiẹ se?—What have you done with yours?
Ẹ̀gbè: Ìbálé kìí fò—All: Virginity does not fly,
       Kín lo mú tiẹ se o?—What have you done with yours?

This song shows that the **virginity** of a woman cannot be lost except through sexual intercourse.

In a traditional Yorùbá community, eroticism is treated with secrecy in most cases. Even among married couples, their love affairs are not to be seen by the people as such, and the use of erotic words is usually limited to the elderly people who are married. Younger couples are in some ways forbidden to talk about sexual relationships, especially in public. The repressed emotional feelings that concern sexuality are kept till the time of **marriage**, during which time the women have the poetic license to express their sexual desires and erotic feelings. The sexual organs of males and females are mentioned without any restriction; they also talk about sexual intercourse without any form of social sanction. Below are examples of this kind of such poetry:

Isan lokó—The penis is a nerve
Òrá lòbò—The vagina is elastic
Jàwàjáwà lẹpòn—The scrotal is soft flesh
Ike nidọ—The clitoris is plastic.

The song above erects a picture, for both the poet and the audience, of the combination of male and female reproductive organs that are ready for sexual intercourse. This stimulates the prospective wife to be in an erotic mood for conjugal duties. The song below also expresses a deep erotic experience between men and women.

Olórí burúkú lokó—The penis is a heady person
Adígbèsè lẹpòn—The scrotal is a criminal
Àfi tó bá wonú òbò sin-sin-sin—It will not desist until it penetrates the vagina "forcefully."
Olókó, sòbò lálejò—The-one-with-penis, entertain the vagina (Twice)

Sexuality is discussed and expressed purposefully for procreation among the Yorùbá. There are many examples of this in Ifá poetry. Below is an excerpt from Ifá poetry.

Ó yèdí pèé, ó bó póró—She opens her thighs widely apart, and it comes out gently,
Ọmọ tuntun lèrè àyèbò—A new babe is the reward of sexual intercourse,
Ìgbà ìdí di méjí la dọlómọ—We have a baby only when we had sexual intercourse.

The Yorùbá thought of sexuality in terms of childbearing because their culture places extremely high value on children. Continuity of the society depends on childbearing, and they opine that sexuality is only legal within the institution of marriage. It is worthy to mention that the incursion of modernism and domesticated religions—**Islam** and Christianity—in the society has changed many of their perceptions about sexuality. *See also* Childbirth; Literature; Restoration Poetry; Seduction Literature; Venereal Diseases.

Further Reading: Ajibade, George Olusola. "Ibale: Perception of Women's Pre-Marital Virginity among Yoruba." In *Local Government and Culture in Nigeria*, edited by Isiaka Olalekan Aransi, 238–47. Chapel Hill, NC: Chapel Hill Press, 2004; Alaba, Olugboyega. "Understanding Sexuality in the Yoruba Culture." In *Understanding Human Sexuality Seminar Series*, 1–12. Africa Regional Sexuality Resource Centre, 2004; Fadipe, N. A. *The Sociology of the Yoruba*. Ibadan: Ibadan University Press, 1970; Johnson, Samuel. *The History of the Yorubas: From the Earliest Times to the Beginning of the British Protectorate*. Lagos: CMS Bookshop, 1921; Lloyd, Peter Cutt. *Power and Independence, Urban Africans' Perception of Social Inequality*. London: Routledge and Kegan Paul. 1974.

George Olusola Ajibade

YOSHIWARA. The Yoshiwara was the official pleasure district outside Edo (today's Tokyo) established under the Tokugawa rule in accordance with the reforms licensing the existing brothels and constraining them to a single area outside the city center. In Kyoto the quarter became known as the Shimabara; in Osaka, the Shimmachi; and in Edo, the Yoshiwara.

In 1605, Edo brothels were moved to the area of Yanagimachi in order to create space for the new castle, and in 1617 a site at Fukiyamachi was designated for the purpose of housing a prostitute quarter. The place, renamed as the Yoshiwara, opened in 1618, and the work on the Yoshiwara bathhouses was finally completed in 1626. By 1657 new brothels were opened (Shin-Yoshiwara), and in 1668 they were populated with unlicensed prostitutes, referred to as the *jigoku* ("the hell women"), captured in a raid and expelled from Edo.

The brothels were classified according to the standing of their inmates. The Yoshiwara courtesans were originally classed (in descending order of importance) as *tayu*, *koshi-joro*, *tsubone-joro*, *kirimise-joro*, and *hashi-joro*, and similarly the brothels were known as *tayu-mise*, *koshi-mise*, etc. After the opening of the new Shin-Yoshiwara, *hashi-joro* and *tsubone-joro* ceased to exist, but at the same time two new classes, *sancha-joro* and *umecha-joro*, appeared. At the end of the eighteenth century, the classes in existence were *yobidashi*, *chusan*, *tsuke-mawashi*, *zashiki-mochi*, *heya-mochi*, and *kirimise-joro* (although that last category was below its earlier namesake in position). At times the Yoshiwara courtesans included also a separate category called *yakko* and recruited from the samurai women, whose three-to-five-year-long service in the Yoshiwara was considered punishment according to the samurai code.

The history of the Yoshiwara is an alternating succession of periods of popularity and decline interwoven with frequent fires burning the brothels to the ground. At times its

"Morning at the Yoshiwara," by Shunman Kubo, ca. 1800. Courtesy of the Library of Congress.

operation was banned at night, and the Yoshiwara women were not allowed to leave their quarters without permission. By 1725 the population of Yoshiwara reached 8679, including 3907 courtesans.

Initially looking up to the Shimabara for its manners and customs, in time Yoshiwara created its own identity. Its inhabitants included *kamuro*, young female attendants to the courtesans (in the absence of the courtesan waiting on the master in her place); *shinz*, thirteen-to-fourteen-year-old female attendants (previously *kamuro*); *yarite*, female managers (mostly recruited from old veterans); *wakaimono* (male servants); *hokan* (male *geishas*); and female **geishas** and courtesans.

Although by 1750s female geishas were already popular in Fukagawa, in the Yoshiwara until 1760 all geishas were male. Around 1760 Yoshiwara began to employ the *geiko* (a type of female geisha) to compete with the dancing *odoriko*. The Yoshiwara geishas were easily distinguished from the outsiders by their formal wear, a monochrome *kimono* with crests under which showed a narrow white collar of their underclothes. Their hairstyle was simpler than that of a courtesan, adorned only with one or two hairpins instead of the elaborate decoration of the latter. The Yoshiwara geishas were also the only geishas who dyed their teeth black similarly to the Yoshiwara courtesans. The Yoshiwara closed down in 1958 and today is an unfashionable district of Tokyo. *See also* Baths; concubines; Harems; Molly Houses; Prostitutes and Prostitution.

Further Reading: De Becker, Joseph Ernest. *The Nightless City of Geisha*. London: Kegan Paul, 2002; Seigle, Cecilia Segawa. *Yoshiwara*. Honolulu: University of Hawaii Press, 1933.

Katarzyna Ancuta

Appendix

FILMS

Barry Lyndon (dir Stanley Kubrick, 1975)
Based on the novel by William Makepeace Thackeray, this long, but visually beautiful movie concerns an eighteenth-century rogue (Ryan O'Neal) who attempts to establish himself among the aristocracy by marrying a wealthy widow. Many of the scenes were filmed only by candlelight, and period costumes and props were used.

Black Robe (dir. Bruce Beresford, 1991)
This movie is the story of a seventeenth-century French Jesuit priest traveling through Quebec to bring Christianity to the Huron.

Casanova (dir. Lasse Hallstrom, 2005)
Heath Ledger plays the title role of Jacamo Casanova in a romantic comedy version of the noted lover's life.

Dangerous Liaisons (dir. Stephen Frears, 1988)
Based on the 1782 novel by Choderlos de Laclos, this movie stars Glenn Close as the Marquise de Merteuil and John Malkovich as her co-conspirator, the Vicomte de Valmont. Both of them view love as a game of intrigue, with surprising results.

Emma (dir. Douglas Macgrath, 1996)
Gwenneth Paltrow stars as the title character, Emma Woodhouse, in this film based on the Jane Austen novel.

Farinelli: Il Castrato (dir. Gerard Ccorbiau, 1994)
Based on the life of the celebrated eighteenth-century castrato.

The History of Tom Jones, a Foundling (dir. Metin Huseyin, 1997)
This BBC/A&E miniseries is truer to the Henry Fielding novel than the 1963 movie.

Libertine (dir. Laurence Dunmore, 2004)
Johnny Depp portrays John Wilmot, the Second Earl of Rochester, a seventeenth-century poet and womanizer. His explicit writing and exploits get him into trouble with King Charles II.

Pride and Prejudice (dir. Joe Wright, 2005)
Condensed, but delightful version of Jane Austen's classic novel. Keira Knightly stars as Elizabeth Bennet.

Sense and Sensibility (dir. Ang Lee, 1995)
Emma Thompson won an Oscar for her screenplay adaptation of the Jane Austen novel. She also plays Elinor Dashwood.

Stage Beauty (dir. Richard Eyre, 2004)
Billy Crudup stars as Edward "Ned" Kynaston, an actor noted for playing the female leads in seventeenth-century England. When Charles II decrees that women are to perform all female roles, his life is changed forever.

Three Sovereigns for Sarah (dir. Philip Leacock, 1985)
Vanessa Redgrave stars as Sarah Cloyce, one of the women tried for witchcraft during the 1692 witch trials in Salem, Massachusetts. This PBS production was shot on location and used some of the actual trial transcripts.

Tom Jones (dir. Tony Richardson, 1963)
Based on the Henry Fielding novel and starring Albert Finney, this movie won multiple awards, including Best Picture, Director, and Screenplay.

WEB SITES

Common Place: www.common-place.org/
An online journal mainly featuring essays and articles on early American history and culture.

Eighteen-Century Resources: http://www.andromeda.rutgers.edu/~jlynch/18th/index.html
Jack Lynch of Rutger-Newark's listing of Internet sources for the long eighteenth century. Includes links to sites on art, literature, history, and other topics, as well as on societies, journals, and people.

History Matters: http://www.history-matters.com/
Covers U.S. history. The site includes primary documents, how historians use primary sources, links to Web sites, teaching assignments, and syllabi.

Lesley Hall's Web Pages: www.lesleyahall.net
Hall, the moderator of H-Sex, provides links to her own work on sexuality, as well as to the Wellcome Library for the History and Understanding of Medicine, archives of Histsex, and other topics.

World History Matters: http://worldhistorymatters.org/
Similar to the History Matters site, but this site covers world history. There is a section on world history sources and one on women in world history.

Selected Bibliography

Anderson, Karen. *Chain Her by One Foot: The Subjugation of Native Women in Seventeenth-Century New France*. New York: Routledge, 1993.

Bloch, Ruth H. *Gender and Morality in Anglo-American Culture, 1650–1800*. Berkeley: University of California Press, 2003.

Brown, Kathleen. *Good Wives, Nasty Wenches, and Anxious Patriarchs: Gender, Race, and Power in Colonial Virginia*. Chapel Hill: University of North Carolina Press, 1996.

Bullough, Vern L., and Bonnie Bullough. *Cross-Dressing, Sex and Gender*. Philadelphia: University of Pennsylvania Press, 1993.

Burnard, Trevor. *Mastery, Tyranny, and Desire: Thomas Thistlewood and His Slaves in the Anglo-Jamaican World*. Chapel Hill: University of North Carolina Press, 2004.

Cavallo, Sandra, and Lyndan Warner, eds. *Widowhood in Medieval and Early Modern Europe*. Menlo Park, CA: Addison-Wesley, 1999.

Cervantes Saavedra, Miguel de. *The Adventures of Don Quixote*. Translated by J. M. Cohen. Baltimore: Penguin Books, 1964.

Cohen, Michele. *Fashioning Masculinity: National Identity and Language in the Eighteenth Century*. New York: Routledge, 1996.

Crane, Elaine Forman. *Ebb Tide in New England: Women, Seaports, and Social Change, 1630–1800*. Boston: Northeastern University Press, 1998.

Crawford, Patricia M., and Laura Gowing, eds. *Women's Worlds in Seventeenth-Century England: A Sourcebook*. New York: Routledge, 1999.

Daniels, Christine, and Michael V. Kennedy, eds. *Over the Threshold: Intimate Violence in Early America*. New York: Routledge, 1999.

Davis, Natalie Zemon, and Arlette Farge, eds. *A History of Women: Renaissance and Enlightenment Paradoxes*. Cambridge, MA: The Belknap Press of Harvard University Press, 1993.

Dayton, Cornelia Hughes. *Women before the Bar: Gender, Law, and Society in Connecticut, 1639–1789*. Chapel Hill: University of North Carolina Press, 1995.

Foyster, Elizabeth. *Manhood in Early Modern England: Honour, Sex, and Marriage*. London: Longman, 1999.

Gerard, Kent, and Gert Hekma, eds. *The Pursuit of Sodomy: Male Homosexuality in Renaissance and Enlightenment Europe*. New York: Harrington Park Press, 1989.

Godbeer, Richard. *Sexual Revolution in Early America*. Baltimore: Johns Hopkins University Press, 2002.

Greenblatt, Stephen. *Will in the World: How Shakespeare Became Shakespeare*. New York: W. W. Norton, 2004.

Hambleton, Else L. *Daughters of Eve: Pregnant Brides and Unwed Mothers in Seventeenth-Century Essex County, Massachusetts*. New York: Routledge, 2004.

Henderson, Tony. *Disorderly Women in Eighteenth-Century London: Prostitution and Control in the Metropolis, 1730–1830*. London: Longman, 1999.

SELECTED BIBLIOGRAPHY

Inés de la Cruz, Sor Juana. *A Sor Juana Anthology*. Translated with notes by Alan S. Trueblood. Cambridge, MA: Harvard University Press, 1988.

Karlsen, Carol F. *The Devil in the Shape of a Woman: Witchcraft in Colonial New England*. New York: W. W. Norton, 1998.

Lang, Sabine. *Men as Women, Women as Men: Changing Gender in Native American Cultures*. Austin: University of Texas Press, 1998.

Laqueur, Thomas. *Making Sex: Body and Gender from the Greeks to Freud*. Cambridge, MA: Harvard University Press, 1990.

Manning, Jo. *My Lady Scandalous*. New York: Simon & Schuster, 2005.

Norton, Mary Beth. *Founding Mothers & Fathers: Gendered Power and the Forming of American Society*. New York: Alfred A. Knopf, 1996.

Norton, Rictor. *Mother Clap's Molly House: The Gay Subculture in England, 1700–1830*. London: Gay Men's Press, 1992.

Peakman, Julie. *Mighty Lewd Books. The Development of Pornography in Eighteenth-Century England*. London: Palgrave, 2003.

Peirce, Leslie. *The Imperial Harem: Women and Sovereignty in the Ottoman Empire*. New York: Oxford University Press, 1993.

Plane, Ann Marie. *Colonial Intimacies: Indian Marriage in Early New England*. Ithaca, NY: Cornell University Press, 2000.

Quataert, Donald. *The Ottoman Empire, 1700–1922*. Cambridge: Cambridge University Press, 2000.

Reis, Elizabeth. *Damned Women: Sinners and Witches in Puritan New England*. Ithaca, NY: Cornell University Press, 1999.

Richter, Daniel K. *The Ordeal of the Longhouse: The Peoples of the Iroquois League in the Era of European Colonization*. Chapel Hill: University of North Carolina Press, 1992.

Ringdal, Johan Nils. *Love for Sale: A World History of Prostitution*. Translated by Richard Daly. New York: Grove Press, 2002.

Roscoe, Will, ed. *Changing Ones: Third and Fourth Genders in Native North America*. London: Palgrave, 2000.

Scholz, Piotr O. *Eunuchs and Castrati: A Cultural History*. Princeton, NJ: Markus Weiner, 2000.

Sievens, Mary Beth. *Stray Wives: Marital Conflict in Early National New England*. New York: New York University Press, 2005.

Smith, Merril D. *Breaking the Bonds: Marital Discord in Pennsylvania, 1730–1830*. New York: New York University Press, 1991.

Smith, Merril D., ed. *Sex and Sexuality in the Early America*. New York: New York University Press, 1998.

Sommer, Matthew H. *Sex, Law and Society in Late Imperial China*. Stanford, CA: Stanford University Press, 2000.

Trexler, Richard. *Sex and Conquest: Gendered Violence, Political Order, and the European Conquest of the Americas*. Ithaca, NY: Cornell University Press, 1995.

Trouille, Mary Seidman. *Sexual Politics in the Enlightenment: Women Writers Read Rousseau*. Albany: State University of New York Press, 1997.

Twinam, Ann. *Public Lives, Private Secrets: Gender, Honor, Sexuality, and Illegitimacy in Colonial Spanish America*. Stanford, CA: Stanford University Press, 2001.

Ulrich, Laurel Thatcher. *Good Wives: Image and Reality in the Lives of Women in Northern New England, 1650–1750*. New York: Alfred A. Knopf, 1982.

Ulrich, Laurel Thatcher. *A Midwife's Tale: The Life of Martha Ballard, Based on Her Diary, 1785–1812*. New York: Vintage, 1991.

Walker, Garthine. "Rereading Rape and Sexual Violence in Early Modern England." *Gender and History* 10, no. 1 (April 1998): 1–25.

Wang, Ping. *Aching for Beauty: Footbinding in China*. Minneapolis: University of Minnesota Press, 2000.

Watanabe, Tsuneo, and Junichi Iwata. *The Love of the Samurai: A Thousand Years of Japanese Homosexuality*. Translated by D. R. Roberts. London: Gay Men's Press, 1989.
Wiesner, Merry E. *Christianity and Sexuality in the Early Modern World: Regulating Desire, Reforming Practice*. New York: Routledge, 2000.
Wilson, Lisa. *Ye Heart of a Man: The Domestic Life of Men in Colonial New England*. New Haven, CT: Yale University Press, 1999.
Wolfthal, Diane. *Images of Rape: The "Heroic" Tradition and Its Alternatives*. Cambridge: Cambridge University Press, 1999.
Wollstonecraft, Mary. *A Vindication of the Rights of Woman: An Authoritative Text; Backgrounds; The Wollstonecraft Debate; Criticism*. New York: W. W. Norton, 1988.
Yalom, Marilyn: *A History of the Breast*. New York: Ballantine Books, 1997.

Index

Boldfaced page numbers indicate main entries.

Abduction, **3–4**
Abortion, **5–6**, 129
Absalom and Achitophel (Dryden), 176
Actors, **6–7**
Adolescence. *See* Childhood
Adultery, **8–9**, 217, 218
Adulthood, 128–29
African slave trade. *See* Atlantic slave trade
Alcohol, **10–11**
American Revolution, 206–7, 243
Anal intercourse, **11–12**. *See also* Sodomy and anti-sodomy law
Aretino, Pietro, 183
Aristotle, 171
Aristotle's Masterpiece, **12–13**
Art: American/European, **13–15**; non-Western, **15–16**
Astell, Mary, 65–66
Atlantic slave trade, **16–17**
Aztecs, 202

Bacon, Francis, 178
Baglivi, Giogrio, 106
Baroque, 13, 14
Bastardy, **18–19**, 112
Baths, **19–20**
Behn, Aphra, **20–21**, 203
Berdache, xvi, 12, **21–22**, 163, 164, 191–92
Bestiality, **22–24**, 216–17
Bigamy, **24–25**. *See also* Polyandry
Birth control. *See* Contraception
Bisexuality, **25–26**

Body, the, **26–27**
Bonny, Anne, 180, 181
Breastfeeding, **27–29**
Brothels, 264. *See also* Prostitutes and prostitution
Buchan, William, 243
Buddhism, 201–2
Burton, Robert, 134
Byrd, William, **29**

Casanova, Giacomo Girolamo, **31–32**, 49, 50
Castlehaven, Earl of. *See* Touchet, Mervyn, Earl of Castlehaven
Castration, **32–33**. *See also* Eunuchs
Celibacy, **33–34**
Cervantes Saavedra, Miguel de, **34–35**
Charles II, 204
Charlotte Temple (Rowson), 215
Chastity, **35–37**, 197, 263
Cherokee, 166
Chevalier d'Eon, **37–38**
Cheyne, George, 106
Child custody laws, 126–27
Child rape, **39–40**, 217, 247
Childbirth, **40–42**
Childhood, **42–43**
China, 47, 82–83, 196, 202
Chinese art, 15–16
Chinese theater. *See* Theater, Chinese
Chocolate, 81
Circumcision, **44–45**

"Circumcision, The" (de Hooghe), 45
Clarissa (Richardson), 215
Cleland, John, 77
Clothing, 27, **45–46**
Coffee, 81
Coleman, Catherine, 7
Colombo, Realdo, 171
Concubines, **46–47**, 173, 218, 222
Condoms, 49, 50
Confucianism, 202
Consent, **48–49**, 198
Consumerism. *See* Household consumerism
Contraception, **49–50**
Cook, James, 74
Corsets, 45–46
Cosmetics and perfume, **50–52**
Courtship, **52–53**, 137
Coverture, 61, 125
Crimes: against nature, 216–17; against the social order, 217–18
Cross-dressing, 7, 37, 38, **53–54**. *See also* Berdache; *Hijra*

Dance, **55–56**
d'Aulnoy, Marie-Catherine Baronne, 76–77
Death, **56–58**. *See also* Infanticide; Murder
Defamation of character. *See* Gossip

INDEX

Defoe, Daniel, 66
d'Eon, Chevalier. *See* Chevalier d'Eon
d'Eon de Beaumont, Charles-Geneviève-Louis-Auguste-André-Thimothée. *See* d'Eon, Chevalier
Descartes, René, 131, 178
Devil, 256–58
Diderot, Denis, **58–59**
Divorce, 8, **60–61**, 126, 225
Doctrine of signatures, 80
Domestic violence, **61–63**, 151
Don Juan. *See* Tenorio, Don Juan
Don Quixote, 35
Dress. *See* Clothing
Dryden, John, 68, 176, 204
Dueling, **63–64**

Eastern Christianity, 244–45
Economics and gender. *See* Household consumerism
Education, **65–67**
Ejaculation, **67–68**
Elliott, Grace Dalrymple, **68–69**, 211
Embryology, 146, 171
Emden, Jacob, 122–23
English Revolution. *See* Revolution and gender
Enlightenment thought on sexuality, 61–62, **69–70**
Epidemics, 57
Erauso, Catalina de, 53, **70–71**
Ethics: philosophy of, 178–79. *See also* Virtue
Eunuchs, **71–72**
Euphemisms and slang, **72–74**
Explorers and missionaries, **74–75**

Fairy tales, **76–77**
Fang Hsûn (Xun), 82
Fanny Hill (Cleland), **77–78**
Fashion. *See* Clothing
Fielding, Henry, 237–38
Flagellation, **78–80**
Folklore. *See* Myths and folklore
Food, **80–81**
Footbinding, **82–83**
Fornication, **83–84**
France. *See* Mixed marriages

Franklin, Benjamin, **85–86**
French Revolution, 206

Galenists, 170, 171
Gaon of Vilna, 123
Geisha, **87–88**
Gender. *See* Berdache; Masculinity; Revolution and gender
Gender roles, xvii, **88–90**, 163, 209, 210. *See also* Berdache; Women
Gilray, James, 90
Gossip: eighteenth-century England, **90–92**; seventeenth-century America, **92–93**
Grose, Francis, 72–73
Guadalupe, Virgin of. *See* Virgin of Guadalupe
Gulliver's Travels (Swift), 226–27
Gwynne, Nell, 7, 211
Gynecology manuals, **93–94**

Haiduk, 162
Hall, Thomas/Thomasine, 27, 97
Hallowell, John, 5
Harems, **95–96**
Harvey, William, 44
Hasidism, 123
Heale, William, 62
Henry VIII, 126
Hermaphrodites, **96–97**
Hijra, 72
Hill, James, 90
Hinduism, **98–99**, 201
Hobbes, Thomas, 179
Hogarth, William, 10, **99–101**
Homosexuality, **101–2**, 121, 128, 151, 216, 219. *See also* Berdache; Lesbianism; Molly houses
Hooghe, Romeyn de, 45
Household consumerism, **103–5**
Hughes, Margaret, 7
Hume, David, 179
Hwames, 163
Hysteria, **105–7**

Implied consent. *See* Consent
Impotence, 78, **108–9**
Incas, 202

Incest, **109–10**, 217
Indentured servants, **110–13**
India, **113–14**
Inés de la Cruz, Sor (Sister) Juana (J. I.), **115–16**
Infanticide, 5, **116–18**
Insanity. *See* Madness
Interracial sex, **119–20**, 221. *See also* Mixed marriages
Islam, **120–21**, 200, 201

Jahan, Shah, 229, 230
Jamaica, 17, 236
Japanese theater. *See* Theater, Japanese
Jeanne des Anges, 133
Jesus Christ, 158
Joseph Andrews (Fielding), 215
Judaism, **122–23**, 201

Kabuki theater, 234–35
Kagura, 234
Kama Sutra, 170, 201
Kant, Immanuel, 179
Knox, Robert, 182

Lacy, Mary, 135
Landes, Joan B., 207
Laws, **125–29**; marriage and divorce, 125–27; sex and sexuality, 128–29
Lesbianism, 158–59, 163–64, 216. *See also* Homosexuality
Libertine, **129–30**, 142, 230–31
Linnaeus, Carolus, 146
Literacy. *See* Education
Literature, **130–32**
Locke, John, 177
Louis XIV, King, 222
Louis XV, King, 37–38

Macbeth (Shakespeare), 219
Madams (prostitution), 189–90
Madness, **133–34**
Makin, Bathsua, 65
Mancini, Hortense, 214
Maritime culture, **135–36**
Marquis de Sade. *See* Sade, Donatien Alphonse François de
Marriage, **136–40**; laws, 125–27. *See specific topics*
Marvell, Andrew, **140–41**

Mary, Mother of Jesus. *See* Virgin Mary
Masculinity, **141–43**
Masturbation, **143–44**, 216
Mather, Cotton, 134, **144–45**
Measure for Measure (Shakespeare), 187, 218–19
Medicine and science, **145–46**
Men. *See* Masculinity
Menopause, 147
Menstruation, **147–48**
Mexico: indigenous women of, **149–50**; sexuality and gender in, **150–51**
Midwives, 41, 42; physicians and, **152–53**
Milton, John, 140, **153–54**, 182, 203
Ming dynasty, 71, 232
Missionaries. *See* Explorers and missionaries
Mistresses. *See* Royal mistresses
Mixed marriages: New France, **154–56**. *See also* Interracial sex
Mohave, 163
Molly houses, 102, **156–57**
Monasteries, **157–59**
Morality and philosophy, 178–79. *See also* Virtue
Mulattoes, 119–20
Murder, **159–61**. *See also* Infanticide
Muscovy, 197
Muskogee, 165
Myths and folklore, **161–62**

Nahuas, 246
Native Americans, 61, 119, **163–66**. *See also* Pueblo Indians, Southeastern Indians
Navajo, 164–66
Neoclassicism, 130–31
Newspapers, 90–91, **166–67**
Noh theater, 234
Nudity. *See* Body

Onania, 143
Onanism. *See* Masturbation
Opera, **168–69**
Oral sex, **169–70**
Orgasm, 58, **170–71**
Orphans, **171–72**

Orthodox Christianity, 244–45
Ottoman Empire, 44, **172–74**, 196

Pamela or Virtue Rewarded (Richardson), 215
Paradise Lost (Milton), 154
Paternity, **175–76**
Patriarchy, **176–77**
Perfectionists, **177–78**
Perfume. *See* Cosmetics and perfume
Perrault, Charles, 77
Phaedra (Racine), 131
Philippines, 248
Philosophy, **178–80**
Physicians. *See under* Midwives
Pinel, Phillippe, 106–7, 134
Pirates, **180–81**
Pleasure, sexual, 170, 193
Poetry, 140–41, 176; Restoration, 203–4; Yorùbá oral, 262–64
Poets, 20–21
Polyandry, **181–83**
Polygamy, 217–18, 225
Pope, Alexander, 131
Pornography, 79–80, **183–85**
Poussin, Nicolas, 3, 4
Pregnancy, **185–87**, 217
Premarital sex, **187–88**, 217
Prostitutes and prostitution, 128, **188–91**, 217, 264
Pueblo Indians, **191–93**
Puritan theology, ambivalence toward sex in, 193
Puritans, 8–9, 18, 33, 36–37, 62, 144–45, **193–94**, 205–6

Qing dynasty, 71, 196, 197
Qur'an, 120–21, 200

Racine, 131
Ranters, 205
Rape law, 195–97, **197–99**, 217, 221, 247. *See also* Consent; Rape/coerced sex
Rape of the Lock, The (Pope), 131
Rape of the Sabine Women (Poussin), 3, 4
Rape/coerced sex, 3, 4, 74, 149, 151, **195–97**, 221; in art, 14; in literature, 77, 78, 140–41,

154, 238; wartime, 192, 196, 251–53
Read, Mary, 180, 181
Religion, **200–203**
Renaissance, 207–8
Restoration poetry, **203–4**
Revolution and gender, **204–7**
Ribeiro, Joao, 182
Richardson, Samuel, 215
Rococo, 13, 14
Romantic love, **207–9**
Romanticism, 130
Rousseau, Jean-Jacques, 78, 177, 179–80, **209–10**
Rowson, Susanna, 215
Royal mistresses, **210–11**
Rush, Benjamin, 134

Sabine women, 3
Sade, Donatien Alphonse François de, **212–13**
Salons, **213–14**
Science. *See* Medicine and science
Seduction literature, **215–16**
Sension, Nicholas, 224
Sex crimes, **216–18**
Sex manuals, 12–13
Sexual assault: of men, 252–53. *See also* Rape/coerced sex
"Sexual orientation," 224
Sexual pleasure, 170, 193
Sexually transmitted diseases. *See* Venereal diseases
Shakers, 177–78
Shakespeare, William, 187–88, **218–19**
Shamela (Fielding), 215
Shandy, Tristram, 44
Sheridan, Richard Brinsley, 91
Shunga, 16
Simpson, Alexander, 64
Skoptsi, 178
Slander. *See* Gossip
Slang. *See* Euphemisms and slang
Slave trade, Atlantic, 16–17
Slavery, 47, 173, **219–22**; interracial relations and, 221 (*see also* Interracial sex)
Slaves, laws regarding marriage of, 127
Snell, Hannah, 54

Snuff, 237
Sodomy and anti-sodomy law, 128, 151, 216, **222–24**. See also Anal intercourse
Southeastern Indians, **224–26**
Sultans, 173–74
Swift, Jonathan, **226–27**
Sydenham, Thomas, 106
Syphilis, 58, 242–43

Taboos, **228**
Taj Mahal, **229–30**
Tantra, 201–2
Taoism, 15–16, 170, 202
Tartuffe (Molière), 131
Tenorio, Don Juan (J.T.), **230–31**
Theater: Chinese, **231–32**; European, **232–33**; Japanese, **233–35**
Thicknesse, Philip, 90–91
Thistlewood, Thomas, **235–36**
Tobacco, **236–37**

Tom Jones (Fielding), **237–38**
Torture, **238–40**
Touchet, Mervyn, Earl of Castlehaven, **240–41**
Transgenderism. See Berdache; Cross-dressing; Hermaphrodites; *Hijra*; Hwames
Turks, 200

Valide Sultans, 174
Van Schurman, Anna Maria, 65
Venereal diseases, 58, **242–43**
Viardel, Cosme, 185–86
Ville, Edward, 67, 68
Virgin Mary, **244–45**
Virgin of Guadalupe, **245–46**
Virgins/virginity, **247–48**
Virtue, **248–49**
Voyeurism, **249–50**

Warren, Mercy Otis, 89–90
Wartime rape, 192, 196, **251–53**

Whaling ships, 135–36
Whitehurst, Thomas, 64
Whytt, Robert, 106
Widows and widowhood, **253–55**
Wilmot, John, Earl of Rochester, 203, **255–56**
Witches and witch trials, xvi, 238–39, **256–58**
Wollstonecraft Godwin, Mary, 65–66, 88, 207, **258–59**
Women, changing images of, **259–61**
Wooley, Hannah, 65

Yorùbá oral poetry, sexuality in, **262–64**
Yoshiwara, **264–65**
Yuan dynasty, 231

Zalman, Elijah ben Solomon, 123
Zevi, Sabbetai, 122

About the Editor and Contributors

George Olusola Ajibade (PhD) is a lecturer in the Department of African Languages and Literatures at the Obafemi Awolowo University, Ile-Ife, Nigeria. Currently, he is an Alexander von Humboldt Research Fellow at the University of Bayreuth, Germany (2004–2006), and he is preparing two book manuscripts, "A Sociocultural Studies of Yorùbá Nuptial Poetry" and "Negotiating Space: Òsun in the Verbal and Visual Metaphors."

Katarzyna Ancuta is assistant professor at the Institute of British and American Culture and Literature, University of Silesia, Poland, specializing in literary theory and cultural studies. She is the author of one book, *Where Angels Fear to Hover: Between the Gothic Disease and the Meataphysics of Horror*, and over twenty academic articles. Since 2005, she has been associated with Assumption University, Bangkok. She is currently researching for a new book on Asian popular cinema.

Rebecca Barr recently completed a PhD on ideas of community in the work of Samuel Richardson at Jesus College, Cambridge.

Melissa K. Benne is a research assistant at the Saint Louis Art Museum and an adjunct professor of art history at St. Charles Community College, St. Peters, Missouri. Her fields of study include gender theory, women in history and art, patronage, and cultural studies.

Mary Block is an assistant professor of history at Valdosta State University, Valdosta, Georgia. She is completing a book on the history of rape law in nineteenth-century America.

William E. Burns is a historian in Washington, DC. In addition to editing *The Medieval Era* volume for *The Greenwood Encyclopedia of Love, Courtship, and Sexuality through History*, he is the author of several books, including *An Age of Wonders: Prodigies, Politics and Providence in England, 1657–1727* (2002) and *Science and Technology in Colonial America* (2005).

Christopher R. Corley is an assistant professor of history at Minnesota State University, Mankato. He has presented papers and published articles and book chapters on the law, adolescence, and parenting in early modern France.

Caroline Dodds is a junior research fellow at Sidney Sussex College, University of Cambridge. She is working on a monograph provisionally titled *Earth Women and Eagle Warriors: The Creation of Aztec Gender Roles and Relationships*, which is a development of her doctoral thesis "Warriors and Workers: Duality and Complementarity in Aztec Gender Roles and Relations" (2004).

Daniel Farr is a PhD candidate in sociology at the University at Albany, SUNY, researching parental aspiration among young gay men. He is a full-time instructor with the College of St. Rose, Albany, New York.

Joel Fishman is Assistant Director for Lawyer Services, Duquesne University Center for Legal

Information/Allegheny County Law Library. Dr. Fishman specializes in Pennsylvania legal history, biography, bibliography, and legal research. He is the author of more than sixty-five books and sixty articles on these topics. He is currently working on *Pennsylvania State Constitution: A Reference Guide* for Greenwood Press.

Andrew K. Frank is assistant professor of history at Florida Atlantic University. He is author of *Creeks and Southerners: Biculturalism on the Early American Frontier* and *The Routledge Historical Atlas of the American South.*

Else L. Hambleton has a PhD in history from the University of Massachusetts at Amherst. She is the author of *Daughters of Eve: Pregnant Brides and Unwed Mothers in Seventeenth-Century Massachusetts* (2004).

Dave D. Hochstein (PhD) is assistant professor of psychology at Wright State University Lake Campus, Celina, Ohio. His research interests include memory for spatial location and the mnemonic characteristics of computerized augmentative and alternative communication systems.

Elizabeth Jenner is a test developer at the Educational Testing Service. She lives in Princeton, New Jersey.

Miriam Jones is an associate professor of English and gender studies at the University of New Brunswick, Saint John, Canada. Her research interests include print and popular culture in the long eighteenth century.

Devrim Karahasan is a PhD candidate in the Department of History and Civilization at the European University Institute, Florence, Italy. Her publications include "Die politische Formierung der kanadischen Metis zur Nation im 19. Jahrhundert" and "Metis als Vielheiten: Die Ethnogense kanadischer Mischlinge in Diskursen des 17. bis 20. Jahrhunderts," both published in *Zeitschrift für Kanadastudien.*

Doug Krehbiel is a member of the Department of History at the University of North Carolina, Wilmington, focusing on legal systems of early modern Europe.

Tonya Marie Lambert is a doctoral student in history at the University of Alberta in Edmonton, Canada. She studies women's history and the history of sexuality, focusing on early modern England.

Mary Linehan is visiting associate professor at the College of Wooster, Wooster, Ohio. She has recently completed a book manuscript, "Vicious Circle: Prostitution, Reform, and Public Policy in Chicago."

Barbara Loranc currently works at the Academy of Technology and Humanities in Bielsko-Biala, Poland. Her interests are British Culture and European Studies. Her most recent publication discusses the subject of the diaspora identities in Hanif Kureishi's novels.

Tanis Lovercheck-Saunders is assistant professor of history and social science at Valley City State University, Valley City, North Dakota. Her interests include American women's history, Ostarbeiter experience in Nazi Germany, and the radical right in American history.

Jo Manning is the founder and director of the Reader's Digest General Books Research Library. Now a full-time writer, she is the author of three novels and of *My Lady Scandalous*, the first full-length biography of the courtesan Grace Dalrymple Elliot.

Wisam Mansour (PhD) is currently an associate professor of English literature at Fatih University in Istanbul. Previously Dr. Mansour held similar positions at various universities in Jordan, Cyprus, and Turkey.

Cathy McClive is currently a Leverhulme Postdoctoral researcher at the Ecole Pratique des Hautes Etudes, Ive section, Sorbonne, Paris. She completed her doctoral thesis on "Bleeding Flowers and Waning Moons: A History of Menstruation in France, c. 1495–1761" at the University of Warwick in April 2004. She is currently completing a book manuscript on blood and menstruation.

Lianne McTavish is associate professor of visual culture at the University of New

Brunswick, Canada. Her book, *Childbirth and the Display of Authority in Early Modern France*, was published in 2005.

DeMond S. Miller is an associate professor of sociology and director of the Liberal Arts and Sciences Institute at Rowan University, Glassboro, New Jersey. Dr. Miller's recent work can be found in *The Journal of Emotional Abuse*, *Space and Culture: An International Journal of Social Spaces*, the *International Journal of the Humanities*, and *The Journal of Public Management and Social Policy*.

Patit Paban Mishra is professor of history at Sambalpur University, India. Dr. Mishra has worked on several projects throughout the world, written over 500 encyclopedia entries for numerous publications, and is the author of many books and articles, including *Cultural Rapprochement between India and Southeast Asia* (2005).

Samantha A. Morgan-Curtis is an assistant professor of English and women's studies at Tennessee State University in Nashville. Currently at work on the manuscript of her first book, she has published in the areas of pedagogy, women's studies, and early modern women. She lives with her husband David and two daughters, Fea and Nemain.

Mihaela Mudure is associate professor at Babes-Bolyai University in Cluj, Romania. She has published essays on seventeenth- and eighteenth-century culture and Jewish literature. She is also a translator from English to French.

Caryn E. Neumann is a past managing editor of the *Journal of Women's History* and a senior lecturer at the Ohio State University at Newark.

Bartlomiej Paszylk currently is the Director of Studies at the Teachers Training College, "The Top" in Bielsko-Biala, Poland. He is also a staff reviewer at a Polish science fiction magazine *Nowa Fantastyka* and a freelance writer mainly interested in the horror genre; his latest publication is an interview with Graham Masterton for the U.S. magazine *Surreal*.

Julie Peakman is a historian, writer, and a former fellow of Wellcome Trust for the History of Medicine, where she studied for her PhD. Her books include *Mighty Lewd Books: The Development of Pornography in Eighteenth-Century England* (2003) and *Lascivious Bodies: A Sexual History of the Eighteenth Century* (2004). She is currently working on her next monograph, *Sex & Civilisation: A World History* (due 2007) as well as on an eight-volume edition of *Eighteenth-Century Whore Biographies* (due 2007). She is also general editor of a six-volume collection of essays, *A History of the Culture of Sexuality* (due 2009).

Jason Powell will receive his PhD in Summer 2006 from the University of Liverpool. His book, *Jacques Derrida: A Biography*, will be released in July 2006. He currently works for the British Army and is affiliated with the University of Liverpool.

Ajnesh Prasad is a graduate student in the Department of Political Studies at Queen's University, Kingston, Canada. His most recent article appeared in *Canadian Woman Studies*. He presented a paper on postcolonial heteronormativity at the 85th Annual Southwestern Social Science Association conference, where he was awarded the Prize for Outstanding Student Paper.

Elizabeth R. Purdy (PhD) is a political scientist and freelance writer. Her research interests include women in politics and general women's studies. She has published in these fields, as well as in history, economics, literature, and popular culture.

Elizabeth Reis is currently writing a book called *Impossible Hermaphrodites: Intersex in America, 1620–1960*. She is an associate professor in women's and gender studies and history at the University of Oregon.

Eve-Alice Roustang-Stoller teaches in the Department of French and Italian at the University of Southern California. She wrote her dissertation on rhetoric in the French Renaissance novel. Her main research interest is the interaction of the discipline of rhetoric and literature during this period. She has published on this subject as well as on other writers of the Renaissance.

Maya R. Rupert is a law student at Boalt Hall School of Law, University of California (2006), and is editor-in-chief of the *Berkeley Journal of Gender, Law & Justice* (2005–2006). Her other publications include "It's All Gotten So Commercial: Abolishing the Commercial Speech Doctrine on the Internet," *Chicago-Kent Journal of INTELLectual Property* (2006); and "Aristotle's Discussion of Temperance and Continence," *The Dialogue* (2002).

Margaret Sankey is a professor in the Department of History at Minnesota State University, Moorhead, and recently published her first book, *Jacobite Prisoners of the 1715 Rebellion: Preventing and Punishing Insurrection in Early Hanoverian Britain* (2005).

Laura Schechter is a PhD student in the Department of English and Film Studies at the University of Alberta. Her major research interests include early modern travel and exploration literature, as well as texts from the period that are written by or deal chiefly with women.

Stephanie L. Schmid is an attorney currently clerking for the Honorable Ronald Gould on the Ninth Circuit Court of Appeals in Seattle, Washington.

J. Shantz is currently teaching at York University in Toronto, Canada, and has authored many articles in *Feminist Review, Capital and Class, Feminist Media Studies*, and *Feminism and Psychology*, as well as in several anthologies.

Bridgette A. Sheridan is a visiting scholar at Brandeis University's Women's Studies Research Center and a visiting assistant professor at Framingham State College. She is currently working on her book, *Gender and the Professionalization of Medicine: Midwives, Medical Men, and the* Querelle des Femmes *in Seventeenth-Century France*. Her article "At Birth: The Modern State, Modern Medicine and the Royal Midwife Louise Bourgeois in Seventeenth-Century France" was published in the journal *Dynamis* in 1999, then translated into Spanish and published in the book *Sanadoras, Matronas y Médicas en Europa* (2001).

Mary Beth Sievens's current research focuses on the popular debate over the meaning of consumerism in the early American republic and the effects of consumer activity on the household economy, familial gender relations, and patterns of household authority. Her recent publications include *Stray Wives: Marital Conflict in Early National New England* (2005); "Divorce, Patriarchal Authority, and Masculinity: A Case from Early National Vermont," *Journal of Social History*; "'The Fruit of My Industry': Economic Roles and Marital Conflict in New England, 1790–1830" in Peter Benes, ed., *Women's Work in New England, 1620–1920: The Dublin Seminar for New England Folklife Proceedings* (2003).

Merril D. Smith is an independent scholar living in National Park, New Jersey. She is the author and editor of several books, including the *Encyclopedia of Rape* (2004) and *Sex without Consent: Rape and Sexual Coercion in America* (2001).

Samaya Lea Sukha is currently a PhD candidate at the University of Melbourne, Australia. She has published extensively and broadly in the fields of humanities and social sciences, with a particular emphasis on Asian studies. Her latest published contribution can be found in the *Encyclopedia of the Documentary Film*, edited by Ian Aitken Routledge (2005).

Konrad Szczesniak is assistant professor at the Silesian University, Poland. He lectures in translation and linguistics.

Rossitsa Terzieva-Artemis is an assistant professor of English in the Department of Languages, Intercollege, Cyprus. Her research interests include modern literature, continental philosophy, and psychoanalysis.

Lana Thompson specializes in medical and forensic anthropology. She is the author of *The Wandering Womb: A Cultural History of Outrageous Beliefs about Women* (1999).

Claudette Tolson is a doctoral candidate in history at Loyola University. She has taught elementary school, high school, and college in various locations in the Chicago metropolitan area, and she has published historical articles for several academic publications.

Deborah L. Vess is a professor of history and interdisciplinary studies at Georgia College & State University. Her area of expertise is monastic history and medieval theology. She has published articles in *Mystics Quarterly*, *The American Benedictine Review*, *The Modern Schoolman*, *Word and Spirit*, and other publications.

Martha Graham Viator teaches pedagogy to social studies teacher-candidates in the Department of Teacher Education at Rowan University in New Jersey. Her research interests include eighteenth- and nineteenth-century social history and pedagogy.

Timothy J. Viator teaches British and U.S. literature at Rowan University in New Jersey. He is editing *The Plays of Colley Cibber*, and he has published essays on theater history and criticism.